Roscommon County Library Service

WITHDRAWN
FROM STOCK

D1136623

TOM JONES

Close up

TOM JONES

Close Up

Lucy Ellis & Bryony Sutherland

OMNIBUS PRESS
LONDON · NEW YORK · SYDNEY

Copyright © 2000 Omnibus Press
(A Division of Book Sales Limited)

Edited by Chris Charlesworth
Cover designed by Lisa Pettibone
Picture research by Nikki Lloyd

ISBN: 0.7119.7549.3
Order No: OP 48119

All rights reserved. No part of this book may be reproduced in any form or by any electronic
or mechanical means, including information storage or retrieval systems, without permission in
writing from the publisher, except by a reviewer who may quote brief passages.

Exclusive Distributors:
Book Sales Limited,
8/9 Frith Street,
London W1V 5TZ, UK.

Music Sales Corporation,
257 Park Avenue South,
New York, NY 10010, USA.

The Five Mile Press,
22 Summit Road,
Noble Park,
Victoria 3174, Australia.

To the Music Trade only:
Music Sales Limited,
8/9 Frith Street,
London W1V 5TZ, UK.

Photo credits:
Every effort has been made to trace the copyright holders of the photographs in this book but
one or two were unreachable. We would be grateful if the photographers concerned would
contact us.

Typeset by Galleon Typesetting, Ipswich
Printed by Creative Print and Design, Wales

A catalogue record for this book is available from the British Library.

Visit Omnibus Press on the web at www.omnibuspress.com

For Elton Thrussell and Frankie Sutherland
for their love, support and infinite understanding

Contents

Acknowledgements

This is not an authorised biography. By default such a book would be obliged to accommodate the wishes of its subject. Our sole aim from the outset was to reflect accurately the ups and downs of Tom Jones' extraordinary 60-year life, to portray him in both a flattering and critical light as appropriate.

We would first like to thank those who gave generously of their time to be interviewed for this book. In purely alphabetical order they were as follows: Richard Adler, Brian Blackler, Nina Blatt, Barry Briggs, Ronnie Cass, Vic Cockerell, Mal Crewe, Marion Crewe, 'Diane', Gaynor Davies, Keith Davies, Anne Dudley, Jackie Evans, Sylvia Firth, Constance Forslund, Tracey Fox, Bill Glaze, Carmen Goglia, Bob Griffiths, Ann Hollowood, Vernon Hopkins, Trevor Horn, Jack Housler, John Hudson, Elsie Huish, Chris Hutchins, Fanita James, Gül Jenkins, Terry Jenkins, Brian John, Darlene Love, BarBara Luna, Jeanne McCarthy, Paddy Moloney, Jennifer O'Neill, Mark Pierson, Ricky Purcell, the Quinn brothers, Les Reed, Lynne Rees-Slade, Johnny Rogan, Jimmy Savile, Jon Scoffield, Tommy Scott, Eddie Seago, Chris Slade, Graham K Smith, Marion Spence-Fox, John Springate, Margaret Sugar, 'Big' Jim Sullivan, Peter Sullivan, Gloria Tait, Jimmy Tarbuck, Ethel Tucker, Leslie Uggams, Derek Watkins, Wendy Watkins, Mike Webb, Beverley Williams, Keith Williams, Robbie Williams, David Winters, regulars of the Wood Road Social Club, Cynthia Woodard and Kath Woodward.

Several interviewees requested anonymity for this book and we have respected their wishes.

Jo Murphy (formerly Jo Mills, widow of Gordon) initially agreed to be interviewed, but sadly after many months of telephone calls changed her mind, citing personal issues and her children's wishes. Others we spoke to at length but similarly declined included Brendon O'Carroll, Mike Gee and Mike Morgan.

We requested interviews with both Engelbert Humperdinck and Gilbert O'Sullivan, but each for his own reason refused, one with more grace than the other.

We first contacted Donna Woodward, publicist for Tom Jones Enterprises, to request an interview with Tom and members of his family back in January 1999. Although this biography is unauthorised, she agreed to limited involvement in order to clarify the finer nuances of Tom's extensive career. After one year of communication no conclusive response was forthcoming and as a result the book has gone to print without any input from Tom Jones Enterprises.

Additional research for this book was undertaken by Barry Briggs, Shaun Chang, Paul Donnelley, Clare Ellis, Edward Ellis, Philip Glassborow, Catherine Huish, Anthony Lewis, John Lutterloch, Paul Minet, Frankie Sutherland, Elton Thrussell and Omamoke Unokan.

Thanks to Rodney Bellamy-Wood, Helen Donlon, Lucy Hawes, Andrew King, Nikki Lloyd and Melissa Whitelaw (Sydney) at Omnibus Press. Special thanks as ever go to Chris Charlesworth, for his encyclopaedic knowledge and personal dedication to dispelling myths. Cheers CC for the curries.

Thanks also to Lynn Coles, Carol Frankland, Mark from The Glitter Band, Des Gray, The Green Fly, Christine James, Yvonne McMahon, George Michael, Graham Muschialli, Dean Powell, David Rudich, Stephanie Schewchuk, Clare Scully, Brian Selby, Vilma Smith, Phil Solomon, Steve Turner, Viking Direct and Nancy Wilson.

Special thanks must go to Chris Hutchins for speaking to us so openly, and exclusively, at a difficult time. Also to Vernon Hopkins for the many meetings and countless phone calls, and for introducing us to The Squires – good luck with the video! Finally to Barbara Newson for proofreading under such a tight schedule, Peter Newson for the photo shoot and Paul Newson for getting us started in the first place.

Prologue

IF I ONLY KNEW

"For me, fame has been a gift. If it limits me from going out alone because of the hassle, then that's a small price to pay for the benefits . . . My voice is a God-given gift, and I'm always aware and thankful for that."

FROM PONTYPRIDD to Vegas and on to Glastonbury, the unchallenged Voice of Tom Jones effortlessly bridges the gap between generations. Commanding respect from his contemporaries through pop's eternally changing faces and fashions, he has shared centre stage with performers ranging from the heights of Jerry Lee Lewis to the high-jinx of Robbie Williams. A self-confessed 'man who loves life', Tom has surpassed every expectation from a career that began nearly 40 years ago in the bar of a Welsh club.

Not least is he famed for the knicker throwing. He commands a truly devoted following who have contributed immeasurably to his success. His enduring rapport with his audience, be they 16 or 60, transcends the appeal of any other performer of his ilk. He is one of the few celebrities to be presented with a 'Star' in the Hollywood Walk of Fame by his fans, while his various appearances for charity have gained him respect from cynics and non-fans alike. As he approaches his 60th birthday, Tom Jones shows no sign of surrendering his title as Comeback King and moreover looks destined for even greater achievements.

The unprecedented vocal assault on the music world began in the early Sixties, when Tom 'temporarily' left behind domestic life in a bleak Welsh coal mining village for a stab at fame singing as Tommy Scott & The Senators. Resembling 'a bricklayer in a blouse' rather than a mop-top Beatle or a rugged Rolling Stone, Tom presented an unlikely candidate for chart success. However, his extra years, experience and tight leather trousers lent his stage act a more mature and raunchy angle, securing him a previously unclaimed niche in bohemian swinging London.

Unforgettable hits like 'It's Not Unusual', 'Delilah' and 'What's New Pussycat' propelled Tom to an extended period of worldwide stardom, which encompassed his own ground-breaking TV series and box-office records throughout five continents. Eventually Tom settled for a 'comfortable' position as a casino crooner in Las Vegas, enjoying to the full his millionaire status and playboy lifestyle.

While his career stalled momentarily under the gaudy neon lights of the gambling strips, Tom continued to capture headlines with his avid dedication to wild all-night parties, countless lusty affairs and alcoholic brawls, all of which provoked tabloid scandals and court cases. Following misguided instruction from his omnipotent manager Gordon Mills, Tom unwisely branched out into country music and unwittingly forced himself into semi-retirement. The roller coaster ride of the boy from the valleys seemed to have screeched to a halt, until the untimely death of Gordon Mills allowed Tom's son Mark to take over the reins and perform a much needed facelift on his father's floundering fortunes.

With the trendy cover of Prince's 'Kiss' with The Art Of Noise, several parodic TV appearances and a publicly heightened social conscience, Tom's star began to shine once more as he hit his fifties. The glamorous granddad uncovered a new generation of worshipful admirers in the Nineties crowd, who served to reinvent him as an alternative icon for the new millennium. Tom still tours relentlessly for up to nine months of the year, tirelessly performing 150 to 200 shows a year. At the start of the millennium we saw him turning more to collaboration with his number one duet album, *Reload*, and film work with a major role in *Agnes Browne*. Once again Tom appears to be 'fashionable' as well as famous, stating recently in the *New York Times*: "I just do what I do. If people think it's hip, well, thank God."

Unquestionably, despite the immense diversity of his incredible career, music will always remain Tom Jones' greatest passion, as he said in 1974: "There's nothing like it. I could give up television and recording if I had to, but I'll stay on stage until I'm 97 if I'm still around and people still want to see me."

1

GREEN GREEN GRASS OF HOME

FREDA AND TOM WOODWARD had always yearned for a son. Their wish was finally granted on June 7, 1940 when a small screaming bundle arrived at Freda's family home, number 57 Kingsland Terrace, in the unassuming Welsh coal mining village of Treforest, Pontypridd.

Nearly a month later on July 1, the baby's birth was recorded at the Pontypridd Registry Office, the proud father's name being passed down to another generation: Thomas John Woodward. The young couple's every-day routine quickly and quietly returned to normal as Freda acclimatised herself to the growing demands of her little family, now completed with the arrival of a baby brother for six-year-old Sheila. Tom Senior continued labouring as a coal miner, pushing himself to the limit each day to feed the extra mouth. In the early Forties a miner's wage was calculated not by the hours he toiled but by the amount of coal hacked from the seam – his newly enlarged family only motivated him to work harder.

Treforest has visibly changed little over the last 50 years. The endless rows of terraced houses still reflect the community's strong, close-knit ambience, vastly disparate to that of the grey, imposing main town in which they both nestle and overlook; Pontypridd, popularly known as the 'Gateway to the Valleys'. Set just 12 miles north-west of Cardiff at the foot of the breathtaking mountains and valleys of Glamorganshire, Pontypridd arose around the junction of the Rivers Taff and Rhondda during the inescapable industrialisation of the 19th century. Initially focusing on the Chainworks factory producing anchors for warships and merchant vessels, the town's main source of income soon shifted to coal mining. A cluster of small pit villages like Treforest sprang up to bolster the larger municipality of Pontypridd, which is known to its residents simply as 'Ponty'.

Life was set out in black and white for the inhabitants. The menfolk would work hard throughout the day to feed and clothe their families, then drink equally hard every night at the many working men's clubs. For the women, life offered little more than the ceaseless monotony of looking after their homes, children and husbands, often simultaneously balancing this domestic necessity with a part-time job. Tom and Freda Woodward both came from traditionally large families of six children, all of whom retained their fiercely proud Welsh roots by settling within a stone's throw of each other. "My father was a coal miner and so were his brothers," the adult Tom Jones has frequently explained to reporters curious about his Welsh heritage. "We grew up in a coal mining community, which was very close. We had many, many cousins and we all lived in the same town. To me, that was being Welsh. It was only later, in talking to other people that I realised how rare it was to have all your aunties and uncles around you like that. But it was great because you never felt alone."

In 1933 women were not permitted to step over the threshold of the working men's clubs except on special occasions. It was not surprising therefore that the smartly dressed Tom Woodward, 23, first met his sweetheart, 18-year-old Freda Jones, at a local dance hall where both sexes mingled freely and swung to a contemporary soundtrack of 'Smoke Gets In Your Eyes', 'Falling In Love Again' and 'Goodnight Sweetheart'. Marion Crewe, sister to young Tom's childhood friend David Perry (also known as 'Dai' or the Anglicised Dave), remembers his parents well. "They were wonderful people. Always dressed well; jewellery, make-up. A very smart man, his father was. Always trench macs, pork pie hats – a handsome looking fella."

On the Saturday nights when Freda was allowed to accompany her suitor to the Wood Road Social Club, regulars fondly remember her party piece; a lively rendition of her favourite ditty 'Silver Dollar', complete with actions and expressions. Tom Snr. looked on affectionately, unable to join in as his voice was already affected by the onset of 'black dust' (pneumoconiosis), the deleterious condition plaguing 10 to 30 per cent of all miners, as the insidious coal dust penetrates their lungs. Regardless of this disturbing predicament and the later pressures of family life, the devoted pair never lost the early blossom of their romance. "You'd never see one without the other, they enjoyed their life," says Marion.

After a whirlwind romance, Tom and Freda married on September 9, 1933, and moved straight into the Jones' family home. Rather tellingly, just six months later their baby daughter Sheila arrived on March 11, 1934. Although it was cramped living alongside Freda's parents, there they remained for the best part of 10 years, during which time Tom was also born. The marriage was sufficiently secure to withstand the admiring glances of Treforest's womenfolk. "My father was a good-looking man, and women would open their doors and call, 'Good morning, Thomas!' I liked it," Tom remembers.

The traditional marital roles of this working-class generation enveloped Tom as he watched his father leave for work at the crack of dawn each day,

4

his mother waving him off with the promise of a hearty meal that night. It was an unspoken rule that when Freda heard the squeak of the gate signifying her husband's return, she must have his dinner on the table waiting for him the moment he walked through the front door. God forbid it should be late or, even worse, she should have prepared a different meal to the requested menu of that morning.

Such conventions were the way of life in the Woodward household as they were throughout South Wales. Both Tom and Sheila absorbed these old-fashioned family values and modelled themselves accordingly on their parents. The naturally passive Sheila was content to step back and allow her spirited younger brother to steal the limelight. Tom idolised and emulated his namesake, dressing up and consequently falling over in his father's mining outfit to Tom Snr.'s great delight: "When he was little he used to walk about in my pit boots with the steel tips and sometimes he'd put on my bowler as well. He did look comical." Although he admired his father's physique and sharp way of dressing, Tom was mostly impressed because in his eyes, the authoritative miner provided for the household and held sole responsibility for any decision-making. "My Dad just refused to be henpecked," he would say in later life.

This is not to say that Freda couldn't hold her own, especially when it came to disciplining her young charges. The adult Tom fondly defends his mother's strict control. "She kept me in good clothes and fed me well when times were not easy. If I got the hell knocked out of me it was because I asked for it." One of the strangest traits he was to inherit from his mother was her strong superstitious leaning. Freda refused to allow shoes on a table or a hat on a bed, and believed it was unlucky if a bird flew into the house. "I remember my mother saying when I was a babe-in-arms that a gypsy came to the door selling clothes pegs. My mother would always give them money. The gypsy looked at me and said, 'I see great things for this boy. He has a round crown on his head – that means he will go all over the world.'"

As a baby Tom was particularly attractive; slightly plump with a mass of tight blond curls. With this cuteness came a certain preciousness, fuelled by his doting family. "They always put him on a pedestal. They would worship him," recalls Marion Crewe.

Tom's formative years were dominated by World War II, as influxes of city children were evacuated to the comparative safety of the Welsh valleys. Although Treforest was far removed from the nightly raids on South East England, German fighter planes who had overshot their target of the Cardiff Docks needed to release their bombs elsewhere on the county of Glamorganshire, so as to be able to return to Europe on low fuel. Along with most children of his era, Tom grew up accepting the alarming noises, beaming searchlights and resonance of the anti-aircraft guns as normal. His most striking wartime memory is of the protective cages into which babies would be placed during air raids, as the adult gas masks were too large to fit infants.

In happier times, Tom was a mischievous baby. His first recollection is of sitting in his pram being watched disbelievingly by a shopkeeper through the window. "Apparently my mother had gone to the butcher's to get some sausages and while she called into the grocer's shop I sucked all the meat out of the sausages. I can still see the grocer's face laughing at me."

Freda would frequently sing to her son and maintains that he was born with music in his bones. "While I nursed him, if music came on the radio he'd start to move like a jelly. And he'd make musical sounds at the top of his voice," she says. Whether these early gurglings were perhaps due more to wind than prodigy was soon eclipsed by the fact that, when Tom was only three years old he was regularly emerging from the living room drapes and treating family and friends to an impromptu performance of 'Mule Train' or 'Ghost Riders In The Sky'. "Obviously parents are always likely to be wise after the event, but I know most of the people back home had an idea that Tom was something special as a singer," Freda later admitted.

When Tom was four his paternal grandfather died, enabling the small family to move the short distance from the Jones household to his grand-mother's larger three storey home in Laura Street. The street is deceptive as the third storey comes from the addition of a basement, a luxury not shared by the houses immediately opposite. Number 44 is the first house in the terrace, situated at the top of a steep slope with an impressive backdrop onto hills and over Pontypridd. The turn of the century house occupied by the Woodwards was divided into three sections, with the adults at the bottom, Sheila at the top and Tom eventually graduating to his own room in the middle. Freda was extremely house-proud and inventive with the decorating, frequently inviting friends over to admire her latest domestic creation.

Young Tom's exhibitionist streak developed as he watched Larry Parks in the sensational film *The Jolson Story* at the local cinema. Al Jolson had been popular during the first half of the century, performing such tunes as 'Mammy' and 'April Showers' down on bended knee, with his trademark blacked-up face now uncomfortably out of date. Tom was enthralled by Parks' melodramatic performance of the self-styled 'minstrel', with his exuberant gestures and immense self-confidence. "I think Al Jolson was a soulful singer," says Tom of the early icon, who was enjoying a revival when the impressionable fan first saw him. "I think that's why he blacked-up to try to look like it, as well as sound like it. That's the way his voice was. And I think I was influenced a lot by that. I liked his energy."

Encouraged by his extended family, Tom's musical flair turned into quite a little money-spinner. He would be taken to the nearby corner shop and while his mother was choosing the weekly supplies, he remembers being "put on an orange crate in the shop and singing to a group of travellers. I just loved to sing, I was never nervous, and there was an added incentive." The grocer insisted that Tom's audience made a small donation for the entertainment. The little boy was inspired by the extra pocket-money: "That taught me an important lesson," he said. Tom would also be taken to meetings of the Treforest Women's Guild, where he would display similar signs of precociousness.

Learning to flaunt his talent in this way stood Tom in good stead when he enrolled at Treforest Primary School, where according to this particular pupil, they "tried for four-and-a-half days to teach us". The school was just down the road and round the corner from his home, hidden behind tall, imposing stone walls. Today a quarter of Pontypridd's primary school children attend Welsh speaking schools, but Tom and his classmates didn't have the opportunity to study their native tongue. Tom never displayed any particular academic leanings and instead preferred to concentrate on his love for music and art, and build on his solo performances. His childhood friend Brian Blackler remembers: "We started school together when we were five and we went on from there. He used to sing every Friday in front of his class and he'd beat the music out on the table."

Tom explains, "The teacher would be sorting out the register, he or she would say, 'You children amuse yourselves.' We'd put on a concert. The kids in the class would get up, tell a joke, sing songs, recite poetry. I would get up and sing." Tom's favourite showpiece at this time was still 'Ghost Riders In The Sky', with its melancholy cowboy chorus, 'Yipee-I-Yay', of which Tom was particularly fond. To an impressionable five-year-old, it conjured up romantic images of the Wild West where men slept beneath the stars and the cries of wild coyotes split the night air. Tom would rarely miss any opportunity to showcase his vocal talents and excitedly joined the school choir where, in his enthusiasm, he would frequently be told off for drowning out the other young voices during the Welsh national anthem, 'Hen Wlad Fy Nhadau', and similarly patriotic songs like 'Men Of Harlech'. Famously, his headmaster was once amazed to hear him transform the ingenuous Sunday School tones of 'The Lord's Prayer' into a gospel-flavoured Negro spiritual.

Tom's flair for music continued to be cultivated at home. "When I was six or seven, we would have family and friends round to the house at holiday times for get-togethers. Everybody had to do something – a sort of party piece. That was a great opportunity for me to show off, so I'd get up on the table and sing – and swivel my hips even then!" Among those particularly supportive of his musical efforts were his many uncles, all of whom sang. His Uncle George passed on some valuable and lasting advice: "Sing to the people's faces – let them see what you are singing about."

With both children now at school, Freda took on a part-time job at a local factory to fill her days. True to the traditional male pride of the Valleys, Tom Snr. was uncomfortable with her new employment. His misgivings came to a head one day when a youth approached the Woodwards as they waited in line for the cinema, and greeted Tom's mother by her Christian name. "My father demanded to know who the boy was. My mother told him he was just a kid who worked in the factory. 'You're not going to the factory anymore,' my father told her. 'If they can't call you Mrs Woodward, then you don't work there.'" Knowing no better, Tom absorbed his father's views, assimilating this outspoken display purely as a protection of his mother's dignity. Eagerly he watched for further instruction on the codes of manhood.

"When I was little I yearned to be a man, to be the best I could," he says. "I have a memory of being a small boy, hearing a noise in the night and my father getting up to see what it was. I remember thinking, 'When I grow up, will I be as brave as that?'" Somewhat surprisingly Tom Snr. did not advise his son to follow him down the pits. "He had this talent for singing, so I thought why the hell shouldn't he use it," he later recalled. "The mining life with all the comradeship was fine for me, but I was much happier that Tom made up his own mind what to do with his life."

As Tom grew older, his preoccupation with singing began to distract him from his schoolwork. Aged 11, Tom quite literally ascended to Treforest Secondary Modern School, which was perched precipitously atop a hill, where he was noted for his increasing absences rather than his diligent attendance. He soon fell in with a group of local boys, among them Dai Perry, Brian Blackler, Alan Barratt, Brian Pitman and the Quinn brothers. Tom began to make a name for himself as a bit of a tearaway, disruptive in the classroom and often playing truant. He recalls how he would particularly torment Mr Bryn, a teacher who bore the nickname 'Mr Fuss' because, "He was always fussing over us. If you were making a noise in class, he used to walk up and down between the desks and as he went past you, you'd think he didn't know you were the culprit, but then wallop, you knew you had been caught!" Scholastic endeavour was not high on Tom's list of priorities, according to Brian Pitman: "He didn't really have much time for school, except that he was always very good at drawing and singing." Tom was also more interested in a game of rugby or football, or training with the gang at the local boxing club.

At the same time, Tom was becoming increasingly aware of girls, and another classmate remembers this healthy fascination with the opposite sex: "The girls were attracted by that rebel thing. I can remember him staggering around wearing white trunks with his comb always stuck inside them. He was always preening himself – but it worked, the girls loved him." Tom's first kiss was stolen during a playground game of kiss chase, when a young girl named Melinda Rose Trenchard caught his eye. Although the two adolescents lived only streets away, Melinda had attended a Catholic junior school. Despite being aware of each other locally, they didn't discover their mutual attraction until they both moved up to the same secondary school. Tom's hormonal changes soon prompted him to look at his neighbour from a different perspective as he watched her play an innocent childhood game. "I can still remember seeing her when I must have been 11," he smiles. "I walked down her street and she was bending down and playing marbles. I saw these great legs and all of a sudden I thought of her in a new light. Afterwards I had to run my wrists under cold water. I was an early starter." Tom's parents had never taken the time to explain the birds and bees to him so the sudden surge of pubescent testosterone was initially a cause for concern . . . "I can remember the first time I got to know myself better – I thought I'd broken it!"

Such intermingling with the opposite sex was cut dramatically short when in his twelfth year Tom was struck down with tuberculosis. A common ailment in the early Fifties, the cure, the drug isoniazid, had only recently been made available in 1951. In spite of this glimmer of hope, TB remained a potentially crippling or even fatal illness which required lengthy periods of bed rest to assist recuperation. "I spent two years in bed recovering. It was the worst time of my life," he remembers. As Tom's condition was contagious his doctor recommended specialist convalescence away from home, but Freda insisted on caring personally for her son. The family's 'best room' was converted into living quarters for the invalid as he struggled with typical symptoms including loss of appetite, fever, fatigue, chills, night sweats and coughing. As the infection begins in the lungs and often leaves a scar, the predominant fear shared by Tom and his parents was that his fast maturing voice and stamina would suffer as a result of this debilitating disease.

Although given regular tutoring in a vain attempt to keep up his schooling, Tom continued to fail dismally at his studies, preferring to while away many hours honing his artistic abilities. He took to sketching and painting the tantalising girls he could see playing outside his window. As the months literally turned into years and Tom passed his thirteenth then fourteenth birthdays, he came to realise that he was missing out on a precious part of his personal development. When the illness took visible effect on his body, Tom became frustrated and anxious that his friends might no longer relate to him. The young rogue popularly known as 'Woodsie' was almost unrecognisable; replaced instead by a tall figure with no trace of his earlier puppy fat, whose mousy hair had darkened to ebony.

After the risk of infecting others had gone, friends like Brian Blackler were allowed to visit to break the monotony. "When he had TB, I used to go over and sit with him and he'd have a little guitar and he'd sing," he says. The strumming could be heard by the neighbours at all hours of the day. Finally, in 1954 Tom's health was restored sufficiently to allow his family to take him and Brian on a much needed holiday to Trecco Bay, Porthcawl. Soon regaining his confidence to perform in public, Tom gave an impromptu concert from the back of a lorry. "Tom pulled out a guitar and began singing to a small group of us," says Brian. "He was always singing. It was then we realised he was going to go places as his talent shone through."

When Tom returned to school he was hopelessly behind. Desperate to become a man and leave this traumatic period behind, his rebellion encompassed further spells of truancy during which he hung around a record shop called Freddy Phaze in the middle of Pontypridd. It was probably here that he first heard the exciting new American music of Bill Haley & His Comets, with their unmistakable 'Rock Around The Clock' and 'Shake, Rattle And Roll'. Over the next couple of years the teenage Tom would experience the strident young sounds of Jerry Lee Lewis and Elvis Presley, his next major influences after Al Jolson. The music of other refreshing American singers who followed in their wake slowly began to infiltrate the outskirts of South Wales, bringing with it the freedom of rock'n'roll's first flourish.

Tom revelled in these exhilarating musical developments and avidly soaked up Radio Luxembourg, the commercial station beamed in from Europe broadcasting 'unhealthy' doses of rock'n'roll in the evenings, and bandleader-turned-disc jockey Jack Jackson's ground-breaking Light Programme pop show, *Record Roundup*. TB had ensured that whether Tom had wanted to or not, he would never follow his father down the mines. Gradually the idea began to form in his mind that a career in music might be his for the taking. After all, encouragement was all around him. "The kids at school used to say, 'You can sing better than anybody. You should be, you *will* be, a singer.' That's what people said and I believed it," he later told journalist Lesley Salisbury. "When I sang I thought, 'God, if I could do this for a living, if I could only sing and not have to do other work, then that would be wonderful; I'd be complete.' "

Tom was simultaneously rediscovering the other passion in his life: women. Regaining his former self-assurance, he reintroduced himself to the girl he had kissed in the playground a couple of years earlier. Melinda, known now as Linda, recalls: "When we met up again after he went back to school, I didn't recognise him at first, but I was immediately attracted to him again." During Tom's extended absence she had metamorphosed into a radiant young woman. Tom's cousin Kath Woodward shared the opinion of most of the little village, "Linda was lovely. A very smart, pretty girl she was. We used to call her Doris Day." Beverley Williams, Linda's classmate illustrates the point: "It was the Teddy Boy era then, and Tom was a big Teddy Boy and Linda was exactly like Doris Day. The stand-up collar, pencil-slim skirt, short, short hair, curly on the top. She'd be in school uniform, but with a twist.

"Tom was in the same year as us, but a lower grade. So we were in the 'A's and he was in the 'D's! There was Tom and Linda, and there was Hazel and John, and both couples stayed together. You could see the partnership then. You knew that they were together and that was it." The young sweethearts rapidly became inseparable in the first giddy flush of romance. "We got together at dances at the youth club and though at this time we were too young to say we were going out together, we always seemed to end up with each other," remembers Linda. Impressed with Tom's musical vocation, his steady girlfriend enthusiastically encouraged him when he bought his first, cheap, full-sized guitar. It was soon understood that the relationship was a serious one, perhaps even with a future.

Impassioned smooching in the local telephone box and the garden shed soon led to the inevitable. Goaded by his gang to overcome the ultimate sexual hurdle, 15-year-old Tom persuaded 14-year-old Linda to 'go all the way'. Tom maintains that this was a natural progression for their loving relationship: "I was never obsessed about losing my virginity because I was fairly sexually advanced beforehand. It happened up a mountain – it was very hilly where we lived, and in the summer time that was the place to be." This advancement in Tom's courting of the young Catholic girl heightened his protective feelings towards her and he fiercely denied to his friends that his belle had been deflowered.

Meanwhile, Tom had fully reinstated himself as one of the lads. Dai Perry was his partner in crime, as Dai's sister Marion Crewe recalls, "Tom and Dave were up to mischief all the time as lads. They used to go round town together, all in black leather, with dark glasses on." The pair were as thick as thieves and one would not be seen without the other. Marion remembers an incident at her wedding where she gave them a piece of her mind. "I gave them both a row, Tom and David, because they'd been in somebody's garden and pinched sweet peas. So they came to the wedding and they had the biggest buttonholes – they were nearly as big as my bouquet! They had all these flowers jutting out of their lapels so I said, 'Take some of those flowers out, you look ridiculous!' But they wouldn't, they thought it was all a big joke." Not content with upstaging the blushing bride at her wedding, Tom somehow always managed to become the centre of attention. Marion continues: "Then I had a birthday party in my house for Dave, and Tom came and he plugged in his guitar, and they're old houses aren't they? Fused every light in my house! There we were, he was still carrying on dancing and singing, and we were looking for somebody to mend the fuse . . ."

Like many young people in Treforest at that time, Tom left school without a single academic qualification. "I finished school at 15 – everyone did unless you went to the county Grammar. If you failed the 11 plus (which I did) you went to secondary modern school and had to leave when you were 15." Unable to go down the mines, he managed to find a job locally as an apprentice glove cutter at the Polyglove Factory on the Broadway in Pontypridd. Albeit essentially achieving his goal of 'becoming a man', Tom soon found the hard, repetitive work an anticlimax. "I worked nine hours a day in a hot, stuffy place packed with people. I stuck it for nearly two years. It was dull."

Tom would daydream while he worked and discuss the growing trend of rock'n'roll. He remembers, "When 'Rock Around The Clock' came out, the other workers thought it was awful. But I liked it. It was exciting to me." One of the few respites from the tedium came at the factory's Christmas party. "They were playing rock'n'roll records and I was the only kid that could jive," recalls Tom, "which was like doing the bop in America. So there I was dancing with all these girls. I thought, 'This is wonderful. This is it. This is for me.'"

For his efforts, Tom took home 38 shillings a week (just under £2).★ His wages would subsidise his ever increasing vinyl collection. "Every Saturday I would buy at least one record from the record shop at Pontypridd. Even when I was married I'd still be there with the lads on a Saturday, with a Teddy Boy suit on, listening to records." He still remembers the first record he ever bought, which became the sensual backdrop to many a lusty encounter. "It was by Clyde McPhatter and it was called 'Treasure Of Love' and I could play it on guitar. It wasn't the first one I nicked mind you, just the one I bought!"

Tom became a true Teddy Boy, enrolling with local ruffians the 'Ponty

---

★ This was a relatively low wage, but fairly reflected Tom's age and position. Still, it would have been ample as he wasn't paying for his living costs and according to Brain's Brewery, a pint of beer in 1955–6 was approximately sixpence.

Teds'. The name 'Ted' or 'Teddy' was an affectionate abbreviation for Edwardian, the style of clothes the boys had adopted as their own. In sharp contrast to the short jackets, baggy trousers, small shoes, wide ties and short haircuts that were a fashion hangover from the Forties, the Teddy Boys would wear 'drape' jackets that stopped just above the knee, and tightly fitting 'drainpipe' trousers often tailored in extravagant fabrics such as velvet. Big crepe-soled or 'winkle-picker' pointed shoes, thin ties called 'Slim Jims' and greased hair styled in a D.A. (Duck's Arse – long on the top in a lavish quiff) finished off the look. Linda, who had also left school at 15 and was working as a drapery assistant, lovingly tended Tom's precious locks.

The Teddy Boys modelled themselves on their rock'n'roll heroes Jerry Lee Lewis, Elvis Presley, Little Richard and Fats Domino, and assumed an aggressive pose. Later Tom reflected, "People think a Teddy Boy is a juvenile delinquent, always getting into punch-ups. I got into punch-ups in my time, but I was never a juvenile delinquent. Teddy Boys were men with big shoulders. We were tough. As a teenager I was bored and didn't know where I was going. The only thing I knew was that I could sing. I was rebellious and hated being young."

Tom and Dai Perry had begun smoking and drinking in public houses at 14 in order to appear older. There was little or no opposition from the local landlords who were only too happy to serve them pints of Fernvale, Rhymney or Mitchells beer. Synonymous with the underage consumption of alcohol was brawling, especially when the Ponty Teds ventured further afield and clashed with other established gangs. Tom remains unrepentant about such exploits. "All of the boys I knocked around with were men. They took pride in acting like it, and a badge of honour was a black eye. Those days, the way things were, you had to stand up and fight for what you believed in."

During one particular altercation over a woman, Tom was unceremoniously head-butted through a fish and chip shop window. He and his ever-present accomplice, Dai, received a warning from two passing policemen. Regardless of the threat of arrest, the fight continued elsewhere, eventually involving Tom's opponent's whole family.

"His father jumped on my back. He had his arms around my throat and I screamed at Dai to get him off," recalls Tom. "Then this guy's mother came flying into the action, his brother ran out of the house and together they beat the hell out of me. Dai didn't get involved because this guy's father was an older fellow and Dai didn't feel he could hit him or the woman, so I got a pasting. I've still got the scar where the guy bit my finger." Indeed Tom's nose was broken several times during this period. The assaults were rough and ready where booting, punching and head-butting were an acceptable way of proving one's masculinity, but using any type of weapon, such as a knife, was considered dirty and cowardly. "I wanted to be a man so no one could push me around. It was just a stage I was going through."

In his boredom Tom turned to petty crime. One day he broke into the tobacconist's shop situated practically on his doorstep. Without too much detective work, the police caught up with the inexperienced thief and found his loot incriminatingly concealed beneath the sofa back at home. Not only had he caused considerable damage during the break-in, but Tom had also disappointed his parents who had previously been blind to his faults. Many years later, Tom was to admit, "I've been arrested for fighting and for breaking and entering. I broke into a shop for some cigarettes. I was arrested and put on probation. It wasn't a big crime or anything – nothing planned, just a spur of the moment thing. I was a teenager, a kid."

2

DO YOU TAKE THIS MAN

CONTRACEPTION WAS NOT high on Tom's list of priorities as he eagerly pursued the courtship of the 15-year-old Linda. The couple truly believed they were in love and that nothing could touch them. "Linda was my first girlfriend," remembers Tom. "Well . . . she was the first girl that I had sex with. I didn't care about contraception – I knew that I loved this girl so I didn't give it a second thought. So Linda got pregnant."

The reality wasn't quite as flippant as Tom would lead us to believe. One cold day in late autumn 1956, Linda and Tom were sheltering from the elements in the telephone box at the end of Laura Street, when the frightened girl divulged her suspicion that she was expecting Tom's baby. His initial reaction was sheer horror. His indifference to sexual precautions would mean that his carefree days as a reckless Ponty Ted were numbered. Eventually, after many tears the stricken twosome resolved that they would stay together as they had always planned. But the hardest part was yet to come: they had to tell their parents.

The ominous gathering occurred not long after in the Woodward house, with Linda's parents Bill Trenchard, a mechanic, and his waitress wife Violet sombrely present. The grown-ups discussed the options open to the disgraced children, who sat gravely waiting for the verdict. Tom was silent while Linda cried quietly. An abortion was out of the question as it went against the Catholic faith practised by the Trenchard family, let alone being illegal in 1956 and physically too late. Instead, the more common solution for underage parents at this time was for the girl to disappear for a few months on a supposed 'holiday', where signs of her blooming pregnancy would not be seen by the gossips of her home town. The child would then be adopted and the clandestine mother could return, her shameful secret known only to her immediate family. The third, and seemingly final option discussed, was that the baby could be brought up by Vi as a sister or brother to Linda.

The adults ranted and raged through the night, totally oblivious to the feelings of the teenagers until, almost as an afterthought, Tom Snr. turned to his son and asked him what he wanted to do. Tom's reply took the adults by surprise: "I said, 'I want to get married to Linda and she wants to get married to me.' My father just looked at me, it all went dead quiet for a moment and then he said, 'Go ahead.' I always loved him for it." Tom's father's attitude might well have been due to history repeating itself, his own marriage having also been born of necessity. After the initial shock of this outburst there was yet more agonising, especially from Tom's grandmother who disapproved vehemently because of their ages. Eventually the two sets of parents begrudgingly came round to the idea, even though it meant waiting until after Linda's sixteenth birthday in January, by which time she would be showing considerably.

Linda and Tom soon had to endure the same interrogation all over again from their extended families. Tom's uncles, who had previously been so supportive of his burgeoning musical talent, spoke out against the decision. Like most of Linda's family, they felt that the self-absorbed pair were far too young to be considering marriage and parenthood, and promptly predicted failure on both accounts. As more and more people discovered the dark secret, it became the scandal on everyone's lips. "It was the talk of the village," remembers Beverley Williams. "It was a five minute wonder . . . It's different today. Years ago it was a terrible thing, it was very hush-hush but at the end of the day they were happy enough, everything worked out right." As January 14, Linda's birthday, came and went, wheels were set in motion for the lovers to wed, even with a semblance of pride. "It made me a man. It gave me more responsibility. I felt strong," says Tom.

On March 2, 1957, the flat and formal atmosphere of the Registry Office on Courthouse Street was momentarily disturbed as Tom wed eight-months-pregnant Linda. Although under different circumstances the betrothed could have taken their pick of many pretty nearby churches, the constraints of pregnancy and opposing religious beliefs dictated the uninspiring location. After the customarily brief ceremony held in the poorly lit marriage room, sparsely furnished with just a few chairs and a table, the small wedding party emerged outside onto the steep hill next to the railway. Around a dozen members of immediate family and friends gathered shortly afterwards for a quiet celebratory drink, although technically the consumption of alcohol was still illegal for the underage Woodwards, particularly for Linda in her condition.

The predicament of the newlyweds soon sobered Tom up. "I got married at 16 and that straightened me out. When you're married you grow up quicker. You have responsibilities and you have to knuckle down." Soon after the wedding Tom and Linda took up residence in the basement of her parents' house, 3 Cliff Terrace – a little cul-de-sac running on a parallel to Wood Road, and just two minutes walk from Laura Street. In order to call on the Woodwards rather than the Trenchards, friends would park on Wood Road and run down a small flight of steps opposite the chapel at the end of Cliff Terrace. They would then bang on the grate in front of the house, above Tom and Linda's living room window, to catch their attention. Bill Trenchard had been suffering from tuberculosis, the same illness that plagued Tom as a child, and it was understandable that Linda wanted to be with her parents as the baby's birth drew near.

In preparation for the coming addition to his family Tom had moved on from the Polyglove factory, taking on a more lucrative position as a labourer for the British Coated Board Paper Mills at the Treforest Industrial Estate, where he worked alongside his future cousin Kath Woodward. Money was tight as Tom and Linda saved for the birth of their child. "I did all the overtime I could, but because I was so young my rate was low," Tom recalls. "I was working night shifts at the paper mill and I couldn't even afford to take the night off when Linda went into hospital. I set off for work on a push-bike as the ambulance was taking her to hospital."

On April 11, 1957 Tom hurried back from work to call the maternity hospital in Glossop Terrace, Cardiff, from the same red telephone box at the end of Laura Street where Linda had first told Tom of her pregnancy. He was rewarded with the news of a healthy son, who in due course they named Mark Stephen. Tom arrived as soon as he could, wearing his ever present Teddy Boy suit. "I walked into the hospital and saw Linda and my son, and I walked out and thought, 'Who can touch me now?' I was so proud. I thought, 'I'm a man! I have a son!' "

Tom, however, was not untouchable. Tragedy hit the Trenchards almost exactly six weeks after Mark's birth, when after a period of hospitalisation Linda's father Bill died from TB, aged just 42. With the distraught Linda at home comforting her widowed mother, and the arrival of an extra mouth to feed, Tom was required to bring in more money for his family. As he passed his seventeenth birthday two weeks later, he realised he had no choice but to approach the foreman for a raise, although that would mean going against the Union's regulations regarding adult wages.

"There were these winding machines in the mill. I'd been watching the fellas work them and the foreman asked me if I could do it. I said, 'I *know* I can.' So he told me that if I went back that night he'd give me the job. I'd already worked the day shift but I went home and came back again that night." But Tom was stopped in his tracks when a Union official stepped in and voiced his objections to a 17-year-old being paid the same rate as the adult workers. Tom was particularly upset by this as the man was actually related to him and was fully aware of the financial pressure Tom was under. Fortunately the foreman decided to take pity on Tom by side-stepping the rule and promoting him from pushing enormous reels of paper to the 'man's job' of working on the winding machine. "So I was put on the machine and at 17 they paid me a man's wage – it was about £12 a week." This meant labouring for a sweaty 12 hours, starting at 6 a.m. every day, drying paper on the heavy machinery, but it was worth it for the extra money. "And we managed fine on that because we lived with my mother-in-law and didn't pay rent. So it was easy."

The fact that Tom was a married father with a full-time job before he was old enough to drive did not deter his increasingly roving eye. "When I was younger my wife didn't mind if I went out – as long as I went home in the end," he chuckled to Lola Borg. "And it was a small town, so if I'd made a wrong move she'd definitely hear all about it. It was the accepted thing then – oh yes, I wasn't in the pub by myself!" Many of the Ponty Teds were in a similar position having married at 16 or 17. "You started working at 15 . . . when you're working you think you're a man . . . you want to be an adult. Getting married is part of it." Like their fathers before them, the young husbands frequently escaped to the drinking dens for some male camaraderie. "There was a pub in Pontypridd called the White Hart and there were no women allowed in the bar. It wasn't that we didn't want women in there because we didn't *like* them – we just couldn't be ourselves. You couldn't tell dirty jokes, you couldn't break wind!" On Saturday nights it was quite normal for the lads, married or otherwise, to stay out late drinking, then congregate in the dozen or so Indian and Chinese restaurants in the nearby town of Cardiff. Curry was the staple diet of the Ponty Teds.

The faded haunt of Tom's family, grandly called the Treforest Non Political Working Men's Club but known to the regulars as the Wood Road Social Club, was the unlikely setting for his professional musical début. Spurred on by his uncles and in particular his cousin Georgie, nicknamed 'Snowy' on account of his brilliant white hair, Tom was lured away from his usual Saturday night out in Cardiff to sing for the men at the social club for the princely sum of £1. Charlie Ashman arranged the performance in which Tom sang half a dozen numbers ranging from the contemporary rock'n'roll of 'Blue Suede Shoes' to the raw, bluesy 'Sixteen Tons', accompanying himself on guitar. Amateur appearances like this were commonplace in the pubs and clubs around the valleys where the lack of television prompted people to make their own entertainment. Although at this stage Tom didn't especially pursue this avenue, his love of drunken sing-a-longs with his pals at the Wheatsheaf Hotel in Rickards Street soon attracted the attention of the landlords, Jack and Joan Lister. Matching Tom's talent with the enthusiastic ready-made audience, they capitalised on the situation and converted the room upstairs into a mini concert hall. Tom, now 18, gradually became known as a regular entertainer in this new arena, singing well-loved standards such as 'My Yiddishe Momma'. Although still maturing, Tom's incredible voice surpassed his peers, and his trademark macho roar was already apparent.

While enjoying the attention he received strumming and singing along to the three chords he knew, Tom felt his act was a little mundane. Deep down he longed for the excitement and comradeship of a real-life rock'n'roll band. He took it upon himself to learn the rudiments of drumming and briefly joined an amateur group called The De Avalons as their drummer. The novelty soon wore off as Tom realised that he missed the limelight of being centre stage. His next opportunity to grasp the microphone again came when another local group, The Misfits, had an opening for a lead singer with a bit of charisma.

The Misfits were part of the growing trend of Concert Parties, an ensemble of up to six acts that would travel the pubs of the valleys and provide an entire night's entertainment. A typical Concert Party would include a comedian or two, a pianist, a band, a girl singer and perhaps a magician or a juggler. Tom was astonished to discover that he could earn the same amount in 20 minutes singing with The Misfits as he could for a whole day's toil at the Paper Mill. One night, to his great delight, he pocketed a staggering £5 and was for once rendered almost speechless.

Over the next two years Tom learnt the tricks of the trade, fortifying his longing to be a professional singer and earn his keep the easy way. The extra money in addition to his regular employment kept Linda quiet, and more often than not she would spend her evenings at home, tending to their baby son.

Accompanying himself on his cheap guitar, Tom sang in public either on his own or with The Misfits whenever he could, learning how to deal with rowdy crowds and hecklers and gamely singing above the noise from bars. In his quest to achieve fame and fortune Tom would optimistically enter talent competitions at venues like the Wheatsheaf Hotel, where on one occasion he performed the song 'Go As You Please'. Once he auditioned unsuccessfully for a televised talent show at the YMCA, but the outcome was a farce as Tom had left his beloved guitar at home because it was raining and he did not have a case to protect it. When he got up on stage and requested 'It's Only Make Believe' in the key of C, the accompanist instead played a much older melody of the same name, leaving Tom flustered and red faced.

Nevertheless Tom held on to his dream, with sound support from his loved ones. Along with Linda's unquestioning acceptance he remembers, "What kept me going was local encouragement, specially from my Dad.

You keep thinking about a lucky break and wondering if it will ever come. It was worse, really, being in Wales, when all the pop music thing was so definitely in London. But it would have taken tremendous confidence on my part to have made the break and gone to London on my own. I had commitments and I felt at least secure in Wales . . ."

Roscommon County Library Service

WITHDRAWN
3 FROM STOCK

A BOY FROM NOWHERE

Elsewhere in Pontypridd, a young bass player called Vernon Hopkins had been striving to promote his up-and-coming group, The Senators. He had teamed up with friends Jeff Maher and Keith Davies who both played guitar, and the three of them would rehearse regularly in Vernon's parents' front room. Once they had established themselves a little with local gigs, The Senators enlisted drummer Brian Price and a singer, Tommy Pittman, who adopted the stage name Tommy Redman. Along with organising the group's equipment, Vernon also worked for the regional newspaper the *Pontypridd Observer*, which gave him the opportunity to sneak in adverts for The Senators' appearances when there was space on the back page. An early break for the budding musicians was a spot on the South Wales television show *Discs A Go-Go* with a couple of other local groups. With such exciting publicity the new faces soon developed a loyal following, and by the time Tom first heard of the group in late 1961, the line-up had already changed, with Jeff Maher and Brian Price being replaced by Mike Roberts and Keith 'Alva' Turner.

The future looked bright for The Senators, but there was one matter vexing the more committed members. The unreliability of their lead singer, Tommy Redman, meant they were often forced to perform as a somewhat less dynamic instrumental group. "On Friday nights we used to play in the YMCA," recollects Keith Davies. "In the breaks Tommy used to go out and have a few pints. And he liked a game of cards. One night he stayed out a bit longer than he should have, playing cards, and one thing led to another and we were struggling to carry the night. This had happened on a couple of occasions before, and it couldn't go on like that."

Tommy's fondness for three card brag had evidently led him into trouble. His initial luck turned into a losing streak and he remained at the pub, determined to win back his money. No matter how desperately the marooned Senators pleaded, there was no persuading him to return to the YMCA to complete the second half of the gig. "Vernon said, 'Well, look, I know a guy who sings in a Concert Party, he's probably

426.211
ROSCOMMON
782
4216409

up in the White Hart – Tom Woodward.' So Vernon went up and got Tom," says Keith.

Furious with Tommy Redman and conscious of the constraints of time, Vernon took the matter in hand. "I raced out of the YMCA and down the length of the High Street to the White Hart, where I knew Tom Woodward would be. When I got there he was sitting at the bar with his powder blue Teddy Boy outfit on, clutching a pint of bitter as usual. When I asked him to stand in for us, he said, 'No, Friday night's my drinking night,' knowing that there was no booze at the YMCA." Vernon finally enticed Tom into filling in for the missing singer by bribing him with a crate of beer, which he would smuggle into the building and ply him with between each song.

Legend has it that Tom bounded onto the stage, greeting Keith Davies with, "Do you know 'Great Balls Of Fire' in C?" and hit it off immediately. The set was completed with a flourish of rock'n'roll standards and Tom later walked off with an equal share of The Senators' £6 fee and an inkling that this could be the group for him.

Vernon was suitably impressed with Tom's performance and well aware of his enthusiasm. "Tom was desperate to get in the band, because we had done local television and I was building things up then. We were doing our own business, hiring rooms and halls, charging at the door. There was energy there, it was really going well."

On the negative side, Vernon sensed the band's misgivings. "The other members weren't fussed, because he was a bit of a tearaway, you might say . . . There were so many good singers around, he didn't stand out particularly. But I knew it, I could see it; I could see the energy. But he wasn't a popular singer with the people because of his looks and attitude." Shortly after Tom's electric début with The Senators, Vernon knew that the messy situation needed to be aired and the choice between the two vocalists had to be made. Following a rehearsal with Tom one afternoon in December 1961, Vernon called a meeting at his parents' house in Rhydyfelin to decide on the singer's future. Mike Roberts the guitarist and drummer Alva Turner joined Keith, who recalls: "There was a knock at the door, and Tommy Pittman said, 'Look, I'm sorry, you know, I didn't turn up . . . I want to remain in the band.' So we had to have a little chin-wag." Vernon swiftly took control. "There was a vote on it," he says. "Two members of the band voted him in, and the other two said 'no' because they didn't like the aggressiveness or his persona. I said, 'I'm the leader, it's my band and I'm going to stick with Tom.'"

Keith continues, "So we called the two of them in, and Vernon said, 'You left us in the lurch and we've been doing alright with Tom. I think I'd like to stick as we are.' I think it hurt Tommy very much, but he'd made a rod for his own back." The decision seemed to go down amicably and the

22

rival singers even left the house together on their way home. Tommy Pittman went on to join The Strollers, a fairly successful rival to The Senators, but Keith believes he always bore a grudge against his friends for being sacked: "It's a sore point with Tommy Pittman, it's something that's festered with him for years and years. But it was down to Tommy, it was nothing underhanded or anything like that."★

Over Christmas 1961 and the following few months, Tom Woodward forged ahead with his new group after formally leaving The Misfits. Early on it was decreed that he needed a catchy stage name; one that blended neatly with The Senators. Nothing the boys could come up with seemed appropriate, so Vernon, lacking inspiration, popped out to the telephone box and skimmed down the surnames beginning with 'S' listed in the phone directory, hoping to link Tom with The Senators. He explains, "I saw the name 'Scott' and thought, 'That's it!' I ran back in and declared, 'Tommy Scott & The Senators' and everyone said, 'Great!' " Keith helped Tom with the next bit. "I can remember down Vernon's house teaching him how to write 'Scott' with a big 'S' and a big 'T', because he liked to sign the autographs."

Back on track, the group resumed their regular gigs, and Vernon continued to plug the new line-up in the *Pontypridd Observer* whenever he could. On May 26, 1962 a small article detailing the rise of The Senators was published on the third page, with the following caption under an early publicity photograph: "The Pontypridd group who are making quite a name for themselves in modern music. Their soloist is popular Tommy Scott, Keith Davies on rhythm guitar, Alva Turner on drums, Vernon Hopkins on bass guitar and Mike Roberts on lead guitar." It is worth noting that in this period singing groups were not the norm, as the British pop scene was dominated by instrumental groups and solo vocalists until The Beatles' astounding breakthrough in 1963. The Senators persevered nonetheless, bent on making their mark locally and, hopefully, further afield when an opportunity arose.

The bookings were handled for a while by Alva's father, Horace Turner. He would arrange their fees and other related matters, as Vernon describes, "He liked it, his son was in the band. It was his little 'perk'." Horace took no commission for his efforts but was delighted to help the group out and immensely enjoyed attending the concerts he'd arranged with his wife, Pearl. This involvement continued even after the departure of his son from the band. Performing without a rhythmic backbone would have been a serious setback for the rapidly improving group, but luckily, the day after Alva left, Mike Roberts happened to stumble across 17-year-old

★ Today Tommy Pittman works as a welder in Treforest, just occasionally singing in public.

drummer Chris Rees in the shoe shop where he worked. Chris was undeterred by the fact that his new colleagues were in their early twenties, and brought with him an even more pronounced longing for fame and fortune, eagerly changing his name to also adopt a stage persona; Chris Slade.

With Horace Turner's help, The Senators evolved into a smooth operation with established shows each week. Typically, they would appear at the Empress Ballroom in Abercynon on Tuesdays, alternate between The Green Fly in Bedwas and the Regent Ballroom in Pontypridd on Thursdays, and on Fridays they would play at the alcohol free YMCA. Other favourite spots included The Wheatsheaf and the Memorial Hall, in Tredegar. The rehearsals continued each Wednesday at Vernon's house, where his teenage sister was only too pleased to supply a steady stream of sandwiches and tea. They would start at 7 p.m. and practise until 10 p.m., when they would nip out to the pub to catch last orders. Such a heavy schedule meant that the boys were exhausted each day at their regular employment, and Keith Davies in particular remembers being sacked from three different places for sleeping on the job!

1962 was an exciting year for The Senators as they gelled as a band and picked up a tremendous following in the surrounding villages. At the beginning of each gig, the musicians would warm up the audience with a couple of instrumental numbers, before Tom made his entrance, whipping the crowd into a frenzy. He worked diligently on his vocal style by listening to other popular singers, like his ultimate idol, Jerry Lee Lewis. The singer/pianist had caught Tom's imagination early on with his outrageous showmanship, wild lifestyle and hits including 'Whole Lotta Shakin' Goin' On' and 'Great Balls Of Fire'. Tom also admired Elvis Presley, the handsome young singer from Memphis, Tennessee, who had emerged not just as the foremost purveyor of rock'n'roll but as a potent sex symbol and idol to a whole generation of teenagers.

Tom elaborates: "I imitated other singers at first, and without being conscious of developing my own style, it happened. Once I was aware of the fact that I did have my own style, I was able to pick out what was good and what was bad about it, and also what other people did or did not like. I worked on getting rid of the things that I thought were bad and continued to build on the things I thought were good about my style." Sometimes, however, Tom found he actually had to work harder on the spectators than on his voice. "In the early days I had some really tough audiences. It's the hardest job in the world to stop a group of Welshmen drinking and try and make them listen to your songs. I had to bawl at them to win their attention and respect. The strength of my voice has its roots in those early days. I was glad to have had that kind of experience. It was very good training."

Tom would also visually stand out from the crowd and the backing boys with his stage clothing. While the four musicians were decked out in matching silver trousers and dark blue blazers, Tom would start off in a contrasting white blazer with dark blue trousers, and then re-emerge for the second half in a dark brown leather ensemble that would stop the girls in their tracks. The Senators were widely considered to be a handsome and tidy group. Chris Slade's girlfriend Lynne, later to become his wife, would avidly follow them to each gig. "They were brilliant, absolutely brilliant," she says. "Every weekend it was the same story, the place was just packed." Lynne and Tom's wife Linda would also attend some of the early gigs, when Mark became old enough to be left with Vi for the evening. Linda found the women's reaction to Tom a little off-putting, as her husband was beginning to attract a regular female following.

Tom didn't just look and sound good; his on-stage movements were pretty risqué too. He claims that it wasn't always done to please his fans, at least not at first: "When I first started singing with [The Senators], and their timing wasn't too hot, I used my arms and body to conduct them as I sang. That's how the movements started." Tom developed a secret code with Vernon and the others, where one movement dictated the tempo and another might signify a dramatic pause. When it became apparent that some of the girls were going to the concerts just to see him wiggle his backside, he began to take it more seriously and looked to one of his role models for guidance. "I had been moving around on stage in school shows and pubs before I saw Elvis, but I wasn't sure if that kind of thing would ever be acceptable. No one else was doing it. I didn't know how far to go with it, and then I saw Elvis and I knew it was possible."

May 29, 1962 was the date of Tommy Scott & The Senators' first major television appearance. They were noticed during their show one night at a ballroom and were invited to perform on a regional show called *Donald Peers Presents* for BBC Wales. The programme was a showcase for unknown local acts, and although very basic, was certainly a step in the right direction for the starry-eyed group. Tom was not allowed to strut his stuff for the cameras as he would for a normal gig, but he was prepared to bend to achieve the exposure the boys craved. The Senators chose 'That Lucky Old Sun', a mellow Ray Charles blues number, for their three minutes of fame, and went down so well that they were booked for a return visit on the next series.

As the year continued, The Senators resolved to capitalise on the boost given to them by *Donald Peers Presents*, and the concept of forming their very own Concert Party evolved over several beers. This would bring in more cash than merely performing alone in local dance halls. Vernon explains, "That was the next progression, to form a Concert Party. To get more money so we could advance the equipment. That went on for two years or so." They enlisted a comedian, a girl singer and a piano player. With Tommy Scott & The Senators naturally heading the bill, the troupe would earn a total of £20 each night, The Senators splitting half of that between them. The Concert Parties were at weekends, thus bringing in extra income for the group on top of their established weekly gigs, and were a huge success. "We were doing well then, we were on course. We started getting photographs and good gear and we thought we've got to get someone to see us," says Vernon.

It was not only females that followed the band around. A mutual friend, Chris Ellis from Nantgarw, came on the scene. Although not a musician, he was extremely supportive of the band and offered his services as 'road manager' for nothing, with the added bonus of his electrician's van to cart their musical equipment from venue to venue. More often than not, Chris and the others would meet with a frosty reception from the staff of the working men's clubs, who watched their enormous rock'n'roll amps being unloaded with nervous apprehension.

The Senators were not the only group disturbing the peace of the valleys. Former singer Tommy Redman had gone on to join The Strollers, who alternated with The Senators each Thursday night at The Regent Ballroom. The third rock group to be featured in the *Pontypridd Observer* were The Sapphires, a Welsh take on The Beatles. Similar bands vying for the headlines of the entertainment pages were Johnny Grade & The Graduates and Danny & The Fabulous Heartbeats. Yet none could really touch the raw appeal and determined ambition of Tommy Scott & The Senators.

The Concert Parties were going well and provided a regular income, but the boys were convinced that they had the necessary talent to take them all the way to the top. Any stab at fame was worth considering. Tom and the band entered another talent show at the Ebbw Bridge Club in Newport but, to their horror, they were beaten by a 16-year-old girl called Susan Howells. Now Susan Virgo, the winner reflects on her victory, "Tom was called Tommy Scott in those days, and he was there with his old band, The Senators. I was singing on my own, and I did the song 'Fireball XL5'. I beat him and won the competition. He had already made a bit of a name for himself around the clubs in South Wales, but I wasn't phased at all by it. I was just a kid and the sky was the limit."

Such an unforeseen insult to their masculine pride was smoothly pushed to the background as Tom's local fame accelerated regardless. The Senators' frontman was spurred on by a new nickname, inspired by his raunchy stage act. 'Tiger Tom The Twisting Vocalist', an affectionate moniker that was to linger up until the late Sixties, became a real magnet to the ladies. "He had bags of sex appeal. Even before he was Tom Jones, women used to fall over him," remembers Chris Slade with some amusement.

Although flattered by the escalating attention, Tom was still capable of being just as star-struck as his new-found fans. One night when his hero Jerry Lee Lewis was playing at Sophia Gardens in Cardiff, Tom watched the show. It was the first professional gig he had attended. Afterwards Jerry Lee exited the venue via a back door and was swiftly whisked away into the night. Tom was hot on his tail as he scrambled into a taxi and ordered the driver to follow the American's vehicle. When the traffic lights turned red and Tom's taxi caught up with the other car he shamelessly jumped out and requested Jerry Lee's autograph. It was an important moment for Tom as he witnessed his ultimate paragon take the trouble to sign a slip of paper for him. Tom vowed then that if he were ever to really make it big, he would do the same for his fans.

As The Senators became more successful and started making between £11 and £15 per night, Tom had been able to leave behind the security of his job at the Paper Mill, safe in the knowledge that even if the financial rewards of the band should slip, he was now old enough to guarantee the 'adult wage' which he had struggled to obtain back in 1957. More importantly, he was now less inclined to work the late shifts as they clashed with the band's heavy schedule.

Instead, Tom engaged in a variety of mainly manual jobs with more sociable hours, including working as a navvy (road construction labourer) and a stint on a building site. "The job I had the longest was on a building site in Newport – that's in Monmouthshire – carrying those hods with bricks in them," he recalls. "I think that's what made me determined to succeed as a singer, as they were really heavy." Tom often jokes, "I became interested in show business the moment I realised how heavy a hod was . . . singing songs is a lot less exhausting than carrying bricks around!" But as Tom became hooked on succeeding at his chosen vocation, his concentration on regular employment dwindled accordingly. He moved on to a different and rather newfangled occupation: selling vacuum cleaners, the latest domestic craze. "I'd go round Pontypridd selling vacuum cleaners in the daytime. A lot of the women I was flogging them to would have seen me the night before in one of the clubs and buy one," says Tom.

Before long he decided to drop the day jobs completely as the majority of the band slowly turned professional, eventually eking out a living solely from playing at the clubs. With a wife and young son to support, Tom was not about to register himself as a self-employed musician and every Tuesday morning would queue religiously to pick up the dole money – a relative pittance of seven shillings and sixpence. Keith Davies recounts that Tom would always have to give Linda the money that he had made from his nights performing as Tommy Scott. At least the other members of the band could have a few pints to celebrate an accomplished evening, but with Linda and Mark as dependants, Tom always seemed to be strapped for cash. Still, while the lack of a fixed income placed a pressure on Tom alien to his more footloose friends, the extra time was welcome to his marriage, which in 1962 was now five years old. "I think at that time they probably saw each other quite a bit because Tom didn't work during the day," contemplates Lynne Rees-Slade.

The day-to-day running of The Senators became more businesslike as the musicians each began to devote more time to their pursuit. Keith Davies relates that Vernon, still dutifully placing adverts in the *Pontypridd Observer*, also devised other means to make The Senators appear more professional: "He made up the first business cards we had. The film *The Young Ones* was playing in the theatre in town and he used the block silhouettes of The Shadows with some red ink." The cards read, "The Senators with vocalist Tommy Scott", placing the emphasis slightly more on a group identity than their normal billing.

Tom also decided to 'do his bit' by receiving specialist instruction for his voice. Vernon lived next door to an ex-operatic soprano who had recently taken up teaching and introduced the two. Tom recalls, "She said if I wanted to become an opera singer, she could work with me. 'As a pop singer,' she said, 'you're singing as perfectly as possible. If you wanted to, you could be an opera singer.' She couldn't understand why I didn't want to. She said that I definitely had the ability and she could make me a fully fledged tenor." But Tom was uninterested in a classical training and instead took a few lessons in which he learned how to control his breathing properly while singing. As a result he emerged a more polished and professional vocalist, and has not forgotten this early and unexpected opportunity: "I have the ability to sing opera, but not the desire. When I was young I loved rhythm and blues and black singers, and thought the rest was rubbish. Now I'm less narrow-minded and more lenient."

In 1962 the charts were interspersed with the sounds emanating from the UK with singers like Cliff Richard and Frank Ifield, and records from further afield in America, with Elvis Presley frequently hitting the top spot in Britain. It was painfully obvious to Tom, Vernon and the others that they were getting nowhere by persisting in the valleys of South Wales, and they had little choice but to establish some kind of link with the pop music Mecca of London. But the Big Smoke seemed a hopelessly long way away as there were no motorways, no fast trains, and the journey by car took an excruciating ten hours.

As 1962 drew to a close, their prayers appeared to have been answered. "We were working at The Green Fly on Tuesdays and Thursdays. We had a residency for £11 a night split between us, and we were really storming there," Vernon explains. "One night these two characters came in . . ." Choosing rather bizarrely to go by the nicknames Myron and Byron, the visitors were in fact called Raymond Godfrey and John Glastonbury. They were songwriting partners based in South Wales who would periodically travel to London in an attempt to seduce the city publishers with their latest compositions.

Not being musicians themselves, Myron and Byron had been advised to present their portfolio in the form of a demonstration disc, recorded with the aid of a group. The odd double act's immediate task was therefore to go in search of some local talent and convince them to help out. They happened upon three groups including Tommy Scott & The Senators, who were all playing at The Green Fly in Bedwas, near Caerphilly. Myron and Byron found The Senators' set the most impressive and exciting, and introduced themselves as soon as the group came off the stage. Explaining their background, the songwriters proposed a mutually beneficial agreement whereby they would take over management of The Senators. The group would then record a couple of Myron and Byron's songs to take to the London publishers, thus furthering the interests of both parties.

After a little discussion, Vernon and the band determined that Horace Turner, the closest they had come so far to a manager, was really only effective in securing local gigs, whereas Myron and Byron were luring them to London with the promise of a record contract. Despite their doubts concerning the integrity of this peculiar pair (as Vernon exclaims: "They were so devious they didn't want us to know their names!"), the boys were so caught up with the thrilling prospect of going to London that they decided to go ahead with the deal. The Senators signed a contract with Myron and Byron in the Thorn Hotel in Abercynon, which was run by the parents of recent recruit, guitarist Dave Cooper and the scene of many a band rehearsal. "So we signed this piece of paper saying that they were our managers. We were known locally by then, we were stars. They saw the potential there. They weren't anything to do with music. They couldn't play, they couldn't sing, they just came along," says Vernon.

Raymond Godfrey, interviewed at length in the 1990 biography *Tom Jones* by Stafford Hildred and David Gritten, describes the following period: "Over the course of the next three months I gave them some songs and used to drive over to see the group . . . We drove over to see them after work. We used to try to rehearse with them because we became aware that we needed a bit more authority. The group was very lax and sometimes they were late and other times they didn't show up at all. Or we'd get there and they hadn't even bothered to set up their equipment." Although the relationship of the two factions clearly wasn't proving ideal, eventually the time came for The Senators to record the demo disc for Myron and Byron. In keeping with the strange scenario, the songs were recorded on a portable eight-track studio in the unlikely setting of the football changing room toilets at the YMCA in Pontypridd. Apparently that was where Myron and Byron deemed that the acoustics were optimal.

The resulting tracks included an original Godfrey/Glastonbury instrumental called 'David's Theme' and songs such as 'Lonely Joe'. Myron and Byron took the tape to London to try their luck once again with the major publishing companies. They met with little success until they approached Joe Meek, a renowned independent record producer who had previously worked closely with the Decca record label, in early 1963.

Joe's biggest hit to date was the instrumental single, 'Telstar', which he had written and produced for The Tornados, and in December 1962 became the first ever rock'n'roll single by a British group to top the American charts. Like his American counterpart Phil Spector, Joe Meek created a 'Wall of Sound', cramming all the instruments possible onto a single track, and for many years was leaps and bounds ahead of his native rivals. Operating from his tiny flat above a shop at 304 Holloway Road, London, Joe Meek would slave doggedly on his creations at all hours of the day, competing with the din of the traffic outside and the nosy neighbours, curious about his erratic behaviour.

On meeting with the Welshmen, Joe felt that Tom's powerful voice and Elvis-style movements were somewhat passé in the light of the evolutionary sounds emanating from Liverpool, but with the foresight of genius he could not fail to recognise Tom's raw, untapped vocal talent. Without hesitation he signed The Senators to a 12-month production contract, via Myron and Byron.

His intention was to lease the master tapes of the recording sessions he planned to hold at Holloway Road to one of the major record labels, most likely Decca, for distribution. These sessions occurred haphazardly over the next few weeks with The Senators repeatedly making the 10-hour journey from Wales to London, each time in the hope that the forgetful producer would have got out of bed, remembered their booking and not disappeared to Cheltenham to record another band instead. It wasn't out of the question for The Senators to arrive at the flat having driven all night, only to find Joe mysteriously absent. Having nowhere else to go and no funds to even buy breakfast, they would literally have to turn around and head straight back to Wales.

However, when Joe Meek did manage to organise his diary, the sessions went well, if a little terrifyingly at times. Chris Slade recalls the unconventional arrangements: "I just remember this grotty, tiny, dirty place – a bit of a strange fella. We thought, 'Joe Meek! The 'Telstar' producer – he must be really good!' But he had a weird way of working . . ." John Repsch, biographer of *The Legendary Joe Meek: The Telstar Man* elaborates: "Whether it was a practical joke, or designed to make Tom and The Senators perform better will never be known, but once during a take he stormed into the studio, pulled out a gun, levelled it at Tom and fired it! There was a loud bang and Tom thought he was done for. It was a starting pistol. Joe walked out leaving a room full of shivering wrecks."

There was something else niggling The Senators about Joe Meek's volcanic temperament. One sunny day, the boys were frogmarched onto the roof of the flat for some publicity photographs supervised by Joe. Chris Slade witnessed a peculiar request from the openly homosexual producer that was to become slightly more graphic than he, or any of the others, cared for.

"I think it was him that got Tom into wearing white all the time," ponders Chris. "I remember Joe Meek said, 'Mmm, Tom, I'd like to try this image just for the photographs. Why don't you go and change into white trousers and don't wear underpants?' Tom went, 'OK.'" However, Joe had not accounted for Tom's naturally dark colouring. "And he changed and came back out. Joe went, 'No . . . I think it's better *with* the underpants, Tom!'"

But Joe's fancy for the hapless singer did not end there. Tom was uncomfortable about Joe's sexual leaning and kept the following story very quiet until 1979, when he spoke on Merv Griffin's US TV chat show: "You see, Joe, I don't think he'd mind, I mean it's open – he was homosexual. It was a bad experience for me because, coming from Wales, there's no such thing, or we don't like to think there is anyway! So, I went to London to record with Joe Meek. I did about five songs with my group The Senators; I was Tommy Scott & The Senators then. So he said, 'Well, tell the boys to pack their stuff up and I just want to talk to you by yourself.'"

Twenty years later Tom elaborated to *Mojo* what happened next. "He said, 'You sound great but I haven't seen you perform. Give me a demonstration of how you move on stage.' And I said, 'I can't do that now. Come see a gig – we'll do a pub or something in London.' He was giving me the come-on – only I wasn't getting it; to me he was *Joe Meek, Telstar*. He was eyeing me from head to toe and said, 'Those jeans fit you well, don't they?'"

"You see, he approached me," he continued to Merv Griffin. "I couldn't understand first of all what was wrong with this man – I thought he wanted to kill me or something! I didn't know what he wanted. *Then* I realised what the story was. So that whole deal fell through because, the deal would have been if I had co-operated with him, I would have had a record contract . . . so I went back to Wales."

In the end Joe Meek recorded a total of seven tracks with The Senators which he was supposed to present to Decca, proposing as the first single 'Lonely Joe' backed with 'I Was A Fool' (the latter a Godfrey and Glaston-bury composition). According to Joe, although Decca showed an initial interest, they continually postponed the release date as they were in the throes of promoting their latest signing, who went by the name of P.J. Proby. As the months dragged on tensions became fraught. "Jones and Co. had grown tired of the long treks up to London," describes John Repsch. "Nor did they like his [Joe Meek's] offhand manner towards them, brought about by his dislike of Tom's two pushy young managers, who called themselves Myron and Byron, and contempt for The Senators, whose musical attributes he rated on a par with Kenny Lord's Statesmen; and his treatment of Tom was not exactly courteous."

While the deal with Joe Meek was seemingly unproductive, another aspect of the boys' visits to London proved profitable. By chance, Tom and The Senators stumbled on the regular haunt of disc jockey, Jimmy Savile, who in 1963 was hosting his popular *Teen & Twenty Disc Club* show on Radio Luxembourg. Famed for 'helping out' rock acts, who could be better to approach than this slightly zany, but extremely hip, celebrity? Jimmy Savile himself outlines the situation: "I was staying in a hotel in King's Cross called the Aaland Hotel, and there comes a knock on my room door. Some very serious-looking chaps were there asking if I'd got a minute to spare, which of course I always had. They told me they were a pop group from Wales and could I tell them how to get on?

"So that was the start of a several week on-and-off relationship, when-ever they came up to town and I happened to be there, then of course it was the next instalment et cetera. I took an interest in them which pleased them no end." Regular pep talks occurred at the café opposite the Aaland Hotel, known then as the Bloomsbury Buffet. Jimmy continues, "It was moral support as much as anything else, because in those days people who had been paid always paid the bills in cafés. Because I was of course the one that was getting megabucks, I just about paid for everybody's meal. But it was a joy and a pleasure. Whatever questions they asked I could give an answer to, because I had been there already. So it was moral support, gastric support and the answering of all their questions."

Raymond Godfrey claimed in Hildred and Gritten's biography, *Tom Jones*, that Myron and Byron introduced The Senators to Jimmy Savile. But Jimmy insists that he has never heard of them, let alone met them, and

Tom refutes their input altogether: "Myron and Byron? They might as well have been called Pinky and Perky for all the good they did me!"

Another popular myth is that Jimmy personally introduced the band to the executives at the Decca record label, thus helping them on the road to fame. Alternatively Peter Sullivan, who at that time was employed by Decca as a record producer, declares that he discovered a tape of The Senators that had been sent in by Myron and Byron. It was one of Peter's jobs to sift through the hundreds of tapes and pick out the most promising songs for a talent contest on Radio Luxembourg, hosted by Jimmy Savile. Jimmy, on the other hand, maintains that he provided limited support and dispels any connection with Peter Sullivan whatsoever. "I have never run a talent show on the radio in my entire life," he says. "I worked on Radio Luxembourg and we only played records that had been released by the Decca Group. We didn't do a talent thing at all, I never have done."

Meanwhile, the relationship with Joe Meek was going steadily downhill. For the best part of nine months Myron and Byron hounded Joe, demanding to know how the Decca deal and début release were coming along, but the producer procrastinated, insisting that it was Decca that was delaying matters. Unknown to Myron and Byron, Joe's relationship with Decca had deteriorated some time before they approached him, which could well explain his unwillingness to elaborate on the situation. At one stage, Myron and Byron confronted Joe claiming to have met with the head A&R man at Decca, Dick Rowe. John Repsch explains: "Matters came to a head one day when Myron and Byron arrived telling him they had just met Dick at Decca – he had denied all knowledge of Tom and *any* release date! After a fine old row Joe duly terminated the contract by tearing it up and slinging it in the bin." Whether or not Joe ever actually gave copies of the tapes to Decca remains unclear to this day, but having torn up the contract he insisted on custody of the music he considered to be his property. All efforts by Myron and Byron to retrieve the master recordings proved fruitless.

The managers returned to Wales with their tails between their legs, disappointed with Joe and reluctant to admit defeat. The dispirited Senators continued performing as normal, but for one of their number the promise of fame had soured. On top of being disillusioned with Myron and Byron and the lack of progress, founder member Keith Davies was finding the financial pressures of staying in the group overwhelming. "We used to go up to London and take a demo tape, and they promised this and they promised that but nothing came of it. We even got to Jimmy Savile and if he had five minutes he'd pop out and see you, but if he didn't, he didn't," he says. "I think that every one of us at the end of the day wanted to get there in the end. Things happened along the way and we went in different directions."

★ ★ ★

A million miles away in Madras, India's fourth largest city, life had certainly taken a different direction for another little Welsh family. Army sergeant, Bill Mills, and his Anglo-Indian wife Lorna were stationed far from the valleys in this exotic coastal metropolis when their son, Gordon William, was born in 1935. Following the culmination of the Second World War the family returned to their roots, settling in the small South Wales village of Tonypandy. Ten-year-old Gordon exchanged cultures, swapping the ways of the Indian sub-continent for a lifestyle that was typically Welsh. Like many young people in the area he left school aged 15 with few career prospects, then followed in his father's footsteps doing compulsory National Service for the army.

After three years he left and became a bus conductor with Rhondda Transport, where he made two lasting friendships which would prove important to his future. One was Gordon Jones, known as 'Gog' to his friends, who became a faithful and longstanding companion. The other, Albert Blinkhorn, inspired Gordon to develop his musical talents.

"I met Gordon during the early Fifties," recalled Albert a decade later. "My brother Terry and [Gordon] were at the school together . . . It was the days of harmonica groups like the Morton Fraser Harmonica Gang, and quite a few people took to playing the harmonica." Gordon himself had been given a harmonica as a gift in the early Fifties and was keen to learn the finer nuances of the instrument. "One night Gordon came to see me along with my brother, and when he learned I played the harmonica he became interested. From then on it was a natural progression." For a while Gordon joined Albert's harmonica group and dutifully received tuition from the more experienced player. "I taught Gordon how to play Glenn Miller tunes. Gordon was a very talented fellow who had a lot of go in him. Like the rest of us he struggled a lot and had a rough time. But he would still go ahead even when he had no money in his pocket," said Albert.

It slowly dawned on Gordon that his new hobby could become a lucrative sideline and he moved on to a group called The Spades who played in a local Concert Party. Fame soon followed when he competed in the British Harmonica Championship and came a close second. This led to the good-looking young musician representing his country at international level in Luxembourg. During his travels Gordon met fellow harmonica player Ronnie Wells, with whom he joined the Morton Fraser Harmonica Gang in 1957. For two years they gained vital experience

34

appearing at theatres all over the world, including pantomime at the prestigious London Palladium. However, as rock'n'roll gathered momentum the world over, Gordon and Ronnie sought the credibility of slightly rawer music and along with another member, Don Paul, left the seven-piece band and founded The Viscounts.

The striped suits and close harmonies of the group appealed greatly to Fifties starmaker/manager, Larry Parnes, who at the time oversaw the careers of successful acts like Tommy Steele and Marty Wilde & The Wildecats. The effect of being catapulted so quickly to fame combined with Gordon's naturally abrupt character often made him appear arrogant, and he made some early enemies as a result. Big Jim Sullivan, a young but exceptionally talented session guitarist, experienced Gordon's abrasive manner first hand. "Gordon was a very cold man," says Big Jim. "I was with Marty Wilde & The Wildecats and Gordon had just come out of the Morton Fraser Harmonica Gang. We used to sit on the stage playing jazz. He used to come up and try and play with us and we'd tell him to piss off. 'Don't make that bloody row round us – we're playing seriously!' "

In awe of the famous guitarist Gordon no doubt felt insecure and proceeded to assert himself when the two were in private. Big Jim continues, "When we were together the front would come down. And this is what he told me: 'I swear, everybody who's done me down in this business, I will buy them out.' " Even though Gordon was still an inexperienced musician without any apparent business inclinations, Big Jim was convinced of his sincerity.

Indeed, far from exuding any strong managerial flair at this stage, Gordon often amazed his colleagues with his ineptitude and absent-mindedness, and was undoubtedly considered to be the most junior member of The Viscounts. Larry Parnes booked the group on to a productive touring schedule but due to pressures from his two largest clients, Tommy Steele and Marty Wilde, Larry was unable to push The Viscounts' recording career any further. Desperate to get ahead, the group signed up with veteran variety agent, Hymie Zahl. Under Hymie's expert guidance they finally achieved chart success with a version of the much covered traditional American Negro song, 'Mama's Little Baby Loves Shortnin' Bread' in 1960. This resulted in a residency at Paul Raymond's Celebrity Club and included gigs at the dubious striptease joint next door. However, following an unwise move to the Audio Enterprises agency, The Viscounts again found themselves searching for a new manager as the ill-fated company collapsed shortly after signing the band. Returning to the security of the variety circuit they eventually joined the talented stable of Eve Taylor who, known as Evie, had fashioned her promotion of gigs on Larry Parnes.

Under Evie's adroit management The Viscounts incongruously bridged the gap between the forgotten days of music hall and contemporary rock'n'roll. According to author Johnny Rogan, they even appeared as the unlikely supporting act for an up-and-coming Liverpool band, The Beatles, who were yet to find fame. In September 1961 the harmonica trio accrued another hit with a farcical cover of Barry Mann's song 'Who Put The Bomp (In The Bomp, Bomp, Bomp)'.

Despite this chart success, it was becoming apparent to the other members of the band that Gordon preferred to apply his talents behind the scenes rather than on stage, as he dedicated his time to perfecting The Viscounts' distinctively stylised harmonies. Gordon wasn't only an accomplished arranger, he was also a promising young songwriter and it wasn't long before he came to the attention of Lionel Conway from Leeds Music. Conway thought Gordon's composition, 'I'll Never Get Over You', deserved better than to languish as the B-side to one of The Viscounts' unsuccessful singles, and when he re-recorded it with Johnny Kidd & The Pirates in September 1963 it reached number five. It was soon followed by another Mills original, 'Hungry For Love'. Gordon also penned Cliff Richard's 1964 Top 10 hit 'I'm The Lonely One'.

With his natural good looks and curly auburn hair Gordon Mills had always been a ladies' man, and in the early days had revelled in the benefits of working at the striptease club. On moving into a well-known London rock'n'roll house in Cleveland Square, Bayswater, famed for its occupants Frank Ifield, Joe Brown and Adam Faith, Gordon encountered fashion model Jo Waring who was vacating the room he was about to take over. Despite his best laid plans for bachelorhood, Gordon instantly fell for the striking blonde. Jo's svelte figure ensured that her modelling career earned her a substantial wage, which combined with Gordon's royalty cheques from his hit songs, enabled the couple to live a comparatively luxurious life in West London. Gordon and Jo were married shortly after they met, and they soon tired of The Viscounts' touring routine which would keep the newlyweds apart for lengthy periods. These changes in his personal life progressively ostracised Gordon from the band, making his split from them inevitable.

Departing from The Viscounts in 1964, Gordon pursued his songwriting career and simultaneously landed himself a job as an assistant recording manager. Astutely, he signed up with the Colin Berlin Agency and proved to be a keen and eager student of the venerable music business masters. Ronnie Wells recalls Gordon's uncanny good fortune in Johnny Rogan's incisive study of pop management, *Starmakers And Svengalis*. "When we used to do cabaret clubs up north there were these card schools, and Gordon could hold his own with good players. We didn't realise this until one morning he said he'd won £50, which was big money then. I wouldn't have thought of Gordon as a manager, but he was single-minded and ambitious and had that all important lucky streak. You've got to have a bit of that going for you and the signs were there in early 1964."

While The Viscounts struggled on for another year before disbanding, it wasn't long before Gordon Mills found his missing link to pop management.

4

CHILLS AND FEVER

IN THE SPRING of 1964 Gordon took his heavily pregnant wife back to his Welsh home. He glowed with pride as he spoke of his exploits to his parents and friends. But what Gordon had thus far accomplished was just the tip of the iceberg, and not even an inveterate gambler such as himself could have guessed that the real jackpot lay so close to his family base in the valleys.

On May 10, 1964, Gordon visited the Top Hat Club in Cwmtillery to see Mandy Rice-Davies with some of his old bus-conducting gang, including Gog Jones and club singer Johnny Bennett. Mandy had lately received instant notoriety following revelations of her role in the scandalous Profumo affair, which had threatened to ruin the Tory government over its implications on national security. Determined to capitalise on her new-found status Mandy was making personal appearances around the country, but although billed for the night of May 10, she had cancelled at the last minute. The other previously booked acts were all duly promoted and Tommy Scott & The Senators progressed to top billing. Gordon had been consciously looking for an act to manage, but never considered he would have much luck in South Wales, as he said to his friends that night: "In Treforest, they're ten a penny, all these groups." But the softly spoken Gordon Mills was yet to meet the man behind the powerful voice of The Senators.

Keith Davies, who had recently left the group, found himself in the spectator party along with Gordon Mills. He remembers the strange turn of events: "When I left the band I still used to go and see the lads every weekend. One particular night the comedian's van that we used to go in broke down and we sort of had to go on as best we could. There just happened to be a spare car. I didn't know whose it was, and Vernon said, 'Is there any chance of giving Keith a lift up to the theatre?' because all the other cars were packed with drums and amplifiers. It turned out to be Gordon and his wife."

Oblivious to the potential of a meeting between his friends and the marginally famous songwriter, Keith remained with the couple as they fought their way into the crowded bar. Although standing room only wasn't an ideal situation for Jo in her condition, they all stayed to watch Tommy Scott & The Senators. Gordon and Jo were immediately impressed as the talented group progressed through a set which included 'I'll Never Get Over You' as a genuflection to Gordon and a dramatic rendition of 'Spanish Harlem'. Tom's entire performance covered several hours, interspersed with other acts such as the comedian Bryn Phillips.

Keith was still socialising with Gordon. "We were just lining up a few drinks at the bar, watching the show, and he said to me: 'I have to have him under my belt.' When I went in and took a load of drinks in to the boys in the interval, I said to Tom, 'You know that guy I came up with in the car? He wants you to go to London with him!' But Tom didn't show a lot of interest at the time. He just sat there talking with the boys."

In fact the group were very excited and quite nervous about the chance presence of Gordon Mills in the club, but they already had two managers and were not aware that they needed a change. For his part Gordon had the foresight to realise that he could help Tommy Scott & The Senators achieve great success. Gordon later recalled the first night with vigour. "He was sensational. That night at the Top Hat he had the audience in a frenzy. All he needed was to get out of that pitiful mining country to where his talents would be more highly appreciated."

All the way back to London Gordon enthused to Jo about his ambitions as the group's manager, and it wasn't long before he met up with the aspiring stars to propose a change of management. Keith Davies remembers that in the end it was Gordon's persistence that won them over.

Tom and the boys realised that Gordon offered far greater potential than the hapless Myron and Byron ever could and so all parties involved met several weeks later at the Hibs Club in Ferndale, Rhondda. Chris Slade explains how clear it was that Myron and Byron should be superseded: "They were trying hard, they didn't have connections like perhaps Gordon had . . . I think they meant well, they just didn't have any idea of what to do."

Vernon Hopkins was equally relieved to be free of Myron and Byron. "Nobody liked them very much anyway. I didn't like them," he recalls. "They were too weird, strange. Not on the same wavelength. They were fooling us anyway from the beginning. We didn't even know their real names until afterwards. It was a release to get away from that because it was so uncomfortable." On a more positive note, everyone was very keen on the band's new manager despite his cocky arrogance. "I think you could see he was such a mega-person, not from a wealth point of view, but who he was," says Keith Davies. "But I think he could be childish in some ways."

Myron and Byron still held a binding contract with the band, but Gordon was anxious to secure a rapid takeover and so hastily agreed to draw up a separate contract offering Myron and Byron five per cent of their future earnings. Conversely Mills drove a hard bargain with the group, demanding a 50:50 share of the profits, an exceptionally high commission that harked back to the days of Gordon's role models Larry Parnes and Colonel Tom Parker, the Machiavellian manager of Elvis Presley. The stage was set for Gordon to lead Tommy Scott & The Senators to stardom; all he had left to do was to find the route.

★ ★ ★

Gordon's first step was to demand that the group move to London. Understandably, the boys were all a little wary at first; it meant leaving everyone and everything that was familiar and safe in Wales. Vernon, eternally optimistic that his future lay in music, did not hesitate to resign from the *Pontypridd Observer* in search of fame, Chris Slade left his job as a sales assistant and Dave Cooper also followed, each certain that Gordon Mills would look after them. Lead guitarist, Mike Roberts, had just commenced his true vocation as a cameraman with a local TV station and so chose to bow out of the band's move. The Senators held auditions to find a replacement before they left Wales, and stumbled upon Mike Gee, 21, who had been dreaming of such a break and gladly gave up his delivery job for Brain's Brewery.

For Tom, the biggest initial worry was the possibility that his new manager had a hidden agenda. "When Gordon saw me and asked me to come to London, we went into a coffee bar," Tom said to Merv Griffin in 1979. "He said, 'Now, if I become your manager, you know I will be in control and you *must* listen to me,' and he put his hand on my leg. So I said, 'Before you go any further, you're not one of those queer fellows, are you?!'" Tom was understandably touchy after the recent incident with Joe Meek, but had nothing to fear about Gordon's intentions.

Collectively, the greatest problem the group faced was anonymity in a metropolis crammed full of promising 'wannabes'. Tom later spoke candidly in the *Daily Mirror* about the band's concerns: "The real danger we saw in going to London was the thought of losing the little bit of security we had built up," he said. "We all had day jobs. I suppose as a group we were becoming fairly well known in South Wales. We didn't want to go and lose it all."

Tom, now 24, had a more difficult decision to make due to his marital status. Although he had not held a steady day job for a couple of years, his quest for pop success would entail leaving his wife and seven-year-old son. True to her upbringing the selfless Linda stood firmly and obediently by her husband, even assuming the role of breadwinner and accepting a job on a factory assembly line to support herself and Mark. Tom was humiliated by the role reversal, but persisted with the move, naïve in the belief that he would soon be returning home triumphant that the little family would never suffer financially again.

By June 1964 Gordon Mills was setting about establishing his new acquisition in England's busy capital, far from their native Wales. As The Senators had no money themselves, Gordon found himself paying for everything from living and eating costs to clothes and equipment. At first he arranged for them to stay in a cheap but comfortable hotel until more suitable accommodation could be found. But before long, Tom, Vernon, Chris, Dave and Mike were relocated from the hotel into a basement flat in Ladbroke Grove, West London ("Go down to the bottom of Portobello Road Market, turn right, turn left and you're there," chuckles Chris today).

The conditions they found awaiting them were far from salubrious. "It was a hovel, if he'd put us in a tent it would have been better!" says Vernon. "It was hell on earth. There were two rooms, three of us slept in one big room, two of us in the other, and a small kitchen and a bathroom. But everything was falling off the walls, it was damp, it was squalid." Gordon paid approximately £8 a week for the dilapidated flat which was situated in an area riddled with drugs and crime. The band members befriended the local prostitutes who would join them at all hours for a cup of tea and a chat in return for a cigarette or two. "We literally lived with prostitutes, which was fine with us, but we never indulged!" remembers Chris.

Gordon, the budding entrepreneur, concentrated on the unpolished appeal of The Senators and decreed that they needed a bolder stage name to appeal to the brash London scene. Accordingly he changed the backing group to The Playboys, leaving Tom's persona as it stood. Brandishing their new image Gordon managed to find Tommy Scott & The Playboys a few gigs at American airbases in the capital's environs and Irish ballrooms within London, but it was a regular spot at Oxford Street's Beat City that was to be the most memorable.

"It was down in a basement, it was a rock gig and I had never felt so hot in my life," exclaims Chris Slade. The main noticeable difference was the stage set-up in the young and trendy club. "I don't know what Tom was like, singing. Drummers and singers have the same problem getting the air in. It was like breathing in from a jet engine. I'll never forget because we were used to being up on a stage, in a club where you were distanced from the people by at least ten feet of stage, whereas there the people were right there in front of you."

As the resident band The Playboys often found themselves supporting more established acts like The Spencer Davis Group, or even The Rolling Stones. By the summer of 1964 the Stones had two top five hits, 'Not Fade Away' and 'It's All Over Now', under their belts. Due to their surly demeanour and all-round contemptuous behaviour they were well on their way to achieving the kind of notoriety that would render them the only serious UK group to rival The Beatles for pop supremacy. Frontman Mick Jagger's crude vocals and flamboyant stage act combined with the group's often controversial songs proved highly successful and they were to bask in a string of British number ones over the next year. Nevertheless, the Welsh rock'n'rollers were unimpressed. "Tom thought that they were a bunch of poofters!" says Chris Slade. "Especially Mick Jagger. I think Tom thought that anybody from London was a bit effeminate."

The apparent culture clash between Pontypridd and London was some-what puzzling for the strapping Tommy Scott. Mick Jagger with his long hair and skinny frame looked more like a girl to the well-built Welshman, who firmly believed that women wanted a real man, not some bony waif: "If you're going to sing a sexy song, then you should be able to act it out that way." Tom sported his tight trousers and blousey shirts regardless, and thrusted his raunchy dancing in the faces of his young audience in the hope that eventually they would change their tastes. Tom described his stubborn determination to Q magazine in 1991: "I was used to playing to people of my own age but in come these teeny-boppers, these bloody kids to see The Rolling Stones. So I'm on stage and I'm doing the thing, and I can see these kids looking at me a bit funny . . . they were looking at me like that because I was very adult for my age . . . So when Mick Jagger came on I could see the difference in me being masculine and him sort of camping it up and the kids were screaming at him whereas with me they'd just look at me funny, even though we were basically doing the same kind of material . . . But I couldn't camp it up, I didn't look that way. I would look like somebody in drag . . . I wasn't effeminate so I knew that was out. I had to do my masculine thing and hope it would work."

That Tom was clearly an anachronism in Beat City in 1964 appeared to have eluded the *Pontypridd Observer* as they proudly reported on the group's progress in London on July 25. The article portrayed them in a very exciting and positive light, describing how the group would play three nights a week on top of their official residency at Beat City. As if to emphasise their up-and-coming status, the paper pointed out that Tom and the boys had all their expenses paid for them as well as receiving a fixed wage for the week. The truth was far less glamorous. Gordon had been able to secure a regular gig at Beat City, but the task of finding an agent and/or a record producer was proving more difficult. Tom's image was too testosterone-laced for the times and he and The Playboys would be turned away from countless auditions with the phrases 'too adult' and 'too Fifties rock'n'roll'. At 24, Tom was simply too old to appeal to the teenagers, who were instead opting for the younger, fresh-faced groups such as The Beatles, the Stones or the anodyne Herman's Hermits.

Gordon would also pay their weekly upkeep but the precise figure in question is a moot point. Some authors have suggested that the group received £1 each per day. Considering that in 1964 a pint of beer was under 10p this would have been comparatively generous for the boys, as well as being extremely expensive for Gordon. The truth is that they were given £1 per day between the five of them, with which they had to eat, drink and live. Vernon amplifies, "Out of that we had to buy food, clothing, toiletries, drinks, cigarettes. So we'd either have a few cigarettes and a pint and go without food, or have food and go without a pint. We were in such a state and dejected that we went for the pints and just a sausage roll between us." But even such a pitiful amount for the boys was still costing Gordon very dearly. He had already invested all the royalties from his previous hits into The Playboys, and had been forced to take out a loan from the bank to maintain the flat and £7 per week expenses.

Chris Ellis, who took a keen interest in the band's progress even though he was back in Wales, would often make the long trek to London to see the lads and spur them on. Despite the dire conditions, Vernon remembers these visits fondly. "Chris Ellis would come up and visit us and he'd bring a food hamper, it was like Christmas. Because we thought fame was just around the corner, we accepted it." The only other link they had with life back home was through Tom's wife Linda. Struggling by with his friends, Tom would often berate himself for leaving Linda and Mark in Wales to survive on their own. Tom spoke candidly about this troublesome era in the *Daily Mirror* in 1969: "Linda had to take a job in a factory to support herself and Mark. She had worked once before in a shop when she left school, but to have to go out to work because her husband couldn't support her really brought me down. It was heartbreaking. There were also a lot of people who did not waste the opportunity to declare our marriage had broken up with Linda being stuck in Wales and me in London." It was obvious to the rest of the group that Tom was torn between his career and leaving his family to fend for themselves. "He used to phone her regularly," recalls Chris Slade. "He did miss her terribly in the beginning, he really did, and he'd get really upset sometimes."

In order to combat the boredom and hunger, the boys would find various pastimes to occupy their many empty hours and they bonded strongly as a group. "A routine developed," Vernon explains. "We'd eat on certain days and survive. We'd sleep all the time, but stay up at night and play cards. We were a team – tomorrow we were going to make it." Chris continues: "Five guys lived in a flat together and starved together and fought together. You get little cliques, but we were all friends and we were all drinking buddies."

Gordon made sure that he visited the flat every day to boost morale in his peculiarly blunt manner, but without any news of record deals the lads remained permanently downhearted and couldn't help wondering why they had given up their steady jobs in Wales. Although they appreciated that Gordon had gone into debt trying to look after their interests, it was difficult not to query his methods. Instead of booking The Playboys at every club possible, Gordon seemed content with their regular appearance at Beat City along with the occasional extra gig elsewhere.

"It was as if he didn't want us to work anywhere," recalls Vernon, who was puzzled at the time. "I don't know if it was paranoia or his way of doing it – keep them low key, don't let anyone see them because if someone else sees them working with a better offer, then his contract [with The Playboys] would go out the window. He had no faith in himself."

Holding the managerial models from the Fifties in the back of his mind, Gordon was also intent on looking to the future. He was juggling several plans at once; securing a record contract for The Playboys, scoring a hit with his earlier compositions, not to mention writing new songs. Gordon was aware that in 1964 there were only a handful of solo artists hitting the top of the charts, Cilla Black and Roy Orbison in particular, as opposed to the myriad groups entering the city. While he felt sure that Tom would be the next great performer to break this trend, he was also conscious that record producers were unlikely to give Tom a second chance without a backing band. Although it was draining his personal resources supporting the whole band, it was probably ultimately cheaper for Gordon to do it this way than to hire costly session musicians. "We were so useful. Rather than being part of it, we were used to the hilt," admits Vernon today.

Gordon knew Peter Sullivan through his circle of musical friends. Peter had been lured away from his work as an assistant producer at EMI by Dick Rowe, the head of Artists and Repertoire (A&R) at Decca. Peter was employed in the offices at Embankment on the River Thames as a producer with the additional brief of acquiring fresh new talent, and in this capacity he signed up solo girl singers Kathy Kirby and Lulu among others. He showed a certain amount of interest in Tommy Scott & The Playboys and was persuaded to go to see them appear in concert back in their hometown of Pontypridd. Gordon was confident that The Playboys were more likely to make a favourable impression on Peter in a place that knew and loved them. "We went back to Wales and hired two coach loads of YMCA fans, and took them to this place in Newport and put a show on," says Vernon, remembering the great lengths to which Gordon went. "So when Peter came down there were four rows of screaming women just in case he wasn't impressed. And it worked. Put it this way, it was crucial. Because he was so impressed with all these girls screaming and shouting, that was the turning point."

After the show that night Peter managed to lock himself out of his hotel and spent an uncomfortable night trying to sleep in his car. Fortunately that unpleasant incident did not mar his feelings about the performance and he returned to London ecstatic about the group. Following company policy, Peter arranged for The Playboys to audition for Decca where they tried different styles, songs and recording techniques. He recalls that although The Playboys were at the audition, it was only ever Tom in whom he was really interested. "Even at his audition for Decca, Tom showed a tremendous amount of talent," he says today. "I'd been to Wales to see him work, in his own environment as it were, and the talent just glowed through." The resulting tape was played to the executives at Decca and a snap decision was made to sign Tommy Scott & The Playboys for three or four single releases, with the option to drop them if they proved unsuccessful.

Characteristically for the star-crossed Welsh group, several weeks passed after the audition before anything of consequence occurred. Finally, on the recommendation of Dick Rowe, Peter introduced Gordon Mills and the band to the imperious music entrepreneur, Phil Solomon. Phil had left his Belfast based family firm, Solomon & Peres, to set up an agency in London under his wife's name, The Dorothy Solomon Organisation. Phil and Gordon became business partners, while Dorothy acted as Tom's manager and agent, but the association turned sour within a matter of months. This was due in part because American producer Bert Berns, who was working with Decca acts Lulu and Them, was dismissive of Tom, insinuating that he was a second-rate Elvis Presley. "Phil's time with Tom was short but sweet. However, Tom was very unhappy with him," recalls Peter Sullivan of the brief period.

Although this was a short-lived relationship, Phil Solomon proposed what is arguably the single most important element in Tom's career: his change of name. A stratagem popularly credited to Gordon Mills, it was in fact Phil who suggested the new pseudonym. In the event, Tom was obliged to change his name anyway after discovering there was already a performer called Tommy Scott. *Tom Jones* was the title of a Henry Fielding novel which in 1963 had been made into an overtly sexual and immensely popular film starring Albert Finney. "It was Phil Solomon that gave Tom his name, that called him Tom Jones," recalls Chris Slade. "He'd signed the contract as Thomas John Woodward, which was his name, and the film *Tom Jones* was out at the time. Phil Solomon went, 'What did you sign there?' and he turned it round, 'What's that?' And Tom said, 'Tom John, that's my name.' Phil said, 'Tom Jones.' Tom told us that story as soon as he came back.'"

Tom corroborated this story himself in a subsequent interview with *The Enquirer.* "There was already a singer who called himself Tommy Scott, so I had to change my name. An agent saw my real name, Thomas John Woodward. At that time the movie *Tom Jones* had just come out, so the agent said, 'Why don't you call yourself Tom Jones?' And that was it." Gordon would always maintain that it was his inspiration to link the raunchy connotation of the film to his rising star.★ Furthermore he claimed that all he had done was remove Tom's surname, thus spawning another prevalent myth: that Tom's real name is Tom Jones Woodward.

As the group's poor run of luck would dictate, there was another band already in existence called John Fred & The Playboy Band. Even though the original Playboys were based in America, Tom's backing group were obliged to change their name. After Phil's stroke of genius with 'Tom Jones', Gordon astutely realised that the character in the movie was a landed country gentleman and seized on the idea of calling them 'The Squires'.

Tom Jones & The Squires finally made it into the studios during the summer of 1964 to record their version of Ronnie Love's 1961 US hit, 'Chills And Fever'. The group had originally demoed the song with Joe Meek and were quite comfortable with the session and its output. Decca, however, were unhappy with the musical quality and Peter Sullivan recalls that while the vocal was strong, they needed to bolster the backing track. He took this opportunity to augment the arrangement by adding a few experienced session musicians.

Big Jim Sullivan, the guitarist used for the second recording, can picture Tom's entrance quite clearly. "I remember this guy who looked a typical kind of Welshman – the big nose, the tight drainpipe trousers and the winkle-pickers coming into the studio. We were all sitting there and thinking, 'Christ, what have we got now?' When he started singing it was like, '*Christ!*'" The tracks were recorded live directly onto tape, but this did not bother the talented frontman. Derek Watkins, the trumpet player, was impressed by Tom's instinctive proficiency at these early recording sessions. "He was very professional, knew exactly what he wanted. He'd

★ The sexy implications of the name bolstered Tom's image, which may not have been the case had he been linked to the other minor celebrities who share this appellation, an astronaut, a water colour painter and a lyricist who wrote the words to 'Fantastics'.

just go in and every take would be perfect. It was just a matter of choosing which one had the best overall sound or feeling."

The outcome of the two sessions was a lively and raunchy song, marred a little by over-production. Tom's vocal performance was dramatic in the extreme but on reflection was not an interpretation that would endear him to a teenage audience. It was just too much for the British pop pickers. Released on August 28, 1964 'Chills And Fever' was a resounding chart failure, despite appearances on *The Beat Room* and a radio début on *Top Gear*. Unsurprisingly, the single made it to number five in Pontypridd's charts, but curiously it actually did well in Australia, reaching number 11 in various regions. But it was the UK sales that mattered to Decca, and more importantly to The Squires, it was the credits on the record that were crucial. Having boasted to all their friends that they had finally made a record, to their dismay their names had been left off. Vernon, as group leader, was especially livid. "This is where the rot sets in with the band, suddenly the record comes out and our name isn't on it." The Squires confronted their singer as to why their names were absent from the single, but his answer was simply, "Ask Gordon".

The failure of their first release came as a tremendous blow to everyone. Unknown to the majority of The Squires Gordon had begun to treat Tom slightly differently to the other group members, taking an interest in his welfare and encouraging him personally. Tom's musical aspirations combined with the added pressures of Linda and Mark living alone in Wales, meant that he became very despondent and sometimes even considered giving everything up and returning to Pontypridd. "He was probably more dejected than us," Vernon reflects. "Probably by then Gordon had befriended him more and said, 'You're the one that's going to make it.'"

Unable to shake his depression, Tom came perilously close to committing suicide. Only after many years did he speak openly about this traumatic experience in an article entitled *The Golden Voice Of The Valleys*. "I remember the feeling so well now, even though it was back in 1964. No hit record, remember; no money – well, very little; and a wife waiting for me back there in Wales, depending with her whole being on me making the grade . . . I was off to see somebody and found myself on the Central Line underground station at Notting Hill Gate.★

"I'd just been on the phone to Gordon, pleading for him to send some extra cash to my wife and he'd agreed, but I knew it was tough on him, because he was literally digging into his overdraft. A great guy . . . but struggling in those days just as hard as we were in the group. I just felt that

---

★ Tom was to tell the *Mirror* in 1999 that he was at Shepherd's Bush station on his way to see Gordon to ask for a loan.

nothing was ever going to happen, and I wondered if I'd have the nerve to wait for a train to come along so I could jump in front of it and end it all. I didn't think, at that moment in time, about it being a cowardly way out, I just thought that it would be a way of ending all the terrible worries I had over my career and my whole future. So I stood there and imagined what it would feel like. Whether, in fact, I'd even make a hash of it. The thought was really there in my head. But eventually, as I waited, I sort of mentally talked myself out of it."

Tom finally stumbled back to the flat where Vernon discovered him, almost hysterical. "I found him in the afternoon and he was sobbing," recalls Vernon. "I said, 'What's happened Tom?' He said, 'I've got to go home.' I said, 'You can't, not now!' He said, 'Linda has had to go to a factory and get a job, I'm fed up and sick of it all.' But I said, 'We've come this far, it's just round the corner.' I was saying anything to keep him going. This went on for a couple of hours."

Tom's insecurity stretched to recurring nightmares about his late grand-mother rising from the dead and voicing disapproval of his reckless ways. The dreams would leave Tom in a broody and fretful mood for the rest of the day, which again, Vernon would have to snap him out of. Vernon was often Tom's pillar of support during these depressing times and they built up a bond of brotherhood.

In a valiant attempt to raise their spirits the group had been hitchhiking to Wales and back or selling some of their few possessions to afford the train fare. Each time they arrived in Pontypridd they faced prying questions about their lack of progress, especially after the *Pontypridd Observer* and other local papers had bolstered their London image so successfully. The stress on Tom and Linda naturally caused ructions, and Linda would often threaten her somewhat credulous husband with the wrath of her late father. "When they used to argue, Linda used to shout for her father, and he was dead, so I think that used to scare him!" remembers Chris Slade. Superstitious beliefs still tormented Tom, as Chris continues, "He used to have a thing about his mother-in-law, Linda's mother. There was a ghost in his house, no doubt about that. Cards used to get knocked off the TV and things like that, and I think Linda's mother was into that sort of thing. Tom's mother's a bit of a medium as well."

Back in London Tom, Vernon, Chris, Dave and Mike would spend much of their time in their dishevelled two bedroom flat; sleeping, playing cards and chatting to the neighbouring prostitutes. The boys were like ghosts themselves, barely existing on their £1 per day and biding their time until Gordon found another means to achieve the pop stardom they so dearly craved.

5

THUNDERBALL

GORDON MILLS had signed with Leeds Music after Lionel Conway successfully revived 'I'll Never Get Over You' with Johnny Kidd & The Pirates, and was now co-writing songs with composer/arranger Les Reed. Les had first met Gordon when he was on the same bill as The Viscounts back in 1958. After losing touch, they were reunited at the famed rock'n'roll house in Cleveland Square and discovered that they could work well together after co-writing a song called 'In The Deep Of Night' for Dodi West.

Gordon had been working alone on a new idea, with Johnny Kidd in mind. Originally conceived as a country song, it was his wife Jo who gave 'It's Not Unusual' its name. Gordon then had the title phrase embedded in his memory, but took a little while to develop the line further. When he eventually hit upon the phrase 'It's not unusual to be loved by anyone', it was easy enough to finish the first two verses. Gordon took his new song round to Les.

"He came up with the idea of the title and the first two or three bars of 'It's Not Unusual', which was great, to start with," Les recalls. "He didn't know where to go from there and so I put it into the bajon rhythm and took it out of the stilted rhythm that he put on to it, and it all came together very nicely. I said to him, 'We need a bit in the middle, an instrumental.' He said, 'I need the voice all the time,' but I said, 'No, let's just break it and put a little instrumental in the middle.' He wasn't keen on that." Nevertheless, Les then added the guitar middle eight and major sevenths to the chords to bring the sound up to date, and the song was completed over three days.

In Les' opinion, Sandie Shaw would be a far more suitable candidate for recording the song than Johnny Kidd. The popular female singer had been discovered by both Les and Gordon's erstwhile manager, Evie Taylor, and in October 1964 was currently riding high in the charts with her cover of Burt Bacharach and Hal David's composition, '(There's) Always Something There To Remind Me'. Famed for her quirky insistence on performing barefoot and her somewhat breathless delivery, Sandie was a popular rival to Cilla Black and Dusty Springfield. Gordon needed to record the track as a demo before he could send it to Evie for consideration, and so he called on The Squires, who by now were all too used to sitting in the bedsit and twiddling their thumbs.

"The one thing we did was recording demos of his songs in the West End, in Denmark Street," enthuses Vernon. "That was incredible because we had £5 each for that. Gordon was still doing songs for different acts to try and get his own songs done, because he needed another [hit] song to get money to pay for everything – he was skint." Sadly, when it came to the crunch, Vernon Hopkins and Dave Cooper were not quite up to standard musically and were dropped for the demo. The recording consisted of Tom on vocals, Chris Slade on tambourine and Mike Gee on lead guitar, also adding some rhythm overdubs. "There was not even time to set the bass gear up," says Chris. "We only had ten minutes to do it, in Regent Sound in Denmark Street. And we did it. On the playback we went, 'That's number one, isn't it!' We just knew, absolutely knew."

After the brief recording session Gordon and the band went to The George pub near the studios to celebrate. Over a few beers, the lads collectively hassled Gordon to give the song to them instead of Sandie Shaw. But Gordon remained resolute as Chris recalls: "Gordon said, 'I've written it for Sandie Shaw!' and Tom had a screaming argument in the pub across the road and said, 'If I don't have that song that's it, you're not going to manage me.' And Gordon still gave it to Sandie Shaw."

At that precise moment Gordon was more concerned about a short-term financial boost than the long-term career of Tom and The Squires. Having unsuccessfully offered 'It's Not Unusual' to Frankie Vaughan through Leeds Music, he and Les took the demo to Sandie's manager, Evie Taylor in the hope that her already established artist would record it.

When they arrived at her offices Evie was ensconced in a critical meeting with the famous pennywhistle player, Des Layne, who was renowned for his summer seasons at Blackpool and went on to appear on *Sunday Night At The London Palladium*. Brashly confident of their demo, Les insisted on interrupting them, much to Evie's annoyance. Despite her protestations, she heard a couple of bars of the song and instantaneously loathed it. Evie obviously did not recognise any potential and Les and Gordon were abruptly dismissed from her office. "The crux of the story," laughs Les with hindsight, "is that she kicked out probably $2 billion, because we were so hungry we would have signed up anything to her at that time: Tom as an artist, Gordon as a manager, my writing, the record – she turned down all that talent for Des Layne The Pennywhistle Man!" Although 'It's Not Unusual' bears striking similarities to '(There's) Always

Something There To Remind Me', Sandie later described Gordon and Les' composition as not being her style. "There's no way I can sing it – it's not my song," and says she was always adamant that whoever had done the memorable demo should record and release it.

After being rejected once again Gordon finally offered Tom the song to record alone. Gordon had privately decided to drop The Squires after the failure of 'Chills And Fever', and instead enrolled a professional group, The Ivy League, to record the backing. Les supported his decision. "I heard [The Squires] on stage and they were OK, they were good for Tom, but I couldn't take a chance in the studio," he says. "They'd been rehearsing that song for months on end, but you don't get that chance in the studio. You've got three hours to get four titles in and you can't have any bad readers or people that play up or play the wrong note."

Tactful as ever, Gordon told the group that their services were not required. "It was explained to us that we couldn't read music, so therefore we were inferior beings!" chuckles Chris today. The recording session took place in Decca's West Hampstead studios on November 11, 1964. Three titles were cut, 'It's Not Unusual', the B-side 'To Wait For Love' by Burt Bacharach and another track called 'One More Chance'. As Decca had only signed Tom for three or four singles this was technically his penultimate chance.

Acting as arranger, Les remembers: "I decided to do 'Unusual' in the Mary Wells style, the laid-back Tamla sound, which just involved a couple of sets of vibraphones and a rhythm section and a backing group. When I took it in to record it with Tom, it was not 'big' enough; the whole thing was too laid back. Tom's voice was streaming through and it was far too big for the backing." Peter Sullivan suggested emphasising the bass hook with brass, hoping to achieve an overall fuller sound. Only Les shared Peter's foresight, as most of those present at the session believed that it would sound unfashionable, but Peter was so sure of his concept that it was doggedly pursued. Tom also disagreed with Peter's choice of adding brass at first, but he enjoyed singing the song so much, that at times the volume of his vocal often eclipsed the other musicians, and re-recording was necessary.

Until the release of the new single, Gordon and Jo were unable to subsidise the group over the quiet festive period and sent the five despondent lads packing to Pontypridd for Christmas. Back in London in January 1965, Tom was pleased with the outcome of the recording session. Les and Peter's visionary determination had produced a brassy bossa nova tune with an exhilarating tempo and a strong melody sung with a force that had not been heard in the charts for several years.

The rhythmic sexuality of 'It's Not Unusual' was considered too

53

extreme for BBC radio and so the record was instead broken by Radio Luxembourg and Radio Caroline, the pirate radio station launched in 1964 and broadcast from a ship in the North Sea. The song rapidly gained an enthusiastic audience and forced the BBC to recant and give the song considerable airplay. The single was released in late January 1965, entering the charts at number 21. Incredibly it reached number one within a matter of weeks, coinciding perfectly with St. David's Day on March 1, the holiday celebrating the patron saint of Wales. On May 1 it entered America's *Billboard* chart where it stayed for nine weeks and peaked at number 10. Overall Tom's record topped the charts in 13 countries. Within just four weeks the single had sold 800,000 copies and projected Tom Jones into overnight stardom.

In the midst of the overwhelming success, Gordon's press release about his protégé carefully omitted the truth on all counts: "He's Tom Jones, he's 22, single and a miner." In reality, Tom Woodward, the 25-year-old husband and father who had never once been down a mine, celebrated his success with a sausage sandwich – the most he could usually afford.

Jo Mills was in hospital recovering from a miscarriage when she heard 'It's Not Unusual' on the 'Newly Pressed' feature on BBC TV's *Top Of The Pops*. Presented as a solo artist, Tom had managed to break through a stifling line-up of bands in the charts including The Seekers, The Animals, The Kinks, Herman's Hermits, The Rolling Stones, Manfred Mann, The Who and ironically, The Ivy League. Tom Jones' more mature approach had obviously found an untapped market, but not everyone approved of his style. As it was evidently teenagers who were buying his record, Tom was promoted at the end of the children's television slot between 5 p.m. and 6 p.m., but he was clearly an adult singer. He appeared on *Blue Peter* and *Crackerjack* without taming his stage act, inciting parents to write in and complain. Tom recalls the havoc he caused: "I did a show which still runs now called *Blue Peter* – sounds like a frozen dick! The BBC were getting letters from mothers saying, 'This man is too raunchy. He should not be on children's television.' It was the way I was moving, you see."

More appropriate was his appearance on *Top Gear*, though it was easy to see why the BBC had received letters of complaint. Tom's Teddy Boy outfits had been superseded by a romantic highwayman look soon after his move to London. He wore tight trousers and billowing, frilly blouses. He had allowed his dark, curly hair to grow longer and was wearing it in a little ponytail tied with a ribbon. Physically he had filled out to become a muscular, well-built man whose roguish good looks tolerated his big nose and crooked teeth, transforming him into an exciting character with an erotic hint of danger about him. To complete the show-stopping picture,

Tom always displayed a rabbit's foot talisman dangling intriguingly from his waistband, and he had not toned down his notorious hip-swivelling.

Although The Squires did not play on the released track they were still being used to back Tom on these performances, dressed in identical outfits and sporting bouffant hairstyles. With a number one hit and numerous television appearances on popular teenage programmes, Gordon finally relented to increasing The Squires' retainers from the £1 a day on which they had survived since the summer of 1964. The new wage was £30 per week, which was some £10 over the average pay cheque at the time. However, it was still less than the standard Musicians' Union wage and, more importantly to Vernon and his friends, Gordon was insisting on remuneration. "We were supposed to be on £40 a week each but it was down to £30 because we had to pay Gordon back for the last nine months," he says. It was not until The Squires had paid back every penny to Gordon that they received their full and proper wage. Although never voiced it was uncomfortably apparent that Tom was being paid considerably more and did not lose the £10 repayment each week to Gordon.

Not content with the monetary stranglehold Gordon levered over his lesser charges, the ruthless manager also changed the line-up to suit the material Tom was singing. He felt that a rhythm guitar was an unnecessary expense as the newly added brass section would cover it up, and consequently Dave Cooper was unceremoniously sacked. The Squires were outraged but there was little they could do or say and, instead, Vernon persuaded Gordon to employ Chris Ellis as an acknowledgement of his endless loyalty. Chris was delighted to be involved after this small victory; this time in the official capacity as roadie for The Squires.

★   ★   ★

The immense success of 'It's Not Unusual' soon began to have an effect on Tom's personal life. He remembers sitting in a pub one Friday when the jukebox selection had just been changed and the regulars played the single back to back. Most of the customers did not recognise Tom and left him smiling contentedly at the bar, but devoted fans could spot his distinctive Welsh features from a distance. " 'It's Not Unusual' had just come out and I was still doing two shows a night and getting nowhere," Tom said in 1999. "I had to dash into a pub between shows to get something to eat. Then one night I came out from the pub eating the last bites of a pork pie, rushing to get back to the stage, and, all of a sudden, I saw all these girls running at me, screaming. They were wild. Before I could get away, they ripped off my leather jacket. A hit record like that changes everything."

On the other side of the coin, The Squires were not experiencing the same levels of attention and were feeling rather isolated and increasingly disgruntled with Gordon. To make matters worse, Tom appeared to be insensitive to the rest of the group's concerns. "One of the biggest effects is that success gives you more confidence in your work. Before, the group was getting fed up and disillusioned but now we all have a contented feeling," he said to the press. Although Vernon, Chris and Mike were finally receiving a decent wage, they not only felt the burden of having to repay Gordon, but were also expected to pay for their accommodation, travel, food and clothes. Furthermore Gordon exacerbated the situation by slowly distancing Tom from the group.

"He sort of prised Tom out of that basement flat and Tom went to live with him and his wife Jo," explains Chris. "It was like, 'Oh, Tom's got this interview, ah, you may as well stay with me tonight Tom.' Trying to get the partnership apart, like getting the husband away from the wife, so to speak. And he'd stay for the whole weekend." Gordon assumed that if Tom exchanged the squalor of the Ladbroke Grove flat for the Mills' more comfortable home, he would sooner or later abandon the sense of solidarity he felt towards The Squires. Gordon need not have worried. With the early profits of sales from 'It's Not Unusual' Tom purchased a gleaming new red S-type Jaguar, leaving the band to drive the unreliable old van they had put up with for years.

If Tom was unaware of how his newly elevated lifestyle was affecting his friends, he did at least remember to look after his family. He had been concerned about his father working down the mines for some time, especially since Tom Snr. had begun to show preliminary signs of chest problems. Thrilled to be able to repay his father's support after 25 years, Tom asked him to retire on the promise of royalties from his first single. His father astutely suggested that it would be best to wait a while to ensure that Tom was not a one hit wonder, but was nevertheless very touched by the thought. Unfortunately the son-turned-superstar was not able to spend time at home with his family to celebrate his achievements as success brought constant claims on his time. "I suppose it has been a bit shattering. It is astonishing how one song can change your life. Suddenly you find yourself in demand from every part of the country. It's flattering and I cannot pretend that I don't like it," Tom remarked at the time.

Gordon had returned to the Colin Berlin Agency and sagaciously signed Tom with his old tutors. With their expertise and the popularity of 'Unusual', Tom Jones & The Squires were invited to perform on numerous television and radio shows. Their first major appearance was on BBC TV's *Billy Cotton Band Show* on March 13, 1965, swiftly followed by slots on *Beat Room* and *Juke Box Jury*. Tom was then flown up to Glasgow to appear on *Scottish Round Up*, but had to travel alone as Gordon had not yet overcome his fear of flying.

Ready, Steady Go! had become firmly established since its launch in the summer of 1963 as *the* programme to start the weekend for the trendy, sophisticated 'mods'. The BBC rival *Top Of The Pops* was first aired on New Year's Day 1964, from a converted church in Dickinson Road, Manchester. Bobby Elliott, the drummer from The Hollies, appeared on that historical first shoot. "It might have seemed chaotic to the production staff, but it was very smooth for the artists," he recalled in *Q* magazine. "Compared to *Ready, Steady Go!*, which we'd done several times, and where you were always getting jostled by kids while you were trying to play, even that first *Top Of The Pops* was a model of organised perfection." Interestingly the songs were not performed live and all the musicians had to mime to their tracks. "We didn't mind that because audio technology in those days couldn't capture a good live band sound for television," continued Bobby Elliott. "The sound on things like *Ready, Steady Go!*, which were live, was appalling. So on *Top Of The Pops*, you just took pride in how well you could match your movements to the record, which was quite a skill in itself."

The young audiences of both shows 'endured' Tom's sweaty mas-culinity mainly because he had an undeniably impressive voice and a positively catchy tune. Even the other acts deemed him incompatible with current trends – when Tom appeared with The Beatles on ITV's *Thank Your Lucky Stars* in 1965, John Lennon delicately referred to him as a "Welsh poof" and provoked him even further by singing to his face a suitably psychedelic pun on Tom's hit, 'It's Not A Unicorn It's An Elephant'. Tom found it difficult to accept John's ridicule and despite Gordon's best efforts to calm him down, it was the beginning of a stormy relationship with the Liverpool group's dominant personality.

Usually, though, Tom did exactly what Gordon dictated, without hesitation. He readily accepted the offer of moving into Carlton Towers with Gordon, Jo and their two Siamese cats 'for the sake of convenience', and greatly appreciated his first tastes of the good life. Just occasionally he would make a vain attempt to stand up for The Squires. While Tom never questioned Gordon's decision to retain them on a low wage, on one particular occasion when he tried to stand up for the musicians, he was silenced by Gordon's vehemence on the matter.

"Gordon was very volatile, he could get these moods," says Keith Davies, who, although no longer a member of the group, would still visit his old pals in London. "I can remember a time when the lads had been asking for a pay rise and we walked past the dressing room door. There was a bit of an argument in the room, and I heard Tom saying, 'Well, they *have* been with me a long time Gordon.' And Gordon said, 'You give them fuck all, absolutely fuck all.'" As Gordon stood his ground, Tom folded and allowed the painfully apparent double standard to continue.

The Squires now realised that Gordon was undermining them at every turn. They were currently supporting a famous solo artist, but were rarely acknowledged as such and only ever seen as a backing group. They had paid their dues struggling alongside Tom in London, but were still only receiving a flat fee per week, regardless of the number of rehearsals and performances. Moreover, the one credit they did receive was not on records but on TV specials, and that in turn warranted a financial commitment to the tax man. The Welsh lads were so naïve that they were unaware of these ramifications and Gordon certainly did not proffer the information, pocketing the extra money himself and leaving the tax implications to fester until a later date.

★   ★   ★

In the meantime Tom was riding on the crest of a wave and his nation-wide fan base was rapidly escalating. Jo Mills found her house swamped by fan mail requiring attention and created the first Tom Jones Fan Club out of necessity. "Within a couple of weeks of going to the top of the charts, bagfuls of post came in," she explained in Hildred and Gritten's biography. "It was so hectic. Bit by bit I began a fan club. I had a hand-run Gestetner machine. I typed a letter out myself to the first fifty fans. I'd never typed before. Eventually we had half a dozen people working for us, and we were deluged with mail."

With the announcement that the official fan club had begun, the Mills' apartment at Carlton Towers, just off Queensway, was instantly inundated with well over 500 applications and Lynne Rees-Slade, Chris Slade's girlfriend, was one of those coerced into helping Jo with typing, stuffing envelopes and sending out the glossy newsletters. Gordon sheepishly corrected his original statement about Tom's age and previous employment but insisted on maintaining Tom's single status, arguing that a married man could not become a sex symbol. This was a common pop tactic, as in the Fifties Marty Wilde had lost a lot of fans after his wedding, and John Lennon had kept his marriage to Cynthia Powell in August 1962 very quiet for the sake of the fans. To emphasise Tom's masculinity the singer was encouraged to talk about his working-class background in interviews. "It's helped me. You have to be pretty tough in this business – physically tough. You come off stage sweating and get into draughts, and you can be exposed to colds and things. The fact that I've done some physical work at one time helps me. I'm strong enough to stand up to things like that," he told the *Daily Mirror* proudly.

Amidst the contemporary pop world which was currently overflowing with groups, Tom Jones was often compared to the few popular solo artists; specifically Elvis Presley and the transplanted American P.J. Proby in the UK. Proby, whose real name was James Smith, was two years Tom's senior and had pipped him to the post at Decca one year earlier. Since then, with their similarly raunchy acts, the two had become fierce media rivals, each claiming to be the original and citing the other as the copycat. P.J. (Perpetually Juiced) Proby described one of his typical 1965 performances from which the comparisons were drawn thus: "I go for the audience as much as possible. It begins with warming-up in which I let them hear my voice while the drapes are still closed. Then I show a glimpse of hand, and a leg afterwards. When at last the drapes are drawn and I start one of my big hits, the audience is already very excited. I excite them even more by following a loud rocker with a ballad. I also do a sexy dance . . . However, it was a pity other people started to copy my act."

The mere suggestion that Tom had copied 'P.J. Probably', as the Welshman nicknamed the American, caused Tom to state emphatically that he did not copy anyone, least of all Proby. But Les Reed, who had worked with both artists, maintains that although the feud was widely reported in the papers there was little truth behind it: "It was complete media hype."

The first time the rivals came head-to-head was at an all-celebrity charity concert on March 21 at the Empire Pool in Wembley, London. Tom was the undisputed crowd-pleaser at that event, but as Proby had the larger, more dedicated following, he was the one chosen to headline a major British tour with Cilla Black, whom Beatles' manager Brian Epstein had discovered working as a cloakroom attendant at Liverpool's Cavern club. Proby, however, had been banned from ABC Theatres throughout Britain as well as ATV and BBC television and radio after ripping his velvet trousers in a pertinent position on stage in Croydon, south London, on January 29, 1965. When Proby insisted on repeating this unendearing 'accident' on the tour he was given a verbal warning by the tour manager, Joe Collins. Blatantly ignoring the warnings, Proby was promptly fired the very next time he split his trousers.

Colin Berlin snatched the opportunity and telephoned Joe Collins to offer the perfect replacement, Tom Jones & The Squires. Rumours persist that Gordon had some involvement in arranging this manoeuvre behind the scenes at Decca, but either way Joe agreed to hire Tom and the group for £600 per week. Despite the singers' irrefutable similarities it took the audiences a while to accept Tom instead of Proby, as Tom recalls: "The first time that I went out on stage after Proby was fired, people in the first few rows were holding up signs with pictures of P.J. Proby. But gradually as the tour warmed up, people put their posters away."

Tom was being recognised more frequently and sometimes found the situation impossibly out of control. "One night I was in a pub between shows, having a drink with Cilla Black. A bunch of kids standing outside though were screaming at somebody . . . I figured it must have been one of the stars on the tour. Later on I walked straight out into the crowd with a beer in my hand, and the people tore my overcoat off and ripped it into tiny pieces. That was my first taste of crowd hysteria and I walked right into it, not knowing it was me they had been shouting at."

The unexpectedly intense wave of Tom Jones hysteria that swept the nation left Tom stranded more than once. One particularly horrifying experience happened in the presence of Chris Slade. "Tom and I nearly got killed once – we got trapped in a crowd. That was on the P.J. Proby tour. That's when we first made it – Tom and I were coming back from the club, minding our own business and suddenly these girls appeared and screamed, 'Ooh! There's Tom Jones!'

"We ran up the road like mad and we couldn't get in the theatre, all the doors were locked, and they just jumped on us. It was terrifying. In the end you're down on the ground, you're being pushed lower and lower, and you think, 'If I'm down there, they'll trample me to death!' It's very possible. I just remember these two big coppers grabbing us, Tom by the hair, and pulling us out." Tom was understandably less tolerant of the infamous occasion when he was followed into a gentleman's cubicle. "Basically, there are two things you do in a toilet and I was literally caught with my pants down," explains Tom. "I was sitting there minding my own business and these girls jumped over the door. There I was with my pants down and around my ankles. I got up and started shouting at the girls and pushing them out of the toilet. The guys travelling with me were in hysterics. I was very nasty though . . . I couldn't see the funny side of it."

Excitement about the four Welsh lads grew at an astonishing rate and for a few months at least Tom seemed loyal to the rest of the band, as reported in the *Pontypridd Observer*: "I have already been offered a tour of Australia, but I turned it down because they only wanted me . . . without The Squires." In the heady month of March 1965 The Squires succeeded in getting their collective name on a vinyl release of the *Tom Jones On Stage* EP. But all was not as it seemed, as top musicians suspected at the time, close inspection revealed that the songs were recorded in the studio with the audience noise dubbed on later, and not live as the title implied.

On April 11, 1965 Tom Jones & The Squires were to be found at the Empire Pool in Wembley for the *NME* Poll Winners Concert, sharing a bill with The Beatles, The Rolling Stones and The Animals. Jimmy Savile remembers his reunion with the Welsh star: "I was collecting Top Disc Jockey Award and Tom was collecting Top Male Singer. He said, 'I never got round to saying thank you. Would you like some of the action?' And I said, 'Like what?' He said, 'Do you want a percentage of the action?' So I said, 'Thomas, thank God you've got a few quid, thank God I've got a few quid. I'll have nothing – it was an honour to give you a lift and one day I may need to call a favour and I know it will be there.' And he said, 'You're damn right it will be there.' If anybody thought I was weird, that confirmed it; not taking a piece of Tom Jones' business!' I know that he has a tremendous respect for me because I wouldn't take any of his bread."

Later that same evening, Tom and The Squires made their début appearance on ITV's *Sunday Night At The London Palladium*. "It was very exciting, it was a live show which elevated people to stardom," illustrates Jimmy Tarbuck, a popular comedian and resident compère at The Palladium until the programme's demise. "Bruce Forsyth, Jimmy Tarbuck, Val Doonican . . . it was a stepping stone show, and if you were a record act, like Tom was, it was a wonderful show to plug your latest hit." Tom was rather overawed by the experience. "Doing *Sunday Night At The London Palladium* in 1965 . . . it was unbelievable, the biggest thrill of my life," he said in an interview with Lesley Salisbury in 1987. " 'It's Not Unusual' had only been out for about a month. I sang three songs and had a speech prepared, but it seemed to phase me and I just spoke right off the top of my head. 'Ladies and Gentlemen, this is the biggest thrill of my life. I've watched this show since I was a little boy and, look at this, here I am at the London Palladium,' – something like that. Next day I was criticised by the papers, who said, 'Tom Jones isn't polished enough for the Palladium.' "

Events were snowballing so quickly that Tom barely had a chance to evaluate his new status. From the relative gloom of the previous year, he was suddenly launched into constant television, radio and live appearances, fan recognition and adulation and his greatest desire: money. Soon after moving in with Gordon and Jo as a temporary measure, Tom summoned Linda and Mark to London to hunt for a flat. For the sake of Tom's image Gordon insisted that Linda should not be publicly acknowledged as his wife, so when they were spotted together she was simply assumed to be a girlfriend.

Jo explained Linda's reaction to her imposed anonymity on the 1991 BBC TV documentary *Omnibus: Tom Jones – The Voice Made Flesh*: "Linda, I think from the very beginning, was made to feel that she really mustn't exist in his [life] . . . and I think it was put mainly by Gordon. It's very sad because she's a lovely person and very warm, and if only she'd got that confidence initially she would have been different, I'm sure." Eventually, when Tom did manage to return home to Wales, the truth seeped out. He tried to justify the situation to the *Pontypridd Observer.* "I never wanted people to believe I was single. It wasn't fair to my wife,

Linda, and son Mark, in fact, I was going to let people know, but about 20 people from Pontypridd wrote to a daily paper and told them."

Although Gordon had firmly believed that the fans would not be attracted to a married man, amazingly it did not seem to deter them. Linda and Mark were of course both happy that Tom was now a famous family man and that they were no longer required to hide from the press. Linda spoke of her relief to the press and Mark, now a chubby little boy of eight, piped up with, "I'm glad everybody knows Tom Jones is my daddy." Whilst Tom was in Pontypridd, his mother, Freda, was always quick to remind Tom of his roots, and made sure that he treated Linda properly and took his turn in fetching the coal when he was at home.

Once their marriage was widely accepted Tom and Linda moved into a flat in west London while searching for a home more suited to their new-found wealth. Tom was a little wary of moving to the south of England on a permanent basis. "I don't relish the thought of leaving Wales but it is something that must be done. It would not be possible for me to live here and organise my career properly," he said to the papers. For Linda however, it was the first time she had moved out of her family home, let alone to another country. She knew no one in London and thus relied solely on the company of her little family and Jo, Gordon and their children, with whom she became firm friends.

Having moved his wife and son from Wales to London, Tom was very concerned that they did not become his second priority after his career and consequently made every effort to pursue a normal family life. Mark was very proud of his famous father but was painfully shy and often embarrassed by all the reporters and fans lying in wait wherever they went. Linda too tried to accept Tom's career as part of her life and began to attend some of his concerts. "I'd stand behind the scenes at Tom's concerts, watching all those women going crazy for him," she remembers. "For a time, it was flattering and even amusing for me, because I knew it was me Tom loved." In return, Tom never forgot that his marriage was based on the strong bond of their teenage love, admitting that if he had been looking for a girlfriend at this stage, he would be convinced that they were after his fame and money, and were not interested in his personality. Tom succinctly summed up his relationship with Linda: "She's always been there for me. We were kids together and she was my first love . . . She knew me when I was this young Welsh fellow who sang but who might not make it. And now that I've made it I want to take care of her."

Gordon's favourite piece of advice to Tom was always: "Put your money in bricks and mortar and you can't go wrong." Tom never knowingly disobeyed his guru and, with his riches pouring in, was soon able to acquire a stylish detached Thames-side house named Rose Bank in

Manny Gate Lane, Shepperton, costing a respectable £7,000. Tom was too busy to assist Linda in the preparation of their new home. "I didn't even have time to help choose the furniture," he said to the press. "I had to leave everything to Linda. Then, when we moved in with Mark, I had just two days there before I had to leave for a tour of America!"

Decorated in a gaudy yet fashionable Sixties style, their front room had a cream carpet, teak furniture and a long settee finished in orange and black Thai silk. The wall was covered in wood panelling and above the television, which was neatly recessed into the wall, were two crossed Spanish ceremonial swords. While Tom had a trendy, masculine living room, Linda found herself blissfully happy in her new kitchen. "It's a pleasure to work in," she gushed. "All the latest cooking gadgets make the daily chores easier, and everything is so well placed and within easy reach." Moving to cosmopolitan London had not remotely touched Tom's ingrained chauvinism as he proudly boasted in *Tom Jones*, Bert Schwartz's 1969 biography: "Cooking's a woman's job. A woman gets pleasure out of cooking because she likes to please her husband or boyfriend. Seeing food she's prepared being enjoyed, this is her reward. I'm on the consumption end of this business."

On the few occasions that Tom enjoyed a rest of any length at home, he tried to lead as normal a life as the fans and media attention would permit. "Success has not changed me as a person, but naturally it has changed the whole routine of my life. My timetable is so tight I virtually have no time at all for myself. My wife feels lonely at times when I'm away, but I don't think she minds because she's pleased to see I have got on, and accepts the price to be paid. We see as much of each other as possible, of course, and she has been really understanding." Tom spent his time around the house in a regular fashion; watching television, listening to records, playing a game of darts or billiards and keeping fit. He particularly liked the *nouveau riche* atmosphere of Shepperton and the relaxed nature of living outside London, yet close to the River Thames. He had a favourite pub in the local square which was also frequented by the Fifties actor, John Gregson. The only negative aspect of Tom's family life was having to get up early in the morning for occasional engagements.

Tom did not have much time to settle into his new accommodation as his whirlwind career raced along at breakneck speed. When 'It's Not Unusual' reached number 10 in the US charts, Gordon felt the timing was right for Tom to tackle the American market in person. On the same billing as old sparring partners The Rolling Stones, Tom was booked to appear on CBS TV's institution, *The Ed Sullivan Show*, in May 1965. The long running television programme had been instrumental in launching many famous acts in America, including Elvis and The Beatles and, before them, Frank Sinatra and Bing Crosby. Gordon scheduled Tom to make five appearances, earning a total of more than £10,000, and at the same time booked him for an American all-state summer tour. For the Welsh lad who had only previously been as far as Scotland this seemed like a fantasy unfolding in front of him. Gordon finally overcame his fear of flying to experience the fruits of their success, and the pair flew out on April 29, for the first *Ed Sullivan Show* appearance two days later.

Nearly a decade had passed since Elvis Presley had been controversially filmed only from the waist up on the very same show because his dance movements were considered too risqué, but Ed Sullivan applied the same censorship to Tom. It was suggested to the singer that he could perhaps move his hips from side to side instead of backwards and forwards. This was the first time Tom had been asked to tone his act down. "They said, 'If you move like that, we'll cut to close-ups.' I cooled it down a little bit, but not to where they wanted it. That's the way it was. If you did any sort of sexual moves, they didn't like it."

As with Elvis nine years previously, Tom's more lewd twists and turns were generally cut out in his performance of 'It's Not Unusual' and 'Whatcha Gonna Do When Your Baby Leaves You'. Tom wore his standard tight trousers and blousey shirt, his hair still long and tied back in a ponytail, but the trademark rabbit's foot was omitted for this performance. He was surrounded by plenty of energetic male dancers, but there was not a Squire in sight. While the rest of the group were at a loose end in London, Tom was reaping the rewards of becoming an international pop star. "The Americans are crazy on British pop stars. The thing over there is to be British, just as it once was the reverse in Britain," he said.

Tom returned to Wales on May 10, where The Squires rejoined him to open a month long UK variety tour at the New Theatre in Cardiff, followed by concerts at the Theatre Royal in Nottingham and the Hippodrome Theatres in Birmingham and Bristol. By June 13, Tom was back in America once more for further appearances on *The Ed Sullivan Show*. Tom's magnetism ensured that he was sought after in all areas of the media and he was tentatively offered a six-year film contract by Universal, but it failed to materialise. In July 1965 Tom and The Squires were invited to Hollywood for a screen test, but again nothing tangible resulted.

While Tom was in the US he was required to do other promotional work for 'It's Not Unusual'. Most Americans had not seen Tom when he first went over, which combined with the power of his voice and the style of his songs, led many to believe that the new singing sensation was both black and American. 'It's Not Unusual' had broken into America's R&B chart and the black radio stations were eager for Tom to appear on their shows. Tom recalls one particular incident: "There was this disc jockey who was amazed because I was white and said I should keep my face off the record sleeves because otherwise I'd lose the coloured audience I'd built up and the sales would drop. But of course I didn't. I was christened 'our blue-eyed soul brother' which I liked. It was a fantastic compliment." Even famous American soul singers were fooled by his sound. Dionne Warwick could not believe Tom was white and Mary Wells said, "I never thought I'd hear a white man sing like that." Tom had always admired black performers and felt that white artists were often missing a certain 'something' in their interpretation. Tom was particularly conscious of the way coloured people moved when they were singing. "I do admire the way coloured artists move on stage. If I go to a discotheque and the person I'm with can't dance properly, I get very bad-tempered."

Because of his tight black curls, swarthy complexion and soulful voice, the question was often raised as to whether Tom's bloodline was exclusively white. "Black people ask me all the time, they look at my hair and say there's got to be something in my family," he was still saying to journalists in 1999. "My publicist once tried finding out but couldn't get very far. I can only go back as far as my grandparents." Most importantly, Tom was never uncomfortable with the race issue and was often quoted retorting: "Where I come from in Wales, we white men dig for black coal and in America your black men pick white cotton. To me it's the same thing. You can be just as much put upon down a mine and singing those songs because you mean them as you can be if you're a Negro picking cotton."

The most important connection that Tom Jones made in America was Lloyd Greenfield. Lloyd was a prominent lawyer in Greenfield Associates of New York City and became Tom's management representative in America – effectively Gordon's right-hand man in the US. He was an intelligent, approachable and devoted family man who did not quite share Gordon's charisma or charm but was far more amiable. "He'd always join in the fun – he was better than Gordon, let's put it that way. Every now and again he'd pull rank," remembers Big Jim Sullivan. Lloyd oversaw the whole operation Stateside from the press interviews and recording sessions to arranging backstage guest lists and major concert contracts. Above all he was able to discern that while the fans each demanded a piece of Tom, the star also needed some rest and time to himself.

While Tom was in New York, an attractive offer came through from Dionne Warwick to show him around. Tom requested a trip to the famous Apollo Theater on 125th Street in Harlem, the spiritual home of R&B and soul music in New York. Chuck Jackson was headlining and at the end of his set he introduced Dionne, and The Shirelles who were also in the audience, to terrific applause. When Chuck asked Tom to join him on stage for the finale and introduced him as the 'Soul Brother from England', the audience almost froze in shock. Undeterred, the clearly Caucasian Tom took the spotlight and launched into a passionate rendition of the classic Ray Charles number, 'What'd I Say?' He received such an enthusiastic reception that the performance was extended for 15 minutes. Tom went on to play in New York's Copacabana Club where he became so popular that the queues started forming as early as 3 p.m. and would trail for several blocks.

Back home, Tom began to mix in elite London circles. One night he reputedly flirted heavily with Diana Dors in a nightclub, and although she suggested that they would make a suitable couple, he replied that he would have been too frightened of her to consummate the relationship!

Somehow, in between all the personal appearances on both sides of the Atlantic, Tom had been able to lay down an album's worth of songs. He would record in the evenings, his preferred time, and would work closely with Gordon Mills and producer Peter Sullivan to ensure that the songs were impeccable. The Squires appeared only at the arduous live gigs, having now been firmly replaced in the studio by some of London's finest session musicians, including guitarists 'Big' Jim Sullivan and also 'Little' Jimmy Page, who in 1968 would form the archetypal heavy rock quartet, Led Zeppelin.

Tom Jones' début album was simply titled *Along Came Jones* and featured a photo of him on the cover as the perfect, dashing highwayman. Whether it was intentional or not, the title mirrored Gary Cooper's 1945 cowboy movie that Tom had probably seen as a boy. Peter Sullivan wrote a synopsis of the album and a description of each track for the reverse side of the record sleeve: "Side One is used as a showcase for the treatment which Tom gives to beat numbers . . . His performance can be described as 'gutsy'. This sums up in one short word the raving dynamic performance Tom manages to whip up . . . Side Two reveals Tom Jones in another light . . . He is by turns, sad, wistful, tender and intimate, delivering the words with a deep sincerity." *Along Came Jones* was released in May 1965 in Britain but despite Peter's hype and Tom's seeming success with the single 'It's Not Unusual', it peaked no higher than number 11 a month later. Although re-titled *It's Not Unusual* for the American market, again the LP did not match up to the namesake single and struggled to reach number 54.

The follow-up singles fared little better, leading critics to ponder whether teenagers were attracted to the catchy song rather than the singer himself. Another Mills/Reed composition, 'I've Got A Heart', was released immediately after 'Unusual', but failed to make any impact whatsoever. 'Once Upon A Time' was their next attempt to enter the charts, just as 'It's Not Unusual' descended from its three-and-a-half month residency, but this rather repetitive tale of biblical love stories lacked the strength of the first offering, and was further hampered by the re-emergence of Joe Meek.

Joe had felt betrayed when the Welsh group signed with the Decca label as soon as he tore their contract up, and noting the success they had achieved since then, fancied a piece of the action. With his attention firmly fixed on his potential profit, Joe revived two of the tracks recorded back in 1963; 'Little Lonely One', which was based on 'Santa Lucia' by The Jarmels, and a B-side 'That's What Love Will Do'. Unlike two years previously, Joe found it easy to entice a major label and the single was rush-released on Parlophone in the UK and Tower Records in the US, just as 'Once Upon A Time' entered the Top 50.

Tom was quick to react and encouraged his fans not to buy the rival release. "This 'Little Lonely One' is something I could well do without," he explained to the media. "I made it a long time ago . . . and tastes have changed a lot since then. They were tough days when the group and I made 'Little Lonely One'. We were called Tommy Scott & The Senators and we really pinned our hopes on the recording session we did with Joe Meek . . . I think it's dated and I'd like to disassociate myself from it." Naturally Joe retaliated: "I have four other tapes of his which I would like to release. Tom auditioned for me and nobody wanted to know about him because it was the time when the group scene was very 'in', and everybody said he sang too well. I originally did him singing 'Chills And Fever', the record that Decca finally released re-recorded. I wouldn't have released this if I thought it was poor . . . I think this is a very good record. He should be glad it is coming out." Despite Tom's protestations his audience were divided between the two singles and 'Once Upon A Time' stalled just outside the Top 30 in the UK, while 'Little Lonely One' reached number 42 on America's *Billboard* chart. It was the last Tom and Gordon were to hear of Joe Meek who violently committed suicide less than two years later on February 3, 1967.

Tom's next single, 'With These Hands', was more respectable, comfortably reaching the Top 20. The revival of Billy Eckstine's bebop hit was a completely new departure for Tom, utilising heavy piano and string accompaniments. The follow-up was a rather more bizarre choice. Composer Burt Bacharach and lyricist Hal David had written the title track for the film *What's New Pussycat*, a Peter Sellers and Peter O'Toole comedy based on the catchphrase telephone greeting. Following an introduction via Gordon, Burt Bacharach took Tom back to his rented flat and played the tune on his piano. Tom was decidedly unimpressed and later complained bitterly to his manager that it sounded like a nursery rhyme. Tom genuinely thought Burt was joking and asked him to play the real song, so Burt tried to explain the idea to Tom: "It's a crazy song for a crazy movie. Don't try to make something out of it that's not there." Regardless of the ludicrous lyrics such as: "Pussycat, pussycat, you're so thrilling and I'm so willing to care for you/So go and make up your cute little pussycat face", Gordon was confident that 'What's New Pussycat' was destined to be a hit, particularly if it was associated with a popular movie that also featured alternative comedian Woody Allen and siren Ursula Andress. Tom reluctantly recorded the song in London and Burt totally immersed himself in the project, even personally producing it which was something he had never done before. Tom was very grateful for the advice and encouragement proffered by the composer and admitted later, "He had me singing better than I'd ever done before."

However tacky 'Pussycat' may have seemed, it revived Tom's somewhat flagging sales and reached number 11 in the UK and number three in the US. Tom went back to America in July to promote the single, appearing on various television programmes including CBS TV's *It's What's Happening Baby*. Then, on August 1, 1965, the Squireless Tom commenced the summer tour Gordon had booked back in March.

The Dick Clark Caravan Tour was a regular event promoted by Dick Clark, all-round entertainer and host of ABC's long-running TV show *American Bandstand*. About a dozen acts travelled the length and breadth of America, visiting 36 cities in a cramped Greyhound bus known as the Caravan Of Stars. The line-up with Tom in 1965 included Sonny & Cher, The Turtles, Ronnie Dove, The Shirelles, Peter & Gordon, The Jive Five and Jackie DeShannon. Tom had not remotely anticipated the sheer gruelling nature of the tour. "In Britain, if you get a hit record, you're playing good venues and doing good TV shows right from the beginning. I sort of got used to that, even though I had only been doing it for a few months at that level. But I thought, 'This is it. This is great.' And then I come to America and that bus, God almighty!"

"It was murder," he told Sylvie Simmons in 1999. "All these different acts in the same bloody bus, and there were no couches, just regular seats . . . The best part of it was people would get out guitars and start singing songs, but the country is so big after so many hours in a bus, arriving just in time to do a show, then back on the bus all through the night. I thought, God, if this is show business in America, you can keep it."

He elaborated further on the tedium in another interview: "I always knew that America was a big country, but when you actually go on the road in a bus trying to cover the country . . . It was one show a day, but the trips in between were so long. Sometimes you'd finish one show and then drive to the next town. It would take you so long you wouldn't have time to book into a hotel, you'd go straight to the job." Another depressing feature about the tour was that it opened Tom's eyes to racism in the southern states. The tour, including the black artists, had stopped off for a meal in a café when some local 'rednecks' walked in, loudly complaining about the presence of the 'niggers'. Tom attempted to stand up for his colleagues, but the police were called when the argument turned violent, and he was told to keep firmly out of it.

As a little light relief after such tension, Dick Clark and Co. would hold 'blow-out parties' every two weeks, which he describes in his book *Rock, Roll & Remember*. At one notable backstage party Tom stole the limelight by performing in a wig and dress belonging to one of The Shirelles. Another welcome break was a brief but exciting trip to Bermuda, where Tom appeared at the Forty Thieves Club.

But undoubtedly the highlight of the Dick Clark Caravan Tour for Tom was the opportunity to meet one of his greatest idols when the party stopped off in Los Angeles, California. Tom was due to sign a contract for his next soundtrack song, 'Promise Her Anything', at the Paramount Studios in Hollywood. As Elvis Presley was filming his 21st movie, *Paradise, Hawaiian Style* on a closed set in the studios, Gordon arranged for the two singers to meet. Tom stood dumbfounded, watching the once outrageous rock'n'roller perform an asinine number called 'Datin' ' to nine-year-old Donna Butterworth in a mock helicopter.

"He looked out of the helicopter at me and sort of moved his hand. One of his guys Joe Esposito, said to me, 'Elvis is waving at you. Why don't you wave back to him?' So I sheepishly waved back." Elvis' manager, the tyrannical Colonel Tom Parker, introduced the two men who spoke for a couple of minutes. Tom can still picture this first encounter clearly: "When I met him he was walking towards me, singing 'With These Hands'. I couldn't believe it! And he knew every track on my album. It was amazing! Here I was, ready to tell him how much he had influenced me and he was telling me how much he liked my records!" Tom managed to ask Elvis how he was able to sing the way he did and was flattered and surprised at the response, "By listening to you!" Tom concludes his initial impression: "This might sound a bit soft, but you know what surprised me about Elvis? It was discovering that he was a real person. I knew he had to be real – everybody is, of course – but somehow I never expected he would be!"

In America and England, Tom received a selection of prestigious awards. He won the Best New Artist category at the eighth Annual Grammy Awards, and was given the accolade of 'Brightest Hope For 1966'. 'It's Not Unusual' was voted one of the best singles of the year and

Tom came fifth in the *Melody Maker* poll Male Singer category behind Cliff Richard, Donovan, Mick Jagger and John Lennon. He realised that in order to maintain this popularity he could not spend as much time in America in the future and stated in an interview, "My long-term career will be in Britain." In October he recorded 'Promise Her Anything' from the Leslie Caron film of the same name, starring Warren Beatty. This again was both written and produced by Burt Bacharach but was not released until the following year and was far less successful than 'What's New Pussycat'.

With his career following its natural course, Tom starred in his first TV special at the end of 1965. It was called *Call In On Tom*, and aired in the UK by ITV on November 17. Despite recent indications to the contrary Tom then briefly returned to America to appear in a charity show at Carnegie Hall in New York with Sammy Davis Jnr. and Louis Armstrong on December 2, and gave his final performance of the year on *The Ed Sullivan Show* on December 12. He also managed to fit in a duet on 'If You Need Me' with Joan Baez for her TV special and an appearance on *The Kathy Kirby Show*.

Tom was then called in at the last minute to sing the title track for James Bond's fourth cinematic adventure, *Thunderball*. The original title song, 'Mr Kiss Kiss Bang Bang' had been recorded first by Shirley Bassey, who had a hit with 'Goldfinger' from the previous Bond film, and then Dionne Warwick, but producers Harry Saltzman and Albert R. Broccoli were nervous about a theme tune that omitted the title. Resident Bond composer John Barry worked hastily with lyricist Don Black on a replacement and Tom recorded the track just weeks before the film's premiere. Tom's robust voice meant that he could reach any note without going into 'head voice' or falsetto. Don Black reported with some amusement that the strain of hitting the song's final high note caused Tom to faint in the studio: "Thankfully, he didn't have to sing it more than once. He got it right the first time. When he sings it live now he takes it down a bit." Tom lapped up his well-earned glory at the opening night of *Thunderball* at Piccadilly Circus' Pavilion cinema, London on December 29, but the song itself reached no higher than number 35 in the UK charts.

6

DON'T LET OUR DREAMS DIE YOUNG

THE DOWNSIDE OF all the travelling back and forth to America was that Tom was unable to spend Christmas 1965 back in Pontypridd with his wife and son, who had returned to Cliff Terrace to see their relatives. Friends and residents of Tom's birthplace were disappointed that their local hero was absent for the festive season, but were hopeful that he would not forget his strong ties to the community and visit in the new year. Now that Tom had attained a degree of affluence it was even harder for him to reconcile his inability to be with his family over the holidays, as he treasured many fond memories of the modest celebrations of his childhood, "We would use the best room in the house and we had turkey – or chicken when we couldn't afford turkey – and ham."

Although missing his folk, Tom had plenty of issues to occupy his thoughts. The single 'Thunderball' had generated little revenue, having made less of an impression on the charts than was anticipated for a James Bond theme tune. It was obvious to Gordon and agent Colin Berlin that they were going to have to consider some other means of promotion to build on Tom's career and secure all their futures. Two critically acclaimed films, *A Hard Day's Night* and *Help!* had been released by The Beatles in 1964 and 1965 respectively, proving that vinyl wasn't the only medium available to rising pop stars. In the early weeks of 1966 Tom was approached by Jon Scoffield, a distinguished and innovative young television producer who was planning a series of 15-minute musical slots to fill the gaps in between programmes.

"They were rather strange," Jon reflects on the resulting product today. "I had an idea of doing a show, mostly in close-up, and Tom was just coming out. We just did two programmes. That was the beginning of Tom and I working together." Tom was chosen as the first artist to feature in the fillers, which were shot in black and white and simply called *Faces*. Jon's personal assistant, Nina Blatt, was present at the filming. "Kenny Powell played piano and a very quiet young man called Tom Jones sang. There were two programmes, known simply as *Faces 1* and *Faces 2*," she remembers.

Tom performed three songs at each sitting and launched the series on March 2, 1966, just one year and one day after hitting the top of the charts with 'It's Not Unusual'. The fairly brutal close shots scrutinising his face helped spark rumours in the press that he had tried to improve the look of his broken nose with plastic surgery. Although the filming was only brief, Tom's natural presence and charisma in front of the camera planted an inkling that was to linger in the back of Jon's mind for some time. Meanwhile, working with other directors and production teams, Tom continued to improve his television persona throughout 1966 by resurfacing in further TV specials, including *Call In On Tom*.

Tom remained under the intense observation of the media and his second LP, *A-TOM-IC JONES*, attracted adverse publicity for its crass cover. The concept of political incorrectness had yet to be realised in 1966, but there was nevertheless something morally unsound, perhaps even gratuitously offensive, about a portrait of a singer posing, legs asunder, in front of a dramatic atomic explosion. Parrot Records, the Decca-owned label distributing Tom's LPs in America, initially refused to release the album as they thought American audiences would still be sensitive after the horrors of the Second World War bombings at Hiroshima and Nagasaki. Eventually the record was repackaged, and released under the same title but with a more tasteful photograph on the cover, with the singles 'Thunderball' and 'Promise Her Anything' replacing lesser known tracks. It was a rare tactical error in Gordon's management of Tom.

The singer was rejoined by his faithful band, The Squires, for a month-long tour of Australia beginning on March 18, sharing the bill with the popular lightweight English group, Herman's Hermits. Tom had maintained a strong Australian following since his substantial hit with 'Chills And Fever' back in 1964, but the notoriously prudish authorities there were less than impressed with the tight clothing that did little to hide his trademark thrusting pelvis. British newspapers gleefully reported tales of Australian police threatening to close his shows as a result of his on-stage sexual antics, especially after Tom appeared shirtless. Tom perhaps didn't take the warnings seriously enough at first, as he joked flippantly to a *Daily Mail* reporter: "It was only because I took my shirt off. Why did I take it off? Because it was too hot."

He was soon forced to pay more attention after his first performance in Sydney was filmed for close inspection by a magistrate. "I remember that the police filmed my first show in Sydney because they thought I was being too rude and raunchy. They said if I didn't cut the raunchy bits out, they would stop the tour," Tom elaborates. "But they viewed the tape and realised I was just dancing and not doing anything rude." Once the scandal had died down, Tom completed the rest of the tour with The Squires in the glorious antipodean sunshine, bolstering his confidence as a 'star' and still managing to sneak in an infamous wiggle every now and then.

Despite the fame and glory 'down under', back at home Tom's singles were not charting particularly well. He was reduced once again to appearing at gigs the length and breadth of the UK with The Squires in order to sustain a steady income. On their return from Australia, guitarist Mike Gee, who had been with the band for just under two years since their move to London, was increasingly perturbed. "He realised that Tom was becoming the star and he didn't want to be 'a backing band'," explains Chris Slade. "He wanted to be one of The Beatles or the Stones." Mike mulled over his concerns with the rest of the boys and finally persuaded them to appeal *en masse* to Gordon for a pay rise, reflecting both their hard work and desired group status. Mike and the others approached Gordon with their request, but the tight-fisted manager refused on the spot. When threatened with the cut and dried choice of either accepting the current wage or leaving, Vernon and Chris backed down, anxious to keep their jobs. Mike on the other hand was not prepared to stay, especially amidst the resulting tension, and left, subsequently joining the bands Plum Crazy and Love Sculpture. Tom was not involved in the fracas, and remained aloof despite Chris and Vernon's rising alarm.

There were other far-reaching problems troubling Tom at this time. The combined effects of Australia's extreme aridity and his serious cigarette habit had damaged Tom's throat so badly that when Gordon sent him to a specialist he was referred directly to hospital. On April 12, 1966 Tom was admitted to the exclusive London Clinic to have his tonsils removed in a straightforward half-hour operation. While the singer was under sedation the hospital's switchboard was jammed by well-wishers and fans hoping to win the tonsils as a grotesque memento. The prized organs later mysteriously disappeared from the clinic.

During the procedure the surgeons recognised tell-tale signs of severe bruising in Tom's throat, and when he regained consciousness he was warned that it was imperative to stop smoking in order to preserve his vocal prowess. Gordon suggested that perhaps taking up cigars instead would reduce the bruising caused by Woodbines, Tom's favoured brand of high-tar cigarettes, as cigar smoke is not inhaled. This gave Gordon the opportunity to enhance Tom's rough and ready image with an aura of refinement and wealth. The doctors had also advised against drinking strong spirits such as Tom's preferred combination of rum and coke, and further informed him that beer was doing little to combat his growing tendency to put on weight. It was recommended that he switched to drinking wine, but Tom disliked the taste and, with Gordon's approval and encouragement, chose champagne as his regular tipple.

For a man brought up in a house where champagne and spirits were regarded as a luxury, Tom took to it like a duck to water. "I always smoked Woodbines and drank beer," he frequently recounts. "My manager said that one day I'd be smoking cigars and drinking champagne. I said, 'I love Woodbines and I love beer, and that's that.' So, what am I doing today? Drinking champagne and smoking expensive cigars." But he was pleased to adopt the new image whatever the expense, as he stated in publicity material at the time: "When you can afford to do that, what the hell. Lots of people say I have changed. The only change as a person in me is that the real me has come out."

Tom spent the week following his operation recovering at his parents' home in Pontypridd. Burt Bacharach had invited Tom to a celebrity dinner in Hollywood, where the *What's New Pussycat* title song had been nominated for an Academy Award, but the recuperation period prevented him from attending. Tom was also forced to cancel a Variety Club Luncheon honoured by the presence of the Duke of Edinburgh for the same reason. Finally Tom allayed his fans' fears that his voice had been damaged with an appearance on *Ready Steady Go!* on May 6, 1966. Tom himself was much comforted that he could still sing, believing that the operation had actually improved his vocal timbre and was aiding his occasional use of falsetto. "Since the operation, I find my voice is standing up to the singing much better than before, which is a relief," he said.

Fully recovered, Tom embarked on a whirlwind summer. He joined Dusty Springfield and The Mindbenders for a charity concert at Blackpool Opera House on May 15. One week later he was flown to Brussels to record a TV show, and then on to Paris where he filmed another television spectacular on May 24 and 25, before setting foot back on home turf. With little respite, Tom returned again to France on July 13, for a whole month of concerts staged mainly on the Riviera. During the same month he attained moderate chart success back in England with a double A-side release, 'Once There Was A Time'/'Not Responsible', which reached number 18 on June 11. In the States he suffered from a lack of exposure and the single struggled to number 58. August saw him guesting on the premiere of ITV's *Bruce Forsyth Show* before travelling to Spain on the 15th for yet another TV special, shot in Madrid, and finally holidaying for the rest of the month.

Interspersed with all this jet-setting, it was hardly surprising that on June 21, 1966 Tom literally lost control. "I had my first car – a red Jaguar. And I was clubbing it a bit too much in London," he admitted to the *Radio Times* in 1992. "I was drinking and driving. So I came out of the Cromwellian one night and I'm going up Park Lane and I just crashed into the barrier." Narrowly missing any vital arteries, Tom's head was split open and he and a 'lady companion' were rushed to St. George's Hospital at Hyde Park Corner in the early hours of the morning. The woman, who was shaken and bruised, escaped relatively lightly, but Tom endured 14 stitches over his left eye. He was fortunate that this incident occurred in the days before breathalysers were the norm in traffic accidents.

Linda was horrified by the whole scenario and spent the night fretting over her wayward husband. But it was his mother, Freda, who put him truly in his place the next morning, as Tom recounted: "We were living in Shepperton and my mother and father were staying with us. So when I woke up . . . with a splitting headache . . . my mother was standing over me. And she said, 'Who do you think you are?' I said, 'Mam, stop it, my head is killing me.' She said, 'You better watch yourself, you're drinking too much, get hold of yourself. This stops right now!' It stopped me – she stopped me right there and then. I was getting out of hand and I knew it and that was that, really." As a result, Tom tempered his errant lifestyle just a little, emerging from the episode with what he now describes as a 'crease' on his forehead to show for the alcoholic mishap.

While Tom was busy misbehaving, Gordon was also causing ructions. He had fallen out with his writing partner Les Reed while they were working on the song 'To Make A Big Man Cry'. Les was keen to expand on his work with artists besides Tom Jones and offered this song, along with others, including demos of 'Delilah' and 'I'm Coming Home', to P.J. Proby. Gordon was furious as he naturally expected all Mills/Reed compositions to go to his protégé. Proby particularly liked 'To Make A Big Man Cry', which was subsequently released and became a minor hit in June 1966. Moreover, unbeknown to Les as well as Gordon, Leeds Music had also submitted the track to Adam Faith, who was facing a career decline, and Faith recorded a non-charting version of the song in October. Livid, Gordon withdrew his original plans for Tom to release the very same number in Europe, with the exception of Spain. Some time later during a concert in Spain, Tom was puzzled to see members of the crowd running their fingers down their faces as if to simulate tears. When he queried their actions afterwards he was told that the audience had in fact been signalling for him to sing 'To Make A Big Man Cry', which – to his amazement – reached number one in the Spanish chart without his knowledge. "Nobody bloody told me it was a hit!" he ranted to the media. "It's fine if they want to make a hit out of a song from an album. The only thing is, I'd like to know!"

Gordon's somewhat temperamental management techniques – and the fact that only the catchiest songs released by Tom succeeded – prompted him to take stock of his star's career. In certain media circles the singer was being criticised as passé as his releases barely scraped the Top 40; sure-fire soundtrack theme 'Thunderball' stalled at number 35 in the UK while in the US, 'Promise Her Anything' collapsed pathetically at number 74. Advance sales of another single titled 'Stop Breaking My Heart' ceased even before its official release. After such an auspicious start, Tom Jones' only resounding smash hit 18 months on remained his signature 'It's Not Unusual'.

To accentuate the problem, Gordon and Colin Berlin's style of press promotion, with Tom and Linda frequently appearing in women's magazines chatting about marriage and family life, was complete anathema to the chart-buying teenagers. Even Tom's increasing television appearances were not aiding his flagging appeal. Outspoken pop personality Jonathan King unleashed a scathing attack on Tom's attempt to become an all-round entertainer. "I don't want to sound anti Jones but what has he got to offer?" he wrote. "He is full of enthusiasm and has a certain animal charm. But he can never be called an entertainer. His television personality comes as near zero as possible . . . No finesse, no subtlety . . . An adequate pop star, yes – an entertainer, no."

Gordon realised drastic measures were needed to secure any hope of a future for his faltering client. "Tom was so strong, too strong on stage, that kids were afraid of him," Gordon later justified in an interview. On close examination he had discovered that Tom's audience consisted mainly of women over the age of 25, who by definition, possessed a larger spending capacity. There was also a substantial gap in the market for the older listeners. "This is when I thought of trying him with a mature audience," Gordon explained. The tight leather outfits, long hair and rabbit's foot adopted for the teenagers were not as tantalising to the older women, who were looking for a more refined eroticism. Gordon leapt upon the idea of clothing his star in a tuxedo, and gave him a short back and sides hairstyle. The change suited Tom as he was now in his late twenties and was well versed in the art of audience seduction. "Women, when they pass 30, are still full-blooded women. And they like full-blooded men. That's what they get from me. I turn them on, excitement like that is a good outlet," he crowed.

The result was phenomenal. Switching venues to theatre circuits and nightclubs preferred by the new target audience, sparks flew. Tom remembers: "What you would expect would happen in a ballroom with teenagers started to happen in these nightclubs with mature people. Women started to go crazy, and back then it was completely different because it had never happened before – adults acting like teenagers and going berserk!" Gordon also prompted a shift towards lighter, ballad material. Tom was not initially keen on the idea as he had always wanted to be seen as a rock'n'roll singer and would now have less opportunity to perform the songs he loved. After a brief period of contemplation, he reluctantly came round to the change. "It's true that doing these ballads might be giving me a square image with the fans. What I'd really like to release is a big blues or R&B number, just to show everyone I can do it. But my manager points out the snags to me and I start thinking maybe he is right and I should stick to the kind of stuff I've been doing."

By modifying Tom's image in this way, Gordon was also knowingly exploiting a certain resentment felt by the older music fans towards scruffy, anarchic groups like the Stones, who lacked a macho or romantic frontman. Tom Jones was always going to be a better singer than Mick Jagger, and with the combination of a grown-up look and a sound reminiscent of a crooner from an earlier era he successfully fitted into a niche long left vacant. Mature women sought a virile male in preference to the trendy bi-sexual aura of Mick Jagger or the cutesy, boy-next-door look of Peter Noone of Herman's Hermits, who appealed to the girls' mothering instincts.* Nobody was going to mother Tom. His obvious manliness and blatant sexuality mixed with the new smooth, sensual songs provided a solid basis upon which to build his future.

★   ★   ★

Meanwhile, in the gambling Mecca of Las Vegas, Nevada, a new casino hotel by the name of Caesar's Palace had just been opened. Taking inspiration from ancient Rome, the sumptuous hotel boasted an abundance of white marble, fountains, statues and waitresses clad in skimpy togas. Andy Williams was the opening cabaret attraction, followed by Anthony Newley and then Tony Bennett. To Gordon's great delight, Tom was sought after as the fourth musical headliner at the hotel. The contract encompassed a four-week stint commencing at the end of October 1966, succeeded by two further month-long periods in 1967. Tom was to be accompanied by only one member of The Squires. "I can't take my backing group with me because of union difficulties, so I'll be forming a backing band out there," said Tom. "But I will have my drummer, Chris Slade, along with me, because he knows the tempo of my songs. I must admit I'm looking forward to it." It was no wonder that Tom was so excited – this phenomenal deal earned him a staggering quarter of a million dollars, as reported in the press at the time.

Back in his homeland, Tom's third UK album *From The Heart* achieved

* A few years later, David Bowie was to become another effeminate antidote to Tom. "I once saw David Bowie in a discotheque in London," remembered Tom. "I couldn't believe it, he looked so pale and fragile. I guess women must want to mother him or something."

moderate success in reaching number 23 in the charts. The sleeve portrayed him nostalgically overlooking the rolling hills and valleys surrounding Pontypridd. As if to reflect the tone of the LP, Tom began to dispel any fears that he might be deserting his native country for the glitz and glamour of Las Vegas with reassuring statements. "I love America and dig the people," he was quoted in Peter Jones' book, *Tom Jones – The Biography Of A Great Star*, published later in 1970. "But in Britain I feel I am really in the centre of the music business. America is so large, you tend to feel you're on the outside looking in. British groups, especially the guys with long hair, are doing well in the States, but I realise so much that I owe a great deal to the fans who have supported me in Britain."

In preparation for recording sessions on Tom's return from Caesar's Palace, Gordon augmented The Squires with a keyboard player called Vic Cooper, who had previously been playing with Johnny Kidd & The Pirates. Having caught Gordon's eye, Vic was badgered on many occasions by the persistent manager hoping to poach him. Eventually Vic amiably gave in and brought to Tom's backing group a welcome touch of Jerry Lee Lewis on the keyboards. Gordon, being Gordon, always strove for the optimum deal, and whilst paying Vic the same wage as the other Squires persuaded him to act as Tom's personal chauffeur for no extra charge. The Squires were still being ferried about by Chris Ellis in their beaten-up old van, but Tom was driven by Vic in a brand-new Volvo sports car, which had replaced his damaged red Jaguar.

Vic soon became firm friends with the close-knit Welsh lads, and as a Londoner he introduced a new dimension to the group. Although in 1966 drugs, particularly marijuana, were common denominators to the music scene, Chris and Vernon were still innocently downing their traditional pints. Tom despised drugs of any description, and with no narcotic experience was unlikely to recognise the tell-tale signs, as Chris recalls: "Tom would never have known if anyone was stoned, and if they were absolutely incoherent, he'd think they were drunk."

So when Vic managed to entice the backing group to dabble on a memorable night just before a concert, Tom was apparently oblivious. Vic remembers: "I made them smoke one, and during the second song, 'What's New Pussycat', Tom was singing and Vernon put his guitar down. He thought it was the end of the whole set! Then Chris started to lose it, and paranoia set in on me. I thought, 'Oh no, what song are we doing?' Then Vernon said, 'I'm on a boat!' I said, 'You're in Sheffield, Vernon!'" Somehow they struggled through the rest of the set, believing that Tom had not noticed, but some years later the singer told *People* magazine, "I remember this bass player I had in one of my bands trying pot and going to pieces on stage. He was just incapable of playing. If he'd been drunk, we could have propped him up against the wall and he could still have played. But he was all over the place. He couldn't even change chord and that shocked me." Gordon chastised the shamefaced trio with the burning accusation, "You're on it!", thus ensuring that this particular indulgence was never repeated.

Tom knew that he desperately needed another hit single. Browsing through his record collection at home, he chanced on an old favourite of his, a Jerry Lee Lewis classic from the album *Country Songs For City Folk*. 'Green Green Grass Of Home' had already been covered extensively by country stars other than Jerry Lee, including the staid Porter Wagoner just the previous year. But Tom felt confident he was able to revive it once more. "It was the right song," he said later. "Some numbers are so personal that they can hardly fail. Immediately there is a bond between the singer and the lyrics and the audience. What makes me specially proud is that it was chosen by me alone . . . and I knew instinctively it was right for me." In a special eponymous documentary honouring the 30th anniversary of his release of the song in 1996, Tom elaborated on the composer's inspiration for its lyric: "The writer was Claude Curly Putnam Jr., who had seen a film called *The Asphalt Jungle* [Marilyn Monroe's first film]. In it there was a gangster who wanted to go back home to his farm before he died – at the end he collapses, bleeding and shot through with holes, onto the green, green grass of home . . ."

Tom approached Peter Sullivan, expressing his desire to make the song his own. Peter was initially dubious that country music was a suitable direction for Tom to pursue, and suggested that the track should be adapted for the pop charts. But Gordon was positive that it was the perfect prototype for Tom's proposed move into ballad material. Les Reed was asked to arrange the song, but he too was sceptical as he felt it had already been overexposed. He agreed to the job on the condition that he could make startling changes to the traditional arrangement, regardless of Gordon's wish for a more conventional sound.

"Tom hated it when he went into the studio," muses Les. "He said, 'What have you done? This is a Jerry Lee Lewis classic! You can't take that country style away!' I said, 'Tom, I'm being commercial. You've got a lot of people out there over 40 years old who are a bit romantic; they love the strings, they love this, that and the other.' He agreed in the end and we put it out." In the event it didn't take long for Tom to appreciate the changes: "Les Reed made this big arrangement of this little song and with me singing it didn't sound country anymore." The alterations pleased everybody and far from pushing Tom into a country corner as Peter Sullivan had feared, the producer now states: "I would attribute all of Tom's success to 'Green Green Grass Of Home' as it opened up new musical genres for him."

Released in November 1966, 'Green Green Grass Of Home' climbed to number one in the UK on December 1, and reigned supreme for seven weeks at the top spot clocking up a total of 22 weeks in the charts. 'You Keep Me Hangin' On' by The Supremes and 'If Every Day Was Like Christmas' by Elvis Presley were among the Christmas releases denied the coveted prime position by Tom's calculated revival. This unprecedented success earned Tom Jones the accolade of becoming the first Decca artist to sell over a million copies of a single in the UK alone. 'Green Green Grass Of Home' was also a resounding success in the US, selling over 1,220,000 copies and reaching number 11 in February 1967. Tom's rendition even attained the royal seal of approval from Jerry Lee Lewis himself.

The incredible impact of Tom's biggest selling record to date has been attributed to many different factors. Fellow Welsh men and women have practically adopted 'Green Green Grass Of Home' as a second national anthem, many mistakenly believing at first that the 'Home' of the title was Tom's tribute to his native country. The choice of release date was timely too, as over Christmas 1966 the British public was mourning the recent tragedy at Aberfan, where a slag heap had collapsed on top of a local school in the small mining village just north of Pontypridd, killing scores of children. Americans also focused their own political and personal concerns on the emotive yet non-specific lyrics. "It affected a lot of people over the world because the Vietnam War was still going on. I've met men since who were in Vietnam when the song came out, and they were crying when it came on the radio," Tom remembers today. "['Green Green Grass Of Home'] goes across the board – kids can understand it, and so can older people. I think it's a unique song, because it never mentions a particular country or city . . . I think everybody, when they hear it, thinks of where they come from."

A little positive promotion from Tom's celebrity friend and admirer, Elvis Presley, famously contributed to the record's success. Elvis and his entourage were touring on a coach when they first heard the melancholy tones of Tom's 'Green Green Grass Of Home' filter gently over the radio waves. A long way from his Memphis home, Graceland, in both distance and schedule, Elvis was homesick and could not help but burst into tears on hearing the evocative opening lines: 'The old home town looks the same as I step down from the train/And there to meet me is my Mama and Papa . . .'. Elvis began to plague the radio station with phone calls begging the disc jockey to play it again and, honouring the star's request, Tom's song was played a total of four times in succession. "It was the best publicity I could get," says Tom wisely. "He was a sentimental guy and said it made him cry."

In spite of the worldwide approval of the tuxedoed Tom's new hit, criticism still penetrated his success. *Melody Maker,* which was rapidly becoming the Bible for seriously inclined rock musicians and fans, cattily described the track as "The song hippies love to hate ... Not since Ken Dodd tickled his way to the top has a number one produced such a barrage of spleen from the self-appointed arbiters of teenage taste!" Spurred on by Gordon and with a modicum of relief, Tom shot back with: "It doesn't worry me because you get criticised in this business whatever you do. I found the song myself, so at least it's proved that I can pick my own winners, and it has ended a frustrating 12-month absence from the charts for me."

The victorious team promoted their newly packaged crooner to the hilt, even persuading Tom to venture down a salt mine in Germany, while back home he celebrated in his favourite haunt, The Wheatsheaf, with all his family and old school friends. When he returned to Laura Street he was met by television cameras and a small crowd, anxious to catch a glimpse of the local hero whose luck had changed. To the residents of Pontypridd, Tom Woodward was still his old self beneath all the showbiz gloss. "They say to me, 'Tom you haven't changed a bit!' and I say, 'Well, what did you expect – horns sticking out of my head?' I'm just a man and it isn't in me to put on airs and graces because of what's happened."

At a time when the moral standards of both the pop world and the war-torn planet seemed to be collapsing, the stability and values offered by sentimental country music such as 'Green Green Grass Of Home' struck an emotional chord with everyone who yearned for a slice of the good old days. To date, Tom's best-known release has been covered by over 113 amazingly diverse artists, including Elvis Presley, Gene Pitney, Joan Baez, Nana Mouskouri, Ricky Valance and the Welsh Rugby Union team, but it is Tom's powerful voice and ardent interpretation that has become the standard version of the song.

Massive success brings opportunities for renegotiating record contracts to an artist's pecuniary benefit, as Gordon Mills surely knew. Music industry gossip suggested that on the imminent expiry of his contract with Decca, Tom's management was considering an offer to sign up with the giant soul record label, Tamla Motown. "I've had a great offer from Tamla Motown and it is under discussion at the moment," Tom was reported as saying in the papers. "The main reason that I haven't done a really bluesy number so far as a single is that I can't get the proper sound in a British studio, and I will not use a synthetic sound. If I stay with Decca, then we might go to Detroit and use Motown as an independent production facility." The fantastic proposition even reputedly hinted at the possibility of using the legendary Motown writing and production team of Holland,

Dozier and Holland, who between 1964 and 1967 produced a total of six number one US hits for The Supremes, not to mention tracks for groups like The Isley Brothers, The Four Tops and Martha & The Vandellas. Details of Tom's rumoured Motown deal have been lost with the passage of time, but without a doubt would have guaranteed legendary status for *any* British artist, even one with an unsteady chart history. Sadly for this particular singer and those who enjoy his diversity, no such contract ever came to fruition, and Tom stayed with the Decca label in the UK and Europe, and their subsidiary Parrot Records in the US.

7

PLEASE RELEASE ME

WITH TOM JONES' revamped career firmly under his belt, Gordon was able to concentrate on helping out an old friend. During his stint with The Viscounts in the late Fifties, he had met a struggling singer called Gerry Dorsey in a working men's club in Coventry. Both The Viscounts and Gerry were planning to perform a song called 'Personality' on the same night, and during the necessary negotiations between parties (in which Gerry backed down) Gordon discovered that he had much in common with the twenty-something vocalist. The pair shared both a strikingly similar background and strong aspirations for a future in the music industry, but both were yet to find their niche.

Born Arnold George Dorsey in Madras, India on May 2, 1936, 'Gerry' (his chosen stage name) was the ninth of 10 children. His father, an engineering consultant called Mervyn and his mother Olive, a singer, brought him back to England in 1947 when Mervyn retired. The young boy was raised in Leicester, and became a keen music student, learning both piano and saxophone from the age of 11. His true vocation though, was to follow in his mother's footsteps, as he discovered he had a notable three-and-a-half octave singing range. Following a failed attempt at a career in engineering and a compulsory period of National Service, Gerry adopted his new name in 1956 and embarked on a life as a full-time singer.

In 1958 he attracted the attention of Decca Records when he won a talent competition, but when his 1959 début single 'Crazy Bells' sank without trace, he moved to Parlophone Records. Unfortunately, Gerry was a 'dance-band' singer, which was extremely out of vogue during the beat group boom of the early Sixties. Two releases on Parlophone including 'I'll Never Fall In Love Again' and further singles on two subsequent labels, Pye and Hickory, all fell by the wayside. When Gerry first encountered Gordon, he was dealing as best he could with failure – a battle that was to continue for the best part of a decade.

After Gerry and Gordon discovered they were kindred spirits they became flatmates, moving initially into a dilapidated, damp and noisy flat in Kensington. From there they made a moonlight flit to escape paying the rent, and soon after relocated to the rock'n'roll house in Cleveland Square. While the friends were trying their luck in the big city, the well-known songwriter Les Reed wrote arrangements for Gerry Dorsey's compositions, which Gerry greatly appreciated as a step in the right direction. When Gordon married Jo Waring in early 1963, Gerry was the best man at his wedding, and on April 18 the same year Gordon returned the favour as Gerry married Pat Healy, a sharply attractive lady with an admirable streak of independence. The four newlyweds got on famously, with Jo designing Pat's wedding dress and Gordon typically arranging for a rock'n'roll group to play cheaply at the reception in return for free food and drink. Immediately after getting married, Gerry and Pat stayed at Gordon and Jo's Notting Hill Gate flat while they searched for a place of their own to live.

As Gordon flourished as a manager, he lost touch with Gerry, whose own career began a downward spiral. His work as a singer was producing very little income and he and Pat barely survived. When their first two children came along, the situation was exacerbated and the little family could hardly afford food. Gerry's health suffered as a result of the stress and lack of nourishment, and one night he collapsed on stage in Manchester. Tuberculosis, the very same illness that had incapacitated the young Tom Woodward, forced the failing singer and family man to retire for 18 months. On his recovery, sheer desperation compelled Gerry to look up his old companion Gordon Mills. When the singer first approached the manager at the end of 1965, Gordon was too busy dealing with what appeared to be the premature demise of Tom Jones. Although he wanted to help out his friend, Gordon was reluctant to take on the extra burden. Gerry was a proud man with a strong ego, but his self-confidence had taken such a battering that he was prepared to wait patiently until Gordon was ready.

Finally, the friendship rekindled and when Tom's situation improved Gordon gave in, agreeing to act as Gerry's manager. It took him the best part of a year to concentrate fully on his newest acquisition, but perhaps the most inspired thing he did during this time was to create a new persona for the flagging vocalist. Leafing through a pile of classical records over the Christmas period, Gordon spied the name of an obscure composer called Engelbert Humperdinck, who had written the score for *Hansel And Gretel*. "As soon as I saw that name I said, 'That's it!'" Gordon reminisced, when interviewed on his find a while later. "It was lyrical, romantic. You couldn't forget it. It had magnetic appeal."

Gordon's plan was to remodel Gerry Dorsey in just the same way that Tom Woodward had so memorably transformed into Tom Jones, changing not just his name, but his image and to some extent even his personality. Unsurprisingly, Gerry was initially appalled, but after so many years performing unsuccessfully under his old name he relented, trusting Gordon's judgement. He said at the time: "It's been a little hard to adjust to. All my life I had a simple name and all of a sudden I've got a monster of a thing to sign and pronounce!" Shortly after his re-christening, Engelbert's attitude proved to be 'in for a penny, in for a pound' and old acquaintances were in for a shock when they thought he would still answer to his old name. Engelbert, now known to his immediate family and friends as 'Enge' or 'Engel', flatly ignored anyone who greeted him incorrectly, and letters addressed to 'Gerry Dorsey' remained unopened. Amusingly, after he became a famous household name, Engelbert was quoted thus in Don Short's 1972 publication, *Engelbert Humperdinck – The Authorised Biography*: "As a matter of fact, I don't think I had ever heard the *Hansel And Gretel* music. But I've got more than his music to thank the German composer for. He's been dead and gone for a long time now, but God bless him for the things his name has done for me!"

"I had to break Tom before signing anyone else, but once I was a successful manager I knew I could help Gerry," explained Gordon. After placing Engelbert in a tuxedo every bit as suave as Tom's, the singer was reintroduced to Decca, following welcome exposure as a last minute entrant in the Knokke Song Contest. Engel replaced Tom at the 11th hour at this event, which was held in the Belgian resort of Knokke-de-la-Zoute, near Ostende. His first release on Decca was called 'Dommage Dommage' and while it received more airplay than the now defunct Gerry Dorsey had achieved in a decade, the single failed to chart in the UK but achieved moderate success across Europe, notably in Belgium. A second attempt called 'Stay' also made little impression in his home country. It was not until Gordon reconsidered a country standard called 'Release Me' (which Tom had previously recorded but refused to release as he didn't consider the song's pleading message 'manly' enough), did Engel's luck start to turn.

'Release Me' had first been unleashed by its composer Eddie Miller in 1950, and was a hit for Ray Price in 1954, but Engel's interpretation owed more to the million-selling 1962 US version by Esther Phillips. A popular rumour surrounding Engel's rendition was that at Mill's request Tom had coached Engel on the vocal phrasing, not that the newly named crooner's pride would ever allow him to admit it. Hot on the heels of 'Green Green Grass Of Home', 'Release Me' reached number one in March 1967 and soon became Britain's biggest selling single that year. Gordon's theory that a solid ballad with an old-time feel would touch the hearts of the discontented masses proved spot on once again. Engel's new schmaltzy theme song stayed at the top of the charts for over a month, even holding off one of The Beatles' finest double A-sides, 'Strawberry Fields Forever' / 'Penny Lane', and ending their run of 11 successive number ones. Engel was also off to a good start in America as 'Release Me' made the Top Five Stateside. His follow-up, 'There Goes My Everything' went to number two in the UK and shortly after, his next single 'The Last Waltz' (the first in a succession of songs written for him by Les Reed and Barry Mason) placed him once again at the top position. In less than a year Engel had become the UK's biggest selling artist of 1967 and suddenly Gordon was in charge of the two biggest solo male stars in Britain, whose record sales were unheard of since the heady days of Beatlemania.

One would imagine that Tom and Engel, who were now popularly referred to by the press as 'stablemates' would clash, both in vying for Gordon's attention and in general public appeal. But Gordon was careful to market the pair very differently, reassuring them that it was the contrast in their voices and their looks which ensured success for both. Tom, although now refined for a more mature female audience, still delighted in thrilling his spectators with overtly sexual dancing and raunchy on-stage innuendo. If he was happy to become 'Mr Sex', Engel was his perfect counterpart as 'Mr Romance'. Engel's swarthy looks and gentle vocals attracted a slightly different crowd, as Gordon explained in Don Short's biography, "Engelbert is a singer with grace and charm, who tends to like romantic ballads while Tom is basically a rock'n'roll singer whose sensual expression is earthy and strident and isn't meant to be as subtle as that of Engelbert's." A healthy media rivalry ignited between the two stars, who were beautifully played off against each other by Gordon in order to boost sales. To this day, fans will only strictly admit to liking either Tom Jones *or* Engelbert Humperdinck – the two rarely mix within one record collection.

Occasionally this opposition would extend into their personal lives. In contrast to Tom's endearing openness with his fans, Engel strove to maintain an enigmatic image, always disappearing after a concert or climbing out of a window in an effort to avoid any contact. His pride might well have been damaged by the younger man's precedence in Gordon's management strategy, and this might explain why he tended to radiate a darker, less sincere image than Tom.★

★　★　★

★ It is worth noting that not one of the 70 plus people interviewed for this book who had known both singers either professionally or personally wished to comment about Engel, although Peter Sullivan ventured a musical criticism: "There was no comparison. Tom was a natural performer whereas Engelbert was contrived." Engelbert Humperdinck himself declined to be interviewed.

Tom Jones proudly clutching the Decca single release 'It's Not Unusual'. *(Popperfoto)*

A young Tom practises his smile for the camera.
(Pictorial Press)

Little more than a child himself, Tom was just 16 wh
he took on the responsibilities of a wife and child.
(Pictorial Press)

Tom Senior and Freda Woodward pose outside 44 Laura Street with a symbol of their son's growing success
(Pictorial Press)

An early family holiday on the beach, circa summer 1966. Tom relaxes with Mark and Linda after his near fatal car crash – note the stitches over his left eye. *(Tom Blau/Camera Press)*

Tom Jones wearing 'those' white trousers on the roof of Joe Meek's Holloway Road Studio. From left to right: Tom, Dave Cooper, Vernon Hopkins, Chris Slade and Mike Gee

Tom and 'girlfriend' Linda flat-hunting in London in 1965. By now they had been married for eight years. *(Popperfoto)*

A woman's place is in the kitchen. *(Popperfoto)*

"Gordon Mills was in the rare position of being a better looking fellow than either of his singers. He could not pass a mirror. He would go and buy himself endless suits," remarked Chris Hutchins of Tom's manager and mentor. *(David Steen/Camera Press)*

Tom: "I always smoked Woodbines and drank beer. My manager said that one day I'd be smoking cigars and drinking champagne. I said, 'I love Woodbines and I love beer, and that's that.' So, what am I doing today? Drinking champagne and smoking expensive cigars." *(Popperfoto)*

Tom, Gordon and Engelbert Humperdinck astride their personalised Rolls Royces in 1969. *(Popperfoto)*

This Is Tom Jones took the world by storm from 1969 to 1971. (Pictorial Press)

om and Sammy Davis Jnr. duet on the episode of *This Is Tom Jones* devoted entirely to them. *(Pictorial Press)*

Tom sings with his all-time idol, Jerry Lee Lewis on *This Is Tom Jones*. *(Pictorial Press)*

Guitarist Big Jim Sullivan shares a quiet country moment with Tom on the set of *This Is Tom Jones*. *(Pictorial Press)*

Tom swings during the concert of *This Is Tom Jones*. *(Pictorial Press)*

After his revived success in 1966 Tom Jones moved from Manny Gate Lane into a new property in Sunbury-on-Thames, called Springfield House. Tom, Linda and Mark's new home cost over £25,000, an astronomical improvement on their last house, and consisted of five bedrooms, two bathrooms, four toilets, and several lounges. As always, Linda set about turning her new residence into a comfortable nest for her family, decorating the house with expensive furnishings. Tom remarked rather gracelessly to journalist Fergus Cashin at the time, "When I go home to my wife, she's always going on about curtains or bloody wallpaper and I maybe couldn't care less. It would be easy to say shut up, do what you like but leave me alone. I've said that, but I also realise that this is her life and she makes the life I live. She doesn't dig parts of the showbiz scene but she goes along with it because it's me. I think that is love and I'm lucky."

Able to concentrate his efforts on his family for the first time in quite a while, Tom readdressed the issue of his father's retirement from the pit. "The only way I finally convinced him was when I asked him how much he would earn until his planned retirement at 65," said Tom. "He didn't know offhand but I said, 'We'll work it out and I'll give you that amount of money to stop work.'" Tom arranged for his financial advisers to reassure his father that he had accumulated enough wealth to be as good as his word. At last Tom freed his father from the crippling coal pits and was able to treat his parents to a luxurious lifestyle in Tom and Linda's old house in Shepperton.

"At first I didn't want to leave," said Tom Snr. of bidding farewell to both Pontypridd and his life as a miner, in a 1969 *Daily Mirror* special. "I had been there all my life. I didn't know any other way of living. Besides, so many things were happening to Tom I didn't know what to believe. But in the end it made good sense. I was happy to quit the pit." Rose Bank, the house in Manny Gate Lane, had become a bit of a shrine for Tom's fans by the time his parents moved in, and the kindly couple were only too happy to offer visitors a friendly cup of tea and a chat. Tom bought his father a white Ford Granada so that they wouldn't feel too isolated from their old friends and finally, at the grand age of 56, Tom Snr. learned to drive. Despite derogatory comments from the ex-miner about the state of English beer, father and son soon became regular drinking partners at the local pub – a family tradition that Tom had missed since his initial move to London.

Freda was especially proud of her son and grateful for the chance to improve her husband's health by removing him from the dangers of the pit. She too spoke of her boy in the *Daily Mirror* special: "He hasn't changed one bit. Tom has great strength of character and I think this has helped him to cope with success." As the nucleus of the Woodwards now resided in England rather than in Wales, Tom was careful to continually refer to his roots in interviews, knowing that his Welshness was at the very heart of his allure. "Why should I alter?" he said, in answer to questions about the changes brought on by his sudden vast wealth. "Some people alter because they feel they have to. I'm still a Welshman from Wales, a small town boy. I've always been that and I always will be."

Christmas 1966 was a far more family orientated affair than the previous year, as on the strength of the money pouring in from sales of 'Green Green Grass Of Home' Tom declined a four figure fee for a concert in Geneva in favour of staying at home. On visiting Pontypridd during this festive season, he was delighted to discover he'd been made president of his family watering hole, the Wood Road Social Club and was given an enthusiastic welcome back. Indulging the passion for classic vehicles shared by Gordon and Engelbert, Tom splashed out on a brand new Rolls Royce as a Christmas present to himself.

Before the close of the climactic year of 1966, one final event occurred that was to change drastically the course of Tom's career. On Boxing Day a quietly spoken but extremely intelligent man named Chris Hutchins joined the fold as Tom's new publicist. Chris had been working as a journalist and was later appointed news editor for the music paper, *New Musical Express*, where he had made quite a name for himself by pulling off some unlikely scoops. His first and greatest achievement in this field was to plague the office of the elusive Colonel Tom Parker with a constant barrage of phone calls, in the hope of an interview. To Chris' amazement, late one night Elvis Presley's eminent manager answered the telephone himself and invited the pushy young journalist to shadow him for 10 days to gain some mind-blowing, not to mention priceless, work experience. A few years later, armed with supreme confidence and an impressive track record, Chris decided to leave the paper and strike out on his own.

"I'd just left the *NME*," Chris expounds today. "Somebody suggested that I set up a PR company. I said, 'Well, if I can get one client I will.' And that client was Tom. I wanted Tom because I'd never seen anything like Tom. From the first time I saw him on television I thought this is unbelievable, there has never been a Brit like this." Chris was horrified when he saw such a manly megastar pictured in women's magazines helping his wife with the housework. Having kept his database from his days at *NME*, Chris found Gordon's number and bit the bullet.

"I rang Gordon Mills and I said, 'I hear you're looking for a publicist for Tom Jones.' He said, 'No I'm not! Who says I am?' Very paranoid was Gordon. But he was intrigued that I called him. I knew Tom had a publicist and I said, 'Ah, forget it,' and I hung up. And I counted the seconds until he rang back." Confounded, Gordon returned the call almost immediately, demanding to know why on earth Chris thought Tom was in need of a publicist. Chris replied that he was in the process of setting up a public relations company. Gordon took the bait, and Chris met with Tom and his manager at the famous London restaurant, The Ivy. Gordon was undoubtedly impressed with the well-mannered PR man's middle-class accent and obvious good connections, and approved of the common ground the three shared, with Chris having been born in Wales. Tom was initially more cautious of the cocky stranger, as Chris recalls: "We eyed each other with deep suspicion the first time we met. But I think he liked the ideas. And I liked the material." After a few hours of Chris' hard sell, both Tom and Gordon welcomed him on board in place of previous publicist John Rowlands, who had portrayed Tom in the damaging domestic light.

Officially commencing work on Boxing Day, 1966 Chris started on a comparatively meagre wage of £25 a week. Gordon could easily have afforded more, but Chris was so eager to have Tom under his belt that he would have represented the star free of charge. Before long he was able to expand his roster, and he formed Chris Hutchins Information to handle a huge variety of artists from The Bee Gees and Engelbert Humperdinck to Eric Clapton and Procol Harum. Chris was to become one of the UK's most sought after publicists, and even indoctrinated the young Max Clifford in the same manner he himself had learnt from Colonel Parker.

$$\star \quad \star \quad \star$$

While 1967 was a successful year for Engelbert Humperdinck, Tom Jones was also enjoying his revival. At the end of the previous year Tom had been voted the Top British Male Singer by readers of *Melody Maker*, successfully de-throning Cliff Richard. "In these polls, you usually get the youngsters voting and I hoped that my sort of family-entertainer reputation wouldn't put them off me," said Tom with relief. Although *NME* were to transpose the top two placements in their Christmas poll, four of Tom's singles were to reach the Top 10 in 1967 and his overall sales weren't far behind those of Engel.

Much of Tom Jones' success could be directly attributed to his talented new publicity adviser. "The only thing I knew about image-making with rock stars was what I'd seen with Elvis," admits Chris. Having witnessed first-hand the mysterious effects of the Colonel's impenetrable force-field protecting Elvis, Chris determined to emulate the same enigmatic presence with Tom. Securing Gordon's approval, Chris insisted to Tom: "You *must* be less available. You've been doing everything – interviews for *Woman's Own* – there's been no control. The copy has been woolly and you've talked about things which are not a sexy image! You've talked about marriage: that's a taboo subject."

The immediate task was to recreate Tom's public image by pushing his wife and son securely behind the scenes, and thrusting the singer's natural sexuality to the fore once again. Chris Hutchins has been much maligned in previous biographies for his treatment of Linda, for driving her out of the public eye and forcing her to become a recluse. But Chris remains adamant that his actions were well-founded. "It was as much for Linda's comfort as Tom's benefit. Linda hated press attention of any sort and she didn't want to be publicised. Tom knew also that it put the female fans off that he wasn't available." Chris further protected Linda by rarely allowing journalists into the Woodwards' marital home and he never required her to attend events. For Linda, this fresh lack of involvement was ironically almost as much of a relief as when the secret of her marriage first came out.

Aside from the physical image building, Chris also concentrated on Tom's perceived star status. The first time the so-called 'miner' actually went down a coal mine was when Chris arranged for a silver disc to be presented to him underground, creating the perfect photo opportunity and promotional stunt. Chris was the catalyst that boosted Tom's fee potential. "I would exaggerate Tom's earnings – exaggerate is to under-estimate what I would do. I would say, 'He's earning £10,000 a night now.' Colin [Berlin] came to me one day and said, 'You know, since you put that story out about Tom earning £10,000 a night, no-one who has phoned to book him has dared to offer less!'" He also utilised Tom's outspoken antipathy to The Beatles (prompted in part by Lennon's 'Welsh poof' allegations back in 1965) to guarantee headlines.

Chris was proving himself to be invaluable and Tom greatly enjoyed reading his own press, generated by such fervent speculation. It was not that Tom was vain, but he basked in the reassurance that he was recog-nised worldwide as a superstar about whom people would pay to read over breakfast. Chris would also write Tom's 'improvised' stage banter and help him with difficult spellings, as Vernon Hopkins remembers, "It's true Tom couldn't spell but that's probably because he lost a lot of schooling when he had tuberculosis."

Tom had sprung back into the public eye after the 1967 new year celebrations with his appearance on the first edition of ITV's *Doddy's Music Box*. Two weeks later he flew to South America for a six-day tour and four TV shows in Venezuela. Chris Slade was planning his wedding to his girlfriend Lynne on February 4, 1967, but neither expected Tom to attend, due to his heavy schedule. However, Tom and Linda managed to fly back to Wales for the church service, and found the area crowded as many fans had arrived assuming that the star would be there. The bride was flustered by all the unanticipated attention, and had to have assistance merely travelling to and from the wedding because of her surprise celebrity guest. The consolation for all the chaos he had unwittingly caused was that Tom was a witness to the ceremony, signing his name simply as Tom Jones.

He was once again headlining at the London Palladium one week later, and on the back of all the hype his next single, 'Detroit City', entered the charts in February 1967. The country-flavoured track, also culled from a Jerry Lee Lewis album, climbed to a respectable number eight. March saw Tom in a month-long stint at The Talk Of The Town, London's major cabaret venue near Leicester Square, now Peter Stringfellow's Hippodrome nightclub. Although already a proven success at the Palladium, Tom was very nervous at the change of scene. "I was terrified on the opening night. There were so many famous faces in the audience. I didn't want to let anybody down." He enthused, "For me, the Talk is the best cabaret hall in the world, and that opening night proved that I could hold an audience for the best part of an hour in the star spot."

Tom considered himself an A-list celebrity by now. When Chris Hutchins first joined Tom, Gordon and Engel he formed the impression that Tom wasn't a particularly confident personality, but this changed with success. "I think the whole bit with the cigars was his way of asserting himself. That's when he felt important, when he had a big cigar in his hand and a big ring on his finger. I think that helped Tom to feel what he was," says Chris. The next status symbol to compound this new found self-esteem was the acquisition of a bodyguard. Rocky Seddon was a former boxer from Liverpool whose career was arrested when he crushed his leg in a car accident. He boasted a remarkable talent for talking his way out of tricky situations and gained a certain notoriety for smuggling hotel cutlery through customs.

1967 was a very productive year for Tom's recording career. His album *Green Green Grass Of Home* came out in April and shot to number three in the UK, while in the same month the single 'Funny Familiar Forgotten Feelings' reached number seven. After spending most of the month of May performing at the London Palladium, Tom released his first genuine concert recording, *Live At The Talk Of The Town*, which went to number six in July. During this month Tom starred regularly in a CBS show called *Spotlight* which was recorded at the Elstree studios, and the press excitedly released details of his planned autumn UK tour – his first for over two years.

On July 21, a stunning new single, 'I'll Never Fall In Love Again', was let loose on the public and climbed to number two in the UK charts.

91

Often credited as Tom's favourite personal performance on record, 'I'll Never Fall In Love Again' had been written and recorded in 1962 by the British skiffle player, Lonnie Donegan. In terms of musical quality, Tom's interpretation of this heartfelt ballad is in the same vein as 'Green Green Grass Of Home' as he swings from meltingly soft and mournful phrases to extreme crescendos of anguish, arguably surpassing his previous year's number one hit in terms of vocal accomplishment. Tom described in a lengthy interview with Alan Smith how he felt unable to record a new song on the same day it was given to him. Typically he would take the song home and study each line for hours on end so that he could form an impression of the songwriter's meaning behind the lyrics. By the time he entered the studio he not only knew the track completely by heart, but was able to put on a display of earnest emotion: "I am not ashamed to say that when I do make records, I tend to close my eyes and just sink into the whole thing. I hadn't realised this until somebody pointed it out, but I've often been known to act out a song, right there in front of the 60 piece orchestra and everybody else crammed into the studio!" Tom's recording of 'Ghost Riders In The Sky' amused many of the session players who chuckled as they watched the famously macho vocalist sway and bounce up and down to the music, pretending to be a cowboy riding off into the sunset.

The session for 'I'll Never Fall In Love Again' proved to be even more spectacular, as Tom remembers: "I suddenly got to a part where I was so caught up in the emotion of the song – I think it's a beautiful number – that I literally let out a sob which came over on the record. I've often done things like that before and they haven't come through. But this did. A gimmick? Corny? I don't think so . . . I just like to put my heart into a song, I don't think there's any shame in that." Two other tracks that moved Tom in this way while recording were 'My Yiddishe Momma' and 'My Mother's Eyes'. But Tom wasn't all tears and torment, and every now and then exhibited odd displays of self-deprecating humour, as one musician recalls, "One of his favourite escapades when he was happy was to go racing down the street, slapping his backside like he was riding a horse!"

During 1967, Tom had the fortuitous opportunity of meeting another of his all-time favourite performers. Both he and the leading soul singer Otis Redding attended each other's concerts in London. Tom had been covering Otis' material for a while in his set, and so was particularly keen to mix with the peerless cross-over artist, who had enjoyed international hits in both the pop and R&B charts. During the meeting Tom was overwhelmed when Otis named him as one of *his* personal favourites too. "He said, which I was thrilled with, 'Man, you are the best soul singer in the world.' Otis Redding saying to me! I mean, I said, 'Please, but no really!' It was great meeting him because he was an innovator."★

The string of hit singles helped finance Tom's first plastic surgery, intended to neaten up his nose. With the 'sex symbol' tag firmly established, Tom was not shy about publicly demeaning himself with respect to his rather exaggerated looks. "I hate my horrible nose," he said, "it's been worked over, bent sideways and patched up more than any other part of me. It got broken so many times in punch-ups that I can't remember which particular incident made it this shape!" While such dismissive outbursts served to portray an endearing modesty and at the same time bolster his 'rough and ready' attraction, Gordon wasn't convinced that the stigma of plastic surgery would be the right sort of image for a lad from the Welsh valleys.

When Tom initially emerged from the hospital with a visibly different appearance, a 'slight' fabrication was made up to put journalists off the scent. Tom was quoted in a press statement: "I had to have an operation for sinus trouble or something. When I came out, I noticed the nose was shorter. They must have cut something out of it." Just in case his fans were worried that their idol had been badly treated by the surgeon, he allayed their fears with, "I prefer my new nose to the old one and my breathing is fine now." No court cases emerged alleging malpractice by his doctors, and fairly soon Tom admitted the embarrassing truth to the *Evening Standard*. "I don't think I could have done so well if I hadn't had my nose altered. I think now that it doesn't look as offensive as it did. Before, some people might have thought, 'Well I quite like his voice but I don't like his nose.' So you have to eliminate all those things that put people off."

Around this time Tom revealed that he had also had his crooked and yellow teeth capped to further improve his appearance. "My nose and my teeth were the only hang-ups I ever had . . . If pictures were taken from a bad angle, they made it [my nose] look ugly and from the same angle my teeth were bad, too. They were decaying, so I had them capped . . . You can't afford in this business to have one thing which is ugly about you." Tom was surprisingly open about this unmasculine display of celebrity vanity and has remained so to this very day, but it has been suggested that he kept secret a prior botched operation on his nose before the surgery to 'clear his sinuses' was first made public.

In the latter half of 1967 Tom was honoured to perform at his first Royal Variety Performance, held at the London Palladium. Unlike other nights at the Palladium, this concert still stands out as a particularly nerve-racking appearance for him, as it was held in front of the Queen. "You

★ Otis Redding died just a few months later on December 10, his plane crashing into the icy waters of Lake Monoma near Madison, Wisconsin en route to a concert.

always get the feeling that if you don't do a good job then you're going to get your head cut off!" he joked to chat show host Phil Donahue some years later. Tom was so nervous that his top lip stuck to his newly capped teeth during his set, but the audience loved him as always and the Queen was reportedly quite entertained by his unrestrained dancing. After the performance, as the stars lined up to meet the Queen, the monarch and the miner's son exchanged opinions on America and personal fitness.

With Tom's new and improved looks and the continuing success of his songs it was hardly surprising that offers for him to act in films began to flood in. "I get at least a dozen scripts a week, but I'm afraid that nothing has been suitable so far," said Tom. "I must be honest and say I usually can't concentrate on reading anything lengthy myself, no matter how interesting, so usually I hand a script over to my manager."

Tom remarked to a pop annual that he would "quite like an adventure story, but I don't just want to do a musical thing – you know, where the hero is lying half dead on a bed and he rests on one elbow and bursts forth with a big ballad about how much he loves his girl!" Ever since Tom's early fascination with cowboy films he had always fancied himself playing the lead role in a Western. Hungarian B-movie producer Joe Pasternak, who had worked with Elvis Presley on *Girl Happy* in 1964 and *Spinout* in 1966, was keen to indulge such a fantasy, regardless of Tom's thick Welsh accent. But Gordon was wary of turning his respectable star into a laughable celluloid sell-out. He explained to Tom the difficulties of transforming a pop personality onto the big screen and the would-be actor agreed that he should not accept an inferior role purely to gain the kudos of starring on the big screen. "I'd rather not bother with films at all than do something like Elvis," he said to Alan Smith. "Elvis has just stayed a teenage idol all his life, and with no disrespect to anyone – I don't want to end up like that myself."

Paramount Pictures Corporation also expressed an interest in Tom, hoping to team him up with Swedish-American sex symbol Ann-Margret, but they were insisting on an immediate start. Sadly the deal dissolved as the time scale would have been impossible, not to mention financially crippling, as it would have meant cancelling too many prearranged concerts. William Jugo then offered Tom a role in a proposed movie called *Lie To Me* which would have taken him to the Bahamas for filming, but this too never transpired. Gordon felt that Tom should not appear in anything less than the starring role, although in retrospect the selection of cameos on offer might well have provided a solid starting block. In the meantime, Chris Hutchins was instructed to whip up a few stories about productions in the pipeline, as it was good press and would hopefully encourage other producers to jump on the bandwagon, but for the moment nothing materialised.

Tom returned to the comforts of his music career touring the UK with the Ted Heath Orchestra in October and November 1967. Based on the fantastic reception, Gordon commenced preparations for a possible repeat performance the following year with Count Basie's big band, again in Britain. With dates either side of America's coast at the Flamingo Club, Las Vegas and New York's Copacabana safely secured for the new year, Tom went into the studio for a week. He took the time to promote his new single 'I'm Coming Home' on *Top Of The Pops* on November 30, and guest on various other television programmes including the *Eamonn Andrews Show* in the first two weeks of December. It was mulled over in the press that the current economic situation regarding the devaluation of the British pound had actually proved profitable for Tom, as a new American million dollar contract would ensure an extra £60,000.

Tom's Christmas single this year, 'I'm Coming Home', continued the winning streak of nostalgic overwrought ballads celebrating the lure of familiar territory. Written for Tom by Les Reed and Barry Mason, the song's recording session remains in the heart of its composer and arranger still. Instead of taping Tom's vocal in a separate booth, Peter Sullivan placed him in amongst the string section, which is traditionally located in the middle of the orchestra. This was a bit of a gamble in terms of volume and clarity, but Peter was confident that Tom was a strong enough singer to carry it off. One live take was recorded which was so breathtaking that there was complete silence at the end of Tom's last note, and moved the musicians literally to tears. Tragically the sound engineer had a technical problem with the tape and had to redo the song, losing the magic of the moment. Still, 'I'm Coming Home' soared to number two in December 1967, spending a total of four months in the charts.

On the strength of his incredible year's run of hit singles, Tom squeezed Cliff Richard into second place in *NME*'s annual Christmas Poll as Top Male British Singer, with Engelbert Humperdinck coming a close third. In the World Section, only Elvis Presley held Tom from the top spot. Gordon Mills and Colin Berlin placed an advert in all the major music papers wishing Tom a 'Wonderful Christmas!' to celebrate his success.

But behind the scenes all was not well with Gordon. Late in 1967 he and close confidant Les Reed prepared for a big meeting at the Dolce Vita restaurant in Soho to discuss a possible future working relationship with the Boulting Brothers, who owned the British Lion Film Corporation. To Les' surprise and consternation the normally self-assured Gordon was vomiting for an hour before the lunch. When Les queried his seemingly over-nervous state, he was horrified to learn that his vibrant friend was harbouring a serious stomach ulcer directly caused by the stress he was under.

8

GOLDEN DAYS

ENSURING THAT HIS records continued to experience high sales meant that Tom was forced to consolidate the last year's work with another speedy tour of Europe. In just 10 days Tom and The Squires pushed themselves to the limit, visiting many European cities. The tour encompassed much of Europe and Scandinavia, including Germany, where the party arrived on January 15, 1968 to appear in two concerts and a television show. Tom then flew alone from Frankfurt to Cannes to receive a prestigious award as Europe's top singer at the Midem Festival, the annual gathering of the music industry. By January 23, he was safely back in England for a performance on *Sunday Night At The London Palladium*, joining the other artists for that night, Des O'Connor and The Supremes. As January turned into February Tom was the guest star chosen to perform in the first edition of his old touring partner Cilla Black's new TV show, *Cilla*.

While riding on the crest of a wave in Europe, Tom had two pressing items on his agenda for the immediate future – consolidating his popularity in the US and making a gradual move towards the glamorous world of movies. Having just shaved off a trial goatee beard, Tom departed for America in the first week of February, taking The Squires with him for the first time. Any qualms that Tom might have had about fans abandoning him while he concentrated on the US were allayed by the great send off from England. His latest album, *13 Smash Hits* (a collection of popular standards as opposed to his own songs as the title suggests), had reached number five in the UK charts and Cilla Black filmed his departure from London airport to broadcast on her show later that week. Once in America Tom undertook some filming work himself, this time for his own TV spectacular sponsored by Kraft Cheese.

On February 15, Tom settled into a two-week stretch at the Copacabana in New York. Remaining in one venue was a luxury for Tom and his band, who were weary of the endless flights and road journeys, but the pace at the famous club was almost as exhausting. Trumpeter Derek

Watkins remembers that they performed each one-and-a-quarter hour concert in a small room which dictated that they repeated the strenuous set three times a night; at 9.00 p.m., midnight and 3.00 a.m. Needless to say, the shows were all sell-outs that attracted many fashionable celebrities including Ann-Margret, Roger Moore, The Supremes, Gladys Knight & The Pips and Aretha Franklin.

As The Squires mixed freely with the session musicians that Gordon had added to the touring party, they began to realise how inferior their wage was in comparison. Unlike Vernon, Chris and Vic, the more experienced players had collectively appeared on much of Tom Jones' released material and superior commercial projects like the *Mission Impossible* soundtrack, but still The Squires felt they deserved more recognition and campaigned to Gordon for a pay increase. He begrudgingly relented to a higher wage of £80 per week while The Squires were in America, which was double their usual salary, but as they were obliged to pay for all their accommodation and general day-to-day expenses (which were far greater in New York), they were still left without any profit. An uneasy comparison was the weekly fee of £82,500 plus expenses commanded by Tom – over 1,000 times more than The Squires.

The Copacabana itself was an enlightening experience for the Welsh lads as it was run by alleged Mafia boss Jules Podell, and many of the patrons were connected to 'The Mob'. Their presence was impossible to overlook and while Tom never pursued any direct connections himself, he was always intrigued by the scene. Big Jim Sullivan remembers the time vividly. "They all had access to Tom, coming backstage; the dons and the hit men. I don't think Tom ever really got involved with them. But Copacabana was a wild, wild place."

Instead of posing a threat, the Mafia's constant surveillance actually brought a measure of security to the entourage. There was never any danger of the party's expensive belongings disappearing – theft was one of the Mafia's most punishable offences. One of the girlfriends of the backing group remembers feeling secure in a hotel run by the Mafia, whereas she was often petrified when they were forced to hang around the more dubious American airports. Chris Hutchins recounts a time when Tom confided in Frank Sinatra that he was concerned for his safety. Frank reassured Tom that wherever he may be, there would always be "one of these guys to look after him" and with that he touched the tip of his nose with his forefinger in a conspiratorial manner. Sure enough, when Tom would play concerts in places like Madison, Wisconsin and Atlanta, Georgia, there was always a shady presence making the secret sign to Tom during the standing ovation.

There was another distinct advantage to the 'Italian Connection', as the musicians would refer to it: the Mafia wives adored Tom and the whole group were showered with party invitations. "They would say, 'Oh I've got a 45 foot motor cruiser parked at a lake. It's fully stocked up, the captain and crew are on it, there's a cook, go out for the day,'" recalls Big Jim. Tom later divulged to Chris Evans on *TFI Friday* that on many occasions he had been offered an Italian lady as a 'gift', but claimed he declined as politely as possible to avoid any further ties.

However protected and well treated they felt, there were occasions when the Mafia's omnipresence caused a sharp intake of breath. "I always remember at the Copacabana club, people used to knock on the door of Tom's dressing room and Chris Ellis used to go and see to them, let them in or whatever," says Big Jim. "This one particular night we were there and this big guy comes to the door and walks halfway through. Chris asks, 'What do you want? Who are you?'" Bearing in mind that Chris was fairly diminutive and the large visitor was obviously not to be reckoned with, Big Jim continues: "Luckily enough Tom saw him and said, 'Hey Sonny, come on in – Chris it's OK.' Later on Chris asked Tom, 'Who was that Sonny guy?' Tom replied, 'He was one of the Mafia hit men – he was out on bail on four murder raps!'"

In March 1968, Tom and The Squires moved on from the Copacabana to Las Vegas, for a month-long stint at the Flamingo Hilton hotel. Although Tom had previously played at Caesar's Palace, it was his début at the gaudy Flamingo, and the first time The Squires as a whole had been to the fabulous casino oasis in the desert, which boasted both live and neon examples of its namesake bird. Chris Hutchins had already been hard at work drumming up promotion for them. "When we announced the Las Vegas deal, the first time at the Flamingo, I got Tom to hold this piece of paper in the air and we put it down as the $1 million contract. It was actually a contract for The Moody Blues to appear at a ballroom in Dunstable [England] for £120!"

Built in 1946 by Benjamin 'Bugsy' Seigel, the Flamingo was besieged by bad luck from its very conception. The notoriously impatient Bugsy was reputedly conned by the builders and the project ended up costing three times its $2 million budget. The grand opening on Boxing Day 1946 was attended by various movie stars and celebrities, but the club was closed less than three weeks later as profits plummeted courtesy of dishonest casino workers. Although it was reopened in March 1947, the resort was still lagging behind the competition by the time Tom Jones was due to play there in 1968. It had since been bought by businessman Kirk Kerkorian as a means for him to gain in both experience and reputation, before building his planned lavish hotel, The International.

Tom's first night at the Flamingo was slightly marred by confusion as –

coincidentally – there was another act called Tom Jones (also inspired by the movie adaptation of Henry Fielding's novel) playing at the Desert Inn lounge. After his identity was established, the next obstacle to overcome was that Tom had been booked as the support act for comedienne Kaye Ballard, who was more typical of Las Vegas cabaret at the time. On Gordon's insistence, and considering the logistics, Kaye agreed instead to open for the new star. Tom explained to her that not only did he have a full band and eight heavy amplifiers to manoeuvre on and off stage, but that the audience would consist mainly of single females, 50 per cent of whom would have seen the show the night before. Kaye was afterwards relieved to have made the swap in the schedule. "In every ringside seat for every show, there was a single woman. And they certainly didn't want to see a comedienne . . . I could never in a million years have followed Tom Jones," she shudders.

When Tom Jones finally played at the floundering Flamingo it proved to be the turning point for both artist and hotel as the singer rapidly became what is known in show business as 'top ticket'. The main showroom seated only 500 people, and even though Tom performed twice a night, hundreds of fans were turned away and the four-week engagement was sold out by the third day. This failed to deter the scores of more ardent admirers who queued for hours in the desperate hope that a seat might become vacant at the last minute. The good news travelled fast and it was not long before Tom was honoured with a visit from his good friend, Elvis Presley. Elvis and his wife Priscilla had driven over 400 miles in order to see Tom performing. "Without any fuss at all, Elvis and his wife came to the show and sat right down at the front," says Tom of the surreal moment. "He told me later that it was watching me on stage in Vegas which gave him the urge to perform again."

During Tom's March stint at the Copacabana, a momentous precedent had been set: the first pair of knickers were thrown as he performed live on stage. "I was sweating," says Tom, "and ladies would hand me their cocktail napkins. One hurled her underwear. I was astounded!" When the veteran showbiz reporter Earl Wilson wrote up the event in his column in the *New York Daily News* the following day, Tom's fate was sealed. Fans from far and wide brought their (mostly fresh) panties simply to launch them at their hero, in the hope of a favourable response. And without fail Tom always gave the response required. A profuse perspirer, he would whip up the audience's excitement by picking up the lacy offerings and using them to mop his sweaty brow, before tossing them back to their delighted owner, often with a lascivious comment like, "I think I know this woman," or worse, "Whose are *these*? I think my Auntie Alice just came in!"

But Tom's lewdness was all in good fun. "It was all part of the atmosphere, everybody quite liked it," remembers Derek Watkins. "Tom would make a big act of it and pick a pair up and flop it on his wet face. Of course all the women would scream and he'd wipe himself down, and if he threw them back at the audience it was like a rugby scrum, everybody was trying to claim them as their own as a souvenir!" The trend extended to the Flamingo in Las Vegas, and before long, venues worldwide. Every Tom Jones concert would be, and still is, accompanied by an explosion of colourful lingerie and at the end of the night Tom's tour personnel are faced with a decision over the fate of those knickers abandoned on stage. The Flamingo's concert promoter claims that during the Sixties he approached the Salvation Army to come and take three boxes of assorted panties and brassieres away, but they refused so the underwear was dumped. More recently in 1993, a spokesman for Tom's management revealed that all 'leftovers' are donated to the charity, Oxfam, who arrange for them to be recycled and turned into children's clothes. "Tom gets thousands of pairs of knickers thrown at him every year. Women can't control themselves when he gets on stage. At least they are going to a good cause."

During Tom's time at the Flamingo in 1968, a name was coined for this most recent public craze, dubbed simply after the hotel's headliner: 'Tom Jones Fever'. The ingenious ploy, created in part by Chris Hutchins, publicity staff at the Flamingo and Tom himself, was a stroke of perfect timing. Just as the rumbles of mass knicker-induced hysteria were echoing through Las Vegas, almost farcical stunts were staged. Bottles of 'fever pills' were placed on each table at Tom's shows, intended not to cure the ladies of their lust, of course, but to make the fever easier to bear. Outside the showroom ambulances would be strategically parked for immediate assistance in the event of a fan succumbing to the Tom-related illness. The Las Vegas radio stations were just as amenable as the hotels, cheerfully running reports of Fever Clinics sprouting up over the town and quoting the Tom Jones Fever Temperature that day. A potentially more dangerous activity than panty-throwing also commenced during this time: the hurling of hotel room keys in the general direction of their idol, accompanied by invitations to him to 'join them later'.

The threat of over-exuberant violence prompted Gordon to arrange for a bodyguard to accompany Tom to and from the stage, and to remain present throughout each concert. Fans had begun to clamber up to touch the singer, tearing at his clothes and his hair, the bravest hiding in the wings ready to leap out when he passed. Jealous boyfriends or husbands also presented a risk. Said Tom of his protectors: "It's pretty frightening, you know, having a couple of men with revolvers walk you on stage, but I suppose someone thinks it's necessary. I don't really want to be ripped to pieces." Big Jim Sullivan is able to verify the extremity of the situation, but with a slightly less sinister twist: "I've seen Tom come off the stage with claw marks down his back where a woman has got hold of him, tried to kiss him and wouldn't let go! He loves it."

On the strength of all this excitement, Parrot Records released an American album called *The Tom Jones Fever Zone* which reached number 14 in July 1968. The record's centrepiece was another Les Reed/ Barry Mason composition called 'Delilah', an unrelenting dramatic waltz punctuated by swirls of Mexican-flavoured brass. Tom's exhilarating vocal explores a tale of murderous revenge, relishing Barry Mason's poetic phrases: 'I saw the flickering shadows of love on her blind' and 'I was lost like a slave that no man could free'. 'Delilah' is the daring story of a man who waits outside the home of his girlfriend, knowing she is being unfaithful. The enraged boyfriend is unable to contain himself when he sees her clandestine lover leaving at dawn, and he stabs her in the cold light of day.

The plot was a little too much for English critics, who felt the song's bloodshed was unsuitable for the charts. In particular, Radio One's Don Moss slated the lyrics as 'violent and unnecessary'. Tom fended off the criticism from New York during a telephone conversation with a journalist from *NME*. "Oh God, there's always something to knock," he sighed. "Of course 'Delilah' has violence . . . It's a song about a man who sees his girl being unfaithful and who kills her in the heat of the moment. It has been known before. 'Delilah' is 'Frankie And Johnny' in reverse. And few people ever complained about that song. It's not as if this is a song that glorifies murder. Far from it. The whole point of it is that I'm sorry for what I've done, and that they're coming for me to give me what I deserve."

Proving that scandal never fails to shift units, 'Delilah' reached number two in March 1968 in the UK charts, and later that year went to number 15 in the US. Some credited its American success to their society's growing tendency towards violence, illustrated by the assassinations of Martin Luther King and Robert Kennedy, and the continuing horrors in Vietnam. The peculiarity of America's moral code was exposed in all its ridiculous glory when Tom promoted the song on *The Ed Sullivan Show* and the lyrics were censored not for their homicidal content, but instead to disguise the fact that the secret lover had stayed overnight: 'At break of day when the man drove away' became 'When the man was across the way'. The song's co-writer, Les Reed, couldn't understand what all the fuss was about, especially with the current musical output of The Beatles' acid-drenched 'I Am The Walrus' and The

Rolling Stones' satanic celebration 'Sympathy For The Devil' attracting relatively little attention. "The BBC were going through a thing at the time and would ban records they didn't like . . . but they never banned 'Delilah' and it really has become one hell of a pop standard," Les justifies today. Ironically in July 1968, Mick Jagger strongly objected when Decca, the label for both the Stones and Tom at the time, initially refused to release their album *Beggars Banquet*. Decca's reasoning had little to do with the controversial lyrical content (subjects including underage sex in 'Stray Cat Blues', bloodletting in 'Jig-Saw Puzzle' and gratuitous lust in 'Parachute Woman'), but everything to do with the artwork, depicting a graffiti-strewn toilet cubicle. Jagger's bone of contention was that just two years earlier the very same label had been happy to release *A-TOM-IC JONES* in England, with Tom Jones posing manfully in front of a nuclear explosion.

Back in more comfortable territory, Tom was kicking up a storm with The Squires at the London Palladium. Journalist Andy Gray commented on May 4, that, "His sexy movements would make any stripper at Raymond's Revue Bar green with envy," noting also that Tom had lost weight while in Las Vegas and that his current musical director, Johnny Harris, had "the most expressive hair in the business". During his brief spell with Tom, the conductor was famous for walking with a pronounced limp and is remembered by Peter Sullivan as "very extrovert, and wild". In time Tom and Johnny both made their imprint on the venerable Palladium, but as Jimmy Tarbuck explains, "The theatre is the star – it's more famous than anyone who's ever performed there. It has a unique atmosphere – you can't put your finger on it. There's such a tradition, the ghosts of all the other performers who have worked there."

★　★　★

While Tom was preoccupied with carving a niche for himself among the greats, Gordon was diversifying his management technique by pursuing other artists. At the beginning of 1968 he launched the easy listening American singer, Solomon King, in Britain with the Top Five hit, 'She Wears My Ring'. Solomon may have possessed a comparable vocal ability to both Tom and Engelbert, but he certainly lacked the equivalent sex appeal and was dropped after just one more single, 'When We Were Young' in May of that year. Gordon followed this by signing the pop singer Leapy Lee and producing his fluke hit, 'Little Arrows', which reached number two in the late summer. After his surprising success the outlandish Leapy's musical career was cut short when he and his friend Alan Lake, the husband of actress Diana Dors, were later jailed for slashing a pub landlord's wrist with a penknife.

Needless to say, Chris Hutchins remembers these managerial dalliances as being minor in comparison to the attention Gordon lavished on Tom and Engel. "He would lose interest in the other acts because none of them was as professional as Tom," says Chris. "Gordon thought he had the capacity to make an infinite number of stars." Nevertheless Gordon was curiously reluctant to further the career of The Squires, whether collectively or individually, regardless of the profit potential. While visiting Tom at the Flamingo, Las Vegas in March 1968 a film producer approached Gordon with the idea of featuring Tom in a movie called *The Gospel Singer*, and suggested also that The Squires' bass player Vernon Hopkins should do a screen test. Taller and more classically handsome than Tom, Vernon was blessed with typical Hollywood looks that were perhaps better suited to the big screen than the singer's rugged profile. But Gordon did not hesitate to block the move in order to protect his protégé's interests, and Vernon was sworn to secrecy 'for the good of the band'. Overall, as each new artist became more unlikely than the last, Gordon began to run out of energy – at least for the time being.

In April 1968 Tom outlined plans for a six-month world tour to the press: "There'll be a big band of about 25 musicians with me. Jimmy Tarbuck will be on the bill and we may try to get another musical act as well. It won't be a wild type of group but on the other hand the audience won't want to see anything too square . . ." Tom commenced the tour in Australia, arriving on April 23, 1968. He was soon revisiting English soil, opening a season at Bournemouth Winter Gardens in Dorset in early June and recording a special programme for Thames TV later in the summer, a show which became renowned for perhaps the most energetic ever performance of Wilson Pickett's 'Land Of 1000 Dances'.

While the media hounds had created a supposed outrage around the adulterous lyrics of Tom's latest hit, 'Delilah', Tom's own personal life had thus far remained under wraps. The tabloid press in the late Sixties was still fairly benign, with scandal-seeking intrusions into the lives of celebrities still some 20 years away. Tom had, in general, managed to escape the prying eyes of the paparazzi and gossip writers who widely portrayed him as a 'straight' pop star. He drank but didn't take drugs, chased women rather than men, and represented no great threat to the establishment.

Still, with the secret of his marriage long since revealed, it wasn't surprising that with the vague whiff of misdemeanour, reporters from the more sensational tabloid press turned and sank their teeth into the much-loved sex symbol. Rumours of Tom's love affairs were rife by late 1968, particularly with the female stars with whom he shared a working relationship. One such 'affair' was with Nancy Wilson, the stylish black American vocalist. Tom and Nancy moved in the same circles, as Nancy headlined shows in Las Vegas, appeared in many TV specials and from 1967 to 1968 hosted her own Emmy-winning variety series, *The Nancy Wilson Show*. The pair appeared on several TV programmes together and their natural electricity on camera sparked erroneous hearsay that they were 'seeing' each other.★

The glamorous blonde singer and TV presenter Kathy Kirby was another target of such rumours. Tom had appeared on *The Kathy Kirby Show* in December 1965 and the association was continued when Kathy toured with Tom in the late Sixties. She was famous for her extra shiny lip gloss, her five hit singles including 'Secret Love' in 1963 and for being a runner-up with 'I Belong' as Britain's representative in the 1965 Eurovision Song Contest. Colin Macfarlane described the vicious calumny of an affair between the TV star and Tom Jones in his 1988 biography, *A Boy From Nowhere*. The romance was supposed to have resulted in an illegitimate baby; a suggestion which both celebrities laughed off as an absurd untruth. According to Macfarlane, Tom joked to Kathy: "Did you hear that we're supposed to have had a baby together?" to which Kathy responded with a withering: "You should be so lucky!" When Tom replied: "It should be a beautiful baby," Kathy apparently retorted: "Not if it looks like you!"

Unfortunately for Kathy the unwanted attention was no laughing matter and she became the target of hate-mail and even abuse during her concerts, when a man in the audience shouted out, "How's Tom Jones' bastard?" Although it's questionable whether the effect of this particular bout of victimisation was responsible, it was not long before Kathy's career took a sharp decline with a broken marriage, bankruptcy, and health problems. Colin Macfarlane states that today she maintains that the lie about Tom's supposed fatherhood was spread by show business rivals, plotting to destroy her reputation.

On the other hand, no-one has ever denied the romance between Tom and Mary Wilson★★ of The Supremes. After 10 number one US hits within 13 releases, the Motown group fronted by Diana Ross, were suffering a temporary chart setback in the summer of 1968, although their TV specials still achieved high ratings in the UK. Mary Wilson was one of the original trio and elected to stay with the group during this troubled time when the increasingly ambitious Ross was threatening to go solo. Tom and Mary became attracted to one another on several occasions in 1967, their first flirtatious tryst being at an award ceremony in Munich,

---

★ Despite the popular misconception that persisted for the next thirty years, Nancy congenially denied any such connection when questioned by the authors.
★★ No relation to Nancy.

Germany. On January 28, 1968 they were both appearing on ITV's *Sunday Night At The London Palladium*, and despite their hectic schedules, the affair flourished throughout the following summer.

Mary describes her initial feelings for Tom with some candour in her first autobiography, *Dreamgirl*, published in 1987. She was aware of Tom Jones the superstar, but was not sure what to expect when her booking agent Norman Wise introduced her to the Welshman: "I opened the door and there he was, dressed in a ruffled white shirt, black tuxedo, and – of course – skin-tight pants. Sparks flew; he was gorgeous . . . I could see instantly that Tom was like no man I had ever met. He was extremely down-to-earth and passionate." Despite the publicity when Tom's marriage to Linda was revealed a couple of years earlier, Mary was oblivious that he had any ties. "Only later did I discover that Tom was married. I couldn't believe it . . . I resolved to break it off the next time I saw Tom, but when that time came, I realised that I couldn't. It was too late." The affair continued whenever the busy couple could steal time to see each other. They visited pubs and restaurants such as Mr Chow's in London regardless of the media attention they attracted.

It was only a matter of time before the truth leaked out. "We were staying at his cabin in Bournemouth when his wife called," Mary says in *Dreamgirl*. "She told Tom she suspected that he had a woman there and that she was coming up to see for herself." Linda had read in the gossip column of *Disc* magazine that although The Supremes had returned to America after a trip to England, Mary had stayed behind to be with her lover in Bournemouth. Linda frantically rang around, asking those who organised her husband's tour where he was staying. When she discovered the secret location of his rented house, she made immediate travel arrangements and arrived in Bournemouth soon after. Mary was long gone, having been packed into a limousine by Tom and sent back to London.

There are two stories arising from Linda's confrontational arrival at Tom's lair. One version of events maintains that Linda discovered a set of eyelash curlers which had been overlooked when Tom was hiding Mary's personal effects, thus giving the game away. But the most commonly told anecdote involves the gourmet meal that Mary had left bubbling in the oven. Linda knew perfectly well that her husband could not even boil an egg and was obviously unlikely to fall for the story that he hastily invented about Chris Ellis taking cookery lessons. Tom assured Linda that it was all in her mind, but his furious spouse remained in Bournemouth to keep an eye on her philandering husband while he finished his last two concerts.

Despite the close call the affair continued, if not intensified. "It was wildly romantic," says Mary, "and yet we could spend hours and hours just talking, which is something Tom rarely did with a woman, or so he said."

The conspiracy began to affect the entire entourage and the musicians began to witness the inevitable friction. "We were driving to LA Airport," remembers Big Jim Sullivan. "We had two big limousines and we were in the back one with Johnnie Spence, John Rostill, Derek Watkins and Terry Jenkins. Tom's [limousine] was in front and I was sitting by the window and I saw things coming out of Tom's car! I thought, 'What the devil's going on?' We get to the airport and Tom's a bit pissed, we'd been up all night, and I asked him, 'What's going on?' 'She found out about me and Mary Wilson. She's just thrown £200,000 worth of jewellery out of the window, so let's go back and get it!'" Unsurprisingly, Tom *didn't* bother to collect the jewellery.

After an adulterous relationship that lasted on and off for a total of 18 months, the couple realised that the affair had become too impractical and emotionally painful. "My relationship with Tom was coming to a close," Mary regrets in *Dreamgirl*. "We both realised that our feelings were too serious for us to keep chasing each other around the world." At one of Mary's parties at her home in Hollywood, Tom finally suggested that they called it quits. "I had to agree. He wasn't going to leave his wife, and I had always known that . . . After that, we kept in touch, and deep inside I still nurtured the faintest hope that things might change. I finally accepted that they never would when he brought his wife backstage after one of our shows and introduced her to me . . . Still, Tom remains one of the very special people in my life."*

Following the publication of Mary's autobiography, Tom had little choice but to admit to an amorous involvement. After a long period of heartache and deliberation Linda, in her typically Welsh way, finally chose to stand by her husband, but only after issuing an unnerving ultimatum. Tom spoke openly to the *Radio Times* in 1996. "I regret I've made her unhappy . . . She can't walk away from me. And I can't walk away from her . . . She threatened once, when that thing with Mary Wilson of The Supremes cropped up. We were in Las Vegas and she said, 'It's over.' I told her I'd hate her to go, but she said, 'I'm packing my bags.' Then she turns round. 'Alright, I'm not going. It would be too easy for you. But I'll cut off your balls if you carry on like this!'"

Newspaper reports of Tom's perfidy brought him a film offer in the role of a passionate playboy, but he was too busy touring and besides, he and Gordon had other on-screen plans. In September 1968 Tom collected his sixth silver disc for 250,000 British sales of 'Help Yourself', an Italian tune

---

* Despite her candour in print, Mary Wilson declined to be interviewed by the authors for this book.

given English lyrics which had reached number five in the charts.* In October ticket touts were selling 25 shilling seats for £20 in Glasgow and the Rank Theatre tour was sold out – a feat unmatched since the height of Beatlemania. In November the press released details of Tom's planned US TV appearances in both *The Ed Sullivan Show* and a spectacular with Nancy Sinatra and Dusty Springfield. However, both appearances were cancelled due to an American musicians' strike. Tom even flew to New York with his agent Colin Berlin for discussions with the American CMA Agency in the hope that the strike would end, but it was to no avail.

Back in Britain, *NME* ran full page advertisements for Tom's new album, *Help Yourself*, and in the classifieds section there appeared a listing for the Tom Jones Official Fan Club, simply care of 'Jo', at a PO Box in Weybridge, Surrey. Tom topped the *NME* Christmas polls, beating Cliff Richard in the British section, but losing to Elvis Presley by only 249 votes in the world category. Despite a bad bout of 'flu just before Christmas, everything was going beautifully for Tom, with Colin Berlin reporting in the papers that he had been inundated with offers for the new year from the London Palladium, the Bournemouth Winter Gardens, venues in South Africa, a feature film and another European tour.

* 'Love Me Tonight' was another modified Italian melody, which reached number nine the following May.

9

THIS IS TOM JONES

"ALL THE SHOWS I've done have been great. Some of them were bad, but all of them were great." The late Lord Lew Grade remains to this day almost as famous for his witty one-liners as he was for his 12-inch cigars and razor-sharp deal making in the world of movies and television. In the late Sixties Lew was the proud owner and controller of Associated Television (ATV), and had achieved millionaire status by personally pre-selling many of his seminal TV series such as *The Saint* and *The Avengers* to American networks through his own American sales company, ITC.

"I first saw Tom Jones rehearsing the *Sunday Night At The London Palladium*," Lew recalled in the 1991 *Omnibus* TV documentary. "He was dressed casually but he performed as if he was doing his actual performance." After noting the ratings for the singer's previous occasional TV programmes, not to mention the intensity of Tom's act at the Palladium, Lew was inspired to initiate a new deal which would turn the lives of all concerned completely upside down. "I called my friends at American Broadcasting in America," he continued for the cameras, "and asked Martin Starger, who was Vice President in charge of all programming for ABC, to come to England to see Tom Jones at The Talk Of The Town." Prior to Starger's arrival in London, Lew attended one of Tom's concerts at the Talk to make sure that his latest hunch lived up to expectations.

Lew carries on the story in his 1987 autobiography, *Still Dancing*: "In 1967, on one of Marty's visits to London, I took him to The Talk Of The Town to see Tom Jones, who had made several television appearances for us and was an enormous hit. Marty was so impressed with his magnetic performance that he gave me an order for 24 one-hour shows to be called *The Tom Jones Show*." Motivated by Martin's enthusiasm, Lew examined Tom's American record sales, and realised that if he could set up and film a series relatively cheaply in England, he would have a guaranteed audience in the US. Picturing returns of £20 million from the States alone, he determined that the deal was to go ahead at all costs, contacted Gordon Mills and set up a series of meetings.

This was a magnificent opportunity for the Jones camp, and Gordon was certain that it was perfect for introducing his principal client to the professional world of television and film. Lew continues: "Whenever Gordon came to see me, he brought Tom Jones with him. Tom liked to smoke a cigar and I used to offer him one of mine each time they visited me. Mills was a tough negotiator and the terms he was pushing were hard. Finally, at the third meeting, while Tom was sitting quietly on a couch in the corner smoking a cigar, I said, 'Gordon that's my final offer, and I'll tell you what else I'll do. I'll give Tom a box of cigars for every programme he does.' Then Tom, who'd always remained silent at these meetings spoke for the first time. 'You've got a deal!' he said."

Tom's weakness for cigars closed a deal that guaranteed him a £9 million fee for a three year contract to film nearly 56 shows, with an option for a further 34 – a figure recorded in the *Guinness Book Of Records* in the Eighties as the largest ever contract to be signed by one individual for a TV series in Great Britain. Behind the bullish confidence of the TV executives and the star himself, there were questions as to whether Tom was quite cut out to host his own slot. To allay any such concerns on both sides of the Atlantic a pilot was shot on September 16, 1968, and was transmitted on Sunday January 12, 1969. It featured Mireille Mathieu, The Fifth Dimension and Juliet Prowse, and included such Tom Jones standards as 'It's Not Unusual', 'Delilah' and his cover of 'Land Of 1000 Dances'. As a result of the prelude, the American rights were successfully bought by ABC TV, making Tom the first British entertainer to star in his own regularly scheduled major network American TV Show. With joint financing from ATV and his own ABC, Lew Grade was ready to commence filming the series proper.

Rumours of Tom's impending TV plans had first broken in the English press back in March 1968 and by the time the deal was confirmed Tom fans were hungry for the finished product. Retitled *This Is Tom Jones*, the hour long slot replaced *Frost On Sunday* in the UK and *Jimmy Durante Presents The Lennon Sisters* in the US, and commenced in the first week of February 1969 on both sides of the Atlantic. Tom was quoted widely in the press about the format of the up-and-coming production and the change in his career direction. "I'll basically be the singing star of the show," he said to the Cincinnati *Post And Times-Star*, "but I want to be involved with everything in it. I think it is important for any entertainer to open new avenues to his career." He was confident in *TV Week*: "I honestly believe the show will appeal to grown-ups as well as to young people . . . I've always thought that adults want to listen to rock music, but it's rarely been presented the right way on television."

Tom's tuxedoed image initiated a new method of presenting a pioneering music programme to the masses. "I don't think adults will accept rock from people with long, unkempt hair wearing jeans . . . The black tie creates a concert or nightclub atmosphere which is more conducive for adults and enables them to relate more easily to the music." He was also evidently pleased to have an influence on the layout of *This Is Tom Jones.* "Every time I've gone to the States to do a guest appearance on somebody else's show, I haven't been able to do what I wanted to do. It's always been, 'do two songs,' and all sorts of restrictions . . . I hope I'll be able to change that."

Tom began filming on January 2, 1969, and spent until April taping his first 18 shows. He was reunited with Jon Scoffield, who both produced and directed the trailblazing series. As with *Faces,* Jon was once again assisted by Nina Blatt, Johnnie Spence was the eminent musical director, Norman Maen was the dance choreographer and Bill Glaze was the production manager. The writers were Tom Waldman, Frank Waldman, Donald Ross and Ronnie Cass, the latter's credits including *The Young Ones* in 1961 and *Summer Holiday* in 1963. It was Jon Scoffield's choice to hire Ronnie, partly because he realised that as the writer was Welsh he would understand Tom's speech patterns better than anybody else. These key people formed the core of a production team that shaped the framework for future variety shows.

Jon was a no-nonsense producer; brilliant, professional to the end and very astute. With his mind racing at a hundred miles an hour, he was at the heart of the operation, masterfully waving his minions off in all directions. "Jon Scoffield is the closest that the Tom Jones/Gordon Mills circle ever came to intellect!" laughs Chris Hutchins now. "A fine talent. I always got the impression that he thought that producing the Tom Jones show was a little beneath him . . . Tom would have been a little in awe of him too because he saw this super-slick show that Jon built around him every week, and Jon did a fantastic job." Jon was able to exert a control where others had feared to tread. Nina Blatt and Bill Glaze both witnessed the producer standing his ground against the long row of financial executives who felt they had the right to sit in the studio loudly voicing their opinions. Finally Jon insisted on their immediate and permanent departure as he felt their presence marred any sense of intimacy during filming – such an aggressive move had never been made before.

One of the most pleasant aspects to emerge from the filming of *This Is Tom Jones* was the overall sense of teamwork, governed by the imperious Jon Scoffield, and sweetened by Nina Blatt. There was a great atmosphere on the set at all times. Ethel Tucker, who worked in the wardrobe department as a dresser remembers that, "Lew Grade was the best boss we ever had," while, as a team, "we would have fun I would say," says Ann Hollowood, who was a costume designer. "Band calls were so exciting – more so than the show because of the atmosphere. Everyone would dance along with it. The electricity was still in the air after the end of the band call; the girls screaming, Tom's voice – that studio was electric," enthuses Nina.

This Is Tom Jones was filmed at Elstree Studios, in Hertfordshire, UK. The studios brought with them an immense sense of film history, housing memories of epics such as *Moby Dick, The Dam Busters* and *Look Back In Anger.* Jon remembers the budget as being lavishly high. "I know my figure above the line [after stage, set, artists, musicians and costumes had been accounted for] was £75,000 a show." This was much higher than any comparable series in the UK, and was on a par with any grand Hollywood affair.

"With this show, which was one of the first shows I did, we just blew out the walls – it became everything," Jon relishes. "It doesn't sound very much now, but it was. For us it was a terrific increase of pace, but it would look incredibly slow now." Completely revamping the series' pilot, a typical programme would start with a close-up of a Shure Unidyne III Microphone. Viewers with a keen eye might note the miniature TJ initials on its side – the mic was a gift from Jon, with the letters embossed in the same font as the show's graphics. After the title flashed up on the screen, Tom would sprint down the stairs through the audience and onto the stage, pausing in front of a backdrop spelling out 'TOM' in king-sized letters. There he would shake hands with the musical director Johnnie Spence. Opening with his signature tune, 'It's Not Unusual', Tom would then segue into an adapted version of the song, 'Ain't That Good News', in which he introduced his guests for the show.

Tom moved away from the stage to perform a couple of large-scale production numbers against a bright pink or blue set, with a chorus of garishly garbed dancers in a variety of psychedelic scenes. Next Tom would present his first guest, joining them for a duet, which was unusual for the time. The guest then had a solo spot to present one of his or her own numbers. Tom would reappear for what became known as the 'quiet spot', where he was supposed to sing an easy listening tune sitting in a chair. Tom remembers that he always found it difficult to sit still at this point, as he was so used to dancing. After this showcase, another guest would join him for a medley before one final production number.

Now the show almost seemed to break in half as Tom returned to the stage to perform the 'concert spot'. "What we did, which was new at the time, was have a concert spot at the end of the show," explains Jon. "That allowed Tom to de-restrict himself from the confines of production, and the confines of the mix of songs that we thought were necessary to make a one hour show. There were three songs; an opener, a big ballad and a closer. That stood on its own."

The lights dimmed as a moving stage propelled the orchestra forward to surround Tom while he typically loosened his bow tie, sending the all-female audience into paroxysms of lust. The front three rows would be purposely filled with particularly attractive women, which was as important photographically as it was for Tom, who unashamedly encouraged the screaming by accepting towels and kisses. Finally, Tom bade farewell in Welsh, taking the opportunity to announce forthcoming tours or albums when appropriate. It was Ronnie Cass' idea for Tom to say goodbye in Welsh, which was not translated for the viewers. This prompted heated feedback from the fans, wanting to know what their hero had said. The correct meaning was, "May you always be well and be happy," the irony being that Tom doesn't speak Welsh himself as Ronnie recalls: "I had to teach it to him phonetically, he didn't know what he was saying!"

"I think we were rather indulgent in many ways," summarises Jon. "I think we did a bit too much production. But I think it was innovative and it did set some form of blueprint." The first half of the programmes each took a week to make, and Tom was busy rehearsing, filming and recording the soundtrack for six of the seven days. Tom didn't mind the hard work, just the morning hours: "That's the only drawback, I don't like getting up early – but if that's the only drawback, I can put up with it," he said. During the week the dancers would practise their production numbers repeatedly and the stars would arrive three or four days before their shoot to be measured for the costumes. The morning of the shoot consisted of a full dress rehearsal and recording of the programme would be completed that afternoon. It was a very busy week for all involved, and that was before anyone even thought about the concert spots. Jon continues, "Every month we shot three or four concert spots in one day. Twelve numbers. We did these shows one after the other through the day with an audience there. I don't think we changed the audience, we just moved them round."

An on-going television series was a new concept to Tom, the daily routine more like a full-time job than anything he had experienced for the last decade. Everyone who worked with Tom recalls just how devoted and patient he was on set. Nina Blatt remembers one particular sequence where Tom was kept sitting and waiting. She went up to him and apologised for the delay, receiving the gracious reply, "It's better than hodding bricks – I'm sitting here with a glass of champagne and I'm quite happy!"

Jon was impressed with Tom's dedication. "I had no complaints. I think sometimes Tom had a short attention span because he liked to get on and do it." Jon suggests that Tom's forte was performing live without the cameras and he was always very powerful in rehearsal. Vic Cockerell, a lighting supervisor on the show, remembers that after a long day's work Tom would remain at the studios for a while but he wouldn't socialise much with the crew. Vic, like everybody else, noticed that, "Every night he'd come off the show and always phone Linda." Linda would occasionally visit the set on rehearsal days, as would Tom's father and various other proud family members.

While Tom may have seemed aloof to some (as Bill Glaze recalls, "I was never aware of Tom as a mate, he was very distant"), he would socialise freely with the guest stars after hours, at local pubs such as the Thatch Barn. "He loved the social side of the show," says Chris Hutchins. "He'd be drinking in the bar at Elstree every night and stars would come out there who weren't in the show just to talk to him, just to be part of it." But the producer did not join in the revelry. "He went his way and I went mine," says Jon. "We didn't make a habit of mixing at all. I think you last longer as a working unit that way – better to get pissed on your own!"

There were times during the filming when Gordon found his control over Tom somewhat usurped. Ronnie Cass witnessed several occasions when the relationship between the star's manager and the show's producer became tense. "It was a bit brittle at times because Jon's a very, very decided director himself with a great style. But he had absolute faith and belief in Tom and that was important because Gordon couldn't be doing with anybody who didn't think Tom Jones was the greatest thing." Jon himself remembers that Gordon's prime concern was looking after his property and he was quite perceptive in gauging what was suitable for his charge. Gordon's presence was dominant at the onset of filming, but he allowed himself to relax as he realised that Tom was in capable hands. "He wasn't the easiest person to work with," admits Jon about his relationship with Gordon. "But he ran along straight railway lines; he didn't throw wobblies."

This Is Tom Jones was always taped twice, once for the English broadcast and again for the American audience. The primary reason for this rigmarole is that the 'line system' (lines being visual signals from which a video image is composed) used in Britain is different from that of the United States. The other reason for the two filmings was that the Americans imposed much stricter censorship demands as they had to assuage their southern Bible belt viewers. An American censor called Elizabeth would sit through the dress rehearsal, knitting and taking notes. "My early TV shows used to get censored," Tom recalled for an interview for *NME* in 1989. "One woman from ABC watched me doing my routine to 'Satisfaction' by the Stones and she said, 'You can't sing that song and move like that,' because she thought it had a bit of a message." Tom was, of course, suggesting sexual satisfaction, just as the Stones had done, but this was not considered suitable for prime time TV in America. The English crew found the American censorship levels very prudish. Even the costumes had to be altered; ankles were not to be seen, while hipsters and crop tops, although fashionable at the time, had to be joined in the middle to cover a naked navel.

Despite the problems generated by differing perceptions of acceptable viewing, Tom's show was such a hit in America that the core members of the crew were flown to Los Angeles to film the next set of programmes. They went over to America in August 1969 to film six shows, returning to the UK in October. After another six months back in England, the winning formula of the two summer months in America was repeated in 1970, producing a further six shows. Tom's first American show aired on October 9, 1969 and featured Tony Bennett and Vikki Carr. Johnny Cash and Blood, Sweat & Tears were to join Tom for his next consecutive shows.

When Tom arrived the ABC network received an unprecedented 30,000 requests for tickets from desperate fans, and even Tom was unable to secure seats for his own friends. "The little groupies would do anything to get to see that show – they would do anything just to touch him," chuckles Nina. Tom explained in Bert Schwartz's 1969 biography: "In America we're trying to bridge the gap between teenagers and adults. It's happening here in Britain. The gap is being bridged. For instance, adults watch *Top Of The Pops*, the teenagers watch it, it's become a family show . . . I think adults want to listen to beat music if you present it to them properly. Now, at 29, I'm not a teenager, but I do a lot of beat music. If you're masculine enough, too . . . you can reach them."

"We all became a little bit hypnotised with what we'd walked into – Hollywood," confesses Bill Glaze. The crew had not realised until now the extent of Tom's stardom overseas. Back at Elstree studios, they were looked upon merely as production staff for Tom's show, but in Los Angeles Tom's celebrity status extended to sprinkle a little fame onto everyone. The crew stayed at the Sheraton Universal hotel, where they were amazed to find five convertible Mustangs waiting for them on their arrival. One night Bill was stopped for speeding by the local police, having alerted them by driving his Mustang the wrong way towards the freeway. Bill explained in his defence that he was English and therefore unused to driving on the right-hand side of the road. On further questioning he verified that his work in America was filming *This Is Tom Jones*. Overcome, the policeman said, "My wife would go without a steak dinner to meet Tom Jones!" Bill replied, "You've got it!" Without further ado the policeman tore up the ticket in front of him and in return Bill ensured that the policeman's wife attended the filming of every concert spot while they were in the States.

The American stars were keen to appear on Tom's show in England. It was good for promotional purposes as it allowed them to 'be seen' in the UK. Inevitably there were some personalities who were unable to spare the time to travel or film, so the show literally came to them. Jon was mainly responsible for choosing which faces appeared on *This Is Tom Jones*, but Gordon and Tom also had a say in shaping the guest list. "In those days, the big singers on American television were people like Perry Como and Andy Williams and Dean Martin," Tom said in an interview for the *Daily Telegraph* in 1998. "ABC wanted me to be like them, but every chance I could get, I would sing something a little different, something harder than the usual stuff of the time. And I would get great people to come on the show, like Little Richard and Jerry Lee Lewis. Back then, no one would let those guys on television."

As far as Tom and Jon were concerned, the weekly invitations were an unspoken agreement. In return for the easier personalities which Jon knew would satisfy ABC's ratings, Tom was allowed to choose the musicians who inspired him most. "It was a trade-off," Tom conceded in a publicity release. "I'd say, 'Look, if I have to have Barbara Eden or Robert Goulet on, I gotta have Aretha Franklin and Ray Charles.'" So when Barbara Eden, the comedienne star of *I Dream Of Jeannie* surfaced twice on Tom's show, she was joined by Wilson Pickett in the first instance and Jerry Lee Lewis in the second. Tom didn't think twice about the presence of Barbara Eden on the latter show; he was far too busy immersing himself in a to-die-for medley with his lifetime idol, encompassing Jerry Lee's classics 'Great Balls Of Fire', 'Down The Line', 'Long Tall Sally' and 'Whole Lotta Shakin' Goin' On'.

The appearance on *This Is Tom Jones* of Janis Joplin, arguably the finest white blues and soul singer of her generation, caused ructions behind the scenes. "She thought I was really straight, like an establishment TV figure because being on bloody TV the rebel side had gone away from it," Tom said to Q magazine in 1991. Bill Glaze recounts that, "Janis Joplin came in smoking grass and said to Jon, 'What key does your boy sing in?' Jon replied, 'Don't worry about keys, he'll do it.'" Unconvinced, the extrovert singer thought she could easily outstrip Tom with her stunning three octave roar during their duet on 'Raise Your Hand'. Tom remembers the result as a real "rock'n'roll scream up . . . and after it she said, 'Man! You can really sing!' She was so surprised."

Another notable American counter-culture act to appear on the show was the 'supergroup' Crosby, Stills, Nash & Young, on October 25, 1969. Fresh from their appearance at the Woodstock festival two months earlier, CSN&Y were at the height of their popularity, the acclaimed CS&N début album a fixture on the charts, but eyebrows were raised at the sight of these long haired, moustachioed musicians in their faded jeans and fringed jackets on mainstream TV. In the event they sang Stephen Stills' keening anthem 'You Don't Have To Cry' and Tom joined them for David Crosby's 'Long Time Gone', one of the best known revolutionary compositions from the era which was later chosen to open the *Woodstock* movie. Crosby was later mortified by the memory of singing with the tuxedoed Tom, but Stills quipped: "I really dig Tom Jones . . . he's got incredible chops."

Tom struck up a fantastic rapport with Sammy Davis Jnr., the black veteran mimic, dancer and singer hailing from the Vaudevillian tradition. Sammy and Tom made such a great double act joking around with each other and zany Jo Anne Worley in Sammy's first brief appearance on *This Is Tom Jones*, that he returned for a second show devoted entirely to the duo. "I ran into Tom Jones during supper at the Elephant," remembers Sammy in his 1990 autobiography, *Why Me?* "I was going to be doing his TV special. We were a good personality combination; we'd do the bumps and grinds together. 'I'd like you to sing "Bojangles",' he said." Sammy had been tutored, aged seven, in his stage routine by Bill 'Bojangles' Robinson, but the true meaning of the song was far removed from this early mentor's success. Although Neil Diamond and The Nitty Gritty Dirt Band had both had hits with Jerry Jeff Walker's composition, Sammy was still wary. "At the studio when Tom's manager brought up the subject I said, 'I can't do that song. I hate it.' I wanted nothing to do with it, with the character. It was the story of a dancer who became a drunk, a bum, and he died in jail."

Sammy explained his reasons to Tom: "The song spooked me. I had seen too many performers who'd slid from the headlines to playing joints, then toilets, and finally beer halls and passing the hat, reduced to coming backstage to see the star . . . The song was my own nightmare. I was afraid that was how I was going to end." But the production team all felt that if Sammy wouldn't sing the song alone, even a duet of 'Bojangles' by Sammy and Tom would be a winning combination. Sammy continues, "They kept insisting, so I said, 'Tom, you sing it and I'll act it.' And working with his choreographer, we devised a way that I could do the movements to show the young guy at the beginning, lithe, a dandy – then, by the end, old and doddering, drunk and pathetic, while Tom was in a jail set, singing that song about him." Between Tom's heartfelt rendition and Sammy's poignant interpretation of Norman Maen's dance pattern, they produced a memorable TV moment. Jon had been oblivious to any concerns Sammy may have harboured about performing 'Mr. Bojangles': "Maybe he had had qualms but he didn't bring them onto the floor. And it became one of his big numbers."

As well as offering a showcase to big names, *This Is Tom Jones* made stars of less publicly acknowledged musicians, in particular Big Jim Sullivan. Big Jim took the idea of having a solo guitar number, along the same lines as Tom's 'quiet spots', to Jon Scoffield, who approved and gradually incorporated it into the show. But like Tom and his choice of guests, there had to be a compromise and Big Jim had to work hard for his slice of fame, performing classical guitar solos in the middle of a rock section, not to mention a festive instrumental of 'Rudolph The Red Nosed Reindeer'.

The statuesque guitarist gained something of a fan base as the series progressed. "What seemed to happen, especially in America, was the guys used to come up to me and say, 'My missus turns on the TV to watch Tom, but I always turn it on to see you!' So I got a kind of male following in the States, which was great," chortles Big Jim. Tom began to enjoy sharing the limelight, typically introducing his pal with "The lad parked here with the guitar is not a guest, he's family – ladies and gentlemen, my guitarist Big Jim Sullivan. Big Jim's a man of few words, he just lets the guitar do all the talking for him." Big Jim often performed country numbers, which enabled Jon to develop the show in a direction that was to Gordon's liking. "We gradually, without telling anybody, let Tom sing more and more country and western numbers," says Jon. "We realised that it was popular – so long as you don't call it 'country and western', because that makes you think of cowboys – you call it a ballad."

In November 1969, Tom forged an alliance for the first time with the Treorchy Male Choir; a well-established Welsh male voice choir that had then been performing traditional music native to their country for over 20 years. Tom had always admired the sense of unity in many men singing together, and suggested to the production staff of *This Is Tom Jones* that his baritone range, with its upper reaches of a double high C, would be a good match for such an ensemble. The Treorchy Male Choir was brought in for a special Christmas edition of Tom's show, filmed at Elstree studios and also featuring guests Millicent Martin, David Fry and Joan Collins. Bob Griffiths, spokesman for the Choir recalls: "We were invited to appear with Tom in November 1969 and we couldn't believe that we would be appearing with such a huge star . . . It was absolutely tremendous. We were mixing with all the stars and we were there for three days." Ronnie Cass devised a suitably seasonal sketch based on 'A Child's Christmas In Wales', in which Tom recited Dylan Thomas' evocative poetry against a background of the Treorchy Male Choir's interpretation of various Christmas carols and other songs associated with the festive season. Ronnie was almost overcome when Tom was so in tune with the Johnnie Spence Orchestra and the Welshmen, that the intricate medley was shot in one take.

Bob Griffiths was impressed with Tom's down-to-earth professionalism. "Tom was a typical valley boy. He was always dressed immaculately – he was a star. But he still remembered his roots back home. He was a gentleman and he treated the boys exceptionally well." To celebrate the success of the filming Tom joined the choir in the canteen. There he indulgently bought a rather expensive round of beer for the 100 plus members. The Welshmen talked, laughed and sang into the early hours of the morning, and when it became too late for the show's star to travel home, he stayed overnight in his caravan based at the studios.

Tom Jones, Gordon Mills, Jon Scoffield and Ronnie Cass were all made honorary members of the Treorchy Male Choir in late 1969. This involved the presentation of a plaque and a special choir tie for each, which they are requested to wear on St David's Day wherever they may be in the world. The fruitful association was continued in November 1970, when the choir was invited back to Elstree to film with Ella Fitzgerald and Rudolph Nureyev. Ms Fitzgerald was so impressed with the choir that she dedicated her special arrangement of 'Just A Closer Walk' to them.

Three months later a section of the choir accompanied Tom on a jovial, alcohol assisted sketch which celebrated the singers' Welsh roots for the *Burt Bacharach Show*, and was also filmed at the Elstree Studios. "The idea was that Tom would be talking to Burt Bacharach about his songs," laughs Bob Griffiths today. "Burt would say, 'Well, where do *you* come from, Tom?' and Tom would say, 'I come from a place called Pontypridd.'" Tom complimented the legendary songwriter by informing him that everyone in Wales knew his songs. When the composer feigned surprise Tom bet him that if they could be transported to any pub in the Valleys, there would be a group of choristers singing Burt's 'Raindrops Keep Falling On My Head'. Bob continues: "They would fade out to a pub scene and there we were, singing the song in Welsh. They had actual beer in the glasses – it's not coloured water! We had done this song about four or five times when Jon Scoffield said, 'No, it's not right.'" A waiter went round and filled the choristers' empty glasses. "After Tom had done about five or six shots, we'd had five or six pints of beer and loosened up a bit. And Jon Scoffield said, 'Yes, that's it, now you've got it!'"

Although *This Is Tom Jones* had finished by spring of 1971, The Treorchy Male Choir returned for a third, slightly less inebriated repeat performance for a special Tom Jones show in December 1971. Despite the discontinuation of his TV series, Tom gladly maintains a professional relationship with the choir to this day and has worked with them on several other occasions. He states in their 50th Anniversary Brochure: "There is nothing like the sound of a Welsh Male Choir, and the Treorchy is one of the finest. They have represented the best of the Welsh voice for generations with honour and integrity. They are our international ambassadors."

Tom was graced with the presence of many of the finest performers of this century on his ground-breaking show. Among the many other diverse guests featured in both musical spots and sketches were The Bee Gees, Paul Anka, Peter Sellers, Nancy Sinatra, The Who, Ray Charles, Sonny & Cher, Wilson Pickett, Smokey Robinson, and Aretha Franklin. Contrary to popular belief, Elvis Presley never appeared on the programme. "He was booked, but never appeared. A contract problem – when he came out of the Army he did a special with Frank Sinatra and the contract said until he did a second Sinatra show he couldn't do anybody else . . . I had everybody else on *except* Elvis," Tom later explained.

As *This Is Tom Jones* developed, Jon Scoffield decided to incorporate an element of comedy into Tom's act, reinforcing Gordon's thinking that a public perception of his star as a skilful all-round performer would pave the way to Hollywood. Comic group, The Ace Trucking Company, consisting of Patti Deutsch, Michael Mislove, Bill Saluga, George Terry, and Fred Willard became an integral part of the show. Jon loved their genuine 'Greenwich Village' type of stand-up performance, which would soon escalate into hilarious improvisation. Although Jon admits today that many thought he was slightly mad in hiring the group to augment Tom's comic routines, they were much appreciated on set and became regulars in the last series.

At first though, the majority of sketches were performed gamely by the star of the show. One memorable early shoot featured a routine where Tom, dressed as an astronaut, sang Frank Sinatra's classic 'Fly Me To The Moon'. The filming took place in America, and was destined for disaster right from the very beginning. Not only did the dry ice cause havoc with the mock spaceship, but for the sake of family viewing, Tom had been asked to don a jockstrap beneath his tight space suit. Never having worn one previously, he put it on back to front and the hapless singer was in agony for quite some time afterwards.

As the new element to the show began to gain momentum, the scriptwriters took the opportunity to introduce contemporary issues to the plots of the sketches, in the hope that credibility would be main-tained. Racial topics were represented in several instances, including a psychedelic performance of the song 'Ball Of Confusion', superimposing

Tom and Norman Maen's dance troupe on a spinning background of newspaper headlines. The dancers carried banners proclaiming "End The Draft!", "Smile ... If You Can" and "Love ... Not War". On another occasion Tom appeared in a 19th century American sketch as a 'Southerner' discussing employment levels of black men and the abomination of blacks being segregated from whites in public places.

Nina Blatt remembers that in the Sixties feminism had become a major issue and even this was tackled, albeit in a sardonic fashion, on *This Is Tom Jones*. Cynicism aside, the very inclusion of such a progressive theme in a programme of this nature was in itself almost unheard of. Guest star Anne Bancroft led the way by appearing in a scene set in a bathtub where Nina remembers the bubbles began to sink at an alarming rate. Anne soldiered on with a forced smile, debating the ideals of feminism against respectful chivalry. The subject was addressed once more in a kitchen scene where Anne played the wife to an exaggeratedly chauvinistic Tom, pretending to gratefully agree with everything her husband says, evidently only too happy to spend her life cooking and cleaning for him. As soon as Tom exits the set she rejoices in the appearance of several brightly clad ladies, who enter the kitchen chanting, "Ban The Man! Women Unite! Girl Power!"

The irony of such a display, of which the Spice Girls would have been proud, may have been completely lost on the show's reactionary star. To his credit though, Tom was often happy to send himself and others up during the topical diversions. In one programme he appeared as a janitor for the fictional 'Funky Records' label. The record company staff were supposed to be searching for a new singer, the joke being that the talented Tom was right under their noses. When they hear the janitor singing while he cleans, they remark, "Did anyone tell you you had an interesting voice?" Tom replies, completely deadpan: "Only my friend Engelbert, but what does he know?!"

Perhaps the most infamous aspect of Tom's sojourn at Elstree was his caravan, and what occurred within. The glorified dressing room was rather romantically described in official publicity material as a "special five room chalet built inside the studio grounds to provide him with a home from home." The caravan, which was used for 'entertaining', was kept very well hidden for security reasons as the site at Elstree was noticeably open and accessible. Only the runners knew of the caravan's secret location next to the wardrobe department. It was widely acknowledged that as ATV were strict about not allowing girls into stars' dressing rooms, the caravan was either Gordon or Jon's method of keeping Tom's wayward inclinations out of the way of prying eyes. TV producer Stewart Morris claimed on the BBC *Omnibus* documentary that, "Tom used to have a driver called Chris Ellis who waited in the wings with towels . . . If Tom spied someone in the audience who he thought was interesting Chris would go around during the show and they would be invited to join him for the inevitable Dom Perignon on ice. And there would be Tom with the towel around his neck in a dressing gown ready to meet them. Chris would stand guard outside the door." Big Jim Sullivan relates: "I remember one lady in particular, quite a famous lady who I've known since she was 14, who I won't name – she came out [of the caravan] and came into the canteen." Here the guest gestured to Big Jim with a nod and a wink that she'd had 'relations' with Tom Jones.

By far the longest affair the caravan witnessed was with the minor American actress, Joyce Ingalls. A model for the Eileen Ford Model Agency and the Sears catalogue, Joyce would later become notorious as the third party in the break-up of Anthony Hopkins' marriage in 1996. According to anonymous sources, Joyce moved into Tom's caravan in January 1970 and declared the trailer off-limits to all visitors. A controlling, on-and-off relationship transpired over the next 18 months and by all accounts Tom was absolutely smitten by his strong-willed new ladyfriend. In the end, his loyalty to Linda overcame the romance and Joyce was dispatched on a plane, leaving the singer for good. Meanwhile, the caravan (the subject of many an 'in-joke' about how its tyres needed frequent changing even though it never went anywhere) was eventually inherited by none other than Engelbert Humperdinck, when he commenced work on his rival show.

This Is Tom Jones rapidly became a world-syndicated TV show. Seen in 18 countries, it regularly topped the JICTAR ratings, and attracted a nomination in 1970 for a Golden Globe for Best TV Actor in a Musical or Comedy (sadly unsuccessful). While the programme ensured a loyal band of regular viewers which enormously enlarged Tom's ever-growing fan base, the critics remained divided about the show's success. Very few were ready to debase Jon Scoffield's extravagant creation. Jerry Coffey wrote a praiseworthy report in the Fort Worth *Star-Telegram*: "Production-wise, Jones' show is probably the most lavish variety outing that has been staged in Britain. The programme is handsomely mounted and Jones has solid musical and choreographic support, and first-class technical credits." He continued by comparing it unfavourably to the high-class entertainment that the American audience was used to. "By current US standards, the show is quite conventional, even a bit old-fashioned, especially in some of the continuity clichés employed to keep things moving." Cecil Smith of the *Los Angeles Times* reinforced the popular opinion that English TV had a reputation for poor quality, but was pleasantly surprised by *This Is Tom Jones*, describing it as one of the "handsomest shows on air".

The programme's host in particular was under intense scrutiny. Some journalists, like Frank Judge of the *Detroit News,* were committed to putting the rising star firmly in his place. "When I saw him he seemed a bit too concerned with establishing himself as an international sex symbol. This tended to get in the way of the show at times . . . In almost every scene, the smooching, snuggling Jones was out to prove that he was quite a swinger." Others, like Bob Tweedell of the *Denver Post* were far more impressed: "Tom Jones . . . combines some of the attributes of Dean Martin, Sammy Davis Jnr., Elvis Presley and Bobby Darin . . . Jones also is a relaxed, at-ease host, and he wasn't required – thankfully – to gush over his guests . . . the Jones show had a certain lilt that makes it a promising new item on the over-stocked variety shelf."

Having established one of his charges on the small screen, Gordon attempted to achieve the same for Engelbert Humperdinck in 1970. Gordon secured what became known as the 'rival' show to Tom's for his more romantic star, and *The Engelbert Humperdinck Show* was likewise networked by ABC in the US and ATV in the UK, and broadcast in 18 countries. The programmes were also filmed at the studios in Elstree, and Engel shared many of the same staff as Tom, as well as inheriting his caravan . . . Despite the budget of about £1.5 million, Engel simply failed to translate onto the screen with Tom's electricity and the show was poorly received. Unable to generate the same kind of audience frenzy in his concert spots, Engel was reduced to lame skits and performing easy-listening schmaltz.

In England, Peter Black of the *Daily Mail* condemned the show in a damning review: "*The Engelbert Humperdinck Show* was the nearest thing I've seen to zombie TV . . . the luckless Humperdinck was projected as a mindless hunk of muscle and looks." Unfortunately, in the US *The Engelbert Humperdinck Show* was scheduled as a replacement for the highly rated Johnny Cash series and paled in comparison. After the initial 13 shows, Engel's option was dropped and the series discontinued. Amazingly enough, Engel's musical reputation survived, and soon after the culling of his TV misadventures, the papers reported widespread interest in his forthcoming US tour, with the same expected gross profit as Tom's tour. Gordon continued to treat his lesser star well, with a reported $2 million guarantee for his extensive US engagements that summer.

Tom's TV career had also run its natural course (for the moment at least), and *This Is Tom Jones* was cancelled after a memorable two-and-a-half seasons at the beginning of February 1971. It was undoubtedly the most phenomenally successful of any show of its genre. The final farewell show was filmed entirely as a concert spot in England and was very emotional for all involved. That was the last many fans saw of *This Is Tom*

Jones until it was released on a specially compiled highlights video in November 1993.

After such a long run, Tom was relieved to be free of the gruelling constraints of a tight schedule and planned to do only a few TV specials after that. He made a telling aside to the audience when he opened four nights at the Hammersmith Odeon, "It's great to be back on the road after being imprisoned at Elstree TV Studios for three months," and was quoted as saying, "That show was never me, but I was younger then and I wanted to keep working."

10

HELP YOURSELF

THIS IS TOM JONES completely turned Tom's life upside down from the years 1969 to 1971. But while filming took up a large chunk of time, Gordon Mills was careful to maintain the pace of Tom's recording and touring. Nevertheless, trips to Las Vegas, Australia and Canada were all postponed during these years, to be fulfilled only when Tom was free of obligations to ATV. In 1969 'I'll Never Fall In Love Again' was reissued on the strength of the success of the series and two albums, *Live In Las Vegas* and *This Is Tom Jones* did very well in both UK and US charts. A 1969 magazine comparing and contrasting the joint appeal of Elvis Presley and Tom Jones (*Elvis & Tom – Who Is The Greater Lover?*) stated that the latter's gross earnings that year were expected to exceed $2.4 million.

With all that testosterone contributing to his typical Welsh pride, Tom did not like to admit to his insecurities, but for several years had housed feelings of jealousy towards those around him. Gordon had instilled in him an expectation to always command the centre of attention, and if his star status was ever threatened, he reacted badly. Standing at several inches over six foot, Vernon Hopkins was considerably taller than Tom, and an obvious target for his envy, especially as the band's frontman had to wear high-heeled boots to measure up.

On The Squires' 1966 tour to Australia, Vic Cooper also found himself inadvertently undermining Tom's position with his cheeky cockney warmth. "About the third day in Sydney, I looked like somebody who was in the charts in Australia," he grins. "We were playing away and we heard, 'We want Vic! We want Vic!' I thought it was a wind-up! It happened on the second show and Tom said, 'What is it with him?' It had never happened before." Chris Slade explains that the adulation enjoyed by The Squires was akin to Beatlemania, with fans favouring their chosen pin-up from the band. "They were doing the group thing, and we thought we were the group and Tom was the singer. So some of the fans would have done that because that's what you do with groups." But Tom was not interested in promoting any kind of 'group scene'. Vernon recalls that Tom would introduce The Squires begrudgingly during the set with, " 'Don't clap too loud because they'll want more money!' – He'd say it as a joke, but he meant it!"

Back in March 1968, while Tom Jones & The Squires were living the high life at the Copacabana, Vic had received a tempting offer that he felt he couldn't refuse. "I was in the Copacabana club and some guy said, 'Do you want to earn a million dollars?' " Although automatically assuming that the proposal was a vast practical joke at his expense, in fact he had been approached by the man behind The Monkees, Don Kirshner, to star in the film *Toomorrow* opposite Australian singer Olivia Newton-John. Vic sent a fond farewell telegram to Tom when the tour moved on to the Flamingo in Las Vegas.

"DEAR TOM REGRET HAVE TO LEAVE BAND STOP AM VERY PROUD TO HAVE WORKED WITH YOU STOP REGARDS TO THE BEST BACKING GROUP IN THE WORLD SQUIRES VIC"

In *Toomorrow* Vic Cooper co-stars as an organist who invents an instrument called the 'tonaliser', which will protect the planet against an alien invasion. The backers of this £5 million science fiction musical, one of whom was James Bond producer Harry Saltzman, hoped for a box office smash on the film's release in 1970. Instead it was an insipid disaster, although it obviously didn't irreparably damage the career of Olivia Newton-John who went on to have several hit singles and star in the hugely successful 1978 musical *Grease*. Despite the overwhelming failure of the film, Vic was still pleased that he had made the break from the underpaid routine of The Squires. He was now free to explore other musical avenues and following the film's demise he chose to pursue a continued alliance with Olivia Newton-John. Today Vic maintains of his split from Tom: "It was the best thing I ever did."

Old ghosts were to come back to haunt Tom at the beginning of 1969. Raymond Godfrey and John Glastonbury, the ineffective management duo better known by their strange, self-chosen nicknames Myron and Byron emerged from the closet to claim their slice of the pie. The deal Gordon had struck with them to secure Tom back in 1964 had stipulated a very generous five per cent of all profits in perpetuity. Myron and Byron decided that since their former client had over the last few years accumulated several million pounds, now would be an opportune time to reap their reward. Both were keen to point out that they had 'financed' the young Tommy Scott, generously supplying a van, a PA system and various other expenses.

The case was initially previewed in the High Court in January 1969 with Mr Brian Neil QC representing the injured parties before the judge, Mr Justice Megarry. The judge was immediately astounded that Godfrey and Glastonbury were seriously trying to claim their five per cent for the past five years and for the rest of Tom's career. The impecunious pair were relying on legal aid to fight the case, and their lawyers were more interested in a quick agreement than in struggling through a lengthy trial against Gordon's high-powered defence. When no one was willing to back the former managers The Squires were individually subpoenaed to testify. Vernon and Co. were more concerned with their internal affairs at the time, but heard later that Myron and Byron had eventually reached an out of court agreement. John Glastonbury told the news-hungry reporters waiting outside on The Strand: "We are very happy about the settlement. It is substantial. What we have done for Tom Jones cannot be measured in terms of money."

The reality of the ridiculous contract in question probably rests closer to Peter Sullivan's summary: "They [Myron & Byron] knew what they were trying to achieve but they hadn't got any idea of the business. They were very naïve and were not experienced in the music business. You could tell by the way they spoke to you." However, the naïveté no longer stretched to The Squires. Vernon Hopkins remembers that after he had testified for Tom, the singer went off in one direction in his limousine and Vernon was whisked off in the other by Gordon, who had indicated that he had an interesting proposition for The Squires. That was to be the last time that Vernon spoke to Tom at length for 17 years.

Vernon is still very bitter about the way he was treated. As The Squires were slowly disbanding of their own accord, Gordon seized the timely reappearance of Myron and Byron to enforce the final split. Peter Sullivan, like Gordon, had never expected The Squires to be involved in Tom's fame. "The Squires were adequate musicians but I only ever intended them to be a backing band," says Peter today. It was this lack of musicianship that has since been cited as the reason for the group's departure, as Tom claims in the *Green Green Grass Of Home* documentary that they couldn't even read music.★

At the time however, Gordon and Tom were neither frank nor upfront with the lads who had stayed with Tom through thick and thin for eight years. Vernon remembers: "When we came back to England this new law came out saying that you cannot just sack anyone on the spot unless there's good reason. They had no good reason for us to be sacked, so Gordon had to find a reason." He recalls Gordon's perfect excuse: "He said, 'Tom's

---

★ Ironically, in the 1999 documentary *60 Minutes II* on Tom Jones, the interviewer reveals that Tom himself can neither read music nor play an instrument properly.

doing television and all that and he's not going to be working for quite a while, but in the meantime get the lads together ... You've got to make a record.' We thought we'd be like The Shadows at last, really get it together."

Vernon eagerly went back with Gordon to hear the song he had chosen for their début as an independent entity – a Joe South number called 'Games People Play', the irony of the title apparently escaping the excited backing band. "We made this record," continues Vernon. "The session was in Barnes after 12.00 a.m. – the cheapest time. So we were there from 12 o'clock to four o'clock in the morning ... He [Gordon] walked out of the studio with a tape in his hand, and within days I opened one of the national papers and there on the middle page was 'Tom Jones & The Squires Part Amicably'."

Melody Maker ran an article about the turn of events on February 8, 1969 quoting a press release from Tom's management: "The Squires have been with Tom right from the start but there were two reasons why they have now amicably parted. First, Tom will be spending most of the year making his television series and any tours he does now are with the Ted Heath Orchestra, as the group aren't going to be working with him for a long time. Secondly, for some time now the group has wanted to try and make it on their own." Intensifying the already deep wounds, Tom was invited to sing at the Investiture of the Prince of Wales in Spring 1969. But as the star was unable to attend, Gordon suggested that The Squires should appear to début their new single, guaranteeing that the manager still made a commission on the booking.

Gordon had created the perfect scenario for dismissing The Squires. In offering them the opportunity of fame in their own right, he effectively separated them from Tom, while at the same time he determined to half-heartedly promote their record thus ensuring failure. Lack of sales could then be used as a legitimate excuse to let The Squires go. As Gordon had always insisted that the group did not have written contracts he was able to sack them without so much as a week's wages, confident they had no legal grounds on which to sue for compensation. "We didn't suss it at the time, [but] the idea was that Gordon got us to do a single and it was like, 'Oh sorry fellas, you've failed, so you're out.' It was that sort of thing," recalls Chris Slade.

Lost and floundering, The Squires tried to recapture their early days performing in clubs in the north of England with a new singer, Michael Davis. But Chris, who had previously been singled out from the rest to accompany Tom at the reopening of Caesar's Palace in 1966, was once again called upon. "Vic left, we carried on for a while," says Chris. "The Squires were sacked. We then got a singer in called Michael Davis. But he used to leave his house as the gig was starting – impossible to work with.

Tom then asked me to go back with him, so I did." Inevitably there was some friction as Chris appeared to be turning his back on his friends. "We fell out a bit to be honest, of course, we were bound to. I was saying goodbye to The Squires and going back to the enemy. But it just really felt like my thing, with Tom."

Chris Hutchins recalls it was an uncomfortable period for Tom, who remained remarkably low-key throughout all the acrimony. "Tom had to be sheltered from everything because Tom never liked to do unpopular things. If anybody had to be fired . . ." Instead the singer busied himself with other events, in particular receiving a Silver Heart Award at the Variety Club on March 11 for his numerous show business achievements. Abruptly turning his back on the events of the previous month Tom flew to Australia in April 1969 to kick off a six-month world tour.

Tom's stage act was highly professional by this stage, but he needed just one final addition for it to reach its zenith – a trio of fashionable black female backing singers who would accentuate the melodies and lend contrast to his Herculean voice. The Blossoms came to Gordon and Tom's attention when they were in a production called *Catch My Soul*, a musical version of *Othello*. The singer and his manager had seen the drama and without hesitation fell in love with the sweet harmonies and charisma of the feisty ladies.

Initially formed at Fremont High School in Los Angeles in 1954, the trio achieved one pop chart entry in 1961 with 'Son-In-Law', an answer record to Ernie K-Doe's 'Mother-In-Law'. After a few line-up and group name changes, The Blossoms settled down as founder member Fanita James was joined by Jeannie King and Darlene Love (who had previously recorded with Phil Spector in 1962 as both a solo singer and part of The Crystals). By 1965 The Blossoms had secured a regular television slot, singing on ABC's popular music series *Shindig*.

In 1968 The Blossoms were privileged to work as back-up singers for Elvis Presley on his critically acclaimed NBC TV comeback special, *Elvis*, and were all set to go on the road with him when he recommenced touring after years in the Hollywood wilderness. In a quirky twist of fate, Elvis' management was taking a little too long to finalise details for the tour and Gordon seized the opportunity to jump in and sign the sought-after singers. Fanita recalls with much amusement how one night years later Elvis popped his head round the curtain during one of Tom's concerts at Las Vegas and declared: "You stole my girls, you stole my pants, now I'm going to steal your thunder!" "The audience laughed and cheered," remembers Fanita. "Elvis came on and gave Tom a hug, then he left – they never sang together."

Fanita worked for Tom from 1969 to 1990, renewing her contract with the rest of The Blossoms each year. Although the group contributed to some of Tom's records early on, their main involvement was as long-standing members of his touring party, as well as close friends. He would always make a point of introducing his "lovely ladies" on stage, where they were set back from the main platform sitting on stools, restricted only to expressive hand movements. Raunchy dancing, of course, would have diverted attention from Tom.

The singer thrived with his overall set now expanded to include a comedian and a big name backing band, such as the Ted Heath Orchestra. Tom's hectic worldwide travels encompassed a whistle-stop tour of the US incorporating 41 cities and appearances at the Copacabana in New York and the Flamingo in Las Vegas, which he opened just 24 hours after closing at the Copacabana. But the strain was beginning to show when a series of concerts was cancelled later in 1969 after Tom lost his voice. Thousands of fans had queued for hours to purchase tickets for the eight-day engagements, but Tom only managed to struggle through three performances before refunds had to be given.

Still, Tom's hold over the arid desert town of Las Vegas was undeniable. In the opening lines to Bert Schwartz's 1969 publication, *Tom Jones*, the American attitude to this most famous British export is summed up in the beautifully dated words of the time. "Ten years ago . . . all that was British was stuffy and severe – for staid and settled people. Today British exports are making America over in new fashions and styles, to the immense satisfaction of both sides of the Atlantic . . . The Beatles were the first of the British pop singing groups to conquer America with a storm of sound and applause. But not the last. The latest of the superpowered musical headliners to reach the American shore is Tom Jones. His arrival could be the most momentous splashdown of the decade, for he promises not only to reign as monarch of the whole popular music world, over more subjects than King George could claim, but also to take more money out of the Yankee entertainment treasury than the King ever thought to grab through his Stamp Act . . ."

★   ★   ★

"If I were to go out with lots of girls, I would lose my wife and my livelihood because I would have lost my roots. I'd be the loser. Look at what I have today; a wife, a son, money, luxuries beyond my dreams. I enjoy this life, and won't throw it away for anything," Tom declared in the interview for the *Elvis & Tom* magazine. The truth was a little less rosy – his public affair with Mary Wilson was not destined to be a one-off. The wide availability of the contraceptive pill and the sexual liberation experienced in the 'summer of love' two years previously, encouraged Tom to play the field, and he continued to make quite a name for himself as a ladies' man.

Darlene Love of The Blossoms was flattered to receive amorous overtures from Tom. She first detailed her experiences touring with Tom and enjoying his attentions in her 1998 autobiography *My Name Is Love: The Darlene Love Story*. "He had been messing around with me almost the whole tour," says Darlene today. "I thought, 'Come on now Tom, I don't need to get into any trouble.' We'd get closer, closer and closer, and I would tell myself, 'If I don't quit this, something just might happen . . .' When you're on the road a long time it gets a little lonely out there sometimes. One night Tom called me and said, 'Why don't you come on down to my room?' I said, 'Why? What's going on down there?' He said, 'Nothing, just come on down for a drink.'

"So I go down to his room and we're having champagne, his favourite drink. And we started drinking and before you know it we're hugging and kissing. Then we were getting in bed. Lloyd Greenfield's room was right next door to Tom's and the connecting door wasn't closed, and that made me very uncomfortable. I did get into bed, I took off everything but my underwear; I left my panties on." But the prospect of being caught by her nearby boss acted as quite a dampener to the couple's heated ardour. "I thought about it and I said, 'You know what? That's all I need for Lloyd to come busting through this door and catch me in bed with you, or for him to know I'm in here!' So in the middle of us getting excited and almost getting ready to have sex, I got up out of the bed, picked my clothes up and went down the hallway. The next day on the plane, Tom looked at me and I looked at him and we fell about laughing! We'd say, 'Al*most!*' "

Darlene's autobiography caused quite a stir within the Tom Jones camp. In it she also implied that singer and Broadway actress Leslie Uggams had a romantic liaison with Tom. In 1969 Leslie was famous for hosting her own TV series *The Leslie Uggams Show* and later went on to star in *All My Children*. Leslie appeared on *This Is Tom Jones* in February 1970 where the two singers duetted on 'Somewhere'. However, Leslie denies any such affair. "I did his TV show and when I was in Vegas one time he was there. There was a group of us, we'd all hang out. Elvis was there, and y'know, but they were the only times I saw Tom. I certainly did not have an affair with Tom Jones. Mary Wilson had an affair with him but I did not! . . . If I did, I didn't notice it!"

While the above 'flings' may seem rather harmless, and whether there is any truth in them or not, according to all reports Tom's sexuality was becoming increasingly out of hand. Described by more than one interviewee for this book as a 'sexaholic', popular opinion seems to be that

Tom literally could not sleep alone. Supposedly, the only time the singer would not request a companion for the night would be when he was so drunk that he was on the point of collapse, apparently a rare occurrence. Tom considered his sexual prowess to be an art form and thought nothing of loudly discussing the previous night's activities over breakfast, oblivious to who might be listening. While acknowledging that his sex drive seemed to be higher than most men, Tom could not understand a woman who was not prepared to become another notch on his bedpost, no matter how politely she might turn him down.

There was never any shortage of willing paramours and Tom never had to resort to a prostitute to satisfy his nightly demands. Even so, precautions had to be taken. Tom would reportedly visit a notorious Harley Street clinic frequented by many rock stars, where his occasional medical problems were kept under control. There was, of course, another risk to his various dalliances; according to an anonymous source, on at least one occasion a woman called Tom's office in a panic and an abortion was quietly arranged.

Tom has always been well aware of the effect his blatantly sexual stage act has on the majority of his female fans. In a 1969 interview he said of his more risqué movements and verbal innuendoes: "I'm trying to get across to the audience that I'm alive – all of it, emotion, sex, power – the heart-beat, bloodstream are all there for the asking. Everyone needs an outlet – I'm the outlet for millions of women." However, he was careful to prioritise his appeal, as he said in the *Omnibus* documentary: "I don't mind being treated as a sex object – as long as it's by females. It's very flattering, I wouldn't want it to only be that. The most important thing is my talent, my voice, the music I'm making. The showmanship is secondary to that."

In various TV chat shows over the years including *Aspel & Co* and *Mavis On 4* Tom has given the off pat simile: "Being on stage is the closest thing to making love," followed by a description of how it stimulates him physically to see his audience's fevered excitement, and the sheer adrenaline rush of performing he finds to be a powerful aphrodisiac. Tom was very frank in a recent interview with *Mojo* magazine. "Well, I don't get an erection when I sing, though you do feel sexy when you're doing a sexy song. When I say it's like sex, it's the anticipation, the excitement, you can't wait to get on stage. Then the actual doing it, you're getting all this emotion and it's pouring out of you, you can cry in one song, laugh in another, almost like going through a sexual situation . . . after you come off stage it's just like after sex . . . it's like *wheeeeww*."

Tom has become more and more outspoken about his sexual preferences as he gets older, particularly in the Nineties. In answer to the question of "What turns you on?" posed by Q magazine in 1998, Tom responded: "Sexually? Well, it's a hard one to admit really. OK, if you want to get down to the nitty gritty . . . let's say I'm watching a porno for instance – and I've analysed it, to see what makes me tick – I do like to see two women together. It turns me on more than anything else. That's what rings my chimes. So I think I might be a bit of a voyeur."* Tom was still not shying away from the gory details as late as October 1999, when he told *Now* magazine: "When I was a teenager I went round with a permanent, you know, erection. I think about sex every day and I can't live without it. If I'm away and on my own I have to masturbate."

Of course, in terms of show business morals there was nothing unduly unusual about Tom's behaviour. Promiscuity is, and always has been, rife within the pop music industry, which by its very nature tends to attract free-spirited individuals with a relaxed attitude towards casual sex. From the first stirrings of rock'n'roll, fans have thrown themselves at their idols in the hope of a night of unbridled passion, and the musicians are often both flattered and easily tempted.

Tom is very open on the subject of his preferred partner. While according to most sources his taste is fairly catholic with a certain partiality for blondes, black ladies and voluptuousness, Tom does not hold back on speaking for himself. In a rapid-fire 'Questions and Answers' interview in the Eighties, he stated: "There are good looking women of all races. As long as they take care of themselves . . . I like a woman to be a woman. I like feminine women. I don't like women who try to be men. There are enough men around without having real aggressive women."

"I like women to look smart," he expanded in Bert Schwartz's early biography. "Actually, I think American women make up better than European women. I always like women to fix themselves up. But one thing I don't like is a Twiggy-type female. If a woman is a woman, that's what she should look like." Perhaps the most incredible fact is that, even in print, Tom is not shy of comparing such an idealistic vision to his wife, Linda. "I was asked what type of women I like, and I said it all depended what you want them for," he is quoted in *Tom Jones* by Stafford Hildred and David Gritten. "You see a sexy chick on the street in tight clothes and look at her and admire her. But I wouldn't want my wife to walk around like that. The type of woman I want is the type of woman who wants to

* One member of Tom's touring party recalls that close members of the group would visit the set of *Top Of The Pops* regularly – not because Tom was appearing, but because blue movies were sometimes shown backstage. Tom's particular favourite was supposedly *The Rent Collector*.

be at home and be a housewife. As far as I'm concerned, my woman's place is in the home."

* * *

As the swinging Sixties stood poised on the verge of a new decade, Tom Jones found himself firmly entrenched in the Las Vegas cabaret circuit. One thousand people a night would attend Tom's three performances and watch the seasoned professional shed an average of six pounds in weight at each show (a combination of excessive perspiration and energy). By the late Sixties over 15 million tourists were visiting the casinos of Las Vegas and spending upwards of $400 million. Tom was a major contributing factor to this astonishing prosperity. He drew in the highly critical crowds who would not tolerate a show that was anything less than excellent, and he never failed to deliver. "The reaction was fantastic every night, which knocked me out because Las Vegas audiences are notoriously blasé," he says today.

On *The Merv Griffin Show* in 1979, the host reminisced with the star about an elaborate Vegas show which opened with a massive image of Tom that metamorphosed into a ramp, which Tom would then slide down to enter the stage. But perhaps the most arrogant example of Tom's advertising was a billboard outside the Latin Casino in Cherry Hill, Philadelphia, which drew attention to his performance with the conceited caption: 'He Is Here'. Tom joked on *The Mike Douglas Show* that his management subsequently had trouble with local Catholic churches, who complained that there could be only one 'He', and it wasn't Tom Jones.

Back in England on respite from Vegas, Tom was to learn an important lesson regarding the consumption of alcohol prior to a performance. "Ah, that happened at the London Palladium," he told the *Sun-Herald* in 1997. "It was in the Sixties and I was doing two shows a night and three on Saturday. During the week I used to pace myself and have a glass of champagne just before the second show. Come Saturday and I'd forgotten there were three shows." Visitors had arrived from Wales and after the second show they began to celebrate their reunion with several drinks. Tom somehow forgot it was a Saturday and carried on downing champagne, thinking that he'd finished work for the evening. When he finally realised there was another show before the night was over, it was too late to turn back and the merriment continued.

"When I went on for that third show, my arm holding up the microphone felt like lead about thirty minutes in. I was trying to hold it up and it was so *tiring*. Everything just seemed so much more difficult, you had to work so much harder at getting it to work. I realised back then the two don't mix." Since that embarrassing episode, Tom has wisely made a point not to commence heavy drinking until his work for the night is over.

Tom was pleased to make his second appearance for the Royal Variety Performance in 1969, this time topping the bill. When Prince Philip was introduced to him afterwards, the Queen's husband quipped, "What do you gargle with, pebbles?" Tom good-naturedly brushed over the comment, but was horrified to learn that the very next day the Prince, renowned for his thoughtless social gaffes, made the following comment at a lunch for the Small Business Association: "Last night we went to the Royal Variety Performance. The last man to come on was Tom Jones . . . It is very difficult to see how it is possible to become immensely valuable by singing what I think are most hideous songs. I would not say this about The Beatles."

Tom was justifiably outraged and the media were quick to capitalise on the sensational story. Tom's wrath was soothed somewhat by his manager and he was politely quoted in the papers as responding: "I don't know what happened. The thing I was annoyed about was that the Prince ran the whole show. It doesn't matter what he thinks about me, there are a lot of people who don't like my music. But the show is for charity. I wasn't doing an audition for the Duke . . . I pay a lot of taxes. I earn a lot of money for this country and I give my services to charity." His diplomacy extended to laughing off the situation when the press queried as to whether he would like a royal apology. Soon after, in order to save face, Prince Philip ordered Buckingham Palace to send Tom an apologetic letter.

When the two met again the following year at a charity benefit at The Talk Of The Town for the World Wildlife Fund, the Prince attempted to set the record straight with a personal explanation. Tom seemed to be happy with this turn of events and reiterated the story of the simple misunderstanding for the press: "He was supposed to have criticised the amount of money I was earning. He told me he wasn't criticising me but that he was at a Small Businessmen's Meeting – they were warning that they couldn't make enough money, that they couldn't survive, and he said, 'When somebody comes along like Tom Jones, when a man can make that sort of money I don't see why you can't do it.'"

As the full impact of *This Is Tom Jones* escalated Tom's popularity worldwide, the extent of his fame attracted unwanted attention from none other than serial killer Charles Manson. Tom shockingly discovered that he had been a target on Manson's celebrity hit-list, along with other big names including Elizabeth Taylor, Richard Burton, Steve McQueen and Frank Sinatra. The popular explanation for Charles Manson's list was that, as a failed singer/songwriter, he was insanely jealous of successful show business personalities, and sought to destroy them as a form of revenge. He commanded a cult following who blindly adhered to his perverse orders. Their most heinous crime was the horrific murder of Roman Polanski's wife, Sharon Tate, and her unborn baby in the Polanski home, scrawling the word 'Pigs' on the walls in her blood.

Charles Manson and 10 other cultists were captured and arrested in December 1969. Until the trial of O.J. Simpson in 1997, no other case in recent American history had attracted quite so much media and public interest. The attorney Irving Kanarch drew attention to the freak-show aspect of Manson's hearing: "There's probably been more publicity in this case than there has been in any other case in the history of American jurisprudence. You have a situation in which the trial is being used for entertainment." During the investigation two 'hit-lists' came to light and were read before the members of the jury. One list had been sent to the *Vacaville Reporter* and concerned those responsible for the felling of the redwood trees, including President Carter and prominent people in the lumber industry. The second list, pertinent to Tom Jones, featured celebrities of whom Manson wished to dispose in order to progress his own career.

"When that Charles Manson thing came to light – the Sharon Tate murders – I was on the list of those who were going to be knocked off," Tom revealed later to the press. According to Tom, Manson harboured plans to murder some of his other celebrity victims by burning and skinning them. But the cult leader had devised a more subtle ploy to trap the star of *This Is Tom Jones*. "They explained the way they were going to do it. One of his followers – apparently she was a very pretty girl – said that she was going to come to a concert and get backstage. If I took her back to the hotel to make love to her, she was going to cut my throat."

For many following the reports of the long and stormy trial, it signalled the end of the peace and free love of the hippy era. Much of the coverage was kept away from the Tom Jones camp, in particular shielding Linda and Mark. However, it was impossible to screen totally the biggest trial of the century, which, with its extortionate expense of $725,000 still ranks as the second most costly in Californian history. Derek Watkins' wife Wendy remembers, "I was so scared, it was really scary. We were very aware of the Manson thing." The case's anti-hero has been imprisoned ever since, regularly attending numerous unsuccessful parole hearings.

In spite of the darker side to life as a celebrity in 1969, Tom's career was on the up and up – nothing seemed to be able to stop him. Those who knew of Tom's humble roots in Wales delighted in the fact that during this year alone the singer's earnings exceeded $2,400,000. This was not necess- arily unexpected for a superstar of Tom's stature, whose concerts were sell-outs and whose records continued to consistently chart well, but perhaps more poignantly the sum was reported as being 50 times more than his father had earned during his career as a coal miner. Tom had already made the record books with his television contract from ATV for *This Is Tom Jones*, and when his deal was renegotiated with Decca in England the same year, he was offered another six-year contract and the highest royalty rate ever set for a recording artist.

One aspect of the success of the US releases on the Parrot Records label can be attributed directly to Tom. The singer thought carefully about the sequencing of his music and requested that the LPs were neatly divided into two sides; one crammed with Tom's favoured rock'n'roll belters and the other showcasing his more gentle ballads. "I came up with the idea based on my own experience," Tom explained in an interview. "When people get into a groove, they want to keep that groove going, they don't want to keep jumping from 'Memphis Tennessee' to 'When The World Was Beautiful', and both tunes were on my first album."

In the golden year of 1969, with numerous awards from the last four years under his belt, Tom appeared to have taken over not just his home country but the rest of the planet besides, and it was time for the singer to find a palace befitting his king-like status.

"I associate Wales more with my youth and childhood than anything," Tom said in a *Daily Mirror* special in 1969. "I had a lot of happy times there but it is difficult for me to go back. I haven't been home for nearly three years. Even then, I discovered a great problem when I went into local pubs. If I ordered drinks all round, everybody thought I was flash. If I didn't, they said I was mean!" It was quite obvious to all concerned that the last thought on Tom's mind was a return to the homeland of which he normally appeared to be so proud. Instead, accompanied by Gordon, Engelbert and their families, he settled on the grandeur of the sprawling estate of St George's Hill in Weybridge, Surrey.

Nicknamed 'Heartbreak Hill' because of the high turnover of famous rock and film star inhabitants including John Lennon, fellow Beatle Ringo Starr and Cliff Richard, St George's Hill remains to this day a conversely magnificent yet peculiar place to live. While it could hardly be described as a 'neighbourhood' with each property required by the St George's Hill Housing Association to possess at least one acre of land, the area is strikingly beautiful in a very English sense. A tennis club and the famous 25 acre golf course both help to attract a high influx of wealthy residents, resulting in many visible security measures, including a small army of grim-faced guards. The restrictions imposed by such riches back in the late Sixties led to an almost total lack of community spirit, with residents rarely glimpsing one another, no children playing together and everybody travelling around in limousines no matter how short the distance they needed to travel.

It seemed perfect for Tom. Although, as Jimmy Tarbuck recalls, he adamantly refused to be drawn onto the golf course ("It's the one thing we disagree on"), Tom was otherwise delighted to move straight into an oak-panelled mansion by the name of Tor Point, which by the early Seventies was worth nearly half a million pounds. Almost simultaneously, Gordon moved into a comparably extravagant property which he nostalgically christened Little Rhondda, and Engelbert paid £45,000 for a slightly dilapidated mansion called Glenbrook, and spent a further £30,000 on renovation.

Tom lost no time in placing his indelible stamp on his new home. Incorporating elaborate security precautions, he installed a pair of mighty electrically operated iron gates, decorating the posts with dragons – the mythical winged monster which has long been the traditional mascot of Wales. Noting the recent arrival of a few extra inches on his waistline, Tom ordered the construction of a health complex in the grounds incorporating a gymnasium, showers, a sauna, a squash court and a huge L-shaped swimming pool with another Welsh dragon fashioned in a red mosaic on the bottom. A portrait of Queen Elizabeth II adorned an inner wall. Indulging his immense passion for films, Tom turned the top floor of his mansion into a private home cinema. Celebrity friends including Jimmy Tarbuck were invited to compete in his 'pool room', which housed an expensive, brand new, full-size snooker table.

Gordon and Jo Mills' house, Little Rhondda, situated half a mile from Tor Point, was no less impressive. Presiding over three acres of land (which was actually relatively small for a property in St George's Hill), Gordon too could now boast his own swimming pool, which unlike Tom's was indoors with an underground viewing gallery. Here, a glass wall below the pool's waterline enabled guests to sit and admire others diving. He and Jo set about their own slightly bizarre decoration, painting entire rooms bright purple, and Gordon began to assemble his own private mini zoo, housing tigers and orang-utans among other exotic creatures. But the single most important aspect of Gordon's new home was the conversion of a single storey, flat-roofed extension into a high-tech recording studio. It was ideally designed to save the busy manager the time and money spent on creating new albums for Tom, Engelbert and his occasional other acts. The studio sat rather incongruously and unattractively next to the beautiful main house, but now Gordon had complete control.

While Gordon was occupied with building, the extra space in the new Jones residence allowed Tom to add to his various 'status' collections with renewed vigour. His accumulation of weaponry including pistols, muskets, knives and swords was now augmented by entire suits of armour.

During this period he initiated a new hobby of investing in fine wines, he bought a yacht, and his garage housed a Rolls Royce, a Bentley and a Mercedes Benz sports car. Tom, Gordon and Engelbert were famously photographed sitting astride their customised Rolls Royces (Tom's number plate spelling 'TJ BIG') in front of ATV studios; the epitome of *nouveau riche* affluence.

In 1967 Tom had bought a racehorse named, rather pessimistically, Walk On By. He was now able to expand this pursuit by putting some money into funding some stables. "I love the races," he divulged later. "For a long time I owned a number of race horses. It's an expensive hobby when you just keep sending cheques to trainers." Unfortunately Tom's celebrity brought difficulties of its own to the racetrack. "The problem with betting on the ponies is that the people at the track were seeing me bet on a particular horse and thinking, 'Ah, Tom Jones must be in the know,' and if they lost they would walk up and just start abusing me!" During their time in Weybridge, Tom and Linda also acquired a black Labrador unimaginatively called Blackie who each day accompanied Tom on a competitive early morning run around the St. George's Hill golf course.

When he wasn't enjoying the benefits of his own personal lounge bar in Tor Point, Tom enjoyed a tipple at any one of the many pubs in and around Weybridge. Chris Hutchins engagingly remembers drinking in The Flintgate in Walton-on-Thames. Tom so loved the atmosphere of this particular pub that, according to Chris, he stayed there for three nights over one Christmas without once returning home. This may well be the same Christmas binge that Jimmy Tarbuck will never forget, at which Engelbert was also present, at least in the early stages. After drinking one too many pints of bitter with killer champagne chasers, Tom and Jimmy had to escort Engel back to Glenbrook because he couldn't stand the pace and collapsed.

Jimmy also recalls another Christmas when he and Tom were both top-drawer celebrities and the pair accepted a somewhat unlikely invitation to judge a fancy dress competition at a local pub. Tom and Jimmy enjoyed being seen simply as normal people, going out for a pint of beer like ordinary men. Chris Hutchins explains that it was in fact relatively easy for a star of Tom's magnitude to enjoy such an outing in Weybridge as the general public would either be completely in awe and leave them alone, or they would want to be seen as 'hip' themselves, pretending it was no big deal to be standing next to the likes of Tom Jones or Engelbert Humperdinck.

Tom initially revelled in his respite from touring and being able to settle into his new luxury home. "It's marvellous at first, like recovering from an illness. Everything's peaceful and relaxing. But it's not long before I'm champing at the bit and longing to get out in front of an audience again." For up to nine months at a time, Tom would be away on predominantly American tours, while Linda would find herself lonely and isolated, especially after Mark became old enough to join his father for the odd holiday. When he was away, Tom would always make a point of speaking to Linda every day on the telephone, but to her immense frustration, she was never able to initiate contact herself, as any call from Tom's 'wife' would be instantly dismissed by hotel switchboard staff as an impersonation.

So Linda chose to stay at home alone, concealed behind the heavy iron gates of Tor Point. Unable to drive and unwilling to join Tom on his tours, she busied herself with her new abode and took comfort in Tom's music and his daily phone calls from America. "I remember my wife and I went over there one morning to see her socially," says Chris Hutchins. "I'll never forget it. Linda was in this big house on St. George's Hill, she was there dancing, dusting – she had a dressing gown on and she was dancing along to Tom's records with a duster in one hand and a bottle of Moët in the other!"

In a rare and revealing interview with Rona Barrett in June 1974, Linda explained how she felt jealous and embarrassed by the female attention lavished on Tom at his concerts and on the set of *This Is Tom Jones*. "There were a lot of glamorous and beautiful girls appearing with Tom in his show . . . So I even began to think I wasn't good enough to be his wife. Soon, I'd become so self-conscious that I wouldn't even answer the front door unless I was wearing make-up and felt I was looking my very best." She went on to credit her husband with noticing this unnerving change in her behaviour and doing his best to alleviate her anxiety. "He helped me sort out my problems – and reassured me that I would never have to worry about him."

As Tom was unlikely to reduce his ever-increasing workload and spend more time at home, Linda came to the conclusion that she would be happier to stay in a place she knew and could make her own. Even when she did travel to America to be with her husband, members of the touring party remember that she would prefer to stay behind in the hotel room most of the time, rather than join Tom in his wildly extravagant parties. Marion, the wife of Johnnie Spence, Tom's popular musical director, was great friends with Linda during this period and describes her as an incredibly sweet, well-mannered lady who loved her tiny family very much. While Tom, Johnnie and Gordon were off gallivanting across the States, Linda, Marion and Gordon's wife Jo would frequently team up and amuse themselves. Often they would meet up at Linda's house and swim in her outdoor pool, favouring Tor Point on a sunny day because Gordon and Jo's pool at Little Rhondda was under cover. Their favourite restaurant was in nearby Fairmile, but the three would equally enjoy homemade picnics on a day trip out with all their children. "They were great times, wonderful times," Marion recalls fondly.

Although surrounded by her select group of friends and taking pleasure from frequent visits to and from her family in Wales, Linda still had an immense amount of spare time left on her hands. One might ask why, with the security of her new-found wealth, she did not pursue a career, or develop a favourite hobby into a money-spinner. The answer could well lie with Tom's attitude towards 'career women'. In a previous biography he was quoted as saying: "I must say there is nothing wrong with them. I just wouldn't want my wife to be one. Women can do what they want and get men's jobs with equal pay. I'm all for that. There has to be female truck drivers, female school teachers, female doctors, female dancers, female strippers and entertainers. They're all fine with me. I just wouldn't marry one."

When Tom and Gordon were in Weybridge they too surrounded themselves with immediate family and close friends, forming an 'inner circle' similar to Elvis Presley's 'Memphis Mafia' and imitatively nicknamed 'The Valley Mafia' or even 'The Tafia'. Tom shared his financial success with his extended family, moving his sister Sheila and brother-in-law Ken Davies down to Surrey to join the rest of the Woodwards. Marion Crewe, the sister of Tom's childhood friend Dai Perry, was 18 months younger than Sheila, and while Tom and Dai would knock about together, their older siblings had spent some time in each other's company. Marion describes Sheila as a "very quiet girl, a very nice person," who had sadly never been able to have children of her own. Sheila and her husband Ken lived in a small lodge in the extensive grounds of Tor Point and Ken was employed by Tom as a general gardener-cum-handyman for the estate. Ken Davies would disgrace the Woodwards when he left Sheila for another woman while they were living in Weybridge – an act deemed so dishonourable by the traditions of the staunchly upright family that they banished him from their vicinity.

On the whole Tom and Linda spent most of their spare time with Gordon and Jo. "Friday nights were great, because Gordon and Tom went to an Indian restaurant in Hammersmith," says Chris Hutchins, remembering a certain weekly ritual. The star and manager would pay for the meal on alternating nights, soon including Chris into their long-standing rota.

Of all the wives, Jo Mills had the highest profile, thriving on the social whirl and causing quite a stir within the group. As could be expected of a former Las Vegas Bluebell girl, dancer and model she was very attractive and exuded immense style and glamour. This enchanted many of the men, as Derek Watkins recalls, "She was a very elegant lady, she would turn men's heads when she walked into a room." The women were sometimes left with a somewhat different impression as Wendy Watkins comments, "She was very aloof."

Once the group was established in Weybridge, the ebullient Jo set about becoming the perfect hostess, entertaining her husband's clients and friends and throwing lavish dinner parties. Unfortunately her well-meaning willingness did not always quite hit the mark. Members of the social circle commented that she would often drink more than was considered acceptable for a woman, prompting her to act in a manner that might be considered unladylike. While it was perfectly normal for the husbands to become embarrassingly drunk, the fact that Jo was the only woman to join them ensured that everyone present remembered it.

Like Linda, Jo did not tour much, partly because of her commitments to their son and four daughters, but mainly because Gordon rarely allowed her to accompany him. It was apparent to insiders that Jo simply adored her husband and tried her utmost to please him, but she found it increasingly difficult to cope with his frequent rages, during which he would often verbally bully her. Gordon would shout at Jo if she got something wrong, which only served to upset her and consequently caused her to make things even worse.*

Jo, Linda and Marion took solace in each other's company during the strained periods when their husbands were on tour. Like Jo, Marion had also previously been a dancer and a model, uncannily at the same agency as Jo. She went on to become an actress, notably appearing in the popular Sixties and Seventies *Carry On* series of British comedy films. Marion had met the exuberant Johnnie Spence at a show in Blackpool where he was a piano player. "I liked him," she recalls. "He had a personality that was sort of shy, but it wasn't shy."

Johnnie was a very accomplished musical director by the time Gordon approached him in the late Sixties. Gordon had heard one of Johnnie's big band broadcasts on Radio Luxembourg one evening and knew immediately that he wanted him to work with at least one, if not all, of his stars. At the time Johnnie was composing film soundtracks for B-movies and Hammer horror films, but he had worked in the pop field with luminaries like George Martin and The Beatles, Ella Fitzgerald and Tony

* Jo Mills initially agreed to be interviewed for this book, but after a three-month period of telephone correspondence, she declined, citing her children's wishes as an explanation.

Bennett. Gordon eagerly signed him to lead his own orchestra on *This Is Tom Jones* and also to join Tom on his regular US tours from the late Sixties onwards.

Johnnie brought with him a great element of fun to the close circle of friends, frequently providing the base for numerous anecdotes. "He was a wild guy," says Jimmy Tarbuck. "Every day was party day for John." In keeping with his party attitude, Johnnie could drink with the best of them. "He was a great character," chuckles Big Jim Sullivan. "We always knew that when John had that one too many he'd drop his trousers. No matter where he was, no matter who was around, there John would stand with a drink in one hand and a cigarette in another, and his trousers round his ankles!" Chris Hutchins recounts that Johnnie was always jovial and would keep everybody laughing with witty one-liners. Session drummer Terry Jenkins boasts of his musical director: "He could entertain anyone, be it a duke or a dustman! Everyone liked him. And a wonderful musician." Marion illustrates how her husband would keep in touch with his band: "Johnnie always made a point of having a drink one night each week with all the musicians."

That Johnnie was multi-talented did not go unnoticed. "He was a fantastic musician, a great arranger," elaborates Derek Watkins. "He was a friend of everyone – a soothsayer, a problem solver; he had time for everybody." But it was with Tom that Johnnie struck one of his greatest friendships. Cynthia Woodard, who was to join The Blossoms later in the Seventies, could appreciate their unique relationship from a singer's point of view. "Johnnie was like Tom's soul mate," she says. "Because he was the musical director he knew Tom's voice. He knew how to bring out the best in him, how to bring the soul out of him and portray a song so people could relate to him."

Aside from the regular musicians, the final member of this 'inner circle' was Bill Smith, Gordon's friend and accountant, who was half English and half Indian. Gordon had found a kindred spirit in Bill, based on their similar Anglo-Indian background, but the numbers man could not have been more different personality-wise. "He was the one who used to amaze me because he still had this kind of Asian humility," says Big Jim today. Bill was a frequent member of the touring party and was included in all the group's events. Chris remembers that they would all go out *en masse* every New Year's Eve. Beginning the evening at Bill's house in Ruislip they would usually end up at the celebrity nightclub, Tramp. If they stayed out too late, which they invariably did, the remainder of the night was spent at the Westbury Hotel.

★　★　★

The inclusion of Gordon's accountant in their social life reflected their growing need for prudent monetary advice. Both Tom and Engelbert were losing thousands of pounds each month in tax to the Inland Revenue. Between them Gordon Mills and Bill Smith devised the formation of a public company to allow far greater tax-free expenses such as running classic cars, staff wages, utility bills and investment in property. The main risk of forming a company whose greatest assets were pop stars would be if Tom or Engelbert dwindled in public esteem, in which case the share value would drop. However, this was a calculated risk as, judging by their past history, the stars were unlikely to fall from favour and the profits gleaned from record sales, live performances and television appearances were constantly flooding in.

Gordon, Tom, Engel and Bill were all to become directors of the company, with Gordon taking on the additional responsibility of chairman. Gordon was by no means experienced in the financial side of business and relied heavily on Bill, whose credentials in the city were crucial to the enterprise. The first executive decision was to name their company. They eventually settled on MAM, which not only stood for Management, Agency and Music, but was an acronym for the person they all loved the most after their wives: their mothers.

Under the new arrangements Tom and Engel became major shareholders, and instead of receiving fees for their performances were issued dividends as a form of 'wage'. In addition the company paid all their expenses. MAM's shares were launched onto the world stock market at a low 66 pence each. They were instantly recognised as a bargain and within a month had increased threefold to £1.85. This rise meant that the value of Tom's 863,750 shares had jumped from just over half a million pounds to £1,597,938 – on share value alone he had made over £1 million within just four weeks.

As the major assets of a public company, it was necessary to insure Tom and Engel's lives for £3 million each, with a yearly premium of £150,000 to account for the liability of travel. By the early Seventies the company was reporting a Stock Exchange value running in excess of £10 million.

MAM's offices were set up on the corner of New Bond Street, opposite the Westbury Hotel which became their home from home on the nights Gordon, Tom and friends overindulged. MAM occupied the top three floors of the building, dividing the varying arms of the business onto different floors. Gordon Mills, Chris Hutchins, Bill Smith, a back-up accountant and a receptionist inhabited the top floor. Chris had put his own company on a back burner on Gordon's insistence and Bill followed suit, leaving his accounting firm to join the budding empire. The floor below them housed the agents whose job it was to secure the best deals for the company's assets. The two 'court jesters', Colin Berlin and Jerry Maxin were to be found there, along with Colin's sidekick Barry Clayman and other agents, each with his own secretary.

The lowest floor seconded by MAM was for Gordon's latest venture, MAM Records, which was run by Michael Jeffery. Forming a record label was the logical next direction to take, now that Gordon had his studios situated conveniently in the extension to Little Rhondda. Similarly Gordon's on-again, off-again dalliances with managing other artists were fully incorporated into the 'Management' of the MAM title. The first act launched on the exciting new label, under the catalogue number 'MAM 1', was the appropriately Welsh rocker Dave Edmunds with his chart topping version of Smiley Lewis' 'I Hear You Knocking'. Originating from Cardiff, Dave Edmunds had coincidentally hooked up with former Squires guitarist Mike Gee, who both featured on the single and played with Dave for many years to come.★

Peter Sullivan had left the Decca label back in 1965 in order to form a company called Air with three other prominent producers including trusted Beatles' aide George Martin. The Air Studios were set up initially in Oxford Circus and then in Hampstead. Peter continued to work for Gordon, Tom and Engelbert being credited as 'Producer for Gordon Mills Productions' and the partnership had flourished for five years until 1970. At that point Gordon suggested that MAM could take over Air and the two companies entered negotiations. However this potential acquisition remained unresolved, as Peter recalls: "MAM and Air were not compatible in a business sense." The parties involved were unable to reach a mutually satisfactory agreement and Peter lost touch with the stars he had intrinsically helped to create. By a strange twist of fate Peter Sullivan, who had initially so vehemently dismissed country music as a suitable direction for Tom Jones with 'Green Green Grass Of Home', now lives in Nashville, the very heart of American country & western music.

Meanwhile Gordon was exerting a strong control over the main MAM shareholders. Now they were all part of the same business, it was inevitable the relationship should shift up a gear. Even though their status had been increased with their shareholding, both Tom and Engel were still very much in awe of their charismatic, authoritarian superior. "He had that arrogance," says Chris Slade on the subject of Gordon's individualistic approach. "It's just like an acquired thing. He was probably very insecure, because people who usually have that arrogance are insecure. Maybe he felt that that's the way he got his power."

★ Equally implausible was the fact that Vernon Hopkins had teamed up as bassist with one of Gordon's erstwhile acts, Leapy Lee, for a number of years.

Gordon's aura of superiority and didactic manner prevented Tom, Engel and anyone else involved in MAM from challenging his command. Even when the stars seemed unstoppable in the public eye, in private they were always mindful to show their manager the utmost respect. Chris Hutchins illustrates an early indication of the developing balance of egos: "I sat in his [Gordon's] office with him one day very early in our relationship, and Gordon went quiet and he looked at the phone. I said, 'What's the matter Gordon?' And he said, 'Tom never rings me.' Now Tom only lived 500 yards up the road and I said, 'Why don't you ring him?' He said, 'That's not the point! *He's* supposed to ring *me!*' And that was the way it was with Gordon. He had to be the boss."

Chris also remembers that Tom wouldn't always bow down to Gordon and the pair of them would have screaming rows, which led to threats of walking out and terminating the relationship. When Tom was outside of Gordon's jurisdiction, notably during the lengthy periods on tour, he was prone to being swayed towards the potential benefits of changing his management, particularly after a few drinks. When Robin Gibb boldly left his two brothers to break away from The Bee Gees and pursue a solo career in March 1969, Chris Hutchins had taken over his management. Tom and Chris spoke on several occasions, with differing degrees of seriousness, about the possibility that Chris could do the same for Tom.

One night in the Penthouse Club in Mayfair, Chris and Tom drunkenly brought up the subject once more. Tom was performing at the London Palladium and Chris suggested altering the stage to have a catwalk running through the audience. As Jon Scoffield was producing the show at the time Chris proposed that Jon might be able to arrange it especially for Tom. "Tom said, 'Right. That's it. You're my manager!'" recalls Chris. But nothing was to come of this discussion as the next morning Tom telephoned Chris, and brushed off the implications of the previous night's conversation with, "Nice little drink we had last night, wasn't it?!" To Chris it was clear that Tom's occasional eagerness to find another manager wasn't because he thought that Gordon was swindling him out of any money, just that more could be done to further his career in the wake of MAM's new business activities.

Gordon divided his time fairly evenly between his two multi-million earners, and although he dabbled in the management of other minor acts, he was not seriously looking to take on another big player. Singer/songwriter Gilbert O'Sullivan had other ideas. He wrote a bold introductory letter to Gordon in 1969 explaining how determined he was to succeed in the world of show business and why, therefore, he had chosen Gordon to manage him (Tom and Engel had at that point achieved between them a staggering total of 23 Top 20 UK singles). Along with his astounding proclamation, Gilbert enclosed a demo tape and a photograph of himself.

This dogmatic approach belied a far more desperate reality in which the 23-year-old Irishman had spent several years recording without success. His début single, 'You', had been produced by CBS under his real name Raymond O'Sullivan, but it had sunk without trace, and after 18 barren months his relationship with the record company ended. Phil Solomon then signed the newly renamed Gilbert O'Sullivan to his label, Major Minor, releasing two singles, but both failed to make any chart impression. They parted company, largely because, like Tom before him, Gilbert experienced a personality clash with Phil.

Gilbert was incredibly similar, in both his physical appearance and personal mannerisms to the entrepreneur he next chose as mentor, but he lacked his idol's worldly knowledge. Gordon was naturally flattered and somewhat intrigued by the bolshie letter. Agreeing to meet Gilbert he was greeted by the slightly ridiculous vision of a childlike man in short trousers, sporting a pudding-basin haircut topped with a cloth cap. Gordon still possessed his extraordinary ability to perceive a potential star and was convinced. Although neither Tom nor Engelbert was impressed when he played them Gilbert's tape, he persisted with the challenge. He could sense the new boy's innate talent, which combined with his enthusiasm, ambition and quirky image he felt would surely succeed.

Gordon offered the rather naïve and equally desperate Gilbert not only a management deal, but an agency contract too. In February 1970 Gilbert happily agreed that Gordon Mills would become his exclusive manager for five years, which would be extended to seven if the partnership proved to be a success. A few months after signing the contract Gilbert admitted to the *Evening Standard*: "When I signed I didn't even look at it. If you respect somebody, and they're going to manage you, then you have to trust them. That's the most important thing."

The signing of Gilbert presented Gordon with a classic case of conflicting interests. Normally a manager is responsible for obtaining the optimum deal he can with a record company, but if the manager owns the record company, how can he negotiate with himself? Similarly, the manager should negotiate with an agent over concert appearances, but again MAM was both Gilbert's management and agent. Gilbert was to suffer extensively because Gordon's stranglehold enveloped every aspect of his career from the recording studio to live performances, and the hapless songwriter received no independent advice.

Unlike Tom or Engelbert who were licensed by MAM to Decca, Gilbert was signed directly to MAM Records. What the eager singer failed to notice in the small print was that while Gordon had suggested Gilbert should cover his own expenses in return for a drop in the managerial

percentage, Gordon was still invoicing him for the 20 per cent management commission. Although Gordon promised to protect him from unfair
exploitation and act solely in Gilbert's best interests, the deal was
extremely restrictive. Gilbert was not entitled to any advances on the sales
of his singles and his royalty rate was a pitiful five per cent in the UK and
3.3 per cent elsewhere.*

He fared no better on the publishing deal. By 1972 Gordon had
obtained the copyright to Gilbert's entire output for the maximum length
of time possible. Gilbert was told that he would have to wait for the best
part of a decade before he could own the copyright to his songs. Instead
Gordon offered him joint publishing terms on a 50:50 copyright ownership basis. Simon Garfield explains the exact details in his excellent study
Expensive Habits: "[The] agreement had not materialised even by May
1974 after nine Top 20 hits and three Top Five albums. A board of
directors meeting noted that in that month a new 50:50 MAM/Gilbert
O'Sullivan copyright ownership company, into which all MAM's existing
copyrights would be placed, would be established 'In recognition of what
had always been an obligation of the company (MAM Music Publishing
Ltd) to Gilbert O'Sullivan as expressed by . . . the chairman (Gordon
Mills).'" Needless to say, the company was never formed and MAM
retained absolute control over Gilbert, permitting Gordon to simply dictate the content of all contracts.

Gilbert was even unable to talk to the media without Gordon's written
consent. As suffocating as the deal may have been when he signed the
binding contract in February 1970, Gilbert O'Sullivan of course had yet to
break into the charts with his own songs, and strictly in terms of reversing
this situation Gordon proved himself a worthy manager in every way.

Lacking Tom and Engelbert's sexual appeal or blistering singing voice,
Gilbert's schoolboy style and demeanour was initially much ridiculed
by the press. His first single under Gordon's management, 'Nothing
Rhymed', was the third release on the MAM record label in November
1970. This intelligent song, with lyrics based on amusing wordplay,
climbed into the Top 10 by December, gaining both teacher and pupil
some grudging respect. The *Financial Times* described his launch on the
stock market as a ray of hope for Gordon's public company which had
declined somewhat after its initial success: "Given the slide in MAM's
shares this year, much may depend on his [Gilbert's] new postage. But as
MAM's publicity describes him as, 'Frail, anaemic looking, usually wears
jacket and trouser two sizes too small, with a very unusual haircut,' we can

* Other labels would probably have offered something in the region of eight per cent with
increments.

only assume that his voice and music must be quite something."

Over the next two years Gilbert O'Sullivan achieved further Top Five hits with 'No Matter How I Try', 'Alone Again (Naturally)', 'Ooh-Wakka-Doo-Wakka-Day', 'Clair' and 'Get Down'. He emerged in the early Seventies as one of the most commercially successful singer/songwriters, briefly challenging Elton John's throne as Britain's premier export in this field. Gordon too furthered his reputation through the partnership and was named as the Top Singles Producer by *Music Week* in 1972.

In return Gordon truly treated his latest protégé like a son. Shortly after signing the contract Gordon literally brought the erstwhile struggling composer into the fold when Gilbert progressed from Notting Hill to join the rest of the MAM clan in Surrey. He moved into the grounds of Gordon's Weybridge estate, occupying a bungalow named Ebony House, which although small in comparison with the others, was still valued at a distinguished £85,000. Gilbert, basically a family man at heart, quickly formed a close friendship with Jo Mills and her five children, leading him to write 'Clair' in honour of their youngest daughter for whom he would often baby-sit.

Gilbert chose a frugal lifestyle, requesting that Gordon pay him a wage of just £10 a week, the same amount he had earned in his previous job as a clerk. He then asked Gordon to pay all his royalties into a company set up for Gilbert to dip into on a rainy day. Rather than purchasing a new car, the ever resourceful Gilbert simply bought Tom Jones' old Mercedes. The relationship among the three singers was unusual. Tom and Engel seemed to thrive on the extravagant lifestyles they had attained, jostling each other for pole position, while Gilbert seemed content to remain quietly in the background. His rapid introduction to fame did not appear to change him, and he was only ever grateful for his situation and complimentary about his manager. The adulation did not stop there as several people have drawn similarities between Gordon and Gilbert, suggesting that the latter was in many ways a clone of the former, particularly in his manner, speech and appearance.

Gilbert has always maintained his carefully contrived image and has amusingly described himself on occasion as a character akin to Mickey Mouse or a commercial product: "I'm a soap powder. I'd love to see myself on sale in shops. It tickles me . . ."★

★ ★ ★

★ Staying true to his cheerful nature, when the authors approached Gilbert O'Sullivan for an interview for this book, his pleasant response was: "I like Tom, I think he's a great singer, that's all I have to say."

As Tom Jones triumphantly entered the Seventies, he produced a flurry of Top 20 hits: 'Without Love (There Is Nothing)' originally performed by one of Tom's teenage inspirations, Clyde McPhatter, which reached UK number 10 and US number five in January and February 1970 respectively; 'Daughter Of Darkness', another sensational Reed extravaganza, which hit UK number five in May and US number 13; and 'I (Who Have Nothing)', an overly melodramatic vehicle showcasing Tom's vocal range which got to UK number 10 and US number 23 in November.

One song that tragically did not materialise could well have made pop history. Despite his long-standing, and some might say justified, dislike of John Lennon, Tom had kept up a friendly acquaintance with Paul McCartney, and had always joked with him about when Paul would proffer a self-penned composition for Tom. During 1969, as The Beatles were falling apart, Paul called Tom to say that he had a song in mind for him called 'The Long And Winding Road'. Paul imposed the condition that Tom could only have the song if it was to be his very next single release. Unfortunately Tom's hands were tied as he was contractually obliged to release 'Without Love (There Is Nothing)' just a few weeks later. As Tom was unable to meet his terms, Paul recorded the song with The Beatles for their final album *Let It Be*. This LP had been intended as a back-to-the-roots conclusion to their career, but Phil Spector's overproduced mix incorporating strings and a choir on this particular track greatly angered Paul McCartney and further contributed to the growing rift within The Beatles. Needless to say, as a Beatles' single, 'The Long And Winding Road' topped the US chart in June 1970. Tom and Paul were not to fulfil a working collaboration for a further 29 years.

In March 1970 the press announced details of a UK tour for Tom, backed by a 35-piece orchestra led by Johnnie Spence, with Big Jim Sullivan on lead guitar and Chris Slade on drums. The other artist on the bill was Jimmy Tarbuck, who was only too happy to provide risqué gags as a prelude to Tom's performance. Five British cities were to be included on the tour and typically all tickets were soon sold out. A charity element was introduced, with revenue from the concerts partially supporting The Kidney Trust and the Newport County Football Club, of which Tom was honorary president.

The tour opened at the Liverpool Empire on March 13. Tom was noticeably slimmer and much appreciated by the almost exclusively female audience, who excitedly sang along to Johnnie Spence's overture medley of Tom Jones' hits. The hysteria was reported in the press by, among others, Phil Symes, who wrote in *Disc & Music Echo*: "Despite long periods in the United States and infrequent singles, Tom Jones Mania is still as strong as ever and shows no signs of declining."

Tom then flew to America to continue breaking box office records, opening on May 22. His set was adapted to include the Count Basie Orchestra, who had just returned from the UK where they had accompanied Frank Sinatra and Tony Bennett. Tom's reported earnings for the 32 concerts were $3 million, with a minimum guarantee of $2,400,000 based on a jaw-dropping fee of $75,000 per night. *NME* indicated that Tom was making as much as $150,000 on top of this fee to appear in New York's Madison Square Garden, while the Seattle Coliseum received cheques totalling $300,000 on the first morning tickets went on sale for Tom's concert on August 1. This incredible popularity extended world-wide with Tom fans emerging from non-English speaking countries as far flung as Israel, Norway, Spain, Sweden, Yugoslavia, Hungary, Holland, France, Finland, Denmark, Belgium and Czechoslovakia.

"I saw Tom when he was a nobody," boasted Gordon Mills in the *Pelham Pop Annual* in 1970. "He agreed I could manage him. Since then it has been work, work, work. Like any businessmen, we started from scratch. Now Tom is the biggest solo entertainer Britain has ever seen. He is bigger than anyone else you can name. He earns more for Britain than any other artist. He has topped the bill in Las Vegas and at the Royal Variety Show at the Palladium. He has conquered the world of show business."

Tom's success naturally ensured that those involved in his career both reaped the financial benefits and endured the frustration of travelling. Lynne Rees-Slade was one of the musicians' wives encountering a typical reaction from her husband Chris. "The thing was, whenever you came to a decision for a holiday, they'd had enough of hotels, they didn't want to stay in a hotel, they didn't want to eat in restaurants and they didn't want what would be a nice holiday for us!" she explains. Tom's wife Linda travelled out to America with the rest of the ladies, but it wasn't a bed of roses for her. "She was a very private person," recalls Wendy Watkins. "She'd obviously join him the same as we all did – we all went out when they were in one place for any length of time. But it wasn't much fun going out on the one-nighters."

During her visits to America, Linda began to feel increasingly out of place and would itch to return home to Weybridge. "She was a very normal person," Wendy continues, "not starry or anything, just like any girlfriend who'd go and visit them. She must have got lonely, like we all did, when your husband's away for any length of time." The majority of the wives would meet up with their husbands either in Las Vegas or Lake Tahoe on the border of Nevada and California; both favourite long-term resorts. In the early days Linda would sometimes stay in the States longer than the rest because Mark was that much older than any of the other children, who were still at an age when they demanded constant attention.

Tom's imperial status ensured that he was easily able to commandeer the ultimate accommodation during longer trips like his eight-week stay in Los Angeles. It became common practice for the couples in the touring party, Tom and Linda, Gordon and Jo Mills, Johnnie and Marion Spence and Derek and Wendy Watkins, to rent houses in America for any stay over one month in length. In true Hollywood style Tom chose the house of one of his favourite actors, Paul Newman, which failed to remain a secret for long and attracted a round-the-clock stake-out by fans and press alike. He enjoyed playing to the gallery and Chris Hutchins staged a photo shoot in which Tom posed as the 'New Man in Newman's bed'.

One of the most memorable episodes during this sojourn in the actor's abode was when 13-year-old Mark, who had still to shed his considerable puppy-fat, bounced straight off his trampoline during a party. There was apparently an almighty thud as he came crashing to the ground, and the numerous celebrity friends present all turned to see what had happened to the red-faced and rather poorly teenager. Meanwhile Paul Newman himself was also suffering, penning a bemused note to Tom saying, "Please tell everyone you are renting my Hollywood House, not my Connecticut house which I'm living in now. There is a constant vigil kept outside here by ardent Tom Jones fans who certainly don't want to know *me!*"

While this was just a regular tour for most, it was to be Chris Slade's final outing with Tom. Chris had taken lessons in reading music and the days of criticism were long since buried. "Chris changed overnight from being good to incredible. I thought I was hearing things. It was like a miracle," recalls Vic Cooper. Chris' talent had been noticed in high places and just before Elvis Presley's 1968 comeback special on NBC, he was offered a job drumming for the great man himself, by Elvis' right-hand man Joe Esposito. Chris' ingrained loyalty to Tom led him to turn down this fantastic proposition, but it was not long before various events embittered the now respected drummer. "That is the biggest regret of my career, that I didn't actually say 'Stuff you, I'm going to play with Elvis.'

"To be very candid, I left because I found out that Jim Sullivan was getting three times what I was getting, and I'd been with Tom longer," says Chris. "I was on £150 a week, which was very good money in those days, but I found out that Jim was on something like £450 a week. And so were the other guys." When Chris approached Tom for a pay rise, Tom responded with his perfunctory, "See Gordon." So Chris duly tackled the manager who flatly refused. "I said to Gordon, 'Another fifty quid, Gordon, what the hell is that to you? Fifty quid a week?!' " Chris believes that Gordon was still thinking of him as a naïve eighteen-year-old who wouldn't complain about surviving on peanuts. Chris walked out to the tune of Gordon's familiar threat: "You'll never work again!"

"After months of silence I got this phone call. 'Better pack your bags then.' It was Gordon. 'What do you mean?' I exclaimed. 'Well, the tour starts in three weeks, better pack up.'" In order to avoid a further confrontation and to retain his drummer on the same meagre wage, Gordon was pretending to have forgotten that Chris had left at the end of the last tour. "He would never have said, 'We'd like you to come back and be Tom's drummer', it was like, 'Do what I tell you!' I said, 'I'm sorry Gordon, I've already signed a contract with Manfred Mann, I can't go.' I hadn't signed a contract." Gordon hung up the phone and likewise the relationship, "All because I hadn't said, 'Oh three bags full Gordon!'"

During 1970 Tom was glad to provide his parents and sister with a well-deserved holiday in Hollywood. Tom Snr., Freda and Sheila were "royally looked after by the hotel managers," according to Derek Watkins, who wryly noted Tom Snr.'s desire to sit around drinking with the lads, just as if he were in his local working men's club back in Pontypridd. Freda and Sheila seemed to prefer to spend their time sitting together quietly and listening to Tom's tales of superstardom. Those who met and mingled with Tom's extended family found them pleasant and unassuming, as Cynthia Woodard of The Blossoms recalls: "Once you've met them you can see what Tom's like and where he comes from." However it did not escape at least one member of the party that Tom's father was so concerned for the welfare of his son that he could verge on the aggressive when he thought a 'friend' of the singer was being sycophantic.

The adulation progressed in leaps and bounds and by the end of the year Tom received yet another string of awards to add to his already substantial trophy collection. Not only was he voted by the popular men's magazine *Playboy* as Entertainer Of The Year and Top Male Singer, but he was also honoured as Entertainer Of The Year by New York's Friars Club, an elite society of American show business professionals. Much to Gordon's satisfaction, Engelbert Humperdinck continued to mirror his stablemate's career by completing a decent season at the Palladium in November and then returning to sell-out performances in Las Vegas. Over the Christmas period Tom starred in a special gala cabaret attended by the Queen. To his fans' and publicists' great delight, he had earlier taken his own family to Buckingham Palace to meet the Queen and Prince Philip. By the end of 1970 Tom had sold over 30 million discs worldwide and it appeared he could do no wrong.

11

IT'S A MAN'S MAN'S MAN'S WORLD

"I DON'T THINK that Britain has realised how enormous Tom is in the States and the rest of the world," proclaimed Gordon Mills in early 1971. "Britain still hasn't given him all the credit he deserves for becoming the world's number one superstar. He can't get any bigger than right now because he's right at the top."

Few could argue with such bravado and the press continued to plug the 'Golden Boy' image. In January *NME* announced, along with another UK tour, plans for Tom's first 'specialist' album on Decca. Tom had for a long time wanted to record a themed album but had met with resistance from record company executives. "I'd like to do some specialised albums," he said. "A rock'n'roll album, a late-night listening album, a rhythm and blues album, a gospel album, a Christmas album, an album of Welsh songs – but the record companies always want commercial. They want a mix."

The new release, according to *NME*, was to be devoted entirely to "late-night listening, romantic songs" and further albums were already planned for the future, including Tom's choice of a rock LP, and a country LP to please Gordon Mills. *NME* and *Disc* were among the papers reporting much-hyped plans for Tom's film début in the summer, the latter publication awarding him with Top Male Singer and third place in the World section.

Tom's new single, 'She's A Lady', a dashing ode to women written by Paul Anka, rapidly became his highest charting track in the States, hitting number two in April, having achieved number 13 two months earlier in the UK. Tom heard the news just before going on stage for a show in Cardiff and was ecstatic to announce his success to the audience as a precursor to performing the song. The composer of 'She's A Lady', however, was surprisingly less than pleased with his creation's fate. "I can tell you this," Paul Anka sniped in a 1999 issue of *Orange Coast* magazine, "I dislike 'She's A Lady' more than anything I've written. I was writing for Tom Jones. It's a chauvinistic song. I hate to say that, but when you're writing for a guy who's very macho, you want to make it as realistic to the guy as you can." The song's parent album, also entitled *She's A Lady*, was released the following month, reaching number nine in the UK and number 17 in the US.

Along with the almost inconceivable prosperity that was being generated into Tom's bank account came the inevitable tax implications. Under Harold Wilson's Labour Government first elected in 1964, income tax for Britain's highest earners had been increased, and when the Tories under Edward Heath were elected in 1970, they saw no reason to reduce this top level. The tax burden was even greater on what was deemed 'unearned income' (interest on investments), a state of affairs that resulted in many wealthy show business personalities leaving the country for more favourable climes. On March 17, 1971 it was reported in the press that Tom had joined the long list of 'tax exiles' who had contributed a minimum of £7 million to the Inland Revenue. Slowly, an idea was hatched by those most affected within MAM, and Tom's desire to uproot and move permanently to America, where they would take 'only' 50 per cent of his earnings, was whispered of in music circles.

For the meantime, Gordon began to develop a system for MAM's high earners which they would exploit to the full in two years' time. Tax laws dictated that British residents could stay a maximum of 180 days in the US before they were obliged to pay American withholding tax on top of the higher rate British tax. Because the 180 day clock reset itself as soon as the Brits left the country, Tom, Engelbert, Johnnie Spence and the rest of the long-standing musicians began to adopt a policy of hopping in and out of America in order to 'save days'. "They used to go to Mexico for 24 or 48 hours and then come back in," explains Marion Spence-Fox.

A new character joined the crew after an incident involving security man Rocky Seddon, which caused him to leave under a bit of a cloud. ("Rocky got more familiar with the star and less concerned with the job," explains Chris Hutchins.) Tom's old best mate from Pontypridd, Dai Perry, was brought in to fill Rocky's boots as bodyguard. Standing at well over six feet tall with broad shoulders and a rugby-player's physique, Dai was from the outset fiercely protective of his new employer and soon became renowned within the group for his paparazzi-directed catchphrase, "No pictures!"

Dai, who had previously been employed as an excavator driver, was in the process of a messy divorce when Tom called him in Pontypridd and proposed the new way of making a living. Even though Dai was petrified of flying, he jumped on an aeroplane for the very first time and joined Tom in America, pleased to leave all his troubles behind in Wales. "He loved it," enthuses his sister Marion Crewe. "He had the time of his life. He's met more people in his lifetime than thousands do."

Unfortunately Dai soon earned himself a reputation for over-zealousness when it came to protecting his charge. "A guy crashed our party in 1971, in Madison, Wisconsin," Tom told Q magazine of a birthday celebration thrown for him by comedian Pat Henry. "Turns out he was the town's bully. He called Dave, my bodyguard, a pumped-up factory worker, and called me a Welsh coal mining prick. I was half-cut anyway, so I smacked him one, then Dave hit him. We did some damage to this fellow because he wound me up so much. We really worked him over. The police were laughing, they thought he'd been run over by a truck." Although it would seem by this account that Tom and Dai found the incident highly amusing, Chris Hutchins remembers that their victim was in fact severely beaten and Tom was forcibly told to hold back from such violent tendencies, as it was extremely bad for his public image.

For Big Jim Sullivan, the entrance of Dai Perry into the group was problematic for a slightly different reason as it spelled the end of the friendly bond the guitarist had shared with the singer. "There was a dampener for me and that was when Dave Perry came on the tour . . . He was one of Tom's old drinking buddies. He was supposed to be a bodyguard but he didn't have the political know-how to be a bodyguard. Rocky, who was with us before Dave, was a real character who could talk his way out of anything. Whereas Dave would just smack somebody, no questions.

"I remember one night I went up to Tom's room and Dave opened the door and said, 'Yeah?' I said, 'I'm just coming in to see Tom.' 'No you can't come in — Tom's busy.' I said, 'Dave, it's *me*! Tom's *told* me to come up to the room.' After that I never used to bother."

In March 1971 Tom toured the UK, proceeding to Europe and then ultimately on to the US in time for the celebrity opening of a new season at Caesar's Palace on April 16. *Record Mirror* noted that Tom performed a 'cleaner' act than that of the previous year, with fewer lewd comments and suggestive wiggles. The Nat Brandwynne Orchestra provided a sparkling overture, followed by a well-received 20-minute set by The Blossoms. Tom finally emerged to sing songs including 'Save The Country', 'Ain't No Mountain High Enough' and 'Shout'. *Record Mirror* also remarked on Tom's outstanding harmony, enthusiasm and good looks.

Now that it was a public company, MAM could claim extensively for travel costs and Gordon spared no expense for the American leg of the tour, leasing a Boeing 707 jet to transport the entire entourage. "In first class there was Tom Jones, The Blossoms, comedian Pat Henry, and Tom's road manager and manager," remembers Darlene Love. Travelling behind in second class were the rest of the musicians and crew. "We would be up in first class and Lloyd Greenfield and Pat Henry would get together. Pat would go into the bathroom and come out with no clothes on and go, 'Does anybody have the soap?' They would get together and cook up things like that on the plane!"

"I probably got closer to Tom than any of the other ladies on the tour," Darlene continues. "I used to sit right behind him, where he gave me wonderful, wonderful foot rubs." The luxury was extended when they landed, as half a dozen limousines were waiting to pick up the artists from the airport and drive them to the smartest hotels in the city. The rest of the crew were rather less glamorously crammed into tour buses which followed along behind.

Big Jim well remembers the chartered plane and the on-board parties. The band would regularly disappear to the back of the plane for a 'smoke'. On one journey they were joined by an American stranger who was very keen to sample the merchandise. It was only later that Big Jim discovered from Tom that the gentleman was in fact the chief of the narcotics squad for the Los Angeles Police Department.

Tom's well-known antipathy towards drugs persisted even though three of his closest friends, Gordon Mills, Elvis Presley and Chris Hutchins, and many of the band members all indulged to differing degrees. Elvis had started taking medication back in the army in 1958 and it was widely acknowledged behind the scenes that he was becoming increasingly dependant on various prescription drugs. "Elvis never took drugs in front of me," claims Tom. "He'd go into a bedroom and come back like he was drunk. I always thought that was a bit funny."

Chris recalls that both he and Gordon had a particular taste for amphetamines and other such stimulants, but they never actually took enough to risk serious addiction. Chris was at a party celebrating the end of filming for a TV special, when he stumbled upon Elvis snorting cocaine in the bathroom. Elsewhere on the premises, Tom was downing champagne like there was no tomorrow. Elvis joked to Chris that if Tom carried on drinking at such a rate he would surely kill himself. Chris relayed this to Tom, who retorted that if Elvis continued to take such vast quantities of pills, he too would kill himself. Chris said nothing, for he was admittedly guilty of consuming both!

Tom is resolute that he has never even smoked a joint, not even without inhaling. All the interviewees for this book support this statement, but there have been a couple of occasions when Tom has unwittingly dabbled with varying results. "The only thing I ever took just once was pep pills," Tom told the *Daily Mirror* in 1992. "I had a busy schedule and I was knackered. One of the guys from the band gave me some pills and said they'd keep me going for 24 hours." But Tom was unprepared for the strength of such a pill. "I did the show but my eyes were popping out of my head and I didn't get a wink of sleep that night."

He then described another unwanted encounter to *Q* magazine. "I was in the Cromwellian one night with a bunch of people and they were handing around [something] like a Vicks Sinex inhaler, and I had a cold so I said, 'Can I borrow that?' And I sniffed it and I thought, 'Jesus! Bloody Hell!' It was like if you were on a roller coaster! The bloody thing was full of Amyl Nitrate!" Amyl Nitrate was the last thing Tom was likely to request as it is widely used as a sex stimulant.

Despite his cigar habit, Tom is repulsed by the whole business of inhaling, smoking and injecting drugs of any description. On several occasions he has talked about attending show business parties hosted by pop stars like Mama Cass and Lulu, in which most of the guests have been involved in some narcotic activity or another, and Tom has been the only one abstaining. He attributes his staunch attitude to his pride in his Welsh roots and the shame he would feel if drugs got the better of him. He explained in the same insightful *Q* interview: "The thing is – I'm positive because I've thought about this . . . if I became a junkie, or what have you, I wouldn't be able to go home. I wouldn't be able ever to go home again. And that's always kept me sane."

Jimmy Savile confirms that from early in his career through to the heights of his success, Tom abhorred the drug taking that has become synonymous with the rock scene. "I have every respect for him for doing the right thing by being serious and sensible about it – knowing exactly where he was going and not being side-tracked by pushing white powder up his nose or anything like that. He's a straight, clean punter."

In the casinos of Las Vegas, Tom was now fully qualified as one of the three big singers, his status fully elevated to join Elvis Presley and Frank Sinatra. Tom placed his standing within the trio thus: "When Elvis stopped working he was replaced as a teenage idol by The Beatles. I'm not so much a teenage idol as he was and my audience isn't the typical Sinatra audience either. It's somewhere between. Now Elvis has made a come-back and he's singing to the same type of audience as I am."

Indeed Tom's appeal was hardly in question. In a memorable article for *Melody Maker* published on May 1, 1971, music journalist Bernard Barry described the Vegas reaction to the world-famous Welshman. "At nine o'clock every morning lines of anxious people stretch past the card tables and roulette wheels – almost as far as the eye can see. They're hoping to book reservations for the Jones Boy . . . No one has caused so much excitement at this hotel since Sinatra played the Circus Maximus showroom. They say the gambling town is in a grip of economic depression, but while Jones filled the hall there was no sign of hard times."

However, Bernard Barry did not continue in the typically flattering manner of most reviewers who witnessed Tom's shows. "And Tom – sad to say – doesn't appear to have an improvisational bone in his body. He's too clockwork . . . and he is like a push button performer . . . His jacket is off before you can say Pontypridd, he smiles, winks and flirts with the girls, begs a drink of water, something to mop his brow with and has a rather disconcerting habit of trying to crack rather bad 'in' jokes with orchestra leader Johnnie Spence." The review then became even more damning. "Sinatra, Sammy Davis, Dean Martin can all get the feel of an audience quickly and bend with their whims, but Tom seems to lack that talent. If the audience heckles, shouts for a song or does anything unexpected, Jones can't seem to cope. Somehow with Tom Jones you feel that if half of the audience was swallowed up by an earthquake during the show he would swing his hip, cock a leg and go into his next number." Had Tom swum out of his depth among the great performers of Las Vegas?

Performing for an audience that ranged between teens and sexagenarians, Tom would bound on stage drenched in what smelled like half a bottle of his favourite aftershave. But his confidence belied the nerves he sometimes suffered prior to the nightly shows. "I get vocally tired and I get nervous in the stomach – you know, butterflies – when I'm really having trouble with my throat," Tom said in an interview for *Tune-In* publicising his performances at Caesar's Palace. "That's my biggest dread at a live show. Before a show I think, 'Oh God, I hope I can do it.' I get a little nervous then. Otherwise I rarely get pressured, I don't get mentally disturbed . . . It took me a long time to learn to deal with hecklers, especially loud drunks, but I feel confident enough now to cope with anyone."

Shortly after the close of the American leg of his 1971 tour, which had been extended until September, Tom relaxed for his first proper holiday in five years. Having had his fill of jetting off to exotic locations, Tom preferred to spend the time at home in Weybridge. Preceding this he had attempted a short break in Mexico, but had been struck down by a brief yet intense attack of food poisoning during which he was fed intravenously, and so instead he returned to the relative safety of Tor Point and Linda's home cooking.

When Tom returned to Britain in October, a crowd of fans were waiting for him at the airport but before he could greet them he was detained in customs for two hours as the presents he'd bought for his loved ones were seized, and he was charged £275 duty. Back in Weybridge, builders were in the process of completing the leisure complex Tom had finished designing while on tour. The swimming pool area was being extended to incorporate a sun lounge and barbecue pit, to complement the sauna, shower rooms, gym and squash court. A tour brochure called

The World Of Tom Jones gleefully pictured the singer assisting the workmen by carrying a full hod of bricks and driving a dump truck. "I was pleased I could still do it – after all it's years since my shoulder took a hod – but I do keep pretty fit and after all that's the idea of the place," he quipped.

The huge takings and generally excellent reception for the 1971 tour had spelled less and less privacy for the exhausted star. Fans had been dressing up as members of hotel staff and literally hiding in wardrobes in an attempt to meet him, and he was reduced at one stage to donning a false beard or other such disguises in order to leave the venue. The pressure of being in constant demand was finally beginning to get to Tom, who was seen spitting at his pianist and angrily kicking a bunch of flowers that had been thrown on stage during a concert in Pine Knob. Later he dismissed the tetchy display as a joke, explaining that everything had gone wrong that night and he had momentarily snapped, but it was obvious to those who knew him that his 'holiday' in Weybridge was not only well-deserved, but extremely necessary. "Privacy is a word that speaks for itself," he said in another tour brochure. "I spend so much time with the public that it's necessary for me to have some time to myself."

★   ★   ★

Having toured solidly for the best part of a decade and devoted any time spent off the road to the recording studio, Tom was becoming impatient to pursue a career on the big screen. He had been regularly approached by film producers ever since 'It's Not Unusual' reached number one, but Gordon had advised him to hold off for a number of reasons. Gordon's first priority was to firmly establish his star as a singer in the top bracket. Nervous about Tom's acting ability and not wanting him to fall into the same trap as Elvis Presley with his banal celluloid outings, Gordon chose to wait for the right vehicle to launch Tom Jones as an actor.

Tom too was concerned, but after gaining confidence with his three year's hard slog in front of the cameras for *This Is Tom Jones*, he felt he was at last able to tackle a starring role and strongly believed that a film career was his best way forward. "I think it's [*This Is Tom Jones*] good training for a film – the first step – and I'd like to make a good film," he said. "I want to get my career fully established. I think you must act. If you don't a singer can't last in making television appearances and singing alone." In May 1971 Gordon Mills brashly announced plans for *The Gospel Singer*, a film starring Tom Jones opposite Charlene Tilton (Miss Lucy in *Dallas*), and in August that year Herb Jaffe, the Vice President of the United Artists Film Studio confirmed that Tom had been signed to a three picture deal.

The Gospel Singer was the fourth novel written by South American author Harry Crews, but in 1968 his first to be published, instantly attracting a cult following. Crews was a volatile character, who by his own admission had been addicted to heroin and alcohol in the past, and he had a penchant for expressive expletives. This attitude was a characteristic of his work, but Gordon and Tom loved the book regardless and bought the rights to the novel. It was to be adapted for film by the respected screenwriter Robert Thom while Paul Anka was approached to write approximately a dozen songs. The film was intended to be shot in Alabama with a projected $3 million budget, but the date of commencement was continually postponed, year after year.

The story revolves around a golden-haired young man from Enigma, a small and backward farming community in South Georgia. The lead character possesses such an angelic voice that his worshipful fans begin to regard him as God's messenger but he is unable to cope with the overwhelming adulation. He tries to draw attention to his flaws to make the townsfolk understand his plight, but his plan backfires as they turn against him and ultimately lynch him. There were two immediate differences between the character and the budding actor as Tom boasted a head of thick, curly dark hair and an unmistakable Welsh accent. The hair colour could easily be altered with a wig although Tom was a little uncomfortable about such a radical change to his looks, which he considered to be a large part of his appeal. But he was keen to impress everyone involved and had even been practising his southern drawl with private tuition from his close friend, Elvis Presley.

It was a heavy plot line to say the least and Gordon and Tom certainly shared reservations on that account. Their initial concerns were the exaggerated levels of decadence and violence in the script, which they felt were inappropriate for Tom's established audience. In particular they were anxious not to offend fans in America's southern Bible belt. But the biggest hurdle they had to overcome was how Tom's devoted following would react to seeing him killed-off on the big screen. Unsure about this point Gordon suggested that the ending be altered so that his star would live, and Tom heartily agreed. As Harry Crews recalled to Hildred and Gritten for their 1989 biography, "He [Tom] loved it that the guy dies in the book, but he didn't want Tom Jones to die in the movie. He didn't want that audience to see him hanging on the end of a rope. He wanted to change the ending so his character didn't die, which is easy to do, but it does hideous violence to the story."

Unable to reach a happy compromise about the fate of the starring role, shooting never actually commenced. In May 1975 filming was on the verge of starting, but by this time Gordon and Tom had lost the rights to make the movie which had been snapped up by producer Larry Spangler and the company, Global Productions. The disgruntled manager and his would-be actor initiated legal proceedings for $100,000 in damages, claiming that they had made an agreement to procure the rights for $35,000. They had been gazumped by another party at the last minute and were now suing for breach of contract.

A couple of years later reports were still filtering through to the press that Tom had completely withdrawn from *The Gospel Singer*, suggesting that instead he had opted to star in a screen adaptation of Lionel Bart's musical *Maggie May*. That film did not materialise either and as the years dragged on Tom tried to explain in a 1981 interview with *Woman's Own* what, or rather what hadn't, happened. "I think I can act, I really do," he whinged. "Gordon and I bought a property called *The Gospel Singer* about 10 years ago, after I read the book and thought it would make a smashing film, and we've been thinking about it ever since. We tried to get some Hollywood people interested in it at that time, but I think it wasn't right, largely because there was a lot of sex and violence and religion in it, and 10 years ago they just weren't ready for that. It was a bit too strong."

Other fanciful on-screen ideas that failed to see the light were a pairing of Tom and Elvis, a film about Tom's Welsh historical hero Owain Glyndwr, and a starring role as the suavely sophisticated James Bond. What is probably every macho actor's dream did not escape Tom, who fantasised about playing the government secret agent, especially after recording the title song for *Thunderball* back in 1966. "I thought I'd make a good James Bond because I saw similarities between myself and the character portrayed by Sean Connery – an agent who can be a nasty bastard if he wants. I can be a nasty bastard if I want. So I asked to do it – well made it known I was interested – but the word came back that my image as Tom Jones was so powerful the audience wouldn't differentiate. It was a big disappointment," he told the *Radio Times*. Tom's grand ideas of being an on-screen playboy, single-handedly saving the world and attracting numerous women were to elude him, as was any chance of film work for the immediate future.

Elvis Presley on the other hand, had grown sick and tired of starring in vacuous movies by the late Sixties and became desperate to perform live once again. In preparation he had started to frequent the cabaret acts of Las Vegas to gain inspiration for a new act. Although Tom had grown up in awe of The King of rock'n'roll the tables were now turned. Elvis would watch the Welsh singer's show, simply amazed that respectable, middle-aged women could be made to act like sex-crazed teenagers. Elvis had himself caused such frenetic reactions a decade earlier, but the God-fearing country boy now felt that Tom was perhaps too overt. Albert Goldman describes this in his 1981 biography *Elvis*: "The only fault Elvis found in Jones' act was its blatant sex appeal. 'I think that's very lewd,' Elvis would frown. '. . . I was never vulgar.' "

Regardless, Elvis was still incredibly impressed by Tom's vocal ability and was often quoted saying, "Tom is the only man who ever came close to the way I sing. He has that ballsy feeling." It is widely acknowledged that Tom's dynamic stage act in Las Vegas permanently changed the direction of Elvis' career. "You know, it was seeing Tom on stage here in Vegas that gave me the urge to perform again," he admitted. Albert Goldman suggested ways in which Tom influenced Elvis at this time: "What Elvis got from Tom was the trick of working the Vegas show stage . . . Tom gave Elvis those head shakes, the vocal accents on the bridges, the freeze poses at the end of the songs, the trick of wiping the sweat with a cloth and then throwing it out in the house."

Elvis took note of all these little personal touches and added his own gimmick, the incorporation of his beloved karate into his act, imitated in both the elaborate costumes he wore and the high kicks punctuating the climaxes to his songs. Tom liked to tease Elvis, suggesting that karate was akin to the street-fighting he had participated in as a teenager in Pontypridd. They would then enter a schoolboy-like competition, alternately demonstrating intricate moves from their respective sports.

Once Elvis had re-established himself in Las Vegas he starred in his penultimate on-screen role, a fine documentary of his 1970 tour entitled *Elvis – That's The Way It Is*. In the film Elvis is shown receiving a good luck telegram which he reads out for the cameras: "Here's hoping you have a very successful opening and break both legs! Signed, Tom Jones."

When it came to their respective choice of music, Elvis freely admitted to singing 'Delilah' as part of his warm-up routine, but was heard to criticise Tom when he recorded an album of standards saying, "We don't do things like that – we leave it to Frank Sinatra." Elvis thought he had found a perfect song for Tom to add to his repertoire once when the latter was performing at Caesar's Palace in Las Vegas. Elvis, who was staying at the Hilton and had come over to watch Tom's act, was so enthusiastic about the song that instead of waiting for the star to freshen up after the show, he followed him straight into the bathroom. With no visible respect for Tom's privacy, The King of rock'n'roll loomed over the shower door and demoed the melody in his unmistakable baritone.

From the late Sixties onwards, the two compelling cabaret acts often found themselves in the gambling city at the same time and took the opportunity to check out the competition. Their respective publicists also capitalised on the high-powered battle. Chris Hutchins' most spectacular coup was when he lined the path to Caesar's Palace with Welsh Flags to detract from Elvis' presence at a neighbouring venue.

There are many accounts of each star being in the other's audience during the Seventies, but contrary to popular opinion and hopes, the two never performed together. On several occasions Tom would introduce his famous fan, who would be sitting with his wife Priscilla in the front row. Sometimes Elvis would even sneak behind the scenes and creep up on stage unbeknownst to Tom. Jimmy Tarbuck, like Fanita of The Blossoms, remembers that Tom would find it very difficult to recapture the audience's attention after the superstar's unexpected appearance.

In tandem with the public display of camaraderie over the years, Tom and Elvis did actually become close friends, spending time together whenever their busy schedules permitted. On one famous occasion, Elvis invited Tom and a few members of his band to stay with him in Hawaii. Once they were settled he provided them with a guitar each and the whole group jammed throughout the night, covering classics from both the stars' early days. Priscilla herself once said that her increasingly eccentric husband seemed more natural when Tom was around.

As Elvis' fixation with drugs and fast food caused him to balloon in the Seventies, he confessed to Tom that he was unhappy with his weight problems, to which Tom suggested exercise rather than dependence on medication. Tom then recalls seeing Elvis commendably riding an Exercycle whilst ludicrously eating a takeaway pizza, purposefully digging at his own declining physique. The good friends would frequently rib each other about their respective sex symbol statuses and manly attributes, with Elvis affectionately referring to Tom as 'Sock Dick', insinuating that his legendary 'package' was not all real.

Overall the relationship was a close one. Elvis displayed his affection for Tom by giving him several elaborate gifts, ranging from his trademark logo 'Taking Care of Business' lightning bolt, blue Lapis Lazuli medallion to a striking black sapphire ring, to which Tom reciprocated with an exquisite tiger's eye ring. Elvis also gave Tom a copy of a book called *The Impersonal Life*, which explored the idea of God existing inside the human being and a prayer book in which he had written a personal note. Sadly indicative of Elvis' abominable handwriting, no one could ever decipher the inscription inside the front cover.

Elvis wished only to protect his friend, be it spiritually or physically. It was with this in mind that he gave Tom a gun with Tom's name engraved on the barrel, saying, "You need more manpower – you need a gun!" Elvis himself carried a two-shot derringer attached to his left leg when he was on stage in the Seventies and urged that Tom should do the same. But, according to Tom, even Elvis could see the irony when in December 1970, President Richard Nixon awarded The King of rock'n'roll a Narcotics Bureau Badge. "Elvis wanted a federal licence for a gun – he was obsessed with guns and he wanted to be able to carry a gun anywhere,"

Tom explained to Q magazine. "So he had an audience with Nixon and then I saw him in Vegas and he said to me, 'What do you think of this? Nixon has made me a Narcotics Agent!' And he burst out laughing and all his bodyguards burst out laughing. He seemed to think it was hilarious."

Tom outlined their relationship to the *San José Mercury News*: "I think he was the only other person I've spoken to that felt the same way about music as myself, as far as versatility is concerned. And we would sit in his suite and talk about music, and he would have his vocal backing group, and we would sing, mostly. Jam. We had a lot in common, it's just he got mixed up with the drugs situation, which I never did."

It is a shame therefore that these two friends and megastars never recorded their combined talents. Undue caution on the part of their overprotective managers is largely to blame. Even when Elvis encroached on Tom's stage act he was never allowed to sing, as Colonel Tom Parker constantly warned him of hidden microphones recording the performance, thus impinging on Elvis' restrictive record contract. Gordon Mills and Colonel Parker were frequently rumoured to be negotiating to bring all their clients, namely Elvis, Tom, Engel and Gilbert, into one management company. The British music press reported at the time that the Colonel might be taking over Tom's affairs in America, in return for Gordon receiving a percentage of Elvis' takings, but a mutually satisfactory deal could never be agreed.

Of course, Elvis was not the only famous singer befriended by Tom at the beginning of the heady Seventies. During a loquacious interview with Sylvie Simmons for *Mojo* magazine in October 1999, Tom describes how his friendship with Jerry Lee Lewis, his prominent boyhood hero, could escalate into unexpected violence at the drop of a hat. "He wanted us to do a TV special called *Tom And Jerry*, which I thought was cute. But I said, 'You've got to talk to Gordon, my manager, about it.' He [Jerry Lee] had this guy called Cecil, and he said, 'Cecil went to talk to Gordon and he won't discuss it.' I said, 'Well, I'd love to do it but I can't give you an answer right now.'"

At the time Tom and Jerry Lee were indulging in a few beverages at the Hilton hotel in Las Vegas. "He's a bad drunk, Jerry Lee Lewis," Tom continues. "A lot of drinks later, he said, 'To tell you the truth, I think I'm gonna set Cecil on him. I'm gonna set Cecil on Gordon Mills.' I said, 'Look, before that, why don't you set him on me?' And I said, 'Cecil come here!' – I was well oiled by then – so Cecil ran in the bathroom and put the bolt on." Tom goes on to tell a sordid tale of fighting, male pride and knuckle-dusters which culminated in Jerry Lee threatening Tom with a champagne bottle. The pair parted that evening with the dispute unresolved, but the next day the sparring duo made up on the telephone and agreed never to discuss their respective management again.

Tom had forged a good friendship with the legendary Frank Sinatra, both men being fans of each other's work. Frank was famously concerned that Tom would lose his voice prematurely due to his 'over-singing' and high-energy performances. On one occasion he invited Tom back to Palm Springs to 'show him a few tricks'. Tom declined the offer, yet conceded that Frank might have a point. "I've got to realise that I'm not 25," he said. "Frank Sinatra told me I was giving it too much, I'd burn myself out. I said, 'I can't hold back, I've got to explode every time I go on.' And I still give it the full whack but I have to hope I don't look ridiculous."

Muhammad Ali was perhaps a less likely celebrity pal of Tom's. Tom greatly admired the charismatic world heavyweight boxing champion, but Ali's initial reason for meeting the singer was due not to his own reciprocal esteem, but because his young daughter was a die-hard fan. Tom would send the little girl signed copies of his records and in return Ali made him a gift of some treasured boxing gloves. The pair often appeared in public together, occasionally visiting each other on their respective territories and at least one time stepping into the ring at the boxing king's compound in Deer Park, Pennsylvania, where they feigned a knock-out round. Their jokey banter was also broadcast on several chat shows and Tom appeared on the episode of the British TV institution *This Is Your Life* dedicated to Muhammad Ali.

Backstage visits by Tom's supreme sporting hero were but one of the many advantages afforded the singing superstar, whose fame enabled him to meet some of the most important people in the world. "Anybody who was anybody would go to see Tom Jones," says Derek Watkins. "He was the number one artist in the world at that time." Wendy Watkins well remembers the time when astronauts Neil Armstrong and Buzz Aldrin, the first men to land on the moon, dropped in on Tom in his dressing room after a concert. "We got to the top of the stairs to go down to the dressing rooms and they wouldn't let us down because the American Secret Service was there," says Wendy. "Nobody was allowed to go downstairs until Gordon came along."

★   ★   ★

At the close of Tom's tour in 1971, a slight undercurrent of unpleasantness had erupted within the touring party. The Blossoms' contract had come to an end and the girls felt they had become an integral part of the show. As so many others had before, they decided to approach Gordon for a higher salary.

Darlene Love recalls in *My Name Is Love: The Darlene Love Story* that when The Blossoms asked for a pay rise they received a racist and derogatory comment from Tom's management. She elaborates on this point today: "Our managers came back to us and told us, 'Well girls, I don't want to hurt your feelings, but this was the remark they made: "Who do those niggers think they are?"' In other words, we ought to be thankful and grateful that we were even working for Tom Jones. That was enough right there to make me say, 'Well that is that.' It was amazing because we had never really had any trouble before."

Darlene was not prepared to stand for such poor treatment and promptly quit The Blossoms. She recalls that before any negotiations to reinstate her old group could take place another trio of backing singers called The Rock Flowers had been hired. Staying with Tom Jones for just one tour, The Rock Flowers were reviewed rather negatively in the music press as "would-be Supremes". Intervention came in the form of further arbitration between The Blossoms and Tom's management, and the group was eventually invited to rejoin the party. According to Darlene, the backing singers were actually making less money when they went back out on the road with Tom Jones than they had been before they left. Founding member Fanita James declined to comment on this bizarre turn of events.

Despite the demise of *This Is Tom Jones* earlier in the year, in October 1971 it was virtually impossible to escape the ever-present image of the tuxedoed singer on nearly every possible popular television show, especially in the UK. Tom stepped in at short notice to host *The Harry Secombe Show* one Sunday when the programme's Welsh star was suddenly taken ill and was unable to film. Jimmy Tarbuck assisted Tom by deputising as compère, and the pair were joined by brother and sister team, The Carpenters. Tom and Barbra Streisand were then star guests in the next Burt Bacharach TV spectacular and Tom was also seen on the BBC shows *Top Of The Pops* and *Morecambe & Wise* promoting his new single, 'Till'.

A poignant Danvers/Sigman/Gaiano composition, 'Till' had already been a hit for Tony Bennett in 1961, The Angels in 1962 and Dorothy Squires more recently in 1970. Tom's recording was praised by *NME*, whose reviewer drew particular attention to Tom's voice and Johnnie Spence's "gorgeous arrangement of sweeping strings". This latest saccharine-sweet offering featured Tom in particularly warblesome mode against a full orchestra and choir, and was a huge success in Britain, attaining number two in the UK charts in November. Tom's American fans were less impressed and the single didn't even dent the Top 40. But Tom was only too pleased to promote it on British television as it made a refreshing change from his lengthy tour, and further appearances were planned for the month of November, including on his old friend Cilla Black's brand new Saturday night series. However, television guides remarked that despite repeated attempts by Eamonn Andrews, the programme *This Is Your Life*, which each week celebrated the rise of a popular personality, was unable to secure Tom Jones as a subject. Gordon obviously felt that Tom had a lot more living to do before such a tribute was shown on TV.

Tom's guest spot on *Morecambe & Wise* in the last week of October was to be one of the most memorable of his career to date. During the programme, he attempted to get through a fairly strait-laced version of 'Exactly Like You' while Eric Morecambe and Ernie Wise, the much loved slapstick stars of the show, performed a typically hilarious dance routine. As the pair hopped, skipped and jumped around him, Tom could not help but burst into fits of giggles during his singing, and like all those big stars who suffered at the hands of Eric and Ernie he took the well-meaning mockery in good grace. His talents weren't completely ridiculed during the programme, as part of the show was devoted to the presenta-tion of a gold record from Decca executive Marcel Stellman for top album sales in Finland. This was the first ever gold disc to come out of the country and was presented to Tom for selling 10,000 copies of his 1969 album *Live In Las Vegas*.

Tom was also experiencing great achievements in other non-English speaking countries; in particular high record sales in Israel, Spain, Nor-way and Sweden. Due largely to the sing-along appeal of his earlier hit 'Delilah', Tom Jones Fever was springing up all over the rest of Europe, including the restrictive communist countries. Thanks to his hit TV series, huge advances of LP copies were requested by various record clubs, and already his singles were widely translated and covered by many diverse foreign artists. Tom's 1971 tour brochure proudly, and somewhat confus-ingly, boasted that Tom's albums were currently fetching upwards of $100 on Russia's black market.

In December Tom's astounding *Live At Caesar's Palace* album reached only a paltry number 27 in the UK charts and number 43 in the US. For reasons which can probably be attributed to the public's growing percep-tion of 31-year-old Tom as a 'middle-aged' singer, the album attracted some negative reviews in the US. This alone was inexplicable as despite the shift in the age of his audience, Tom's star was still shining as reflected by his recent UK hit single, 'Till'. The 14 songs on the album included this latest release, two medleys and further hits like 'I (Who Have Noth-ing)', 'Delilah' and 'She's A Lady'. Frank Sinatra's 'My Way' and Simon & Garfunkel's 'Bridge Over Troubled Water' were also covered in a live set, interjected with female screams and shrieks from the excited audience. The excellent material stood testament to the sheer power and energy of Tom's explosive voice, ranging from rootsy soul to sheer glitz as he raced through a typical Las Vegas performance recorded earlier that year.

Things weren't running quite so smoothly back at Tom's family home in England. Mark had been raised almost single-handedly by Linda as her famous husband spent little time at home, dedicated as he was to his career and socialising. Linda was exceedingly reclusive and although Mark went to school, he too fell into a fairly solitary way of life. It was difficult for him to mix with other children, partly because he was naturally shy, but also due to his awkward looks. At 14 Mark was as gawky as any teenager, with a pale complexion, untameable curly mousy-brown hair, sudden towering height and a lingering weight problem.

As the son of a superstar, Mark's appearance left him wide open for unflattering tabloid speculation. One such critic, Lester Reisman, wrote for the magazine *Movie Stars* a cutting and horribly exaggerated description of the unfortunate adolescent. "Hidden from the general public, and known only to a few of his closest associates, Tom Jones has been waging a battle to save his 14-year-old son Mark's life. According to previous case histories of medical science, if some drastic action isn't employed soon, the heart and perhaps some vital organs of the boy will be affected. For Mark is a victim of a serious weight imbalance which presumably cannot be controlled . . . He tips the scales at well over 225 pounds."

Reisman then twisted a comment Tom had made about his son a few months earlier to sound like he was defending him against such wild criticism: "Mark has never been thin. He's a heavyweight. He was a big baby. He just has a bit of leftover baby fat, that's all. Both my wife Linda and I tend to be stocky. It's our Welsh peasant background." One can only begin to imagine how such ludicrous comments must have affected the self-confidence of the already reserved teenager.

It had always been apparent that the young Mark worshipped his celebrity father, and he would sit in with him on recording sessions and TV filming whenever possible, even occasionally joining him on tour as a 'holiday'. Mark found it particularly difficult when Tom was away for such long periods at a time. His mother was unable to offer much comfort, insisting that he must attend school, receive an education and be with children his own age. By 1971 it was obvious that things in the Woodward household weren't all that happy.

Christmas 1971 was a spectacular affair. *The World Of Tom Jones*, an official publication brought out early the following year, painted an idealistic picture of Tom skiing in Zermatt, Switzerland. "I had never been to Switzerland before," said Tom. "It was one of the prettiest places I have ever seen in my life. The chalets looked beautiful, especially at night in the reflected light of glistening snow." The MAM brochure, written and compiled by Chris Hutchins, told an amusing anecdote about the events of the skiing trip, which was accompanied by a series of photos of a warmly wrapped-up Tom, in the style of a cartoon strip and entitled 'Fun In The Snow In Switzerland'. The singer, accompanied by a small entourage, was travelling under a pseudonym and it was not long before the high-jinx began. "Tom found himself locked out on the balcony in a hotel in the village of Zermatt at midnight," wrote Chris. "It was a prank played on him by friends when the party arrived for a few days skiing shortly before Christmas."

Things then began to become more complicated: "The trip had been arranged with the greatest secrecy with Tom travelling under another name, but his face is as international as his voice and within 48 hours of his arrival Zermatt was invaded by photographers. Unable to ski anymore Tom made a dash for Rome, where another set of photographers followed him from hotel to restaurant and on to nightclubs."

This was the officially released story. The truth of the matter was far more entertaining. "Tom would stay at the Westbury if there was someone with him, and not go home," Chris says today. "One night we were in Tramp and he said, 'Where are we going to go tonight?' I said, 'Well, the Westbury; you're booked in.' He said, 'Well where am I gonna go in the morning?' I said, 'Home,' and he said, 'Chris, we've been out three days and three nights, I can't just go home! Linda will be furious!'"

Taking charge of the situation, Chris hit upon the wild idea of going to Heathrow Airport and jumping on the first plane that would take them out of the country. To convince Tom, who really didn't need much convincing, Chris suggested that they took the photographer David Steen with them so that they could take pictures for the next year's brochure – the perfect excuse for a last-minute disappearance. Tom readily agreed. Then the pair realised that the only thing standing between them and freedom was that their passports were back at their respective family homes. Thinking on their feet they gave Chris Ellis their keys, and the road manager willingly crept into their houses in the middle of the night and stole the passports while everyone was asleep.

Tom, Chris Hutchins, Chris Ellis, David the photographer and a small, excitable gaggle caught a plane to Geneva at 7.00 a.m. After three days and nights out on the town they were feeling a little the worse for wear and vowed to stop drinking and clean up their act. Of course, the first thing the British Airways staff did on recognising the pop singer was to give him a complimentary bottle of champagne, and the party started all over again.

Chris continues: "We get to Geneva and I've alerted a guy from the record company that we want to go to somewhere in the mountains. He's picked Zermatt, but he says, 'There's no train until 3.00 p.m., so the record company would like to host a lunch.'" More alcoholic indulgence naturally followed at the lunch, and again in the restaurant car of the connecting train. Chris Ellis then produced a bottle of brandy for the final little train climbing up the mountain to Zermatt itself. But the group, who to all intents and purposes were behaving like a pack of naughty school children, were about to be rumbled.

"There was a bunny from the Playboy Club amongst the group. We were there for two days and we had a good time. We got the pictures, having all got our anoraks and snow boots! When we come back to the hotel the second evening the manager says, 'Mr Jones, the paparazzi have arrived from Rome. They've heard you're here and that there's a Playboy Bunny in the group.' So Tom looked at me and said, 'What'll we do?' I said, 'Well, they've all come from Rome . . . let's go there, there'll be no problem!'" The combination of a popular celebrity, a drunken crowd from the music industry and a 'lady of entertainment' would have spelled the end of any supposedly harmless trip for the men when their wives saw the damning photographs in the tabloids the next day, so the group leapt on the last train down from Zermatt, catching it by the skin of their teeth, and left the paparazzi stranded in the cold skiing resort for the night.

The fun continued as the merry assemblage returned first to Geneva and then flew through a storm down to Rome. They booked into the Excelsior Hotel, still clad in their anoraks and snow boots. "Where do we go tonight?" they inquired of the doorman. "The 21 Club," came the prompt reply. So they checked in, went upstairs, washed their hands and came back down the stairs, having neglected to change from their anoraks and snow gear.

"We get to the 21 Club and they let us in because it was Tom Jones, but they wouldn't have normally because it's a strict dress code there," marvels Chris. "They show us to this table in the corner. The centre of the room is taken up by a huge table with this group of immaculately turned-out people. I think Peter Sellers was at the table, but certainly Michael Caine was, and there were all these glamorous women. Nobody wanted to acknowledge us because we were this smelly, dirty-looking bunch of guys, but Michael Caine comes over, he has a white tux on."

The pristinely dressed actor, who was accompanied by an elegant lady, barely raised an eyebrow when Tom asked, "Where are all the women in this town?" Without missing a beat, Michael Caine looked the ravaged rock singer up and down, and replied in his famously deadpan tone: "Tom. It takes me half an hour to get all this gear on. Then I've got to help her get all her gear on. Then I've got to come down here and wine her and dine her for two and a half hours. Then I've got to take her back to the hotel and spend another 20 minutes getting all her gear off. The least the women can do is come and find *me*!" Not wishing to intrude on

Michael Caine's territory, Tom and his friends returned home to face the music the very next day.

★   ★   ★

Now in his thirties, with a thundering career, an understanding wife and an adoring son to his credit, Tom Jones had everything he ever wanted in life. Despite the refinement that vast wealth can eventually nurture in even the most unsophisticated of men, Tom retained the rather traditional views instilled in him by his Welsh upbringing, especially with regards to women, but some aspects of his life were undeniably changed. His blasé attitude towards money became a typically complacent response from someone as comfortably affluent as he: "Money is something you only think about if you haven't got it. The greatest thing it has done for me is to give me independence to do what I want to do."

"I suppose I am a lavish spender – if it's something I want," Tom told the press in 1972. His spending sprees were well-publicised, particularly his ability to amass several thousands of pounds on champagne bills alone when partying at a club, and he was often criticised for championing the aesthetic of the *nouveau riche*. When Bill Smith first congratulated Tom on his millionaire status, Tom asked him to prove it. The accountant then had the arduous task of cashing in all of Tom's shares and banking the profits in order to show the star a statement with a seven figure balance, only to convert the money back into the original stocks once Tom was satisfied with the proof.

Ultimately though, Tom was not really interested in looking after his accounts, and was content to place implicit trust in others to make the most prudent financial decisions on his behalf. He explained his situation to *Melody Maker* in May 1972: "Most of my earnings are channelled into MAM – and I am, of course, a large shareholder in the company. But I couldn't tell you how much I gross, or even what my dividends amount to. The company secretary would probably know, but I don't want to. As long as I have enough, I'm not interested in how much it is." Chris Hutchins confirms that, "Tom never wanted to know about money," and providing he always had some ready cash, he never worried about being mismanaged or conned.

Tom didn't believe that his new-found wealth would separate him from his old friends back in Pontypridd, but there are several people still living there today who can bear witness to Tom's casual attitude towards repaying old debts. Back in the Fifties when he was struggling to support his new wife and son with a low-paid manual job and occasional gigs in social clubs, Tom had borrowed £10 from The Green Fly's Christmas fund. A spokesperson for this social club says that Jimmy Moran lent Tom what was then a sizeable amount of money in good faith but was never repaid, and others have since accused Tom of borrowing LPs and not returning them.

The most incredible account comes from Vernon Hopkins, who witnessed proof not long before they parted company, that Tom had truly forgotten about their previous shared poverty. "One day I got a phone call from Tom. He said, 'I've got some suits here for you. They'll be a bit short on the leg for you, but you can lengthen them. I've got half a dozen of them.' These were just day suits which had been in his wardrobe for a couple of years, he was going to throw them away. I hadn't got a suit to rub together. I thought OK then, I'll go and pick them up.

"So I went up to Tor Point. It was very regal, like a mansion. He said, 'Here they are. You can have them.' Then he says, 'How much are you going to give me?' He was living in total wealth and I was earning £40 a week. The suits had cost £80 each and Tom started bartering! He said, 'Give me 25 quid for the lot, a fiver each.' I was paying a fiver for my accommodation! But I was so desperate – I had to owe him the money and pay him back weekly."

Tom had little trouble adjusting to the opulent lifestyle and had acquired Gordon's taste for fine wine and haute cuisine. "I like white wine with fish, red with meat, a large cognac and a Cuban cigar. And then if the night goes on, champagne . . ." he elaborated to the press. Tom explained to *NME* how he felt about drinking at home: "You know when I was a kid in South Wales I used to dream of having booze in the house. That to me was unbelievably posh, to have alcohol *in your home*. Now I've got two bars in my house and I have to avoid the bloody things. I have to walk past them. I steer clear of the drink during the day, but in the evenings when we have the family over we have a few. That can go on a bit."

Tom was always mindful to intersperse his more exotic tastes with food and drink reminiscent of his past. "I love the national Welsh lamb dinner, but I must confess that my international all-time favourite is raw oysters and clams, and my favourite meat dish is peppered steak . . . and I do have a weak spot for the Welsh local brew, Brains Beer." When it came to champagne, Tom was something of a connoisseur. "My favourite tipple has to be Dom Perignon," he told *Now* magazine, "which is a Moët & Chandon champagne that first appeared in 1921. OK, it's very expensive, but you have to remember that only the finest grapes are used." Among his other preferred dishes are Indian, Italian and French delicacies, and he is a self-confessed cereal and fresh fruit freak.

After expensive food, drink and cigars, Tom was predictably passionate about music, but he did have other hobbies, as Chris Hutchins elucidates. "He had an amazing intellect when it came to the things he wanted to study. Obviously music is one, but history was astonishing." Tom would often talk to Chris about one of his favourite historical figures, Owain Glyndwr, the Welsh nationalist who had successfully defeated Henry IV in the early 15th century. While Tom immersed himself privately in history, he was not comfortable about speaking on the related subject of politics.

Regardless of the fact that he was not a songwriter himself, Tom consciously avoided cultural critique or topical comment in his choice of musical material. Unlike Bob Dylan, John Lennon or Mick Jagger he did not feel the need to make a political or social statement with his songs, and appeared content to simply entertain the masses and project his sex appeal across to the audience. The Fort Worth *Star-Telegram* once complimented his knack of skirting any political pressure with an otherwise interesting selection of recordings: "He's not a writer, but he's got incredible taste in covers, in finding songs obscure or well known and making them his own. And he's always mixed his influences and stayed at least on the fringe of contemporary music."

Tom strongly believed that current affairs and music should be kept separate. Back in the late Sixties he had sniped in an interview, "When I see them [fans of political songs] with their banners and their sandals, I feel like telling them to get off their backsides and do something. They do nothing. They're bums." In 1972 he responded to the question, "What do you feel about pop songs which also attempt to be social commentary?" posed by *Melody Maker* with, "I don't believe in it. I don't think popular singers should use their influence to convey political messages, when they probably don't know enough about a situation. Message songs don't appeal to me, and I don't think a musical platform or a jukebox is a place for social comment."

Tom's personal political leanings were something of a contentious issue. He was raised, as most mining families were, to be a staunch socialist, and appeared to respect these roots even in the Seventies when his wealth and social standing were more suited to the ideals of the Conservative Party. Whether Tom genuinely believed in the nationalisation policies and social welfare reforms heralded by the Labour Party, or whether he was stubbornly sticking to his guns, was open to speculation. Chris Hutchins remembers one particularly heated argument they had over politics on tour in the early Seventies. "He went for me. We were talking about politics and I was one of those people who was born a socialist and became a Tory, and he really had a go at me for that. There could be friction, but basically everybody wanted to keep Tom happy. So if it blew up it was very rare and very spectacular."

Tom himself concedes that he can lose control of his temper, and that it is perhaps his most unpleasant characteristic. "I avoid arguments and confrontations like the plague because I know that if I snap, it's terrible – I throw caution to the wind. Fortunately, I don't snap easily, but I know that I can, and that when I do I erupt." Chris was personally wary of this flaw. "I've seen his black moods. Particularly when we'd both been drinking, but they were few and far between. And Tom's face would turn black, literally black."

★　★　★

At the beginning of 1972 Gordon Mills organised a 170 day world tour for Tom, which was widely regarded as his most comprehensive and impressive to date. When Tom was asked by *Melody Maker* if he found the demands of such an extensive tour exhausting, his reply was: "I enjoy it, and tours are set up in such a way that they are never arduous. For example, I don't have to attend functions, and so on – I'm only expected to sing. Charter planes are used, to allow me to fly when I am ready instead of having to get up earlier to make a scheduled flight. That way I have no difficulty in completing even a six month tour."

In conjunction with the February press releases announcing the upcoming dates, Gordon also insinuated that following the culmination of the tour Tom would almost definitely begin work filming the screen version of *The Gospel Singer*. An alternative version printed by the papers stated that provision had been made to interrupt the tour should Tom's movie début be brought forward from its scheduled commencement in October.

To launch Tom on his expedition, which was timetabled to end on September 8, 1972, a new single was released in March. 'The Young New Mexican Puppeteer', written by Earl Shuman and Leon Carr was not initially Tom's cup of tea. "I once recorded a song called 'The Young New Mexican Puppeteer' about peace and love and a fella making puppets," he told the *TV Times* some years later. "I liked the song but it didn't work. And then I thought, 'Hell, there's no sex in this!'" The conga-driven number, full of funky flourishes from flutes and Mariachi horns, was what could be described as an 'energetic ballad'. Its story-line included references to Abraham Lincoln, Martin Luther King and Mark Twain; intriguing subject material for a singer who was so adamant that politics and music don't match. This was a far cry from Tom's usual love-torn territory, but he conceded and made it his own. "I didn't see why I had to be sexy all the time," Tom reasoned, "but it didn't make women twitch, see, and that's what works. You can't bite the hand that feeds you."

Despite his reservations, the curious choice of 'The Young New Mexican Puppeteer' was unleashed on the public and declared in Britain by *The Mirror* as a 'chart cert'. Indeed, the single had climbed to a respectable number six in the UK charts by May, but failed dismally in the

States, reaching only an embarrassing number 80. Its parent album, *Close Up*, which included other colourfully titled songs like 'Witch Queen Of New Orleans', 'Woman You Took My Life', 'I Won't Be Sorry To See Suzanne Again' and 'Kiss An Angel Good Mornin'' was released in June and went to number 17 in the UK, but only number 64 in America. Still, the tour pressed on.

While Tom and Linda maintained a special set of friends that they would mix with, Tom also became close to the regular members of his touring party. Many musicians stayed with the singer throughout the Seventies, accompanying him on his annual US tours and around the rest of the world. The core players naturally became good friends and formed a strong bond with Tom as well as each other. Guitarist Big Jim Sullivan, who had played on Tom's sessions since The Squires had arrived in London, was perhaps the closest of this group to the frontman. Today he admits that his solo spot on *This Is Tom Jones* and the ensuing fame went to his head for a while and he would often compete with Tom on lavish spending sprees. Trumpeter Derek Watkins remembers that Big Jim would buy suits in vast quantities, out-doing anyone else in the group, including the star himself. Wendy Watkins also recalls their extravagant contests: "They used to have competitions about who could spend the most in the hotels, whose bill was the most. Jim generally won it!"

Derek had also been present at Tom's initial Decca recordings in 1964, adding the signatory blasts of brass on 'It's Not Unusual' and later on 'Delilah'. Officially joining the touring party in the late Sixties for The Squires' last European tour, he benefited greatly from having Welsh roots, and consequently fitted in easily with the group. Derek still works occasionally with Tom today, his most recent stint accompanying Tom on his 1999 promotional TV appearances, but he harbours fond memories of the once-in-a-lifetime experience of touring with one of the Seventies' most famous sex symbols. "I'd never been to America before, and to be treated like that, in that sort of entourage . . . it was like The Beatles. Everything was done for you – what a wonderful way to see the world."

Terry Jenkins, Tom's drummer, was trained by the late great Kenny Clare, who had performed on the *This Is Tom Jones* series. Kenny had asked Terry to cover for him on one rehearsal for the programme in 1971 and both Johnnie Spence and Tom were so impressed with the new drummer that when he reappeared for a recording session in 1972, they asked him to join the tour permanently as Kenny was unavailable. By sheer coincidence Terry, like most people involved in the Tom Jones story, was also Welsh.

John Rostill, formerly of The Shadows, was the bass guitarist in the early Seventies up until his accidental death on November 26, 1973, and along with Big Jim, Derek and Terry, he completed the solid kernel of

Tom's backing. The four key musicians were as thick as thieves and would rarely be found too far apart. With this friendly camaraderie came superior performances as they could all predict each other's next musical move. There were of course line-up changes through the years for various different reasons, and one by one they all left, the magic never quite recaptured. Alan Jones stepped in on bass guitar after the sad loss of John Rostill, Mike Morgan replaced Big Jim when he finally bowed out in the mid-Seventies and Trevor Bastow played the keyboards in the band from the mid to late Seventies.

To counterbalance the overwhelming and predominantly Welsh testosterone on stage were the American female backing singers, The Blossoms. As one of the founding members, Fanita James was the acknowledged leader and chose the other harmony singers. She too experienced several line-up changes as although popular Jeannie King remained with The Blossoms throughout the Seventies, it proved hard to find a permanent replacement for the gap left by Darlene Love. Alexandra Brown temporarily filled in, followed by Viola Jewel (known as 'Pumpkin') and Deborah Wilson, each staying for a couple of years at a time. Finally, in April 1976 Fanita discovered Cynthia Woodard, who fitted in perfectly as a long-standing member of The Blossoms.

The backing singers all enjoyed cooking and when they were in their respective hometowns they would prepare lavish regional meals for the crew, who would visit regularly. Everyone was very respectful and fond of the only females on the tour, and looked out for them at all times. Los Angeles was constantly besieged by racial tension following the violent Watts riots, and when the Sylmar earthquake caused considerable damage to the city in 1971, Tom telephoned Fanita at her home in Inglewood just to check that she was all right. The Blossoms themselves liked to think they were a little more reserved than the rest of the raucous crowd and did not partake in any of the wild parties on tour. But when the notion of the female trio being the 'nerds of the group' (Darlene Love's expression) was put forward to some of the other musicians, it prompted a hoot of disbelief followed by much knowledgeable smirking . . .

Behind the core musicians and backing singers would be an accomplished touring band. In 1970 Gordon excitedly signed up the Count Basie Band, but although they were excellent in their field, they did not fit in easily as Big Jim explains: "When they were playing jazz it was fabulous, but as soon as they started playing any of Tom's stuff it was like squeaking reeds and out of tune . . ." Friction sparked between the band and Tom Jones' regular musicians, so the following year they were dropped in favour of the Jeff Sturgess Universe, which proved to be a more successful partnership.

Derek recalls that the Tom Jones touring party would quite literally take over an entire hotel, with the star enjoying the luxury of a suite on the top floor, the main musicians having a whole floor to themselves and then the accompanying band would be lower down, almost as if the musical hierarchy was reflected within the lodgings.

However, the on-stage benefits of transporting so many people around the world did not prove cost effective for MAM, and so Gordon let the supplementary band go, retaining only the 12 or so necessary musicians. This greatly annoyed the touring party as it meant that they were then required to pick up in-house bands at each venue, which naturally incurred extra rehearsals and an unavoidable drop in quality.

"It was like a well-oiled machine," says Big Jim of the whole touring process. "It just kept on grinding on. And if a bit fell off, it was replaced by somebody." Big Jim clarifies that after the days of high class back-up such as The Count Basie Band the entire package was streamlined down to the very basics. "What Tom used to do was to take a drummer, bass, lead trumpet, lead guitar and conductor on the road. Everything else was built up with bands which would rehearse."

It was Lloyd Greenfield's remit to handle everything on the American leg of Tom's travels for Gordon. As American tour manager he would organise work permits for the band and ensure that all concerts and transport arrangements progressed effortlessly. He was greatly appreciated for his talent of smoothing ruffled feathers and generally keeping the party in good spirits. "Lloyd was so friendly. He was the comedian of the tour. He was the one that was always carrying on and acting silly and crazy," says Darlene.

Although Lloyd had complete control in the US, Gordon would occasionally fly out and check up on business. Gordon did not like to travel alone, but his wife Jo had to stay at home to look after their five children and house in England, so wherever Gordon went, he was accompanied by his old school friend and former work-mate, Gordon 'Gog' Jones. He had introduced Gordon to the idea of having his own private zoo in Weybridge, and the two often went on safari in South Africa, sometimes joined by musical director Johnnie Spence. Gordon rented Gog accommodation on his land and treated him like a comedic sidekick. Unlike the high-powered businessman that his ex-colleague from the Rhondda buses had turned out to be, Gog was a simple soul who couldn't handle the frenetic pace of Gordon's lifestyle. Tragically, he committed suicide by feeding the exhaust fumes into his car. "He was one of the casualties of Tom Jones' success," concludes Chris Hutchins.

Tom too had a personal assistant travelling with him. Through all of Gordon's purging, Chris Ellis had survived by changing his role from roadie to that of Tom's general right-hand man. Chris would handle all the odd jobs from runner, driver and bodyguard to dresser. The streetwise Big Jim says, "Chris was alright, he was a bit of a whipper-snapper." Chris' most distinguishable feature was his impenetrable Welsh accent as Norm Crosby, a comedian who occasionally toured with the group in the Seventies, often joked, "Chris was a nice bloke – shame he never learned to speak English!" Chris left in the mid-Seventies, around the same time that many members of the original group began to move on, and was replaced for a brief spell by Larry Richstein, Jeannie King's husband, who was known as Nifty.

Aside from the amazing memories, each and every person on the annual tours would part with a memento from Tom. This tradition was customary within the more upmarket parts of the pop world, and Elvis in particular was renowned for splashing out on impressively extravagant gifts, such as a car each for the entire Memphis Mafia. Tom was not that ostentatious, but he would give everyone involved from the musicians to the roadies a small gift, be it jewellery or perhaps a piece of porcelain. "Tom always used to give us very nice presents at the end of a tour. It was usually something gold. Massive great chunky rings," says Derek. Big Jim confirms, "At the end of the tours we used to get a trinket. One year we had a ring with the Welsh dragon on it." Tom would go to great lengths to ensure that the gifts were perfect, and his generosity to his friends and colleagues was faultless. One year he gave everyone an ounce of gold worth $1,000 and another time he sent 40 gold bracelets off to be engraved by hand, only to order 40 replacements from the Far East when the first batch were lost in transit.

With Gordon's approval, PR man Chris Hutchins was always mindful that minimising exposure would maximise demand, and that too much publicity might induce media saturation and complacency. Chris was also well aware that Tom was prone to the odd social blunder, the best example being his more traditional views concerning the rising wave of feminism. Shrewdly selective publicity thus dictated that in the early Seventies, Tom was never to be seen on TV chat shows and radio interviews were not recorded live. Tom's apparent reticence did not go unnoticed in the press, who printed pictures of the star with captions pondering that if Tom was so amenable to the photographers, why wouldn't his management let anyone interview him?

Tom was not totally screened from reporters, it was just that Chris picked the interviewers very carefully. He well remembered the time when, as a young journalist, he had been thrown into the deep end by Colonel Parker with a surprise meeting with Elvis Presley. On one occasion when he worked for Tom, a popular music paper had bullied Chris into allowing one of their staff to accompany the star on a brief tour. Chris had agreed on the proviso that he would be given a full preview of the article and would have the final say on whether or not it ended up in print. He was only too glad of his precautions for the finished report by the young female scribe – which was never published – portrayed Tom Jones in a wildly sexually active manner. Chris vetoed the piece immediately as it would have spelled the end of the public's perception of Tom as a decent gentleman, let alone the ramifications for Tom's marriage to Linda.

In May 1972 *NME* correspondent Preston Whittaker was invited to travel across the Nevada desert with Tom and his entourage. In Whittaker's interview Tom talks eloquently on the sheer spectacle of the reception his tour is attracting that year, and the consequent restrictive security measures. Whittaker remarks in his article that, even as late as 1972, Tom's early life is being kept a closely guarded secret – the implications being that his humble roots, living in poverty with The Squires, had long since been swept under the carpet. He alludes to Tom's sense of humour, reporting that the singer had recently split his pants, P.J. Proby style, at the Westbury Music Fair in Long Island. His scarlet briefs had been revealed for all to see, allowing Tom to quip to the audience, "Well, at least you know I *do* wear underpants now!" before going to change.

The most interesting part of the *NME* write-up was an endearing description of Tom giving an impromptu concert, strumming a miniature $5 banjo and singing an hour's worth of a capella material like 'Mamma Don't Allow'. The performance took place in a deserted restaurant in Havasu in front of only a handful of people, and was movingly described by the writer as the 'human touch' to the singer. A picture of Tom with said banjo appeared in the following year's MAM brochure, *Body & Soul*.

The interview concluded with Tom admitting that he was finding the US part of the tour very long, and it would probably be his last before his film career took off. As Tom confessed that even his one-week holiday would be spent in a recording studio, he came across in print as quite down and dejected, probably realising too late that he had a bit too much on his plate.

During the 1972 tour, Tom made a joke on stage that inadvertently upset some of the members of his entourage. Racism directed at black Americans was still raging underground in the US. Although it had been denounced by successive American Presidents, including Lyndon Johnson in 1965, the Ku Klux Klan was beginning to revive with renewed vigour in the Seventies. On stage in Las Vegas Tom turned to his black backing group, The Blossoms, placed a white handkerchief over his face and ominously intoned: "Be out of town by midnight!" The obvious reference to the Klan was seen by white members of the touring party as a joke that anyone could have made, but The Blossoms took understandable offence, as the murderous witch-hunts of the Klan were certainly no laughing matter.

Colin Macfarlane describes in his biography how the singers refused to perform any more shows with Tom. After a brief telephone call, Elvis Presley dispatched two planes to Nashville and Los Angeles to pick up some replacement backing singers for his friend. By the time they arrived, Gordon and Tom had mended the bruised relationship with The Blossoms but the extra singers were kept on for the rest of the week, and according to Colin Macfarlane, 'entertained' the two megastars each night after the show. When asked to comment on the embarrassing episode for this book, Fanita James maintained that Tom had only meant the comments as a joke and only one of the girls was upset. "It was obvious and unprofessional of her to take offence on stage as it disrupted the show," says Fanita, who conceded that the resulting situation was a bit tense, but it was resolved the same night without further unpleasantness.

The only matter that really troubled Gordon about Tom's 1972 tour was the odd dichotomy of the performer's profile on the different sides of the Atlantic Ocean. While Tom's singles and albums were continuing to chart well in the UK, for some reason he now seemed to be attracting far less public recognition in Britain than in the States. Indeed, the demise of *This Is Tom Jones* seemed to have prompted some observers to regard him as a 'has-been'. Conversely Tom's US chart placings were appalling by any standards, yet his status in America had been elevated to legendary, on a par with Elvis Presley and Frank Sinatra.

The practical result of this changing perception of the singer was that Tom was spending nearly 90 per cent of his time in America, where Gordon could always be certain that the concerts would invariably be jam-packed. Tom spent most of his time in Las Vegas, but he was consistently breaking box office records all over the US, with venues charging up to $20 per ticket, the high price reflecting the deeper pockets of his audience. *Variety* reported in May that Tom had grossed $300,000 at the Deauville Star Theater in Miami, forcing one of their rival venues to cancel for the evening due to insufficient advance bookings.

In Las Vegas Tom would be performing two and sometimes three sets each night, and during this period he abstained from drinking alcohol altogether. He had begun to experience worrisome throat problems brought on by the dry desert heat, and his habitual heavy drinking was only making matters worse. "The only thing I had to watch was alcohol because it's so dry here, and alcohol dehydrates you anyway. So I learned after a while not to drink alcohol when I was here for a month," he said to journalist Mike Weatherford. "I cut it out completely. If you're going to

(Terry O'Neill/Camera Press)

Chris Hutchins: "We eyed each other with deep suspicion the first time we met. But I think he liked the ideas. And I liked the material." Publicity on the run. *(Hulton Getty)*

'hose are *these*? I think my Auntie Alice just came in!"
rry O'Neill/Camera Press)

"Mr Romance" and "Mr Sex" on horseback.
(Terry O'Neill/Camera Press)

One for the ladies... *(Terry O'Neill/Camera Press)*

Tom shares a gourmet meal with Mary Wilson, of The Supremes. *(Pictorial Press)*

That kiss. Tom with Marjorie Wallace on *Happiness Island*. *(Terry O'Neill/Camera Press)*

"Fun In The Snow In Switzerland..." *(Horst Tappe/Camera Press)*

Childhood friend and bodyguard Dai Perry, known for his no-nonsense catchphrase: "No pictures!" *(Terry O'Neill/Camera Press)*

Elvis Presley: "Tom is the only man who ever came close to the way I sing. He has that ballsy feeling."
Tom and his most famous fans, Priscilla and Elvis Presley. *(Hulton Getty)*

Tom with The Blossoms in 1978: Fanita James, Jeannie King and Cynthia Woodard. *(Richie Aaron/Redferns)*

Queen of the "tour widows". *(Mirror Syndication Int.)*

Tom spars with teenage Mark, who by now accompanied his father around the world. *(Terry O'Neill/Camera Pre*

The personalised £700,000 private jet purchased by MAM in 1973 to transport Tom and his entourage.
(Richie Aaron/Redferns)

Coast To Coast – Tom's second TV series shot in Vancouver in 1981. *(Pictorial Press)*

Woodward family portrait: Mark, Tom, Alexander and Donna. *(Rex Features)*

The man behind Tom Jones... *(Jerry Watson/Camera Press)*

do two shows a night for a month straight in Las Vegas, alcohol's got to go. My cousins would come out from Wales, where I was always known as a beer drinker. And my cousins said, 'If the boys back home could see you now!' "

In 1972 Tom's dream of appearing in a film finally became a reality, though the film in question was about as far removed from reality as Tom now was from Pontypridd. *The Special London Bridge Special* was a crazed concoction of celebrities thrown together in a psychedelic dream sequence, cooked up by producer/director David Winters. "I was driving in America and I saw some signs that Chevrolet had out that said: 'See The USA In Your Chevrolet' which was their advertising campaign that year," explains David about the creation of his bizarre idea. "It showed you people driving and going to places in a Chevrolet and so I thought, 'Well, that's great. There's got to be some places in America that I can create a show around.' Then I read that the London Bridge was being brought to America."

As it turned out, the American who bought London Bridge thought he was acquiring the famous drawbridge-operated Tower Bridge and so was rather disappointed with his purchase. Regardless, the impressive construction was relocated to span Lake Havasu, Arizona and David developed the concept of filming a star-studded TV special focused around the bridge and its new setting. Accordingly he approached Chevrolet for sponsorship and secured a lucrative deal.

"It was a fantasy love story," says David of his initial idea. "I originally wanted Barbra Streisand and Rex Harrison to do it. Chevrolet wanted younger people and they gave me a list of possibles. As things happened it wound up with Jennifer O'Neill and Tom Jones." Jennifer had launched a fitful film career in 1968 and was currently in vogue for having starred as Dorothy in the 1971 coming-of-age film, *Summer Of '42*. Tom, however, had only appeared in his own TV series and various specials, which hardly qualified him as an actor. David was aware of Tom's limitations and bore them in mind when scripting the role. "He was a big star. He represented a youthful, sexual, energetic image and Chevrolet thought that was good. And he wanted to get into films and have a chance to act a little bit . . . I didn't really ask him to act. There wasn't very much for him to do. I just really wanted him to be himself, and to be charming. It was very easy for him."

In a bid to attract ratings, David persuaded an incredible list of celebrities to appear in the film including actor Kirk Douglas, the politically controversial ballet dancer Rudolf Nureyev, brother and sister pop duo The Carpenters, Hermione Gingold as the lady bus conductor, Elliot Gould as the villain, the legendary Charlton Heston, and even painted by noted artist Feliks Topolski and sculptured for Madame Tussaud's London waxwork gallery.

Still, the Americans could not get enough of their adopted superstar and for the second consecutive year he was named 'Singer Of The Year' by the American Guild of Variety Artists. As Tom had now returned from his tour, which had finished on September 8, he was unable to attend the televised ceremony hosted by Ed Sullivan in Las Vegas, and instead a clip was filmed for the audience, with Tom accompanied by two blonde actresses and singing while being chauffeured around the landmarks of London in an open-topped Rolls Royce on a freezing cold night. This could well explain why music journalist Chris Charlesworth witnessed Tom spluttering from a cold on the opening night of a three-week homecoming stint at the London Palladium, the singer reduced to sucking lozenges on stage and prolonging the breaks between songs with lengthy and uncharacteristic jokes and anecdotes.

12

DARK STORM ON THE HORIZON

BUSINESSWISE, everything was looking healthy, and as 1972 drew to a close MAM was reporting praiseworthy pre-tax profits of £2,569,000 – a vast step up from the previous year's £158,000. Around this time MAM also had a Stock Exchange value reportedly running in excess of £10 million. Gordon had decided to branch out and expanded his entertainment empire, investing in some 10,000 juke boxes and arcade games such as fruit machines and one-armed bandits, which MAM then leased to pubs and hotels all over the country. Other coups included the take-over of the powerful Harold Davidson Agency and the recent signing of UK vocalist Lynsey de Paul. New ideas such as investment in hotels, concert promotion and publishing were already well under way.

With the unexpected assault on the pop charts coming from Gilbert O'Sullivan and Lynsey de Paul's three top twenty hits on the MAM record label over the next three years ('Sugar Me' had reached number five that August), Gordon's brainchild enterprise was flying high. "He was developing the leisure industry," explains author Johnny Rogan. "He had an expansionist mind. At each stage he rose to the challenge." During the developments MAM had by no means forgotten its roots in the music industry, and authorised Engelbert Humperdinck biographer Don Short noted that in 1972 MAM also managed singer Mary Hopkin, balladeer Jimmy Young and DJ Tony Blackburn, not to mention Tom, Engel and Gilbert.

While it seemed to all intents and purposes that nothing could stand in the way of MAM's omnipotence, dark clouds were threatening on the horizon. "The idea was to build an empire with Gordon as its chairman, and Gordon didn't like board meetings, and it didn't really happen," says Chris Hutchins. His opinion is backed up by Gordon's wife Jo, who declined an in-depth interview for this book but stated: "Gordon was not a businessman. He was a music man, but he had to become a businessman as chairman of a public company."

Chris goes on to explain that while Gordon was capable of paying immense attention to detail, for example spending hours choosing the livery of the £700,000 private jet purchased by MAM in mid-1973, he was guilty of making a series of poorly judged decisions with regard to far more important matters. As a result his hastily concocted empire slowly began to crumble around him, the malaise affecting friends and associates on his company board alike. "Bill Smith was a nice man, but no great entrepreneur," says Chris. "And Tom didn't like being part of a public company in which he was an asset alongside Engelbert Humperdinck and Gilbert O'Sullivan. He really didn't like it. It just made him the property of the public and meant that he belonged to them."

In fact, after a year or so, none of the artists felt comfortable about their standing within the company. They had initially been persuaded that going public would be a good idea, simply because they would pay less in tax and realise more of their earnings. But it left them with the feeling that their future was out of control. Another niggle with the running of the company, which few shareholders had noticed in amongst the small print, was the existence of an alleged off-shore, tax-saving company called Ebostrail. An inside source revealed for this biography that the ghost company, which was set up in the Caribbean, bled MAM of all the money Tom and Engel made during certain stints in the US. Ostensibly, for whatever figure MAM disclosed to its shareholders, a similar figure was syphoned into Ebostrail.

★   ★   ★

In 1973 Tom performed his first ever concerts in Japan and the Far East. The star, who was being fancifully nicknamed 'Tom The World Lover' by the Japanese media, sent the following message to his fans in the souvenir brochure printed for the event:

> "Hi, Japanese Fans,
> It's been a long pending subject for me to realise the tour to Japan and, now, I am pleased to have this special occasion of visiting your beautiful country in February. I have been only appealing to Japanese fans through television shows and records, however, I am pleased that I can have the first ever concert in Japan to sing for you in person. I'm sure that my shows will be exciting ones and we can all have a wonderful time."

Gordon's power complex was beginning to get out of hand, and Chris Hutchins, who accompanied Tom on this tour, remembers that the manager drove such a hard bargain with the Japanese promoters that the ticket prices escalated out of control. As an example, tickets at The Festival

Hall in Osaka ranged from an astounding 20,000 yen (approximately $55) to a mind-blowing 100,000 yen ($277). Although a certain percentage of the takings was hastily redirected to various charitable causes, the tour was not as successful as it could and should have been, and Gordon's pecuniary greed only ensured bad publicity in these foreign quarters as a result.

Still, Tom's 'mini' tour of Japan, during which he also performed a televised concert at Budokan in Tokyo, was an exciting event, and Tom was to visit the country once again the following year. Having long since become used to each other's extended company, those involved in the 1973 trek had a whale of a time, and when the expedition progressed to China the fun really began.

"We used to pull Dai Perry's leg a bit," smiles Chris Hutchins. "He was a nice guy, but he was a bit thick! Tom did a concert in Hong Kong and the promoter had laid on the usual party with loads of pretty girls. One of our number had taken a particularly pretty girl back to his room, and he came back 10 minutes later, saying, 'It's a fella! It's one of those transvestites!' Dai came over and said, 'What's the matter?' "

The PR man could not resist taking the gullible bodyguard for a bit of a ride. "I said, 'Dai, there's been a bit of a problem . . .' Dai said, 'What's that then?' Tom was looking at me. I said, 'She's hooked on one person. She's crazy about *you*!' 'Oh, alright then!' he said."

Chris just had to take it one step further. "I said, 'Hang on a second, Dai, this is *not* the normal sort of one-night stand girl.' So he went off to court her, and needless to say, it was nearly two hours before Dai came back steaming . . ."

Tom's studio output in 1973 was far from prolific, with just one single released on his return from the Far East; a brassy recording of 'Letter To Lucille' which stalled at number 31 in April's UK charts and number 60 in America the following month. June saw the release of a new album entitled *The Body And Soul Of Tom Jones*, which fared just as poorly with the same UK chart placing at number 31 and an unimaginably poor number 93 in the US.

The album was a strong collection, Tom's treatment of recently discovered singer-songwriter Bill Withers' tracks, 'Ain't No Sunshine' and 'Lean On Me' in particular proving that he hadn't lost his touch. Johnnie Spence's polished orchestration stands head and shoulders above other such contemporary offerings, and The Blossoms compete admirably with the luscious swirlings of strings. The cover of the LP was a portrait of Tom by Californian artist, Shel Starkman, who had originally painted it for his wife Donna, a huge Tom fan. The gaudy artwork, which today could be described only as a remarkable example of Seventies bad taste, had such a fantastic reception at the time that Tom's American label, London Records (another Decca-owned company replacing Parrot) arranged a Stateside tour of the original picture. Despite this enthusiastic publicity, its relative chart failure was premonitory.

"The hits stopped in 1973," Tom said years later. "We had hit on a formula with Peter Sullivan, my recording manager at Decca, but he went off and formed a public company with Beatles producer George Martin and suddenly became very expensive." The end of MAM's association with Air had pretty much spelled disaster for Tom's studio success. "[Gordon] reckoned we could make hits with other people," said Tom, who was unsure of upsetting the balance of the winning team. "We kept trying things with different producers but that formula thing is like a puzzle, and when you lose parts of a puzzle you lose the whole thing."

To compensate for Tom's chart failure over the last couple of years, Gordon had made the conscious decision to concentrate on his talents as a live performer rather than a recording artist. Tom's lifestyle now involved almost incessant travelling. His records continued to be released, but on a far less regular basis – although he still managed a greater output than other artists who spent years in between recordings. But the singer wasn't complaining.

Tom settled easily into a routine of wealthy extravagance, and was content to tour the United States almost indefinitely in the style and comfort of MAM's private plane. It did, after all, offer the opportunity for more frequent philandering. Since the early days of fame, Tom's legendary womanising had been a constant source of gossip, and by now the popular opinion was that the singer maintained at least one girlfriend in each town he visited on the repetitive US domestic tours. Much of this may have been wishful thinking, fabricated events or pure speculation, but one fan, who wishes to remain anonymous, has told her story for this book. She has chosen the alias 'Diane'.

"It was June of 1973, I was absolutely crazy about Tom Jones. He was really at his peak of popularity about this time, but I was still on the young side to be a fan of his." Tom was playing at the open-air summer venue, Musicarnival Theater in Warrensville Heights, Cleveland, Ohio. Diane had obtained tickets in the eighth row for one of his concerts and was determined to steal a kiss from the famous sex symbol. "On the fourth or fifth song I decided to make my move, which was quite out of character for me because I was painfully shy. I went down towards the stage and the bodyguards told me to go back to my seat. I said, 'No' and started screaming for Tom. He acknowledged me and the next thing I knew I was in the middle of the stage with him."

Stunned by the sudden turn of events, Diane remembers that Tom treated her to a passionate kiss as he would with many of his fans during a concert, before she left the stage. As she was walking away Tom pretended to swoon as a result of the kiss and called after her, "What did you say your name was again?" Diane repeated it and Tom voiced the aside, "Guys, write that down for future reference."

Diane had barely caught her breath when "about 15 minutes later, a gentleman showed up at the end of my row motioning me to leave with him – when he [Tom] says 'write that down for future reference' it means go get that girl from the audience!" The bodyguard told Diane and her chaperoning sister the touring party's arrangements for the evening. "We met the limo at the designated spot and got in," recalls Diane. "It was full of his musicians and back-up singers. It was here in the limo that I met Lloyd Greenfield. He kind of took me over and showed me and my sister up to Tom's hotel suite."

Tom was staying at the Bluegrass Motor Inn and in Tom's suite there was an open bar and some food. Tom had showered and changed by the time he approached Diane. "He immediately came over and sat down next to me and talked to me and my sister for the next hour and a half." They made polite conversation and then, "My sister and I got up to leave and I asked him to autograph my programme. He pulled me aside and asked me if I could come back tomorrow afternoon alone." Diane eagerly agreed and arrived at the hotel at two o'clock the following afternoon. She describes how the bodyguard, Dai Perry, took her through to Tom's room where he had just woken up. "He walked me through the suite and into Tom's room. There were maybe 10 humidifiers going – it was like walking into a rainforest. We made some more small talk and then he said he couldn't stand it anymore, he had to kiss me."

Through their brief conversation the day before, Tom had correctly gauged that Diane had led a sexually sheltered life. "I don't think he had a particular thing for virgins although he seemed to like the role of teacher." Withholding his passion no longer Tom took Diane to bed with him, but due to the medication he was taking for a touch of 'flu, they did not have intercourse. Diane left after some heavy petting and light conversation, nonetheless ecstatic at the experience and yearning for the following year when Tom would return to Cleveland. Sadly the concerts scheduled for the next summer were cancelled with just five days notice as Tom was once again ill. Diane could hardly tolerate the thought of waiting until 1975. "I really thought I was going to die," she says. "Another year seemed unbearable."

The idea of Tom having what Darlene Love aptly describes as a "booty scout" was not a new one. It is common practice for celebrities in all walks of life to procure women through aides. Aside from the archetypal spotting of a pretty girl in the crowd and having someone invite her to the after-show party, much the same would happen when Tom wasn't on tour. According to various sources, many of his close-knit circle of friends, including Chris Hutchins and Chris Ellis, would frequently be dispatched to a nightclub to find Tom a lady companion for the night, the incentive for carrying out this delicate task being that if she had a 'friend' then the scout would also be rewarded.

Darlene Love, having once so nearly consummated her friendly attraction for Tom, describes in her autobiography an unforgettable scene at one of Tom's extravagant and excessive parties. She and fellow Blossom Jeannie King watched aghast from the safety of the landing at the top of the stairs. "We felt as if we'd just stumbled on a porno film. Naked men were chasing naked women everywhere. And in the middle, on top of a round glass table, a woman who must have weighed maybe 200 pounds had one man underneath her and a couple of others taking turns on top."

Following her experiences with Tom, Darlene joked to the authors of this biography: "Tom was the kind of guy that if a woman said 'No' to him he would say, 'Well, OK,' then, 'Bring in Mary, bring in Sue!'" Today Darlene describes Tom as being quite discreet about his affairs because they mostly took place at his parties. During Darlene's stint with Tom, the backing singers would normally refuse any invitation to such an event. But there is always an exception to the rule.

"One night Tom and his road manager actually did come and get us. They came to our room and told us to come down to the party. We told Tom, 'No, we're not coming to your parties because we hear they are *something else* and we don't indulge!' Tom tried to explain to us that nothing goes on, they're very nice, those are all rumours. And we said, 'OK,' so we started going to their parties and they were OK, sitting around, laughing and talking after the gig was over . . . But then we did see quite a few women going in and out of the bedroom – they weren't in there very long, then they would send somebody else in . . ." Darlene goes on to say that it became a standing joke that the women would be brought in as soon as The Blossoms had left for the evening.

"There were some crazy parties, there were some crazy things. Some incidences which were just mind-blowing," Big Jim marvels today. "I wouldn't want to experience them again. You can use your imagination, we were all involved! You'd walk in a room and you'd have 600 bums staring at you!" Chris Hutchins can only remember one actual orgy, and volunteers that they weren't so much orgies as 'selection parties' . . .

While this was not necessarily the kind of atmosphere into which to introduce a child, Mark Woodward, aged 16, finally joined the touring party for good in mid 1973. "I've often asked him if it's difficult being my son, but he's got a strong personality of his own and I've only wanted whatever made him happy," Tom told the *TV Times* in 1989. "When he was 16 I was travelling a lot and not seeing him much. We were out to dinner one night and I could see he was moody. I asked him what the matter was and he said he wanted me to be with him more. I talked to his headmaster, who said: 'Let him leave school and take him on tour with you.' He's been with me ever since." Chris Hutchins believes that it was actually Mark's idea to leave as he didn't care much for his education and wasn't a remarkable scholar. Either way, Chris wrote a letter to the school explaining the situation, and the general consensus was that Mark would be happier if he were to accompany his father around the world.

Mark fitted easily into the new way of life. He was not in the least star-struck by all the celebrities he encountered and was simply glad to be with his father all the time. He was an independent lad and did not show any jealousy or possessiveness over his father. Furthermore Tom expected appropriate behaviour from his son as Wendy Watkins recalls: "Tom was very strict with Mark, particularly with his manners ... Mark had to watch his p's and q's. He had to behave in a certain manner." Being the only youngster within the group Mark was well looked after, particularly by The Blossoms, who all acted as surrogate mothers. He was into heavy rock music, and was fanatical about football. Chris remembers that Mark would spend an hour-and-a-half on the phone to England while someone played the radio commentary for Leeds United games to him.

Previous biographers have suggested that Mark was disliked and even mocked by members of the fold, but everyone interviewed for this book has only fond memories of the teenager in a man's world. However bizarre it must have seemed to have a youth with them at all times, no one in the entourage questioned Mark's presence with Tom, although Lloyd Greenfield in particular was taken aback. "I think some of us around Tom felt that this was not a natural life for a teenager ... I don't think he [Tom] thought that through," remembers Chris.

Being on tour and treated like 'one of the lads' exposed Mark to the idiosyncrasies of the group, and abruptly forced him out of his mother's protective cocoon. Tom's philandering was by far the most delicate subject the entourage felt they had to shield Mark from. At first the conscientious father was discreet about his female companions and illicit exploits, but because it was such a regular occurrence his precautions lapsed with time. "It just somehow seemed so natural suddenly that Mark had to accept it ... his son would just be one of seven or eight men round the table at breakfast," says Chris.

It was, of course, around the breakfast table that Tom would openly discuss his previous night's activities, often with those who had been responsible for finding him a willing companion. Tom's rumoured 'sexaholism' meant that his employees would often find themselves looking for a suitable night-time partner for the star, sometimes at three o'clock in the morning. Big Jim Sullivan confirms: "Members of the entourage went out in the middle of the night in Caesar's Palace to pick up a bird for Tom."

Although Mark's education had been stunted, the majority of Tom's circle of friends regarded him as highly intelligent, and it came as little surprise when the teenager began to actually work for his father. Tom had spoken well of his son in a *Daily Mirror* special four years previously: "He knows everything I do. If I discuss something – a deal or something – with my wife, I discuss it with him there. He's interested in my job . . . I'd like to see him in show business, because I think it's a marvellous business to be in. He needn't necessarily be a performer. He could be in an agency or with a recording company. He's interested in music and aware of the business. Though he's only 12 he can tell a corny song from a good one."

Now Mark was 16 he was old enough and strong enough to take on several responsibilities within the touring party, and he was pleased to become at first an extra 'minder' for his father, using his height and size to great advantage. Later, when Chris Ellis and then Larry 'Nifty' Richstein decided to retire from the scene, Mark became a roadie, and shortly after, a lighting supervisor. Tom was extremely proud of his son's budding career, boasting that he was the best lighting supervisor he had ever had, and that with all the additional time they were now spending together the pair were more like brothers than father and son. The apprenticeship that Mark served on the road as a teenager would stand him in good stead for the future.

Mark obligingly emerged as a younger version of his dad, similar in facial features and manner, and sharing both a fondness for alcohol and a disdain for drugs and drug-users. According to biographers Stafford Hildred and David Gritten, he also inherited Tom's penchant for black ladies as he gradually came out of his shell and began to mingle more at parties. "The time I remember meeting him, a group of black singers/dancers called The Love Machine was opening for Tom. Mark was clearly involved with one of these girls," recalls 'Diane' of the young Romeo.

Tom's ever-growing revenue from touring enabled him to indulge himself with the ongoing purchase of new cars. In 1973 he invested in a custom-made reproduction of a 1935 Auburn Speedster in cream with brown leather. Plans were also discussed about buying an entire farm in the English countryside of the Cotswolds. Linda received gifts of elaborate and extremely expensive jewellery, but understandably, its value to her was considerably less than her husband's physical presence, and rows would inevitably erupt with increasing regularity.

Tom too had a bit of a temper and, spurred on by the ever-vigilant Dai Perry, scenes could rapidly escalate, especially when they'd been drinking. One particularly rowdy 'going home' celebration occurred on a flight back to England, the aftermath of which was reported with great delight in the media soon after. Tom and his entourage were travelling with Pan Am, with whom he had previously maintained a good relationship, as they had provided substantial sponsorship for *This Is Tom Jones*.

The drunkenness of Tom's party caused an uproar, but the real trouble started when an angry passenger asked Tom to quieten down and, getting no response, hurled her coffee all over him. Tom responded by throwing his brandy back at her, and a veritable brawl ensued. At one point a uniformed man was knocked to the ground by an incensed Dai Perry, who told him that he would not be getting up until the plane had landed. The papers took great delight in printing the man's stiff response: "The plane can't land without me – I'm the captain!"

On arrival at Heathrow the plane was met by police and Tom's party was detained for two hours in customs where yet again he was obliged to pay excess duty, this time to the tune of £850. The on-board shenanigans were quickly hushed up as much as possible and a spokesman for Pan Am made the following statement: "This whole affair is most regrettable. We have been carrying Mr Jones and his party on most of his round the world tour and this is the first time anyone has complained about them." But Tom was unrepentant, admitting that celebrations on board had become overly raucous but offering no form of apology.

Alongside fame and fortune came not only the obligatory media scandals, but frequent invitations to attend or even host star-studded events. With 19-year-old Marjorie Wallace, Tom got both.

In autumn 1973 Tom was invited to judge the celebrated *Miss World* beauty contest. With the rise of feminism and general common sense, this televised extravaganza is now vastly outdated, but in the early Seventies it was an immensely popular parade of bikini-clad girls vying for the title of the world's most beautiful woman. The award brought with it lucrative sponsorship and a year's worth of travelling to exotic locations, meeting exciting people and representing the 'ethics' of the *Miss World* pageant. The downside was that the girls were supposed to be as pure as the driven snow, and to remain so for the duration of their reign.

When the offer came through for Tom to reside on the panel of judges, Gordon put his foot firmly down and refused – his superstar was by now far too famous and classy to appear on a show which had traditionally attracted only B-list celebrities. Chris Hutchins remembers with a smirk that the offer was instead put to Engelbert Humperdinck, who graciously accepted and never found out he was only the second choice . . .

Marjorie Wallace was the first American to be crowned *Miss World*, and her country looked on proudly as she smooched with Engel for the cameras at the ball held in her honour in November 1973. Although Chris Hutchins actively encouraged the crooner to make a move on the pretty teenager as it would be good for publicity, the pair sadly didn't connect. But the link between Marji, as she was affectionately known, and the MAM crowd continued and in December that year she was finally introduced to Tom Jones.

Although the standard story goes that Marji first met Tom backstage after one of his appearances at the London Palladium, she was actually set up with Tom by Chris, who took her to a club called Hatchets in London's Piccadilly, where the singer was waiting. By all accounts they hit it off immediately, fuelling intense media speculation that was unsuccessfully played down by the organisers of the *Miss World* competition and guardians of Marji's career, Eric and Julia Morley. They were already a little too late. The fact that Tom Jones was supposedly happily married to Linda, and Marji Wallace was the steady girlfriend of famous racing driver, Peter Revson, did not go unnoticed by the press.

Still, the electricity between the couple sparked a deal with the BBC to film a spectacular show in the New Year, to be entitled *Tom Jones On Happiness Island*. The plot went along the less than imaginative lines of 'pop star meets the most beautiful girl in the world' in the idyllic setting of Barbados. Hand in hand they strolled along the beach, pausing for a passionate kiss before Tom serenaded Marji with the Bread ballad 'Make It With You', a title just begging for reckless interpretation by the media. Julia Morley was incensed and attempted to put a stop to the scene, but the lustful embrace was filmed and duly broadcast to the world.

Sightings of the celebrity 'couple' outside of working hours incited yet further tabloid interest, and Vi Trenchard defended her daughter and son-in-law perhaps a little too vehemently to reporters: "Who isn't after Tommy? Everywhere he goes he is chased by women. Miss Wallace is just one of the crowd. She means nothing to Tommy. There's only one girl in Tommy's life, and that's Linda. He only has eyes for her. Linda's not a bit worried about the tales of Tommy and this Wallace girl." The truth was that Marji had to be told that any possibility of a 'serious relationship' with Tom was impossible.

At 19, Marji was perhaps too immature to deal with the responsibilities heaped on her young shoulders by the *Miss World* organisation. On a trip to England Marji famously became involved with football hero, George Best, which climaxed dramatically in court, with Marji accusing George of stealing her fur coat and expensive jewellery. During the media scramble which ensued, revelations abounded about Marji's 'love diary' in which she supposedly rated all of her lovers on a scale of one to 10. (Tom scored with a top rating of nine out of 10, but Best earned a yellow card with a meagre three.) George Best was eventually cleared on all accounts, but the disgrace was too much for Eric and Julia Morley, and the *Miss World* crown was taken away from Marji after only 104 days. Amusingly, the following year Helen Morgan claimed the coveted *Miss World* title for the UK, but she too was dethroned when it was revealed by the press that she was in fact married with a child!★

Marji consoled herself with a planned career as a TV actress and later as spokeswoman for the Wella beauty corporation, but just a fortnight after being stripped of her title, tragedy struck. On March 22, 1974 Marji's long-term boyfriend Peter Revson was killed in a horrific car crash caused by suspension failure while he was testing the F1 Shadow at Kyalami in South Africa.

Marji was understandably distraught and turned to Tom for comfort. He had been instructed by Gordon to keep the affair low-key, but the couple had seen each other on a casual basis only over a period of some months, and had stayed in touch by telephone. When Tom was unable to offer any tangible alleviation for Marji's loss, it was the last straw.

Chris Hutchins remembers that the touring party were in Las Vegas when word came from Marji's hometown of Indianapolis that she had attempted suicide by taking an overdose of some pills she had allegedly found in Tom's bathroom, and was hovering between life and death. The entourage made the difficult decision not to tell Tom the news before he went on stage that night, but when the show was over he was properly informed and was deeply distressed.

The pianist Liberace was in the audience that night and personally assumed responsibility for taking the troubled singer's mind off his woes. He took Tom and some friends to the bar in Caesar's Palace, where an area was roped off for celebrities. Among other tricks, the colourfully camp Liberace tried to ease the situation by blindfolding his guests and offering them an array of soft drinks. They were then made to guess the name of each drink they consumed – Chris recalls that each and every person involved in this game failed, due either to a decline in his taste buds or more likely to the lack of alcohol involved! Thankfully, the next day Tom received the information that Marji had survived, although she remained on the critical list in the Indianapolis Hospital for several days.

Despite the tragic implications of the last few weeks, the press were

---

★ As is their standard policy, Julia and Eric Morley refused to comment for this book.

having a field day and the following statement was issued on Tom's behalf: "Tom is very happy that Marji is getting better and feels that things are being said about her character when she is not in the position to defend herself." Although throughout their association Tom and Marji had sworn that they were merely good friends, it was hardly surprising that the publicity caused a strain on Tom's marriage.

Over the years Tom has become more outspoken in interviews on the subject of his high-profile affairs with Mary Wilson and Marji Wallace. To journalist Mike Cable he spoke about Linda's reaction to the speculative reports her husband had attracted during the *Miss World* scandal: "As long as I always go back to her in the end she's OK. Mind you, I still get a lot of stick if I'm in the papers for the wrong reasons. She's not *that* understanding! When I went out with Marjorie Wallace a couple of times and Linda found out, there was hell to pay. She was frightened that I was going to run off with her but when I assured her that I wasn't, it was alright. Not that she ever lets me forget it. Even now, whenever Marjorie comes on television in America, Linda still goes on about it . . ."

★   ★   ★

In 1974 Tom's chart career limped on, with a *Greatest Hits* compilation achieving a fairly respectable number 15 in the UK but a diabolical number 185 in the US early in the year. His new single, the bouncy 'Somethin' 'Bout You Baby I Like' reached number 36 in the UK later in September. In spite of the disappointing US chart showings, the tour brochure publicising Tom's appearances at Caesar's Palace that year proclaimed him to be the world's highest paid entertainer.

Tom spent the beginning of the year in Britain, undertaking his first UK tour for three years. In January he hit the headlines, singing in the Halmaen Club in the village of Usk, Monmouthshire. Tom was truly returning to his roots with this appearance at the Welsh working men's club, which was packed with miners and their wives wearing their Sunday best. Tom said to the delighted reporters: "When I sing in Vegas, I'll see Presley or Sinatra in the audience, and it's flattering to know they're out there applauding me. But it means so much more to perform here and spot familiar faces from the old days, boys I used to go drinking with when we were lads. I know I earn a lot of money now but the feeling I get here when I go on stage is just the same as when me and the band – Tommy Scott & The Senators, as we were known in those days – were earning £12 a night between seven of us and changing in the gents toilets."

The truth behind the façade was somewhat more prosaic. The jollity of Tom's trip around Britain belied the fact that it could well be his last for many, many years to come. By 1974 Tom's typical earnings were over £5 million per year, and although the singer's tax bill had been lessened through the formation of MAM, it was still a crippling figure. Tom had returned to America when the Labour government came to power in March, but was still required to pay 84 pence for each pound he earned to the British Inland Revenue. The obvious answer was for him to become, along with Engelbert Humperdinck whose earnings were equally high, a tax exile.

"It wasn't that I objected to paying British tax," said Tom to the Birmingham *Evening Mail* in 1987, "but with all my earnings coming from America by then, I was paying 84% in Britain plus 15% holding tax in the States. Really I had no choice." When Harold Wilson's newly elected Labour Party's plans for taxing the rich were revealed, Tom was abroad. "In February of that year, I got a call from my accountant Bill Smith saying: 'You will have to seriously consider not coming home, because they're going to kill you with the tax.'" Tom considered his options, well aware that he was travelling back and forth to the States, where his presence was more amply rewarded. What was the point of retaining a base in England? "It wouldn't have made much sense to keep doing that. The tax was 98% on unearned income, 84% on earned income and 15% withholding tax in the States.★ So for two years, I just kept on the move until I got my Green Card."★★

During the years from 1974 to 1976, Tom, Gordon, Engelbert and all the musicians intrinsic to their success found themselves in a form of domiciliary limbo, and made good use of the 180-day plan formulated back in 1971. While this may have seemed a haphazard and uncertain way of life as Tom awaited his Green Card, those involved used the travelling necessities as a way of seeing the world, and quite literally had the time of their lives.

"While we were in the States we could only stay there six months – we used to have to get out," recalls Big Jim Sullivan. "We used to go to all sorts of places. We went on John Wayne's yacht down the Gulf of Mexico for a couple of weeks, and the Bahamas and Bermuda, all to get out of the

★ Tom was not exaggerating. In 1975, one year after coming to power, Harold Wilson's government alienated all British high-earners by raising the taxes from 75% to 83% on earned income over £20,000 while lowering the threshold to £19,000. Tax on investment interest remained at 15%, making the total taxation a maximum of 98%. Although this was the year that Margaret Thatcher took over from Edward Heath as leader of the Conservative Party, it would be four years before she and Nigel Lawson reformed tax allowances to encourage high-earners back to the UK.
★★ The Green Card is a US work permit which enables non-US citizens to work, and live permanently, in the US.

tax. This one particular time in Bermuda, we'd been there for two or three weeks, and we went to this nightclub. The three of us, John Rostill on bass, Kenny [Clare – teacher of Terry Jenkins and occasional drummer] and myself got up as the rhythm section, and Tom sang the blues – Howlin' Wolf, you know. It was fantastic."

Derek Watkins particularly enjoyed the trips aboard John Wayne's boat, *The Golden Goose*, with Big Jim and John Rostill, and still winces at the memory of John Wayne firing a gun to announce that dinner was ready. The whole point of visiting the vessel was to get out of territorial waters, and when the musicians faced the decision of whether to go home to save tax days or to set sail on this boat, they invariably chose not to return to England.

Tom too had to spend time in exotic locations like Barbados and Mexico to avoid the monetary implications. He would make arrangements to see his wife in 'neutral' countries like France and Belgium but sorely missed his family home in Weybridge. Verging on the faintly ridiculous, Tom, Gordon and Engel had just invested in a 1,300 acre farm in Sussex but all were unable to physically visit the site, simply because of the maniacally evasive tactics that were necessary to avoid tax.

Still, the fun persisted and in June 1974 Tom had a surprise 34th birthday party thrown for him in Las Vegas, which was attended by, among others, Joan Rivers, Sonny Bono, Dionne Warwick, Debbie Reynolds and Liberace. A prank had been played on the birthday boy earlier that evening during a performance, when a hotel security guard dressed as a woman chased Tom around the stage before picking him up and putting him back in the spotlight. Gordon arrived especially for the celebrations and led the orchestra during the concert in place of Johnnie Spence. Tom only realised the difference in personnel after he had completed the opening number.

Around this time reports began to surface in the tabloids that Tom had ballooned to 15 stone. Having given up reporting on young Mark's portly appearance, the media hounds decided instead to focus on his Dad, announcing that a massive transformation was taking place as Tom trained his way back to fitness. While this was all very much exaggerated in order to sell newspapers, in all truth Tom had battled with his weight since 1966 in an effort to appeal to the masses. During the filming of *This Is Tom Jones* the cameramen were not allowed to film Tom from below as it would reveal his double chin, and a work-out programme cunningly titled 'Operation Superstar' was launched to help Tom stay in shape. When questioned on this matter, Tom would typically shrug and admit to fluctuating by approximately 10 pounds in weight then jest that the tightness of his figure-hugging trousers kept the flab at bay.

Another shocking report this same year concerned Tom's brush with death in a bathing incident. During a day-saving holiday spent in Acapulco, Mexico, Tom decided to venture far out into the sea. When he surfaced for long enough to look around him, the intrepid swimmer found he was more than a quarter of a mile away from the coastline. As he struggled unsuccessfully to return to the shore, Tom began to panic, thinking he wasn't going to make it back. "I thought to myself: 'What a bloody fool you are. Everything you've achieved means nothing if you drown now because of your stupidity.'" When Tom reflects on this frightening experience, he remembers how he felt his strength ebbing away and began to prepare himself for the worst. Suddenly, seemingly out of nowhere a giant wave picked him up and threw him through the air and onto the beach!

"I landed with a crash and just lay there gasping for air. I'd made it but I'd known real fear. And I didn't feel a lot better for the experience when a Mexican found me on the beach and told me: 'Señor, do not swim here. It is where we shoot sharks.'"

As 1975 beckoned, Tom and his usual entourage embarked on a whistle-stop tour of South America, performing in a total of 10 countries in 12 days. The motley crew had a fabulous time, partying at discos every night and refusing to leave until the cleaners arrived. Spirits were high and those involved were inebriated most every night. However, when Tom arrived in South America, there were concerns as to the current volatility of the continent, not least the temperament of the people and the indiscriminate methods of law enforcement. Engelbert Humperdinck had performed there prior to Tom's visit, and had been detained in customs while the authorities scrutinised a bottle of pills he was carrying for the purpose of calming his nerves.*

When the tour party arrived in the Venezuelan airport of Caracas, fans had been queuing for hours to catch a glimpse of the pop singer, and he was immediately pounced on by a rabble of paparazzi. Dai Perry, Tom's trusted bodyguard, swung into preventative action. "Dave's job was to not let anyone get too close, they could have a knife, a gun or anything," explains his sister, Marion Crewe. "So they got off the plane and this fella, this cad, they told him not to get too close and he ripped a chain from around my brother's neck, so he hit him!" Dai himself later confirmed in the press: "They were hitting us and kicking us from behind. I retaliated, I just turned round and let him have one."

* Previous Tom Jones biographies have also suggested that this part of the tour was clouded with a threatened kidnap of 17-year-old Mark, but research on this topic turned up no supporting evidence for such a claim.

The injured party was Manola Olaquiaga, a photographer for local paper *El Universal*. Without hesitation he pressed charges against the Tom Jones group and filed a law suit claiming a staggering $65,000 in damages. "We knew we were in trouble because when we went into Caracas and Tom did the concert, the bodyguards were muted, [whereas before] they had been great fun throughout the tour," recalls Chris Hutchins. "We especially knew there was trouble when the bodyguards who had been in the room with their guns pointed out suddenly were *outside* the room with their guns pointing *in* . . ."

At the hotel Tom's party was informed that Olaquiaga was requesting Dai Perry be detained and not allowed to leave Caracas. For Gordon, who had endured several bust-ups involving the temperamental bodyguard to date, it was the final straw. Such violent behaviour was unsuitable for Tom's public image, as was having the singer's name splashed across headlines in connection with events like the recent Pan Am scuffle. So the manager decreed that whether Dai had been acting in Tom's best interests or not, he must be asked to leave the party.

The entourage were then faced with the question of how to remove Dai from the potentially dangerous situation. "We mounted a military-style operation to get Dai out of the country, and get him via Miami back to London before they could arrest him," explains Chris. Marion confirms the termination of her brother's employment: "You can't retaliate in these South American countries otherwise they put you in jail and lock you up. So they shipped him straight to Florida and he was there for a while. He got a bit cheesed off with Florida, he wasn't sent home so he just got his own way back here. He'd had enough then."

Back in Caracas the tension was mounting despite Dai's departure. "That didn't satisfy anybody, the authorities wanted Tom to answer to the charge," says Chris. "It was very, very unpleasant. Instead of leaving the next day as we planned, we were under house arrest for three days." The only solution that Gordon and Chris could come up with was to contact British Prime Minister Harold Wilson, for whom Chris was working infrequently as a press aide, and appeal for help.

Ironically it was Harold Wilson's government that had forced Tom and the others into tax exile just months earlier. MAM's existing relationship with the Prime Minister was shaky to say the least, due to a chance meeting between Gordon and Wilson at a party thrown by Chris some time before. One of the Government's first problems on reassuming power in 1974 was how to approach the civil war that was currently raging in Rhodesia (now Zimbabwe) following Ian Smith's Unilateral Declaration of Independence. Gordon's wife Jo originally came from Rhodesia and her husband, fuelled by alcohol, had some typically hawkish ideas about how the Government might best handle the racial issues involved. After a while the Prime Minister refused to listen to his views, whereupon Gordon pompously asked Chris to throw out his most distinguished guest!

Fortunately for Tom, the Prime Minister did not harbour a grudge, and when the urgent cable arrived imploring his assistance, he tried to set the official wheels in motion to free the virtually imprisoned pop star. To a certain extent his hands were tied due to the explosive political situation in Venezuela, and it was also apparent that any intervention from the British Embassy was going to take time. That was something Tom Jones did not have.

Chris continues the sorry tale: "What happened was about three o'clock one night, the mood had become very sombre and we were sitting around. We were really serious and worried, nobody's laughing, nobody's joking and there was no womanising going on . . . We were told he [Tom] would appear before a certain judge at half past six in the morning. And if he had $9,000 I think it was, in cash, the judge would release him and we could get on the one plane that went to Miami. If we missed that plane he would be hauled back in and the whole procedure would have to be gone through again."

"It was like a bad dream," said Tom later, having duly deposited the money in a briefcase the following morning. "Until they took the aircraft steps away and closed the door I was half expecting someone to grab me by the arm and escort me out again." The relief shows on his face in the famous photographs of Tom landing at Miami airport, wearing handcuffs and being jostled by two armed guards. Never one to miss a publicity opportunity, Chris had decided it would be best to play up the incident but make light of it at the same time.

The Venezuelan fiasco aside, the tour was not without its happy moments. Drummer Terry Jenkins first encountered his wife-to-be, Gül, partially thanks to Tom. The singer had temporarily lost his voice, and because of their problematic tax situation, Terry and some other musicians escaped from America and stayed for a brief period in Barbados.

"We met in Barbados when Tom got laryngitis, that was when we were working in New York," says Terry today. "And by sheer accident, Gül happened to be on her own on holiday. It was a bit of a whirlwind romance. The following January we were doing a South American tour down in Puerto Rico, and Gül came to visit me.

"One night we were sitting around the pool having a few drinks and I said, 'Let's get married!' And somebody said, 'Yeah, great idea, let's have a party!' So she said, 'Fine, OK.' So we had to find a judge!" The following morning on January 28, 1975 Terry and Gül were married in the hotel suite. The whole band attended the ceremony, Mark took the photographs, and to his immense pride Tom was given the honour of being best man, although he got away without making a speech.*

Back in Weybridge, Linda Woodward had recently surprised those friends who thought of her as increasingly reclusive. She spoke on the subject of marital bliss and domesticity in a rare interview with Rona Barrett. "I do all the heavy, heavy cleaning and cook all the meals," she said stolidly. "When we grow old in the tooth, we might have servants. But while I have the energy I will do most of it myself."

Linda was also determined to show the world that despite the unwanted attention drawn to her marriage by Tom's association with Marji Wallace, her bond with the Welsh singer was still strong. "I feel alive when he comes in through the door, whatever the hour, the day, the month or even the year. I'll always be here. He knows that. And so do I."

★   ★   ★

By the summer of 1975 it had been two long years since the lady who has chosen to be known in this book as 'Diane' had her first sexual encounter with Tom, and she had been virtually counting the days to his return. As before, Tom was appearing at the Musicarnival Theater in Warrensville Heights in Diane's home town of Cleveland. "I had great seats for the concert – third row. I believe Tom was there for six nights and I had tickets for three of those nights. After several songs, he spotted me in the audience. He said, 'Haven't we met?' I went to the stage. Tom looked at me and said so sweetly, 'I remember you. It's been a while.'" Tom appeared delighted that Diane was at the concert and said to her, "I'll see you later Diane . . ."

Based on her past experience Diane expected to be collected by one of Tom's bodyguards, but when he failed to show up, Diane and her friend went back to the Bluegrass Motor Inn where Tom was once again staying. "As we made our way to the lobby, I was suddenly grabbed by a gentleman. He said, 'I have been looking for you everywhere. Tom is upstairs waiting for you.' He escorted me up to Tom's room . . . he was waiting for me, all alone."

After the long-postponed deed Tom went to the bathroom to apply some ointment, which slightly baffled the young lady. "I later found out from other women that this is kind of a ritual, I don't know what it is but

* Over the years, several other such unions took place among Tom's touring party, including guitarist Mike Morgan to his sweetheart Wendy; a surprise wedding between John and Margaret Rostill in Las Vegas; and Big Jim Sullivan who embarked on his first marriage (out of four) to a member of a backing group previously employed by Tom Jones.

I'm assuming it kills germs." She continues, "When I was leaving he told me to let Lloyd Greenfield know I would be there at the following Friday and Saturday's concerts and arrangements would be made then." As Diane watched the concerts on those two nights Tom flirted openly with her from the stage, prompting some of the other women present to ask her if she knew the star personally, which she found both flattering and embarrassing. "I only objected to the groupies that would try and scheme to see Tom or buddy-up to me to get information."

Diane then returned to Tom's hotel, going straight up to his suite where his customary party was being held. "At one point during the evening, one of the ladies made a rude comment about Tom's wife. I heard it and that woman disappeared from the room so fast. She was escorted out by one of Tom's bodyguards." Diane explains that Tom needed to feel total trust in the people around him. "He told me early on that he didn't want any photos of us together because that could cause trouble."

After their second encounter in 1975, Diane was not to see Tom again for over a year until he returned to Ohio in the autumn of 1976, playing at a new venue called the Front Row Theater, in Highland Heights. Once again their meeting was the same: "I was waiting for the perfect moment to stand up and give Tom the bottle of Dom Perignon. We had already made eye contact and as soon as I stood up he acknowledged me. He asked how I'd been . . . It was almost as if he wanted everyone to know he knew me. He made the usual small talk and I of course asked for a kiss. Tom was always delightfully sweaty and cupped my face with his hand and gave me that wonderful, deep French kiss."

This time Diane was collected by a new member of Tom's entourage, Burke, who took her to the penthouse suite of The Bond Court Hotel. "We sat around the room waiting for Tom. He came out of the other room and sat down on the couch next to me and we started watching TV. All of a sudden his son Mark startled me from behind, on purpose, just to scare me. He was really rather obnoxious . . ."

Certainly Tom did not shy away from showing his affection for Diane in public. Eventually he led her through to the bedroom. "The first thing he asked was if I was on birth control pills. I was and told him, 'Yes,' but I could have been lying. He was so trusting in that area, probably because he had no intention of wearing a condom."

Spurred on from meeting Mark and feeling close enough by this time to Tom, Diane dared to broach the subject of his wife, Linda. "I asked Tom if she knew what he was doing on the road. Tom said, 'She doesn't ask me what I do on the road and I don't ask her what she does when I'm on the road. We have an agreement.' " The next night Diane was taken to Tom's suite by Burke as before, but she was concerned for the singer's well-being as she had the beginnings of a sore throat. "He gave me this tiny little lozenge and told me to suck on it. It was called a 'vocalette' or something like that. It's what Tom is continually popping in his mouth during concerts." After what Diane describes as their 'usual business of sex', they rejoined the rest of the party and sat down to dinner. "Tom was hungry and I was a little taken aback by his table manners – the way he held his fork and how he didn't chew with his mouth shut!"

Tom returned to the Front Row Theater in October 1977 and as always, Diane was able to get prime seats for three of the performances. Well-versed in the routine by now, Diane was taken by Burke to the Chagrin Marriot hotel to be with Tom. Sex with the singer had always been exciting for Diane, not least because he was many women's greatest fantasy, but also because he was very skilful with a lot of stamina. "He was a very caring lover in bed, tender and deliberate. He didn't talk much."

Tom enjoyed the pleasures of both intercourse and oral stimulation and would often indulge several times a night. As this was the fourth year of wanton meetings with Diane, Tom wanted to introduce a few sex toys into their lovemaking. Diane was unhappy with this and refused, which at first did not appear to cause a problem.

"Then Tom started talking about me having sex with another woman. He had all the arguments to convince me this was a very normal thing to do, but I felt very uncomfortable about it. I asked him if he would like doing it with another man, and he said, 'No,' because that was totally different. 'Women are soft and gentle to touch and it feels like that to another woman,' he said." Unconvinced, Diane declined again, but Tom persisted and attempted to experiment in other ways that she felt were unpleasant and also halted. "He never pushed any of these issues, but I felt things in our relationship had really taken a turn. On top of that I was newly married . . . I never tried or asked to go backstage again."

During her time with Tom, Diane made friends with several other girls who visited the entourage while they were on tour. She has no regrets and today adopts a detached attitude towards the time she spent with Tom and the other relationships of his that she learned of. "I think when you start to assume anything in a relationship with Tom it is over instantly. I know one-nighters were really popular with Tom though. Too many nights might give a girl ideas, like he actually cared for them . . . Tom never gave me anything except his time. I never even considered asking him for anything either. I really felt and guess I still feel that was one of the reasons I got to go back for repeat visits. I was never demanding or acted like he owed me anything.

"If I had to do it over again, I would. Looking back on the entire experience I guess I might wish the relationship wasn't just about sex, but it was. It would have been nice to actually know Tom . . . [but] my memories will always be good ones."

13

ONLY IN AMERICA

THE CLOSE OF 1975 saw the sad departure of the very man who had smoothed over the troubled South American events at the beginning of that year. Chris Hutchins had been based in Los Angeles with his wife Jan and the rest of the MAM people for the best part of two years, but now Jan put her foot down and demanded that she and their family return permanently to England. Gordon Mills was having none of this and told his trusted PR man to convince his wife that it would not be possible. Torn between his marriage and his friends, Chris steadfastly refused and on New Year's Eve Gordon phoned him at his home in Richmond no less than four times. The fourth and final time Chris told him their business association was well and truly over, and hung up on him for good.

By this time, and by Chris' own admission, he and Gordon were both acting erratically, due mainly to the influence of drugs and drink, but also the unreality of living within the penumbra of Tom's reflected superstardom. Chris was relieved that the stress of being part of "the circus" was finally over and he hoped that being in London again might help him resume a normal lifestyle. He had been MAM's press officer for almost a decade, from Boxing Day 1966 to New Year's Eve 1975, and when he put the phone down on Gordon for the final time, it was the last time they ever spoke to one another.

In the summer of 1975, Tom's popularity was ebbing away in Britain and the Tom Jones Appreciation Society, which had originally been run by Jo Mills, folded due to lack of interest. As Tom was now rarely spotted in his home country there was no longer any need for a fan club, especially as 'chapters' of varying sizes were being established all over the States. It wasn't until a further two years later that Sylvia Firth took over the running of the 'official' UK fan club.

Also put on hold for another two years was any new studio output from Tom. Aside from a host of hits collections commemorating a decade's worth of material, no new albums were released until 1977. For the immediate future the 35-year-old performer settled into a repetitive

209

routine based around his US travels and his long-standing stints in the casinos of Las Vegas.

"I don't like a lot of time off," said Tom of the touring that kept him away from home for up to 10 months of the year. "I can get lazy, and start overindulging in good food and good wine. What I do keeps me disciplined." Tom's tours had been organised since the early days by an agency called Creative Management Associates (CMA), headed by Buddy Howe, who became a great friend of Gordon's.* Each year CMA would produce a potential itinerary for Gordon, who would examine the various options, converse with Buddy over any discrepancies and then agree a schedule.

During their travels, the musicians would stay in the same hotel as Tom, and were not allowed to reveal its location to any members of the press or the public. CMA would do their utmost to keep the accommodation facilities as far away from the concert venues as possible. However, such precautions did little to deter the die-hard fans, who would follow the cars all the way to the hotel after the shows.

Anyone braving a visit to Tom's suite had to endure some unusual impediments. Because of the risks of dry air and smoke to his priceless voice, the singer would almost always have at least three large humidifiers constantly humming away in his room. "I lost my voice in Berlin in 1967 and since then I've carried a humidifier in my trunk wherever I go," Tom informed *Smash Hits*. "It's a bloody big black trunk and the steam is good for my voice." A former bodyguard was later to reveal to the press that Tom's humidifiers gulped an incredible 20 gallons of water every night, making the room as steamy as any rainforest and very difficult for the untrained to breathe in.

Aside from the attention heaped on his vocal cords, Tom was also keen to keep fit while on the road, and the advance planners would locate all the exclusive health clubs along the journey so that Tom could train to his heart's content. His daily routine was a strange one, based largely around his nocturnal habits and the substantial amount of sleep he required to ensure a decent night's performance.

Normally Tom would go out for a run to keep himself fit, but in the dry desert heat of Las Vegas this would have been potentially harmful to his voice. Any other sporting activity might disrupt his career with an injury, so instead Tom would ensconce himself in the gym, followed by a moisturising sauna. A Las Vegas health club trainer, boxer Mike Caplin, was favourably impressed by his famous student, stating in Tom's 10th

---

* Buddy Howe's deputy was Norman Wise, the very same booking agent who had introduced Tom to Mary Wilson all those years ago.

Anniversary Tour Souvenir Book: "I have never seen a guy outside the ring in so good a condition. And he can take more hot steam than any man alive – he is in that cabin for 25 minutes. Some of the other guys go in there to try and rap with him but the most they can take in that heat is two minutes. That's Tom – he can outlast them all!" By all accounts including his own, Tom loved his lifestyle. "Touring? It's just like being patted on the back all the time. I love that thing of coming off stage after all the excitement and thinking, 'Christ, you've done it again, Tom' – it's magic."

In the mid Seventies the aesthetic of Tom's performances had extended to the mildly pornographic, with the star thinking nothing of an appearance at The Lido Club, where he sang 'Old Fashioned Strut' in front of a line-up of topless dancers in skimpy gold thongs. The ladies' assets were barely covered by their strategically placed swinging tassels and Tom appeared to be having the time of his life, adding to his performance the rapturous ad-lib: "You know I want it and I've got to have it all night long!" Notably, a fan club called the Tom Jones Old Fashioned Strutters was in evidence in New Orleans, presumably inspired by the song and not this particular display.

In addition, press reports described Tom's on-stage 'humour' at this time as being, "a little on the raw side; one minute he's reciting an embarrassingly naughty ditty about the birds being ripe for the plucking and the next he's stripping off his mauve jacket and waistcoat and asking the audience what they think of his tailor." Tom would set about kissing each and every delighted female on the front row of his concerts, literally rolling around the stage in mock ecstasy and making full use of the various items of erotic lingerie flung in his direction.

At Caesar's Palace, Tom would perform two shows a night, each about an hour in length, the second finishing at around 2.00 a.m. Tom would then eat a full dinner and stay up partying either in his dressing room area or suite until 8.00 a.m., when he would have his breakfast and finally retire to bed, not to be disturbed until late afternoon. When he arose he would snack on cereal and fruit, declining a proper meal until his performances were over. This was a typical day in the life of Tom Jones during the weeks he spent in Las Vegas. Tom rarely ventured out of the permanent twilight of the casinos, where purposely no clocks are displayed, and almost never went on any extra-curricular trips out of town. "Las Vegas is like home to me. The only trouble is, it's a bit like working down the coal mines of Wales – I rarely get to see the daylight!" he quipped at the time.

"In Vegas you felt like a house band because you were working there six times a year, for two straight weeks at a time," Cynthia Woodard says today. "We would look forward to that, rather than being on the road doing one-nighters." She recalls that in the Seventies the ensemble would submerge themselves in Las Vegas for up to half a dozen stretches each year, with trips to each US city in between. She describes how the majority of the audience would be made up of familiar faces, be they in Las Vegas or New York. Like many performers of his stature, Tom had such a devoted following that they would travel to wherever he was currently playing.

As he was busy running MAM and looking after his other interests, Tom's monthly sessions in Las Vegas were the only times that Gordon would join the party on tour. Long gone were the days when the manager felt it necessary to chaperone his most successful charge. "Gordon would come to Vegas because he liked to have a flutter and all that," says Derek Watkins frankly. "He would come and keep an eye on everything, make sure it was alright."

★   ★   ★

In February 1976 a British White Paper was published that proposed a possible decrease in the devastating rate of tax paid by the country's wealthier citizens, but no substantial tax cuts actually transpired. It hadn't escaped Gordon and Tom's notice that overseas ticket sales for his stage act consistently poured American revenue into the British government, and it seemed all the more unfair that he should then be taxed by the very country that benefited.

During 1975 Tom had been residing mainly in New York, but when the decision was finally made for him to move to America permanently, he chose the sunny Californian way of life and hunted for a suitable property in the exclusive enclave of Bel Air, north of Los Angeles. The 'City of Angels' was an ideal base in which to settle as the show business quota there was far higher per square mile than any other city in the world. Linda faithfully accompanied her husband to their new surroundings, perhaps for once denying the anonymity afforded behind the gates of Tor Point.

They weren't alone in moving abroad. At the same time Engel acquired the 'pink palace' once owned by Jayne Mansfield in the same area, and Johnnie and Marion Spence moved to the sweltering heat of Lake Encino. For some time now Gordon and Jo had been experiencing problems in their relationship. When Gordon moved to Holmby Hills, just off Sunset Boulevard, Jo chose initially to stay behind in Weybridge, although she did then travel out to Los Angeles shortly after in a last ditch attempt to save her floundering marriage.

Key members of Gordon's empire remained in London to run MAM's British interests, although they were all frequently to be found visiting their friends in Los Angeles. Bill Smith took over the daily control of the London offices in Gordon's absence and Colin Berlin and Barry Clayman also stayed behind, the latter eventually forming BCC Entertainment which to this day promotes Tom's concerts. It was up to the musicians whether they chose to move permanently or not, and most stayed resident in the UK, renting houses in the US when necessary. The singular Gilbert O'Sullivan typically continued his frugal lifestyle in Weybridge.

Although it was of course very exciting to up sticks and move to America, Tom was heartbroken to put his beloved English residence on the market. Publicly he had no qualms about blaming the government for his departure, but he was still sad to leave his home country and Tor Point, especially as he had fared far better in the British charts than it seemed he could ever hope to in America.

When Tom had lived in his native Pontypridd, the entire population of the town had been around 2,000. In Los Angeles the number was within the millions and the culture shock would have been quite substantial if Tom hadn't first lived in London and then New York. When interviewed on the difference between the countries, Tom listed the biggest improvement as the favourable weather, and stated resolutely that he was going to retain his Welsh accent no matter what.

In the month of August 1976, Tom, Gordon and Johnnie Spence all moved into their respective Los Angeles abodes and cheerfully bustled around comparing and contrasting each other's new living quarters. The price Tom paid for the house he finally decided on, which had previously belonged to crooner Dean Martin, differed considerably according to which newspaper you read. The general consensus was that it had cost him $1 million though some reports suggested he paid a further $3 million in renovation expenses. Tom quipped to the *Observer*, "The house is just like me. Conceived in 1939 and finished in 1940."

Tom's new home was also strikingly similar to Tor Point. Situated at 363 Copa de Oro Road, Bel Air, the red brick structure was fashioned in a mock 18th century style complete with wooden panelling inside. The house had been built at the very top of Copa de Oro; a Spanish name meaning 'Cup of Gold', which was coined to reflect the millionaire status of its inhabitants. Tom immediately set about shipping all his furniture from Weybridge over to the new location, and soon enough for added security he had installed his trademark electronic gates adorned with Welsh dragons.

The frontage of Tom's new home was particularly stunning. It stood in an acre and a half of well-tended gardens, and at the front of the house in the cobbled courtyard, there was a decorative fountain that had been shipped all the way from Italy. At the rear was the obligatory swimming pool, measuring an ample 25 x 45 feet in length, and once he had settled in properly, Tom added a small gymnasium housing his rowing machine and punch bags, a squash court where he enjoyed regular matches with his son, and a jogging track for his daily run.

Once it had been transformed into the palatial style to which he was now accustomed, Tom seemed only too pleased to allow journalists into his American home and many detailed descriptions of the house's interior have since appeared in print. The most striking feature on entering the front door was a huge sweeping staircase in full *Gone With The Wind* style; perfect for the superstar to make a grand entrance. The staircase led up to three en-suite guest bedrooms and a master suite, which was dominated by a king-sized four poster brass bed. For some time Mark, who was just entering his twenties, lived in his own two-bedroom apartment built over the huge garage of the Bel Air mansion. Tom's parents also moved to Los Angeles during this time, with his mother endearingly transporting the bed in which Tom was born.

Downstairs housed the dining room with an extravagant twelve-seater English dining table, a breakfast room and an old fashioned kitchen with a red brick hearth harbouring a large gas range. Tom also had a big sitting room which he decked out with paisley and green leather sofas in keeping with the ornate character of the house. He had a well-stocked, mahogany panelled library, and next to that was a room devoted entirely to billiards, with its own hi-fi system for background music. Tom once mentioned on film that the price of Dean Martin's property had included an American pool table but its British counterpart, the larger snooker table, sadly didn't fit.

Tom was proud to display his collection of gold records and photographs of himself with various celebrities on the walls of the hallways. Linda added her own personal touch to the exhibition; a plentiful assortment of china animals. The finishing touch to this dream home was a room featuring its very own cinema screen, cosily fitted out with a stone fireplace, a beamed ceiling, and fittingly for a house previously occupied by Dean Martin, a well-stocked bar.

Soon enough Tom felt perfectly at home, and was fiercely proud of his new abode and its lavish decor. "I don't think success really changes you; it only brings out what is basically there to start with," he said, defending any possibility that his status had gone to his head. "It's like people saying that money changes you. It doesn't. It only lets your real character come out because some people are suppressed. They can't say what they really feel because their position doesn't allow it. But I had no reason to hold anything back."

Before the move to America, the wives or girlfriends of the Tom Jones camp had often considered themselves 'hard done by' when it came to visiting their counterparts overseas. Biding their time during rehearsals and so forth, the tour widows were well used to amusing themselves without their husbands' presence. "We all got on very well," says Wendy Watkins. "We used to go to see the shows together, the lounge acts and things after the shows had finished. Very often though we'd go into the dressing room after the show and it was just us, there weren't very many people there at all."

"I loved Linda," says Johnnie's wife Marion gently. "We had so many laughs, she had a great sense of humour. We had a lot of fun. We spent a lot of time together because if Tom was away, so was Johnnie." When it came to moving to Los Angeles, the regular shopping excursions were replaced with nostalgic trips to remind them of home. "We found an H. Salt fish and chip place on Santa Monica Boulevard," laughs Marion today. "We used to go and pick fish and chips up and go to the beach and eat them!" Once those who moved permanently abroad were firmly ensconced in Los Angeles, the three couples, Tom and Linda, Johnnie and Marion, and Gordon and Jo, would get together regularly for dinner. Johnnie and Marion in particular would host special barbecues, in typical English fashion not caring in the least whether it was rain or shine.

On moving permanently to America, Linda suffered terribly from homesickness. She took great comfort from the fact that when Tom stayed at his new house for any length of time, he gave his wife 100 per cent of his attention. Although the seemingly never-ending accounts of philandering may suggest otherwise, his devotion to Linda was never in question – his love for his wife was there for all to see. When Tom was not around, Linda liked to surround herself with familiar objects, which is one of the reasons why the couple shipped their beloved furniture over from Weybridge instead of buying new furnishings in California. She also formed a lasting bond with the cook Tom now employed on a permanent basis.★

Although Tom and Linda stuck to the Welsh tradition of keeping personal troubles within the family, it was really no secret that Linda, uprooted and missing her familiar haunts, felt uncomfortable in Los Angeles. Asked about her daily activities, Tom sometimes innocently portrayed her as a little materialistic. Whilst stating that she would amuse herself in the same way in Bel Air as she used to in Wales, he would also describe how she enjoyed the rewards and lifestyle of having anything she

---

★ This appointment contradicted somewhat Linda's statement to interviewer Rona Barrett just the preceding year, suggesting that she and Tom had no need to employ servants until they reached old age.

wanted, whenever she wanted. Tom would tactfully make a point of never discussing any marital problems with his friends, but Big Jim Sullivan perceived one aspect fundamental to the Woodward bond. "I think that there was something still there amongst all of the rest of it – I think Tom still had a little soft spot for his missus. I think that comes from the old Victorian type of attitude: 'You must stick by your wife.'"

"It's funny, but I can't imagine myself growing old in America," Tom stated in an interview with the *TV Times*. "I like the pub scene in Britain, the village life, walking down to have a pint with the boys. You don't get that here. We don't have many American friends – it's mostly family. My wife likes to keep a low profile, so we don't entertain much and we don't go out much. I don't know what I'd do if I had to retire here."

On those rare occasions when Tom found himself with some time on his hands, he read voraciously, acknowledging that it was only the absurdity of his lifestyle that allowed him to indulge in a habit he was unlikely to have developed had he remained in the mining towns of South Wales. "I read avidly," he told journalist Donald McLachlan, "just about anything I can get my hands on, but mostly biography and history, non-fiction. See, I am on planes or in hotel rooms so much that a lot of my time is spent *waiting*, and I can't go for a walk or anything like that. I take books with me everywhere I go and I have acquired a broader general knowledge than I ever dreamed about."

When it came to home comforts Tom went from the sublime, with his beautifully furnished luxury mansion, to the ridiculous. Tom somehow heard on the grapevine that the red telephone box which had stood for so long at the junction of Tower Street and Laura Street in Treforest was about to be replaced by a newer model. As this was the very site where Tom had romanced Linda and first heard news of Mark's birth, he contacted the relevant authorities and bought it for £250. After five hours work releasing it from the pavement, the telephone box was finally wrenched free and sent over to the alien setting of Bel Air, the shipping costs amounting to a reported £50,000.

"When I was 18 if you dialled Pontypridd 3667, the chances were you'd have got me in that box. That was my first home. My first office. I courted girls from it. And my family began in it (not literally mind you), and it is as much part of my life as my first gold records," justified Tom of this slightly eccentric acquisition. He promptly set it by his outdoor pool, installed an American phone and used it to store his swimming towels.

It wasn't just Tom's lifestyle and place of residence that were changing in 1976. In March the recording giant EMI concluded a licensing deal with MAM Records which was applicable worldwide, with the exception of the North American continent. From that month onwards, Gordon's major artists Tom, Engel and Gilbert appeared on the MAM label, but were distributed by EMI. For North American releases Tom parted company with London Records, having been under Decca's control for nearly 11 years, and signed to Epic, then part of the CBS empire, in the hope that they would improve his flagging record sales. Anything would be better than the abominable chart placings he had suffered in America since 1972.

As Tom was unable to visit his home country due to the tax implications, he chose the closest capital and played two concerts at the Palais de Congres, Paris in mid-March. Those Brits lucky enough to afford tickets travelled across the English Channel to catch a rare glimpse of their idol. Tom netted more than £55,000 for the performances in ticket sales alone and so in between dates was happy to sing for charity at the picturesque Lake Geneva, in Switzerland. However, Tom's most notable engagement by far this year was a controversial tour of South Africa.

Tom had first been approached to play in the racially segregated country back in 1965, but largely due to his loathing of apartheid and the harm it would have done to his image at the time, no trip had transpired. Then in early 1968 reports appeared in the music press announcing a 21-day South African tour that May.

Because of the South African government's policy of separating the blacks from the whites in public places, including concert venues, members of the Musicians' Union in Britain were banned from any professional dealings with the country. This would have prevented any of the musicians in Tom's usual touring party from making the trip. Tom was not a member of the MU and was therefore free to consider such an offer, and in the early part of 1968 Gordon flew to Johannesburg to begin negotiations.

In December 1964 British singer Dusty Springfield had hit the headlines when she performed four concerts in front of mixed audiences, having apparently found some loophole that enabled her to do so. At a fifth show, however, she was served with a deportation order and forced to leave the country. It was perhaps with this precedent in mind and also the onset of the hectic filming schedule for *This Is Tom Jones* that Gordon had decided to hold off from any Tom Jones South African tour for the best part of a decade.

Finally in 1976 Tom's own refusal to compromise appeared to have paid off when arrangements were made for him to give a concert in front of a multiracial audience. Reportedly, this would be the first time a white pop singer would legally make such an appearance and was to be a major coup both in assisting the bridging of the divide in a cultural sense, and boosting the Welshman's public image in the rest of the world. This was the year that saw the worst violence between the police and the black inhabitants of the Soweto township since the Union of South Africa had been formed in 1910, but despite the country's unrest, the South African reaction was generally good. However, Gordon made much the same mistake as he had with the 1973 tour of Japan, forcing the promoters to push the ticket prices too high, which naturally affected the number of people able to see the star in concert.

Unfortunately for Tom, Gordon was unable to ensure the desegregation of every audience, and although Tom did indeed perform for a mixed crowd on three separate dates, the other five concerts were restricted to white attendance only. Tom was outraged, having originally decreed he would sing in front of all races or not at all, but ultimately he was persuaded to see that some progress had been made and went along with the arrangements. He was accompanied by an entirely American band, which drummer Terry Jenkins notes was more than a little ironic; certainly in the Seventies the American Federation Of Musicians had a far higher percentage of black members than the Musicians' Union in the UK. The only familiar faces sharing the experience with Tom were The Blossoms as they were American, but equally faced the problem of being coloured themselves. Fanita James remembers the trip well, describing herself and her colleagues as "three little black girls scared to death over there" and recalls that they had a white bodyguard for protection. Special arrangements had to be made for The Blossoms to be allowed to stay in the same whites-only hotel as Tom, and restaurants would have to be alerted in advance that the party was of mixed race.

Back in the UK, opinion on Tom's semi-groundbreaking tour was divided. While it was one thing to herald a major breakthrough in public relations in music and between countries, it was also possible to see Tom's visit as an approval of the discredited political situation. Were the motives behind the tour purely honourable, or was his management guilty of simply spotting a good PR exercise, while simultaneously taking advantage of the dearth of internationally renowned performers in South Africa and thus ensuring a healthy revenue? Either way, Tom still holds the dignified position of being among the first white artists to officially perform for an entirely mixed audience in that country, for which he is rightly proud.

Of course, whenever Tom's musical moves made the newspapers, so did the latest rumours about a film début, and this year the popular favourite was the possibility of the singer playing the lead in a cinematic adventure about the 18th century English horse thief and highwayman, Dick Turpin. For some time Tom had been keen on the dashing role and on one occasion he had sent Chris Hutchins out to buy five copies of books on the subject, in the hope of turning them into a film. Sadly the murmurings in the press were attributable only to hopeful hype, and Tom was unable to fulfil his dream, at least not for the foreseeable future.

Moving from the romantic to the risqué, the gossip then suggested that another possible starring role for Tom would be in a celluloid adaptation of Jackie Collins' racy novel, *The Stud*. The best-seller had first been published back in 1969 and now its authoress was making plans for it to appear on the big screen, as a vehicle to revive her famous sister's flagging career. The plot ran along the lines of a rich lady (to be played by Joan Collins) betraying her elderly Arab husband by having an erotic affair with a handsome young man named Tony; the 'stud' of the book's title and the role intended for Tom Jones.

Tom had enjoyed previous connections with the Collins family. The sisters' father Joe had chosen Tom to replace P.J. Proby on the formative 1965 tour with Cilla Black. Tom had also shared a friendly banter with Joan on an episode of *This Is Tom Jones* some years later. Consequently he was only too pleased to become involved when he was approached to read the script by co-producer, Terence Deane.

But when Tom opened the pages, his face fell. *The Stud* seemed to him to be one long sex scene after another, involving his character in bisexual encounters, foul language and drug abuse. Whatever real-life mischief Tom's rock'n'roll lifestyle may have entailed, he was not prepared to portray himself in this manner on-screen, and refused point blank to have anything further to do with the film. Not only was he concerned that his fans would see him in such an extreme light, but he was also unwilling to risk the wrath of his mother, whom Tom has described as hating seeing sex depicted on television. "We know what goes on, we don't need to see it," said Freda.

To the authoress and her staff, Tom cited the required obscenities he would have had to utter and the gratuitous sexual content as his main reasons for turning the part down. Jackie Collins was horrified, stating the immortal words to the press: "It's certainly not porny and I'm flabbergasted that Tom should have any scruples about playing the role of a superlover!"

Somewhat surprisingly, Tom's run-in with Jackie eventually evolved into a friendship, and the singer was amused to read the sleeve of her 1977 book, *Lovers And Gamblers*, where the plot description heralded the main character, rock/soul superstar Al King, as being a mixture of Elvis Presley, Mick Jagger and . . . who else but Tom Jones. Tom knew not what to make of this latest development and kept relatively quiet, but Jackie has always lived by the following admission: "I write about real people in disguise. If anything, my characters are toned down – the truth is much more bizarre."

Dick Turpin and *The Stud* aside, after several fitful years it seemed as if Tom might finally make his screen début. In the early part of 1976 it was announced that he was to play the part of a hired assassin in a film tentatively called *Yockowald*, which was spelt differently depending on which paper you read. Producer Clarence Greene and director Russel Rouse (both since deceased) were to supervise Tom in this non-singing role set in a Los Angeles ghetto, and a substantial stretch of Tom's concerts were cancelled to allow time for the filming.

There are conflicting reports as to what happened after the shooting of *Yockowald* commenced in the summer of 1976. Biographers Stafford Hildred and David Gritten were able to interview Clarence Greene before his death in 1995 and the producer regretfully recalled that he and Rouse had secured finance from a Canadian investor through an American bank. Almost immediately after work began on the project, the bank was sold to a Japanese company and the funds were then either cancelled or exhausted. Filming was abandoned just a few weeks into the schedule and despite Tom's panicked request to MAM, Greene and Rouse were simply unable to assemble enough money to finance the project further. "It kills me just to think about it," Clarence Greene told Hildred and Gritten. "I think Tom Jones would have been a big movie star had we been able to make *Yockowald*. He was absolutely great in the part."

Gloria Tait, now a Los Angeles based agent, appeared as an extra during the brief period of shooting for *Yockowald* in 1976. She and a friend who had also applied for a small non-speaking part were informed the day before the filming that it would take place in the troubled area of downtown Los Angeles, and they were to arrive dressed as 'street people'. By this, the two young actresses assumed that they should resemble prostitutes, which was not actually director Russel Rouse's original intention, but caught his imagination enough for them to be promoted to actually standing next to Tom himself.

Gloria recalls that filming took place throughout the night, from 6.00 p.m. to 6.00 a.m., because that was the cheapest time to film. This meant that she and her friend were standing in an unpleasant location dressed in the worst possible garb, and to their dismay they heard real-life gunshots fired as they shivered in the cold, waiting for the cameras to roll. "We worked 18 hours for $50. We ended up doing many, many scenes right next to Tom," she says today, fixating on the more agreeable aspect of her ordeal.

"The interesting thing that happened was there was a Mexican executive producer and he was hustling us to see if we knew anybody who had money to put into the movie! From what I understand the fellow from Mexico took all the money and went back to Mexico and it never got released." Whatever events actually transpired to prevent *Yockowald* from continuing, everyone agreed that it was a great shame for Tom as the role would have been ideal and he was totally committed to his part. Flummoxed yet again, plans for his film début were shelved and MAM swallowed the bitter pill of embarrassment one more time.

As the topsy-turvy year of 1976 drew to a close, Tom featured on a distinguished edition of the popular music programme, *Midnight Special*. The 200th broadcast occurred on December 17, 1976 and the audience was packed full of members of Tom's Californian fan clubs. This television appearance was notable for Tom's duet with the incorrigible Sly of Sly & The Family Stone – a singer famed for his vast intake of drugs. As they sang Sly's hit 'Everyday People', they held hands and bounced up and down to the music. Tom then duetted with Lynn Anderson on 'Don't Go Breaking My Heart' and The Blossoms on a raucously entertaining version of The Miracles' 'Love Machine'. While today this performance makes for great television, at the time those behind the scenes of the *Midnight Special* criticised Tom in their anniversary book for being too awkward during his duets, and vastly over-singing his part to the detriment of his vocal partners.

14

BUSINESSMAN BLUES

FOR TOM JONES the year of 1977 began on a high. The staff at his new record label, Epic, were determined to improve on the poor chart ratings that had haunted Tom for the majority of the decade. To this end the marketing department decided that their new acquisition needed a new image, one in which Tom would be steered towards country music. It proved to be a successful strategy and his first single release in three years, the easy-going 'Say You'll Stay Until Tomorrow' reached a respectable number 15 in the US charts. Perhaps because of its long and somewhat outdated association with cowboys and the Wild West, country music is a peculiarly American culture and although there are pockets of country fans in the UK, it has never quite caught on. This might explain why back home, Tom barely scratched the Top 40 with what was to them a surprise offering. Still, Tom was not out of the woods yet in his adopted nation, and his album entitled *Tom Jones Greatest Hits* barely struggled in at number 191 in the US charts.

Putting his cinematic disasters of the previous year forcibly behind him, Tom spoke boldly in MAM's official publicity material of a possible return to television work. "I enjoy doing live shows better than anything else," he said. "But if a TV series comes along, and if the idea is a good one, then I would do it." Could this mean the return of a series along the lines of *This Is Tom Jones*? "I had my own TV series for three years . . . and that gave me ample opportunity to work in that medium. I wanted a short rest from television and I wanted to spend more time making actual contact with the public. In the future, I will be doing more guest appearances and my own specials," he stated confidently.

If Tom had been looking to make more 'actual contact with the public', then he was in for one hell of a shock. His wish was about to be granted more vividly than he could ever have imagined possible.

In January 1977, Billy Weinberger, the boss of Caesar's Palace, placed a call to Chris Hutchins saying he was in London, and suggested the pair of them met up for a drink. The irony of the meeting place – the Westbury

Hotel opposite MAM's offices – did not escape the company's former press aide. Chris recounts the bizarre rendezvous: "He said, 'I understand that you're not going to be with us in Vegas this year? I was talking with Gordon about you just the other night. He wasn't very complimentary about you . . .' " As far as Chris was concerned, the parting of ways had marked a sad ending to an era, but it had happened amicably enough. "I said, 'What do you mean he wasn't very complimentary?' Billy said, 'He said, "I made him, and I'll destroy him." ' "

Confounded, Chris excused himself, went to a payphone and called his friend Mike Malloy, who was at that time editor for the *Daily Mirror*. Ever since Chris had left his previous employment the year before, Mike had been hounding him to tell the story of his exploits with the MAM organisation. Up until this point Chris had honourably refused, but the very thought that Gordon was badmouthing him to his friends and even claiming to have created his very talent, wiped any previous feelings of loyalty to his erstwhile employer clean away. He reached Mike Malloy while Billy Weinberger was still sitting at his table, and agreed to run an in-depth series for the paper, purporting to "put straight the fallacies and half-truths of the lives and careers" of Messrs Jones, Humperdinck, O'Sullivan and Mills. The title of this series became known simply as *The Family*.

Chris' first article appeared on Saturday April 16, and gave details of serious marital disputes between Tom and Linda involving undignified temper tantrums. The following Monday Chris disclosed 'The Truth' with regards to Tom's supposed affair with Marji Wallace, supported by a large photograph of the couple kissing. On the next day he began to attack the other famous members of 'The Family' and by that afternoon MAM had issued a High Court writ against Hutchins and the *Daily Mirror* seeking an injunction to prevent any further material being published, and claiming damages for libel and breach of contract.

It was no small affair, the plaintiffs being Thomas John Woodward, Arnold George Dorsey, Raymond O'Sullivan, Gordon William Mills, Management Agency & Music Ltd and G W Mills Ltd, all represented by solicitors Balin & Co. The defendants were Christopher Neville Hutchins, Chris Hutchins Information Ltd, Daily Mirror Newspapers Ltd and Mirror Group Newspapers Ltd, whose defence was put forward by solicitors Nicholson, Graham and Jones.

The case hinged on whether or not Chris had been guilty of a breach of confidence. In addition to his most recent contract which had been signed on April 21, 1970, a confidentiality agreement in the form of a letter had been sent by Lloyd Greenfield to MAM's employees in the middle of the American tour of June 1972. The obligations therein stipulated that nobody was allowed "to make any statement or give any interview or pass any information to any third party touching or concerning" the principal members of the MAM group, namely Tom, Engel and Gilbert. The timing of this restrictive additional clause to the original contracts was probably prompted by several events: in 1972 Tom and Engelbert were popular after their respective TV series, Gilbert O'Sullivan had joined the MAM fold and was proving to be increasingly successful, and Gordon's creation had recently been floated on the stock market as a public company.

All staff were required to sign the letter agreeing to these terms. When it was presented to Chris for signature he objected. It was common knowledge that he had always planned to write his memoirs and any such agreement would preclude this project. He was told in no uncertain terms that if he didn't comply, he would have to return home. So Chris duly signed but on returning to London went straight to Bill Smith, who was by then MAM's managing director, explaining that he felt he must resign. Bill then located the offending correspondence and handed it to Chris. With Bill's full consent the PR man then tore up the letter in front of him, retaining the pieces.

The court, presided over by Judges Denning, Lawton and Bridge discharged the injunction, in part due to Chris producing as evidence the torn-up loyalty agreement. They agreed that not only were the terms of the letter unreasonable and unclear, but its destruction, in full agreement of the managing director, surely rendered it of no consequence. An additional opinion cited by all three judges was that, if the plaintiffs actively sought positive publicity for certain events in self-promotion, then they must also expect negative publicity as a natural by-product. In the case of the revelations of *The Family*, the judges decreed that it was more important for the British public to know the truth about the public company than for MAM's employees to be obliged to withhold 'confidential' information.

The series was allowed to continue, and *Daily Mirror*'s readership increased after interest was heightened by the legal proceedings. For the 10 days the story ran, the *Mirror* sold 180,000 extra copies per day. Never had such a damning exposure of pop stars attracted so much attention. Alongside tales of Tom's legendary womanising ran stories of Engelbert's egocentricity, vanity and underlying insecurity, Gilbert's paralysing reticence and Gordon's ceaseless slave-driving.

Gordon's outrage was well-documented in the press, and there were even rumours that he had issued a death threat. Chris recalls: "I did get a phone call from a man in Newcastle, who was a hoodlum I knew Gordon had associated with in the past. He said that Gordon had said, 'If you get a chance to end this man's days I'll pay handsomely.'" Chris believes that had Gordon truly meant it he would not be alive today.

The reactions from Engel and Gilbert were speedy and dismissive. Engel haughtily remarked to the papers: "I have nothing to hide and can hold my head high," while Gilbert's defence was: "I have done nothing to be ashamed of or which could possibly upset me if it were publicised."

Tom on the other hand took more time to reflect on his former confidant's exposé . "Hutchins betrayed a trust," he said to *Music Week* in March 1978. "We were – or I thought we were – good friends, and I didn't think he'd stoop so low. I told him that conversations we had with other stars when he was in my company were between us, and yet he published verbatim a conversation we had once with Frank Sinatra during which Frank just mentioned that he was thinking of buying an hotel. Some of the American papers picked up some of the stories, and I told my wife what he had done. She just said that she didn't want to read any of it or hear anything about it. It will be best if I never meet Chris Hutchins again."

"I thought it was an honest account," says Chris today. "In Tom's case I thought it furthered the job I'd been doing anyway." Today the only thing he regrets with regards to the whole sorry incident is having unintentionally hurt Tom in order to reap revenge on Gordon after Billy Weinberger's fateful comment. Far from having been 'broken' by Gordon Mills, Chris went on to become one of Britain's foremost show business columnists, and has written books on Princess Diana, Athina Onassis, Elvis Presley and The Beatles among others.

As a result of the debacle, Gordon tightened the reigns on his employees to protect his company from further embarrassing disclosures. "He wasn't insecure; he was furious," states author Johnny Rogan. "He was locking the door after the horses had bolted. It was a very family-orientated, close-knit organisation – he felt betrayed." The loyalty aspect of working for MAM was drummed into the staff with increased vigour. Mike Morgan began working with Tom as his lead guitarist in 1973 and moved on to become musical director, staying with the band for a total of 17 years. He was quite frank about his allegiance when approached for an interview by the authors of this book, stating that he had promised Tom faithfully never to speak to the media about their time on the road together. However, he continued to say that if Tom's current management wished to release him from his contract and provide guidelines on which he could talk, then he would happily oblige. Other former members of the touring party were notably restrained when talking about this period of their employment, presumably with this 'loyalty clause' at the forefront of their minds.

The contracts that Gordon required Tom's musicians to sign were highly restrictive. They were only ever hired for one year at a time like The Blossoms, but equally they had to ask for Gordon's authorisation before undertaking any other work. Terry Jenkins confirms this point: "I had a 12-month contract with Gordon Mills and I had to get permission if I worked with other people [in the studio] – I was allowed to do that. Gordon could put me with people if he wanted, he could send me out. I was under contract to him. The only thing I wasn't allowed to do was to perform with anybody else on the stage."

Derek Watkins felt strongly that the stipulations in Gordon's professionally binding agreement were quite unusual and could occasionally cramp his musical flair and leanings. "He wanted me to sign a contract and work exclusively for him. I actually didn't sign a contract with Gordon – I would sign a contract for the length of the tour with MAM. When the tour finished I was a freelance musician again. What Gordon wanted with me was to pay me more money just to exclusively be his property. He *would* allow me to work outside and do freelance work, but he wanted half of it, which I didn't think was a fair deal. So I declined his offer, which I think he found quite astounding."

In order to replace Chris Hutchins, Gordon turned to publicity specialists, Rogers & Cowan, who competently took over, appointing George Kirvay as MAM's new PR man. After the day-to-day relationship Gordon had shared with Chris, suddenly dealing with a large company took the all-important publicity element of Tom, Engel and Gilbert's respective careers dangerously out of Gordon's hands. So it was not long before Rogers & Cowan were replaced by John Moran, whose background was in public relations for US politicians. Gordon didn't mind John's lack of experience within the pop music field; he was far more relieved to have found a willing replacement who would answer to him, and him alone.

Many of those close to MAM were of the opinion that the entrepreneur's interest in business was slowly waning, especially those intimate friends who were aware of the intricacies of Gordon's character. He had harboured a guilt complex over the deterioration of his elderly father's health ever since a family trip with Jo and Bill Mills to South Africa. Gordon and his father were preparing to go riding and to make his horse run, Gordon struck it on the side. Instead of trotting forward, the horse violently kicked Bill who was standing directly behind. Whether this unfortunate incident was responsible for his subsequent ill health no one could know, but nevertheless Gordon shouldered the burden of blame which in turn aggravated his recurring stomach ulcer.

The obsession with animals that took hold of Gordon in Weybridge

showed no sign of abating in the late Seventies. Unable to relax sufficiently for a regular beach holiday, each year he would go on a South
African safari, accompanied by either Johnnie Spence or Gog Jones. On
these trips he would invariably befriend an orphaned animal, the more
exotic the better, and transport it to his private menagerie which had been
relocated in part to his Los Angeles home. The dictates of impracticality
had meant that Gordon had already donated seven of his orang-utans and
five gorillas to the San Diego Zoo. Gordon was not averse to using the
animals to play pranks on his house guests. More often than not, an article
of clothing would be removed by an excitable simian adoptee, and tiger
cubs famously patrolled the ladies toilets for comic effect.

The manager liked to marry his business and pleasure interests and as a
consequence, it was Tom who was frequently portrayed in the press as an
animal conservationist. For one publicity stunt Tom was required to have
his photo taken with an enormous tiger at an hotel. Gordon boldly
entered the tiger's cage first, followed by a visibly quaking Tom and then
David Steen, the intrepid photographer. David was a large man, over six
foot tall, but he was totally dwarfed by the irate tiger who, incensed by
David's purple trousers roared, stood on its hind legs and slammed its paws
down onto David's shoulders. The unexpected attack was enough to force
him backwards to land in the water trough. Gordon found this highly
amusing, and needless to say, the photo session was abandoned.

Ollie, the one-eyed orang-utan, was also the source of many a tale
recounted at dinner parties. "He found him [Ollie] in really bad condition
in a private zoo," remembers Wendy Watkins. "He had very scrunched-
up toes which would never improve. It was the way he'd been kept in
such a poor condition. Gordon took him over." Visitors to Gordon's
house would have to endure Ollie's manic mood swings which often
extended to more than just Ronnie Cass' relatively mild experience:
"Ollie clamped his hand down on my son's leather jacket and tore the
thing off. My son screamed, '*Get him off!*'"

Although Gordon employed a stand-by trainer, Ollie was still prone to
fits of violence, as *The Special London Bridge Special* producer, David
Winters, is never likely to forget: "An orang-utan grabbed one of the
people that worked for me by his testicles! It was very scary. My guy was
sweating. He had him right up against the cage, and the orang-utan's face
was right up against *his* face. Gordon was saying to my guy, 'Don't move,
don't make any moves, because he can actually rip them right off you
know!' The guy that took care of Gordon's animals then went behind the
orang-utan with a spade and hit him on the head. And that shocked him
enough to let go of my guy."

Whatever fun and games were inspired by the inmates of Gordon's private zoo, there were some who felt that he was devoting too much time to his precious animals . . . and too little to the stars he had so carefully fostered.

While the rivalry between Tom Jones and Engelbert Humperdinck received its fair share of press comment, it was covered in a generally good-natured manner and served to promote both stars. Behind the scenes, however, there were some genuine cracks in the relationship which had been visible for quite some time. Contrary to popular opinion, Engel had only ever desired the same tangible trophies as his opponent – bigger, better and brighter rewards were not actually on his agenda.

Reports comparing the two singers' records, TV series, Las Vegas performances, cars, houses, spending sprees and respective images weren't of interest to Engel. It didn't matter how many pairs of knickers were tossed up onto the stage. He had always felt second best and all he wanted to do was to match his usurper.

Engel was insecure, and it certainly didn't help when Tom would seize on any publicity opportunity to emphasise the fact that they were of two different musical moulds. "It's the only thing that bothers me," said Tom of the endless comparisons. "I can't see it. He's a balladeer, I'm more of a rhythm and blues singer. I reflect that in my songs. Humperdinck can't. He hasn't got it in him." After the initial boom in Engel's career in 1967 and his ill-fated TV series, he had followed in Tom's footsteps and ensconced himself in Las Vegas, becoming a regular favourite with the crowds who flocked to see his more gentle, romantic stage act. Like Tom's, Engel's career had also faded somewhat as a singles artist yet he continued to eerily mirror his antagonist when in this period he too had a surprise Top 10 American hit with 'After The Lovin' '.

Although Engel fretted about his looks, in particular the greying of his dark locks, he still managed to attract plenty of sexual attention, and he too was dogged by allegations of extra-marital affairs in the press. Over the years paternity suits arose from Diane Vincent in 1974, who settled out of court, and later Kathy Jenner, who claimed $1 million in child support for her daughter. Engel's wife Pat stood by in the same faithful manner as Linda, while the hapless crooner was often heard to joke that he had amassed more paternity suits than tailored suits. It was extraordinary just how many similarities Engel actually shared with Tom – he had also once been the recipient of an unwanted homosexual pass by a West End pop manager, an incident uncannily reminiscent of Tom's brush with Joe Meek.

It is not surprising that in the wake of the constant comparisons and Gordon's increasing disinterest, by 1977 Engel felt it was time to move on and change his management. "With Engelbert it was an ego option,"

Chris Hutchins reflects. "He felt that Gordon wasn't giving him enough time and attention. He's the most self-centred man in the world." It took one heated argument with Gordon to seal his departure, but no one could quite believe that the party could ever break up after so many years.

Engel explained his frustration to the press. "I felt trapped. My talent was being held back and I felt at last I had to do things my way . . . I got sick of people asking me about Tom and Gilbert. Look at it this way – no man, not even Gordon Mills, could look after two entertainers like Tom and myself." His disillusionment can best be explained by the brutal fact that Tom and Gordon were simply closer friends than Engel and Gordon, even though they had been best men at each other's marriages. To his further annoyance, he could not make a clean break. Gordon was too canny not to have contractually tied one of the company's major assets to MAM for a substantial number of years.

Although Engel's dramatic exit was shocking enough for the MAM entourage, especially so soon after Chris Hutchins' public muck-raking, the unthinkable then happened. On August 15, 1977 the much-loved Johnnie Spence died suddenly of a heart attack.

Everyone was devastated. The autopsy revealed that by rights he should have passed away six months earlier, but evidently his will to live was so strong he had surpassed this sentence. As a mark of the respect they felt for their musical director, Tom, Gordon, Gilbert and Terry Jenkins were pall-bearers at his funeral.

Shortly afterwards, Gordon spoke with Marion, his widow. "Gordon Mills said to me once after Johnnie had died, 'Johnnie did something really bad, Marion.' I said, 'What are you talking about?' And he said, 'He left me.'" Support for Marion was fiercely strong within the group, demonstrated by a constant stream of visitors to her house and caring telephone calls. Johnnie had just finished the score for the *Spiderman* movie and had been looking forward to expanding his career within the world of film soundtracks.★

But the misery was not to end there. The very next day the whole world went into mourning when 'The King' died at the age of 42. Elvis Presley's lifeless body was found on the bathroom floor of his Graceland home in the afternoon of August 16, the cause of his death a combination of long-term drug abuse leading to bodily malfunction and an eventual heart attack. "I was slightly in shock over Johnnie's death," Tom recalled

---

★ The musical director Johnnie Spence was replaced temporarily by Trevor Bastow, followed soon after by Jack Parnell in March 1978. Jack was an accomplished conductor and jazz man who had previously worked with Ted Heath, and had been musical director of ATV, directing the pit band for *Sunday Night At The London Palladium* throughout the Sixties.

later. "I was thinking about that at the moment somebody came up and said Elvis died. It was like, 'What's happening? What's going on here?' I was shaking. It was terrible."

Many years later Tom spoke at length to the *Daily Mirror* about the closing days of his relationship with the virtually drug-dependant icon. "He had pushed all his friends away from him when they tried to warn him about what he was doing to himself. I phoned him but he didn't answer. The bodyguards who had grown up with him told him that he was destroying himself, but he didn't want to hear it so he fired them. Those guys would have died for him. Two of them, Red West and Sonny West came to me. They told me, 'He's gonna die.' But he wouldn't listen. So I rang him." Tragically Tom was unable to get through to his old friend. "I might have been able to save his life, but it wasn't to be."

Tom's greatest regret and a huge source of loss for the music industry was that the only film of Tom and Elvis singing together, albeit home-made, had since been lost. "We were at his house one day, just fooling around playing guitars and singing," said Tom. "Joe Esposito took an 8mm film but when Priscilla tried to find it she couldn't. No one knows where it is."

Beleaguered by such traumatic events, it is not surprising that reports began to surface about Tom's yearning to return to more familiar territory. His homesickness was much publicised in the press and Tom often expressed his simple wish to sup a pint of ale in a traditional English pub. He had not set foot on British soil for over four years, and as a consolation he began to frequent the Shakespeare's Head in Santa Monica, California to enjoy a drink and a game of darts with his long-time celebrity friend, Jimmy Tarbuck. Tom admitted to the papers about the 'stress tests' he and the others had been required to undergo following the two deaths close to the group. The results of the tests showed the singer to be healthy, but it was recommended that he keep up his rigorous fitness programme for both physical and mental reasons.

One positive element was to emerge from the *annus horribilis* that was 1977. Back in the UK devoted Tom fan Sylvia Firth negotiated with Rogers & Cowan to re-establish the official British fan club, which was grandly re-christened the Tom Jones Appreciation Society. "We started it in August 1977," says Sylvia today. "There had been an official one run by Gordon Mills' wife in 1965 which disbanded in 1975 because he had gone to America. They said they hadn't got enough news for us to have." To this day the Tom Jones Appreciation Society remains a strictly non-profit organisation with a steady influx of members joining each year, notably after each tour or hit single. The fan club holds regular raffles of Tom-related memorabilia to raise money for his favourite charities. "We used to have an open house here at my home in Luck Lane [Yorkshire] once a year to celebrate Tom's birthday when there were 100-150 members – but of course the society grew! I couldn't possibly host anything like that now there are hundreds of members." Over the years nearly 2,000 people have passed through Sylvia's books from countries as far flung as Canada, Japan and Sweden.

★　★　★

It is difficult to comprehend how Tom must have felt after the sudden deaths of both Elvis Presley and Johnnie Spence, combined with the gradual and bitter decline of the MAM entourage as key members of the group left the fold under a visible cloud. In early 1978 Tom first spoke of a sorrow that was closer to home. "Linda had a miscarriage after Mark and the doctor said she'll never be able to have another baby. I'd love to have more children. It's a terrible loss that we can't manage it." Linda had always wanted a daughter to complete her tiny family, and although she was slowly coming to terms with this sad impossibility, typically she had kept her private life to herself and must have been taken aback by her husband's candour.

On the business front, the MAM boat was now rocked yet again by another major player. Gilbert O'Sullivan's fame had reached its pinnacle during the period from 1970 to 1975 when he achieved seven Top 10 hits in the UK, but like Tom and Engel he too had suffered a serious downturn in chart success thereafter. For much of the decade Gilbert had remained relatively quiet, seemingly satisfied to stay hidden in the background while his colleagues basked in the limelight. But the Chris Hutchins scandal had focused press attention on Gilbert again, and along with Engel's accusations against Gordon, most likely encouraged him to take stock of his own situation.

Having experienced a long stretch of lean years before becoming a star, Gilbert had realised the fickle nature of the business he practised and had wisely chosen to be thrifty with his fortunes. Sadly he had not been so perceptive when it came to signing contracts or reading the small print in the first place.

By 1978 it had become impossible for even the most imaginative accountant to reconcile the vast discrepancies between Gilbert's sales figures and his actual income. According to Simon Garfield in *Expensive Habits*, Gilbert's début album *Himself* had sold almost one million copies, grossing MAM some £2 million and the follow-up LP, *Back To Front*, had exceeded three million sales providing MAM with a further £1,700,000 gross. Gilbert's two greatest singles, 'Alone Again (Naturally)' and 'Clair' grossed £900,000 and £600,000 respectively for MAM, but for all of the above Gilbert was only netting a pitiful 3% of his contribution to MAM's profits.

Although he was painfully aware that his hits had ceased a few years prior, by rights Gilbert should have been able to continue living in the same simple manner on the money he had stockpiled for a rainy day. When he discovered that his mortgage had become unsecured, despite his lack of luxuries and unhealthy but cheap diet of sausages and beans, he finally caught on to this imbalance. He bared his concerns to the press: "I got the biggest fright of my life when they showed me a statement of how much money I needed to live as skimpily as I do. The rates for this house are fantastic, and the cost of food – even when you eat as little as I do – is frightening." But money should not have been a problem for the provident Gilbert.

To make matters worse, the songwriter lacked any obvious solution to rectify his financial straits. In every aspect of his career, he was contractually bound to MAM, and yet he was unable to demand that his work received promotion, or record or perform elsewhere. In addition, the initial promise of joint ownership of his songs had never materialised. In short MAM had Gilbert over a barrel and regardless of the money owed from his back catalogue, he just wanted to be released from MAM's stranglehold.

Loathe as he was to sue his former mentor Gordon Mills, Gilbert was left no choice. All the same, he was informed that short of re-writing sections of the law, his chances of success were slim. Furthermore it would be an exceptionally lengthy process, possibly lasting up to four years, with the running costs escalating to hundreds of thousands of pounds. Still Gilbert was determined to see that justice prevailed. He was introduced by the publicists Rogers & Cowan to a lawyer named Charles Negus-Fancey and the two men got on so well that he went on to become Gilbert's business manager. Negus-Fancey encouraged him to resume composing again and they approached CBS for a new record contract, fully aware that this was in direct breach of Gilbert's existing deal. MAM threatened litigation for a while, but dropped their case early on.

Although proceedings began in 1978, Gilbert's action against his former manager lasted a total of seven years with the first High Court date set for April 1982. Gilbert was to finance the extended lawsuit by selling his home in Weybridge and maintaining his economical living.

★   ★   ★

Having lost two of his greatest musical acquisitions, Gordon's managerial touch appeared to be slipping somewhat in the late Seventies. Yet he was constantly being approached by artists, both famous and hopeful, all desperate to secure the services of such a prosperous entrepreneur. Recognising years ago that his own stage career was not destined to be, Gordon had developed into a unique manager, gifted with both tremendous vision and an ability to realise the maximum potential of innate talent. "Gordon wasn't a great musician," says his former writing partner, Les Reed. "That's nothing against him; he could play a very good harmonica, but if you put a score in front of him he couldn't read it. But he knew what commercialism was." Composer Ronnie Cass adds, "He had this wonderful psychological magic about him that made him a natural impresario. He was always three steps ahead. He exuded confidence."

Three things underpinned Gordon's multi-faceted character: his often complex personal psyche and traits, an astute and cunning business mind, and a ruthless, bolshie arrogance. Chris Hutchins was one of the few people close enough to be exposed to all the dimensions of such a man.

"There was a certain amount of competition," says Chris, speaking on the delicate balance of power between Gordon, Tom, Engel and those who achieved a certain standing within the MAM administration. "Gordon regarded himself as the kingpin of the whole operation. Really we knew that without Tom's voice the organisation wouldn't exist. But Gordon had style, he knew more things than Tom, he dressed better, he was more handsome and he would like to think that he had the best looking woman on his arm.

"Gordon was in the rare position of being a better looking fellow than either of his singers. He could not pass a mirror. He would go and buy himself endless suits. In Beverly Hills we went to a very expensive shop called Georgio's and Gordon would buy the [contents of the] shop, but he would scream at the man who owned it. 'I want that shirt in stone!' The man said, 'What colour is stone?' 'Stone! *Stone* is *stone!*' That was Gordon, he would be so frustrated.

"He could be a bully, a verbal bully. And he could be utterly, utterly charming . . . I have seen Gordon reduce many people, including myself, to tears."

No one could argue with Gordon's natural flair for management and money-spinning ideas. His staggering management deals with his major players were virtually unheard of and guaranteed him millionaire status on equal terms with his clients. One simple, but extremely lucrative, sideline he practised from his early days as a songwriter was to compose many of his artists' B-sides in order to gain half of the mechanical royalties of those that became hits. This ruse has been commonly employed by pop music managers since the Sixties, with manager Larry Page writing all the B-sides for The Troggs, and Cilla Black's late husband Bobby Willis penning all her flip-sides. Gordon also capitalised on his stars' substantial European audience, encouraging

Tom in particular to record foreign language versions of Gordon's own songs, including 'Not Responsible' and 'The Rose' in Italian.

Yet his ruthless streak earned him few friends. "I always thought that Gordon Mills was living his life through Tom Jones," snipes Jimmy Tarbuck. "Gordon Mills never had a career; he had one hit record. [He was] petty and didn't like anyone getting near Tom or getting close to Tom."

Back in the early days Gordon's artists always had to be number one, and if they didn't achieve this top spot then he would actually ring up the record company to demand an explanation. If the unfortunate employee on the end of the line told him that the sales figures had simply not reached the relevant criteria, then Gordon would yell, "Count them again!" Chris was present for many a verbal ear-bashing directed at whoever picked up the phone. "I remember Gordon screaming down the phone at a radio producer when they were doing the billing for a radio show that Tom was appearing in. Gordon was saying, 'What do you mean Dusty Springfield is closing the show? Tom is more important than Dusty Springfield! If Tom doesn't close the show, he doesn't *do* the show!'"

Record producer Peter Sullivan confirms that he and Gordon would have fierce confrontations about anything and everything to do with work, be it the choice of song, the style of song, its recording method, or even the future promotion. Unlike his adversary, Peter strove to keep the disputes behind closed doors. "Gordon was a hard-nosed man but we were always able to resolve our problems because we both had a great deal of respect for each other," he says.

Obviously, there was a vast difference between Gordon's victims and those he respected. Back in the days of The Squires, Vernon Hopkins has no doubt that he was always destined to be disposable, no matter how pleasant Gordon seemed on the surface. "He was amiable. But very cunning, very dark in the end because all that was on the outside. It was a plan, a master plan."

Strangely Gordon would sometimes show uncharacteristic desperation when a talented musician or party member threatened to leave, as occurred in the cases of Chris Slade and Chris Hutchins. Gordon would proffer an extravagant deal or contract as an olive branch to entice his people to stay on, but he was usually too late as the individual had already reached breaking point and made up his mind to leave. He could have saved a lot of torment if he had only conceived a preventative method from the outset rather than an irrational, belated cure. But few would question his authority although Derek Watkins recalls, "I think he enjoyed people standing up against him. He would obviously try and wheedle a way round to . . . not owning you exactly . . . but he was a very astute businessman."

Somewhere under the gruff exterior lay a man with a heart, albeit glimpsed only rarely. Nina Blatt, production assistant on *This Is Tom Jones*, will never forget sitting with Gordon Mills in the midst of one of Johnnie Spence's parties and the manager confiding in her, "I hate being a heavy – I hate all the fights."

Although Gordon's aspirations in the pop world were often insightful, as time went on it became apparent that he did not possess especially good long-term business acumen. Desperate to revive Tom's former glory and fed up with the non-event that was his cinematic career, Gordon formed a production company for the acquisition and development of material for film scripts and TV specials. Although Tom did work in front of the cameras, no finished product would ever actually materialise from the production company itself.

★   ★   ★

Tom's second TV movie after *The Special London Bridge Special* was filmed in June 1978. Dubiously titled *Pleasure Cove*, the script was given to Tom by writer and producer Lou Shaw, who had previously worked on *Crypt Of The Living Dead* and *The Bat People*, and director Bruce Bilson whose glowing CV boasted *Wonder Woman*, *The Six Million Dollar Man*, *M*A*S*H* and *Hawaii Five-O*.

Tom was to guest star in the pilot for a proposed TV series akin to the formulaic fun portrayed in contemporary US favourites *Fantasy Island* and *Love Boat*. His character, Raymond Gordon, was a dastardly crook, using a holiday island hotel called Pleasure Cove as a temporary base. Tom's thick Welsh accent was amusingly explained away as 'English' in the script. The role required him to fall in love with the main character played by Constance Forslund, appear on a nudist beach and narrowly escape death when his boat is overturned in the vicinity of a large, evidently inflatable shark. Tom was joined by other notable celebrities in the cast including Joan Hackett, Shelley Fabares and Harry Guardino. His partner in crime was played by experienced TV actress BarBara Luna, while a young David Hasselhoff competed with Tom for the female attention.

Connie Forslund, who had previously appeared on TV series such as *Chips*, remembers that they shot the majority of the scenes on location in a luxurious Santa Barbara hotel in just three gloriously sunny days. The remainder of the action was filmed in a park in Pasadena and around Los Angeles over the following three or four weeks, which was typically quick for a TV movie and allowed no time for deliberation. The budget was fairly standard for a piece of its genre and although the sets were not particularly lavish, they were certainly well presented for the era.

"Tom was absolutely charming, adorable," Connie enthuses today.

"Great sense of humour, a little nervous about his first [major] acting role though he needn't have been because *Pleasure Cove* wasn't about the acting . . ." BarBara Luna initially took on a more cynical stance. "I remember when Tom Jones was cast that, shamefully, I had a preconceived idea that this was a rock'n'roller. I thought, 'Oh my God, what are we in for? He's not going to know all his lines, he'll be drinking and drugging every night – it's really going to be a big headache!' And he shocked me, he really did. I never saw him pick up a script. He knew not just the work for that day but he was prepared to do it all. He was very impressive in that he was very believable, that he knew how to hit his marks. He gave me the feeling that he had a lot of experience."

Given the extent of Tom's fame in America in the late Seventies, Connie was concerned as to how to portray their 'courtship'. "I knew we were going to have to do one swing dance and one contemporary. Although I'd been a dancer, I didn't have a clue how to swing dance and I suggested to Tom that we spent an hour or two with the coach. He assured me I'd have no problem and just to turn when he squeezed my hand.

"The trouble was that I could make neither head nor tail of his hand squeezes, so we spent a lot of the time colliding with one another! Then we had to go to the table for the kissing scene, which took several hours to film . . . and they couldn't use a lot of the footage because we really got into it as the hours passed! He's a very accomplished kisser and I became somewhat unaware of the hundreds of people standing around filming. The awful part was we were told the next day that open mouths and tongues don't really look very sexy in close-up . . ."

During filming the stars warmed to Tom as he displayed a human side to his superstar status. In one particular scene, almost the entire range of characters were required to tread water for a long period of time. "I think you can see from the film that it wasn't exactly a warm, sunny day," says Connie, "and even if it had been, the Pacific Ocean around Los Angeles is always very cold, especially about a mile out to sea, where for some reason they decided to shoot. The waves were big enough that I couldn't even see the boat at times and there was a strong rip tide pulling me further out to sea . . .

"The next day they had the good sense to shoot right near the shore and simply point the camera out to sea. But it was still absolutely freezing. That was when Tom, teeth chattering, up to his neck in frigid water, uttered that phrase I've never forgotten: 'It's not the cold I mind, it's the damp!' It was such a masterpiece of understatement that we all just roared." The humour can be shared by any viewers of the finished scene as it is plainly obvious that, as the actors and actresses begin to tire of the constant movement simulating treading water, they actually forget to keep their arms and legs moving and allow their shoulders to mysteriously rise above the shallow water.

Pleasure Cove was first broadcast on NBC on January 3, 1979. The pilot was never taken up and developed into an ongoing series as intended, which on one hand was a surprise given Bruce Bilson's excellent track record, but on the other, as Connie herself admits, its concept was rapidly becoming out of date on US TV. "It was such a typical pop genre piece of the late Seventies," she summarises. "Of course it lacked dimension and reality, but that was the fun of it!"

In the meantime, Gordon was still determined to keep all his irons in the fire, and harking back to the days when he built a studio in the grounds of Little Rhondda, he and Tom set about establishing a Hollywood based recording studio on Cahuenga Boulevard, called Britannia Sound. While this undoubtedly saved him money in recording fees, the success of the studio itself was unremarkable, possibly due to the high standard of the competition in the area.

On the whole work continued as usual for both Gordon and Tom throughout 1978. One notable concert was a special collaboration between Tom and foot-stomping rock diva Tina Turner in Washington. The Welshman opened the show with lively up-tempo numbers, but was then impressively upstaged by the entrance of Tina. Sporting a large pair of wings, she accordingly swooped across the stage, flanked by an array of feathered dancers. The two huge voices duetted on 'You Got What It Takes' and 'Nutbush City Limits', enjoying an explosive connection with both holding their expressive own.

As 1978 drew to a close events had turned full circle. Tom was once again Gordon's sole concern but whether their fortunes would improve was in the lap of the Gods.

★   ★   ★

In conjunction with changing his PR representation, Gordon and Tom agreed to address the singer's public image. Whereas before Tom had deliberately been held away from the increased media scrutiny encouraged by non-singing TV appearances, now Gordon felt the time was right to introduce the 39-year-old star to the competitive arena of the US chat show. One of the very first programmes to feature Tom in an informal television setting was *The Tonight Show*, hosted by stand-in Dick Clark, on which Tom was ostensibly promoting *Pleasure Cove* and his new album, *Rescue Me*. When questioned by the ex-Caravan Tour star as to why Tom appeared so infrequently on TV, his reply was simple: "I don't have a lot to talk about."

Tom went on to explain that after having done so much intense television work with *This Is Tom Jones* he had decided to give it a rest for a while. During the same period the singer also appeared on *The Merv Griffin Show* with a young Jay Leno, reminiscing about the time at Caesar's Palace when the comedian had opened for Tom, and had to cover for an extra 20 minutes because Tom accidentally split his trousers.

Regardless of his fluctuating fortunes, a constant throughout the Welshman's career was the number of fans who avidly followed wherever he travelled. Drummer Terry Jenkins is among many who witnessed first hand the lengths to which Tom's security guards would have to go with the more expressive audiences. "I remember one time at Madison Square Garden, they made the boxing ring into a stage and the audience was all round us, and there was only one corridor to go out of. At the end of the show everybody pushed forward and they came over the barriers. Tom was physically passed out by the security guards."

Sometimes the palpable fervour of Tom's devotees became potentially dangerous, if not painful, when they managed to slip past the bodyguards. "I remember another time on stage," reminisces Tom. "There I was, singing away, when suddenly a girl climbs up on stage runs up to me and grabs me by the short and curlies. Well, I didn't know what to do. I was singing in a high voice for about two minutes. The security guards couldn't pull this girl away, she was hanging on for dear life!" Tom's encounter with this particular fan was not to end there. Some years later Tom recognised her familiar face in the front row of another concert. When he asked, "Where have I seen you before?" she simply clenched and unclenched her fist . . .

One very famous incident occurred in Atlantic City, New Jersey. All the tables were pushed together for the show and a voluptuous member of the audience heaved herself up onto a table. As The Blossoms looked on in horror they saw her perform a death-defying sprint across the tabletops towards the stage. There she paused to remove her bra and expose her nakedness to the band. "In the same place, another lady in the audience had a heart attack," says Fanita James seriously. "They pulled her up onto the stage behind us and started working on her right there." Sadly the over-excited lady, one of Tom's more elderly followers, passed away at the scene.

"The fans were just hopelessly devoted," continues Fanita. "They would give us, The Blossoms, presents because they figured that we were the closest they would get to Tom. I was given an oil painting of The Blossoms once." Cynthia Woodard adds, "You would see the same faces from town to town and year to year. We became friends with the regular ones, we'd get talking. Sometimes, they would even take us out to dinner!"

Darlene Love, who had been with The Blossoms in the earlier part of the Seventies, remembers more of the threats than of the niceties that could occur. "When we worked in the theatres in the round we would have to sort of sit in the aisles, and women would actually come up to us and be mean and tell us to get out of the way. One lady even went so far as to push us. She went a little far and we had to say, 'Excuse me, but we're part of the show – we're not sitting here just to be sitting in the middle of the aisle!' We actually had to end up having security stand behind us while we were working.

"We even had people come up to us, especially ladies, and offer us money, anything we wanted to actually tell them where Tom Jones' room was. The ladies were a mess." Darlene previously wrote in her autobiography that mothers would bring their daughters up to the stage as 'sacrificial virgins' pleading, "I want Tom Jones to be my little girl's first."

Some admirers, having acted impetuously on their extreme devotion, have become immortalised in Tom's own history. "There was this one woman in Texas who used to follow me across America," Tom told teen pop magazine *Smash Hits*. "Her name was Donna Blood. She tried to pass herself off as Mrs Tom Jones and I don't know how she did it, but every night, wherever I sang – she'd be there in the front row . . . Anyway, one day I decided to confront her and see what it was all about and she pressed me into a room so we were all alone and she started pleading . . . 'You don't understand. I love you. I have to be with you. I've always loved you. I need you.'

"It got so bad that we had to get her locked up for the night wherever I was playing so she'd stop molesting me," he continues, tongue slightly in cheek. "But she'd get out of jail and follow me to the next town!" An equally obsessive fan with a slightly less doom-laden name was Barbara Anderson, who became renowned for embezzling more than $100,000 from her employer just to follow Tom around the world. In 1991 Tom then suffered the attentions of an infatuated stalker who attempted to land herself a job working for him. Once again, Tom took the bull by the horns and confronted his tormentor.

"My people couldn't shake her off and she started turning up at my shows," he said in an interview. "So finally I said to my security man, 'Bring her into my dressing room and I'll talk to her.' I said, 'Sweetheart, I don't really need another secretary,' and she said, 'But I'll do anything, absolutely anything for you.'" The young lady eventually began to cause even more of a nuisance by posing as Tom's wife and finally the police became involved when they discovered that she had financed her exploits on her father's credit card.

While many fans try to pretend that they are someone else to gain an intimate audience with Tom Jones, one woman had trouble coming to terms with Tom's own identity. He described the hilarious mix-up as follows: "I had a Hungarian woman who kept writing to me saying that I wasn't the real Tom Jones but an impostor. Anyway, one night she met up with me and said, 'You can't fool these people, you know you're not Tom Jones but my husband Boris from Budapest, so come back to Hungary with me.' We had to get her locked up as well . . ."

Perhaps the most famous British fan is Liverpudlian Jean Nicholls, who turned to Tom for inspiration when naming her son and grandson, Scott and Thomas respectively, and her two Yorkshire Terriers, Delilah and Rhondda. The respectable wife and mother was caught on more than one occasion in Tom's grounds, prowling with intent to take photographs. Still in the UK, the lady chairman of a fan club approached Jack Housler, the current owner of 44 Laura Street, requesting a snippet of grass from Tom's old garden to raffle for a charity of the fan club's choice. When Jack politely informed her that the lawn had long since been cemented over, she pleaded with him to just find some grass and send it to her in an envelope. Jack's grass actually came from the turf of the British Airways site where he worked and he heard a couple of months later that the bogus greenery had fetched over £500.

But the bizarre stories are not limited to the female fans. Jack Stahl, pastor of the Progressive Universal Life Church in Sacramento, California was given the dubious honour of being voted America's Strangest Man by the *Strange Universe Show* in 1997, having cited Tom Jones as the only true deity. "I received my calling when I was seven years old, I remember it like it was yesterday. Back in 1969 when the Tom Jones television show first appeared, I would sit in front of the TV watching this gyrating god. I knew from that moment on he had to be worshipped." An average day for Pastor Jack involves lighting the candles on his Tom Jones altar and performing exorcisms with a signed photo of his hero.

Of course, not all of Tom's admirers are infatuated to the point of irrationality, and invariably he has become close to many of them, particularly if they have followed him for a substantial number of years. A much quoted fan by the name of Ursula Alioto (incorrectly credited in Stafford Hildred and David Gritten's biography as the Vice President of the Milwaukee Fan Club), has met her idol backstage over 30 times. She is also an active voice within the devoted Tom Jones internet community, and frequently and openly discusses her many meetings with him online.

"While I didn't actually sleep with Tom (that would have been difficult as there would be no sleeping with all the vaporising/misting machines he had set up around his bed for his voice) – I was in his hotel room with him for most of the night back in the late Seventies. We talked for hours about his life, my life, astrology, fate and other things. We did more than talk . . . we drank copious amounts of Dom Perignon and 'made out' . . . I was struck by how different he was off stage . . . much less bawdy, and more 'normal.'" ★

One prized possession many Tom Jones fans still give their eye-teeth for is an article of sweat-saturated clothing discarded at a concert. Rather than taking off his jacket and tie specifically to titillate the ladies in the audience, Tom claims that he has to loosen his clothing to let his neck expand and enable him to breathe properly for his powerful performances, although this fails to explain why his shirt has to be undone to the navel!

It's not just the top half of his clothing he has problems with either. Tom has always worn threateningly tight trousers, but they tend to split and have to be replaced after just one or two outings. His tailor explained early on that although all the seams are double-stitched, the excessive perspiration and consequent dry cleaning to which the garments are exposed causes the seams to rot and weaken. There was nothing more the tailor could do, except provide every suit jacket with several pairs of trousers.

The fact that Tom comes off the stage every night literally dripping with moisture poses other limitations on his attire. "I only wear black on stage because it doesn't show the perspiration as much," says Tom. "I sweat so much that if I wore loose pants they'd look bloody awful."

Tom's choice of stage suits have always been the source of much discourse for his fans. "I like to change my wardrobe every year and have to find clothes that fit comfortable [sic] and give me the freedom of movement on stage." As he approached the Eighties Tom began to change his style from the traditional tuxedo-style outfit, to one influenced by the Matador look with high-waisted trousers, a frilly shirt and a Bolero jacket.

Accompanying the tailored outfits, Tom wears a fair amount of jewellery, more than one might expect for a miner's son from Pontypridd. When they were first married Linda had given her husband a plain silver crucifix which was suitably fashioned to cross the boundaries of their differing religions. "I started off with a small one but that got ripped off by a fan," explained Tom. "So she [Linda] got me a bigger one and that got ripped off and eventually I ended up with this thing. So if this one ever goes I'll have to wear one the size of a bloody great anchor!"

Jon Scoffield well remembers the clashes of taste he used to have with Tom when they were filming *This Is Tom Jones*. "He had a great fondness

---

★ After some deliberation, Ursula declined an interview with the writers of this book, stating: "I cannot say that I was intimate friends with Tom Jones. Nor was I president of his fan club, but merely a member. I did meet him several times and spent some time with him through the years, but nothing recently."

for jewellery which I thought was a bit over the top sometimes – I had to sort the rings out!" Aside from the necklace, Tom sports several solid gold, jewel-encrusted watches and bracelets along with numerous chunky gold rings, although strangely he does not appear to favour a wedding band of any description.

As befitting a sex symbol, Tom has always paid great attention to his personal grooming. The distinctive fragrance of Zibalene, an extremely expensive bath oil, would linger in his wake in the Seventies, and later his preference changed to a bespoke cologne called Secret de Venus, which had interestingly originated from a ladies' perfume.

His physique is a primary concern and Tom's daily fitness routine includes running, swimming, playing squash, lifting weights and riding an exercise bike, finished off by either a sauna or a massage. "I've got my own gym in the cellar of my Bel Air house where I use 100 lb. weights to tone my stomach muscles, do sit-ups and punch a heavy bag," he says. "I take 30 vitamin tablets daily, and make sure our cook gives me plenty of the good food I always used to eat in Wales – things like hearts and kidneys. I also use a steam bath to keep my vocal cords in good shape – you see, I can't get them insured."

As Tom approached his forties, the subject of his health often cropped up in interviews. "I try not to abuse myself too much. I like to drink occasionally, and I like to smoke cigars. Being in show business, I think, keeps you young also." He often seemed to labour the point when it came to his weight problems as he said elsewhere, "I'm identical to my father shape-wise. The only trouble is that I put on weight easily. I have to watch what I eat – I love chocolate but I force myself not to nibble. I still love a pint of real ale but that's an indulgence as well, so when I'm in Wales and go to the pub I'll have a Vodka with a slimline tonic – even though I get a few funny looks. The older you are the tougher it is."

Films have remained one of Tom's favourite pastimes since childhood. With the advent of the video cassette recorder, he was able to watch movies in his own home. He converted one room in his Bel Air mansion to house a magnificent 8 x 12 foot television screen and an impressive stereo system. Tom is often quoted saying that his favourite movie is *A Christmas Carol*, but he is also particularly fond of older classics and cowboy films. "The best Western ever made was *The Wild Bunch*," he pronounced. "But I also love a movie called *Red River*, starring John Wayne before he became a caricature of himself. And *Wuthering Heights*, the version with Laurence Olivier, is fabulous stuff."

Tom drastically increased his video collection almost overnight, as he waggishly detailed to *Smash Hits*: "[I've got] 2,500 of the bloody things. I bought them from my local video hire shop – this fella was selling up the stock and he did a deal with me. Have I watched them all? Two and a half bloody thousand?! I'll never get through them all. I'll have to leave them to someone in my will!" Being born during the Second World War, Tom often cites war veterans Sir Winston Churchill and Field Marshall Montgomery as his heroes. He watched the exhaustive award-winning *World At War* documentary series repeatedly when it was released on video.

Sadly for Tom, his own film career had faltered once again after *Pleasure Cove* and in the summer of 1979 he had to retract another statement after prematurely announcing plans for a film called *When The Lion Feeds*. It would have been a period adventure set in 19th century South Africa but like so many of Tom Jones' other cinematic prospects, it never quite got off the ground.

While Tom was again obliged to channel his energy into his concerts in the late Seventies, it seemed to some that his public comments were becoming increasingly lewd. "I not only suggest sex, I practically demand it," he boasted to the press. "When I'm performing, I'm like a guy who has a girl cornered in a motel room with my body blocking the door. I get turned on and frankly my show is like an orgy in pantomime."

Tom's outspoken male chauvinism was well documented. The strong views on sexual equality he outlined to Preston Whittaker back in 1972 had not changed. "I would support it only in as far as women getting as much money as a man in the case of them doing identical jobs. But in my book, equal means the same, and men and women are not the same. They shouldn't want to be treated the same, and I don't believe that most do."

Despite this outdated, even reactionary, stance, Tom agreed to a request from America's National Association of Women to appear in Washington DC at a benefit concert to raise funds for the Equal Rights Amendment. The singer joined Tina Turner at the $100 ticket event and managed to keep his sexist comments to a minimum.

But the respite in Tom's notorious attacks on female equality was brief, and shortly after the show he was heard to say: "A woman's job is to serve her man. But men have let women go too far. They give them equal rights, and I don't believe in that." He continues to this day to maintain his beliefs, saying to the *TV Times* recently: "The man should be the provider and the husband should make the decisions. I think women are happier that way. They really like to lean on a man, to depend on him."

15

RESCUE ME

THE YEAR OF Tom's 40th birthday saw a move to the Polygram record label. His most recent hit, 'Say You'll Stay Until Tomorrow', had been over three years ago and in the mid to late Seventies Tom had seemed to be content singing a mixture of middle-of-the-road, Californian soft rock and ballads. In 1979 he released an album called *Rescue Me*, a half-hearted attempt to get into disco which simply hadn't worked due to his ill-suited voice and advancing years. Perhaps the most ludicrous massacre on the LP was a disco re-working of Andrew Lloyd Webber and Tim Rice's 'Don't Cry For Me Argentina', lasting a tortuous six minutes and 18 seconds. Aside from the dubious delights within, the album's sleeve was in extremely poor taste, picturing Tom smiling out from between a woman's legs. The inside cover featured an oiled-up, bare-chested Tom looking mean and muscular with the same woman now at his feet, clutching his bulging thigh. *Rescue Me*'s artwork was held up in front of Tom by at least one chat show host for ridicule by the audience.

It was no surprise therefore when Tom left disco behind the following year with his move to Polygram. He was given a five-album deal and since his only recent chart success had been in the country mould, it was decreed that his first album with the new label should follow suit. Although it wasn't in his contract to solely record country albums, Tom was to become a fully fledged advocate of this genre for the remainder of his Polygram contract.

Of course this change in musical direction did not suit all of his fans. Indeed in the UK Tom eventually became so deeply unfashionable that several of his country albums weren't even released. Tom was quick to leap to the defence of his new sound, explaining to journalist Pete Mikla: "I've always done big ballads, rhythm and blues, rock and country. No matter what I do, though, it's not going to shock anyone. I have never come at the audience from left field. My fans don't have to worry that I'm all of a sudden going to dress up like a cowboy and sing only country music just because I record one country tune."

The insecurity provoked by the uncertainty of Tom's new career path was suddenly compounded by an unexpected attack from his old sparring partner and ex-stablemate, Engelbert Humperdinck. By sticking with his romantic forte and releasing the LPs *After The Lovin'*, *Miracles* and *Last Of The Romantics*, Engel himself had in fact substantially outsold Tom since his departure from the MAM family. The sales of these albums and others had far exceeded those of his old adversary and the Epic record label had chosen to renew Engel's contract for a further four years, while simultaneously dropping Tom Jones and prompting his move to Polygram.

As Engel was also receiving greater critical acclaim than his rival it seemed somewhat unnecessary for him to choose this moment to launch a spiteful feud. How much of the excitable reports were hype to boost the respective singers' record sales and how much were actual venom is a matter for conjecture, but for a while the printed stories of clashes between the Vegas giants took on renewed vigour.

"Engelbert was due to play Indianapolis," said Tom. "I was scheduled to follow him in three months so my name was outside the theatre as a coming attraction. Engel refused to go on until they had taken my name down. Absolutely refused. I guess he feels I'm a threat." Engel also started what was to become a life-long castigation of Tom through impersonations in his concerts. Typically he would make derogatory quips about the number of handkerchiefs or socks Tom would stuff down his trousers, then imitate him singing the first verse of 'Delilah', exaggeratedly thrusting his hips and punctuating his performance with nasty asides.

Engel continued the unpleasantness in the media. "After I left Gordon Mills, my career really soared," he said. "Tom resented that. He's never forgiven me for 'breaking up the team'." But Tom denied the rift. "There was never any feud at all," he told *Woman's Own* magazine in 1981. "Before Eng split with Gordon we were good friends. I mean, we used to see each other socially. We were pals. Now, well, we've just gone our separate ways, separate paths. I don't have any bad feelings towards him at all, not one. But I know that he felt Gordon was promoting me over him and he was always my shadow . . . Eng was unhappy, and he did what he felt was right for him. So I respect that, of course."

Marion Spence-Fox believes that the bitterness was probably press hyperbole and mainly for effect: "I think they were friends really. I think that underneath all the papers saying they're feuding, basically they were friends." But intriguingly, when Engel was approached to be interviewed for this book, a spokesperson for Manhattan Management inadvertently suggested that Engel's refusal was due in part to a very real personality conflict between the two stars.

Meanwhile, life was looking fairly bleak for Tom's own manager. An inside source has revealed that by this period Gordon was beginning to curse ever having set up and floated MAM as a public company. The on-going pressure of repeating and exceeding the previous year's profit margin was becoming increasingly tough, especially as by now he had lost both Gilbert and Engel, and Tom alone wasn't shifting enough records to pull him out of the woods. The only sure way of sustaining income was to put his tried and tested major act into Las Vegas cabaret for months at a time. If Tom was by now a little bored with the set-up, it wasn't really open for discussion.

The MAM staff that remained in the US were all feeling a little homesick, and for Gordon's wife Jo, life away from England was becoming unbearable. Over the last three years she had battled to rekindle the dying embers of their marriage but it was now obvious that there was no hope of a reconciliation, and so she moved back to the familiarity of Weybridge, filing for divorce. Around the same time, Linda's mother, Vi Trenchard, began experiencing problems with her health, and Linda, too, moved back to the UK, albeit on a temporary basis, staying in Wales to look after her mother. But for Tom's wife there was never any question of a divorce.

The men had to keep working, no matter what was happening in their personal lives, and Tom's new country angle was publicised by a slew of promotional chat show appearances. In January 1980 he guested on the primetime American shows hosted by Merv Griffin, Phil Donahue and Mike Douglas. Typically Tom would plug his latest album or single, performing a couple of songs in the TV studio. He would talk about his rise to fame, explaining both his Welsh roots and accent, his friendship with Elvis Presley, his touring lifestyle and exercise routine. Tom would also repeat the little white publicity lies that had rolled off his tongue for so long. When Phil Donahue asked him what his full name was, Thomas John replied without hesitation: "My real name is Thomas Jones Woodward". On an edition of the *Tonight* show when Joan Rivers was standing in for Johnny Carson, Tom stated that he had been married for a year before his son Mark was born, presumably a sop towards America's moral majority.

A departure from the normal chat show routine occurred on *Good Morning America* when they elected to focus on Tom's relationship with Mark, now in his early twenties, who had been touring as a lighting and wardrobe man with his father for half-a-dozen years. He had grown into a slimmer but less confident version of Tom and the men were filmed playing pool in the billiards room of the Friars Club in New York. Tom proudly described how they enjoyed going out to discotheques together and when the interviewer asked Mark whether he had inherited his father's famous sex appeal and was causing a stir with the ladies, Mark mumbled: "If it happens, it's lucky for me, you know."

Eventually it did indeed 'happen'. Donna Marie Paloma, who had previously worked as the secretary for the actor and comedian Bill Cosby, had become romantically involved with Tom's group of touring musicians. She had initially set her sights on Mike Morgan's drummer brother, Barry, and had moved from New York to Los Angeles to be with him. Donna was four years Mark's senior, but they nevertheless became attracted to one another. As Mark was good friends with Barry, the secret couple were unable to pluck up the courage to make their relationship public for quite a while. Having finally broken the news to the drummer, they announced their engagement towards the end of 1981.

Tom's next country album was entitled *Darlin'*, and the cover photograph, which featured Tom smirking from beneath the wide-brimmed cowboy hat he had promised never to wear, left no-one in any doubt about the style of music therein. Released in March 1981, it reached no higher than a woeful number 179 in the American charts. Even Tom's live performances were suffering from technical glitches. When he was performing at Caesar's Palace in 1980 the giant sign declaring 'TOM JONES IS HERE' spontaneously burst into flames, costing the casino a cool $1 million in fire damages.

On all accounts the briefly bearded Tom threw himself wholeheartedly into the country routine, appearing on one of Dolly Parton's TV shows, duetting with her on 'Green Green Grass Of Home' and finally enduring the certain embarrassment of the voluptuous country superstar throwing her knickers at him.

While Tom's albums sold fairly well in the US country charts, they rated poorly elsewhere, and overall the sales were nothing in comparison to the success he had enjoyed in the early Seventies. Tom was suffering from the dichotomy of performing raunchy cabaret in Las Vegas to exhilarated sell-out audiences, while releasing a totally different, and rather limiting style of music on vinyl. Inevitably the imbalance began to affect his self-esteem. "When I'm on stage and people are there it comes home to you all the time. You hear the applause. So they keep on reassuring you. But when you record something you have faith in and it doesn't sell, you wonder. You think, 'What's wrong? What am I doing wrong that it's not selling? Why do I feel that it's a good record and the people aren't buying it?' So you question yourself."

Still, Tom was to try a new medium. One new marketing opportunity in the early Eighties was the rise of the video, either as a short promotional tool for a single, or a method of bringing a whole concert into a fan's living room. Unfortunately, Gordon's attempt to take Tom into this growing new area took the form of a straightforward and rather uninspired video of live concert footage, entitled *Tom Jones Live in Las Vegas*. The video was unremarkable, with unimaginative camera shots and a surprising lack of knickers thrown onto the stage.

But all was not lost. In a further attempt to recapture past ratings, Gordon referred back to the medium that had properly secured Tom's superstar status at the end of the Sixties. It had been almost exactly a decade since the demise of *This Is Tom Jones*, and a new TV contract offered a great opportunity for the 41-year-old singer to rejuvenate his flagging career. During the months of April and September 1981, Tom filmed a new series of half-hour television shows in Vancouver.

"When you've got a hit TV series and records in the charts, you're about as far to the front as you can go," said Tom, recounting his former glory. "That's got to level off. Straight variety is not working on television any longer . . . So if you're not on television that much and not played on the radio that much, they wonder where you are."

Tom's new series was directed by Perry Rosemond, written by Paul Wayne and produced by both, with Gordon Mills overseeing a portion of the action. The music was separately recorded at Pinewood Studios, and each episode would run along a very strict set formula. The name *Tom Jones* would simply flash up on-screen during the opening sequence, although the actual title of the series was *Coast To Coast*.

The opening to each programme would be a lively, up-tempo dance number, with Tom clad in a casual outfit and backed by four female dancers in revealing costumes. After the first number Tom would banter with these ladies, Terrell, Victoria, Jackie (later to be replaced by Deborah) and Candy. The latter was, to Tom's evident delight, the youngest aged only 18. Candy's introduction to the series serves as an excellent example of the sheer banality of Tom's interaction with the girls, with the singer uttering the immortal line: "Candy is dandy but liquor is quicker", to which the teenage dancer was scripted to offer the verbal warning: "Underage glamour could land you in the slammer". The petite brunette Terrell was clearly Tom's favourite, and she and Tom would regularly whisper what were presumably X-rated jokes to each other during this part of the show each week, before indulging in a full, open-mouthed kiss.

After these excruciating on-stage flirtations with the dancers, Tom would sing a solo number, and then introduce his guest for the week. A brief chat would ensue, invariably tinged with sexual innuendo if the guest was female, which was generally the case, and overly flattering if the guest was male; a macho back-slapping session that would always concentrate on Tom slightly more than the guest.

The two would then duet, and the guest star would be afforded a solo spot to plug his or her latest single. For the penultimate segment, Tom would reclaim the show and zip through a series of four song styles. Grandly coming down the stairs having changed into a lurid sparkly jacket (a different colour each week), Tom would sing a standard of the time and then make his way down to the front of the stage. There he would sit on the stairs for a 'quiet spot', performing a gentle country ballad. To kick-start the momentum again Tom would stand up, whip off his sparkly jacket and throw it into the audience. With his shirt now unbuttoned to the navel, he'd launch into a powerful number chosen primarily to demonstrate his extreme vocal abilities.

Finally Tom would stand centre stage and thank his guest, who briefly reappeared for a hearty embrace. Tom then recited a reflective quotation before, flanked by the dancers once again, he closed the show to a spectacularly choreographed version of a contemporary song.

As with *This Is Tom Jones*, an impressive guest list was secured for *Coast To Coast*. Gladys Knight's performance proved a successful pairing of the two voices, with a duet on 'You Gotta Be Mine' and a tender lip-licking kiss as a farewell. A teenage Brooke Shields went down a treat with Tom, who harboured fond memories of her sensual film *The Blue Lagoon*. Juliet Prowse, who was notable for her appearance on the pilot for *This Is Tom Jones* some 13 years earlier, reappeared, duetting on 'I Get A Kick Out Of You'.

Cybill Shepherd, who had been linked with Elvis in 1966, the year before his marriage to Priscilla, was at this stage a minor actress yet to move on to *Moonlighting* and *Cybill*. She guested on Tom's show, making quite a splash in a large purple dress and singing 'Our Day Will Come' with the star. Another actress who tickled Tom's fancy was the six foot plus Susan Anton, who was much taller than the host even in her flat shoes. After the obligatory flirting, Susan snidely re-christened the programme 'The Tom Thumb Show'.

Two interesting male guests included the composer of 'She's A Lady', Paul Anka, who contrary to Susan Anton was visibly tiny and worryingly orange, and songwriter, pianist and film scorer Isaac Hayes, who performed a very loose sketch with Tom.

Tom was unmistakably in his element on screen, and although the series was unquestionably repetitive and unoriginal, he was an amiable host who obviously enjoyed his work. "One thing I have learned is that one should relax more on television," he said. "It is different in a theatre, where you have somehow to reach out and hit the back walls with power. I used to think the same in front of the television camera . . . go out and belt away hard, put on a terrific show each time by working at full pitch. Now I feel more relaxed."

The series was aired in January 1982 in the US and Canada, and soon after to the rest of the world. Sadly it could never hope to emulate the universal appeal of *This Is Tom Jones*, but it went down well with his existing fan base nonetheless. Unlike Tom's first TV show which has yet to be released in full on video format, *Coast To Coast* was repackaged in October 1999 in a set entitled *The Ultimate Collection*.

★　★　★

Intent on keeping up appearances on radio as well as television in 1981, Tom was featured as the guest DJ at WHN Radio New York on May 21, and a slot on *Live At Five* for NBC. He also donated a pair of his boots to a San Franciscan radio station, raising $200 in a celebrity auction.

Shortly after Tom completed the filming for *Coast To Coast*, his personal life was complicated by family issues. Although in 1975 Tom's parents had been thrilled to move to Bel Air with their superstar son, they missed the familiarities of home and by the late Seventies had returned to Wales. As Tom was still unable to visit the UK due to tax reasons, in order to see their son his parents would fly out to Los Angeles whenever he was there for any substantial length of time.

"I brought them over here when Linda and I moved permanently, but Dad just couldn't settle," Tom told journalist Donald McLachlan in 1981. "And Mum? Well, she wants to be where he is. But they come over and see us as often as they want – usually twice a year."

Tom was concerned for his father. Although Tom Snr. had been freed from the mines earlier than his planned retirement, he was suffering from a combination of miner's asthma, called pneumoconiosis (also known as 'Black Dust' and caused by industrial residue accumulating in the lungs), and emphysema from his nicotine addiction. Tom had arranged for some of the best doctors on both sides of the Atlantic to help look after his father, but on one trip to see his son, Tom Snr. became unexpectedly trapped in Los Angeles, unable to fly due to his advancing ill health.

Tom Snr. never recovered and passed away on October 5, 1981, aged 72. Tom's only comfort was that he had been able to spend his father's last week with him. The grief-stricken Freda made the decision to remain in America to be with her son and family, and so Tom Snr. was buried nearby in Los Angeles for them all to visit.

Emotionally shattered after such a personal loss, Tom felt that his life had been turned upside-down. He was unsure whether he could continue with his Las Vegas season, on the basis that it wouldn't be fair to his fans if his heart wasn't in it. But his mother reasoned with him. He tried to express his feelings in a TV interview a few years later: "I didn't know what to do, I was so emotionally upset. I was supposed to go to Vegas for two weeks, I couldn't do it . . . Songs take on a different meaning when you've lost somebody you love, you read more into the songs, lyrics become different . . . But time is a healer. My mother said give yourself time and when you feel like it again, do it. So I did, but it was difficult at first."

Fortunately, 1982 was to be a happier year for the whole Woodward clan. Tom and Linda celebrated their 25th wedding anniversary on March 2, and just five days later on March 7, Mark and Donna were married. The antithesis of his parents' downbeat ceremony, Mark's wedding was an elaborate affair, set in a plush Beverly Hills hotel with over 200 guests attending and a lavish sit-down dinner for all. Initially Linda refused to attend due to her virtually paralysing reclusiveness, but thankfully changed her mind at the last minute.

Tom's gift to his son and daughter-in-law was a beautiful house in Beverly Hills close to his own. After the recent death of his father, Tom made a concerted effort to spend as much time as possible with his family, with Mark and Donna visiting for dinner almost every night. Donna would join the men in discussions about the latest tour or other work-related matters, while Linda felt increasingly isolated. The newest Mrs Woodward was aptly described by Marion Crewe as "very businesslike, she's got her wits about her".

Having reconciled his temporary disinclination to continue touring after the loss of his father, Tom resumed his heavy annual schedule for much of 1982. Meanwhile, Gordon Mills and MAM faced the culmination of Gilbert O'Sullivan's fight for freedom and a hefty sum in back royalties, the High Court hearing having been set for April 1982. On the advice of his lawyers Gilbert had dropped his allegations of deceitful accounting or other financial malpractice and was now simply asking the courts to declare unfair the contract he had signed a decade before.

The impending lawsuit aside, MAM had suffered a severe downturn in fortunes since losing both Gilbert and Engelbert Humperdinck. Pre-tax profits had dropped approximately half a million pounds and the shares had almost halved, dropping from 180p to 95p in the previous 10 years. By 1982 almost two-thirds of the company's income was generated by its 16,000 amusement machines and jukeboxes.

In addition to demanding the immediate return of all copyrights on his songs, Gilbert was suing MAM for £7 million of the £14.5 million he felt he deserved in both back royalties and damages. Most of those involved in this high-profile case, not to mention the music industry in general, squirmed in their seats when Mr Justice Mars-Jones cited damning evidence which proved that between 1970 and 1978 MAM grossed approximately £14.5 million from five of Gilbert's singles and seven of his albums. The artist received only £500,000.

The judge agreed with Gilbert that he had been "fleeced" and bought at a "bargain basement price". As Simon Garfield quotes in his excellent analytical book, *Expensive Habits*, the Judge concluded, "These figures give some indication of the scale of the exploitation of this young man's talents." This was all capped by the fact that, in his naïveté, Gilbert had not taken independent legal advice before signing the offending contract.

In their defence Gordon Mills and Bill Smith, backed up by Decca executive Dick Rowe, claimed that the contract had been perfectly normal for its time and that without their expert management, Gilbert would not have achieved such success.

The Judge did not waver and released Gilbert from all his contractual ties with MAM, allowing him to recover his master tapes and every penny that Gordon had unfairly made from his music, including compound interest and his legal costs. Simon Garfield succinctly sums up the final settlement: "He received an astounding award of publishing and recording profit, estimated by MAM's counsel to stand, after interest as high as £7 million pre-tax. This amount and the copyright award had never been seen in the industry before. It was a fantastic shock."★

At MAM, Gordon's stubborn arrogance kicked in and he launched an immediate appeal. Reiterating that they had remained within the law at all times, his legal team argued that the court's decision did not take into account the benefit Gilbert had received from such skilled supervision. As if the implications of financial deception weren't enough for Gordon to bear, his personal life was also becoming rather complicated. Jo Mills had finally accepted the demise of their marriage back in 1979, effectively leaving Gordon free to play the field.

He met his soul-mate, Annie Toomaru, during his tortuous year of 1982. "She was lovely, absolutely gorgeous," recalls Les Reed of the Tahitian businesswoman who had previously run her own travel agency. Soon after linking up with Gordon, Annie was drafted onto the MAM workforce as an administrator dealing with the fan clubs. She took an active role in the development of the clubs worldwide and was appreciated for her patience and measured diplomacy as she streamlined the various Tom Jones chapters in America to become more user-friendly.

Annie's introduction coincided with the sad passing of another much-loved member of the group, Jeannie King. The long-standing Blossom and wife of Larry Richstein had suffered heart problems since an operation

★ The unprecedented judgement in favour of Gilbert O'Sullivan sparked understandable panic within the music world, most notably initiating a copycat trial in which Elton John brought (and lost) a greater case involving even higher sums of money against the redoubtable music publisher, Dick James.

some years earlier, and suddenly became ill during one of Tom's tours. She stayed behind in Las Vegas to see the doctor while the rest of the party moved on, but tragically died on March 28, 1983, just five days later. She was 44 years old, an age that mirrored those of Johnnie Spence and Elvis Presley six years earlier. Jeannie was just one year older than Tom.

In order to assist her grieving family in the wake of their loss, Tom donated a personally autographed, velvet Givenchy jacket to his fan clubs to raffle in Jeannie's memory. All proceeds of the $3 tickets were divided between her grieving family and the Heart Fund. Jeannie was irreplaceable in The Blossoms, followed in lesser succession by Stephanie Spruil, Debbie Wilson, Myrna Shilling and Angela Lewis.

Professional life for Tom now saw a move deeper into country music. While he remained with the Polygram label, his base was transferred to the Nashville office of Mercury Records, then Polygram's US outlet. Here he was awarded the honorary title of Nashville Deputy Sheriff in recognition of his services to entertainment. Although Tom has always maintained that he likes all genres of music and prefers to record a healthy mixture, he seemed resigned to the fact that the only way he could make an impact on the charts was with country LPs, *Tom Jones Country* in 1982 and the forthcoming *Don't Let Our Dreams Die Young*.

Tom's hits in 1983 were the singles 'Touch Me (I'll Be Your Fool Once More)' which reached an encouraging number four in the country charts, and 'It'll Be Me' which, accompanied by a promotional video, also went into the specialist charts, this time attaining number 34. While it was pleasant enough to achieve success in these targeted music genres, the songs had limited Tom's overall audience to the extent that many observers believed that he had in fact retired by the early Eighties. The star was always quick to explain his perceived change of direction: "When I recorded these two country albums, [fans] didn't even say I like the switch or I don't like the switch. To them, there was no switch. I'm still singing those love songs, except there's a country flavour."

As he justified himself further in the papers, the truth began to seep out. "It's difficult for a non-songwriter such as myself," he said to journalist Bob Andelman. "I just don't have the talent to write songs. I've got to rely on other people and sometimes they just don't come your way. The country stuff was coming in and I thought, why not, I'd done country music before and had success with it," he continued, citing examples such as 'Green Green Grass Of Home' and 'Detroit City' to reinforce his argument.

Satisfied that he had explained his move into country music, in the same interview Tom continued to reason why he then could not break the mould. "[Polygram] feel I'm doing well with it, and why change horses in the middle of the stream? Now when I put a country record out, most of the stations play it. So if I was to make a pop album, I would lose the country audience, the country stations. And then if you want to make a country album after that, you've got to start all over again. Until something really strong comes along pop-wise, I'll stick with country."

Tom tried desperately to convince anyone who was prepared to listen that he was not strictly a country singer. He would later admit to listening to artists like Hank Williams, Garth Brooks and Clint Black, but protested that his taste and sound continued to cross all musical barriers from country to pop and R&B. "I also like rockabilly music as well, like Delbert McClinton," said Tom. "He's on the border too. He's never really been considered a country singer, and he's never really been considered an R&B singer."

Regardless of the music he was recording, Tom ploughed on with the endless touring as if nothing had changed. He incorporated a few of his biggest country hits, 'Say You'll Stay Until Tomorrow' and 'Touch Me (I'll Be Your Fool Once More)' into his act, but the majority of the shows consisted of Tom Jones classics from the Sixties and covers of Seventies standards.

The women still threw plenty of knickers, but now they were accompanied by the occasional cowboy hat. The manner in which Tom played and paraded around with the lingerie and other missiles had become something of a self-parody, and he would often delay the show for up to 20 minutes while he made exceptionally lewd comments, accepted various gifts brought up to the stage and handed out endless kisses to his hungry fans.

During this period, with precious few other promotional opportunities, Tom's publicity agents seized on any gimmick they could to get their boy into the papers. It was in this vein that they claimed he had kept a count of the number of room-keys thrown on stage over the years, and had just received his 5,000th key at Caesar's Palace. Another feel-good story around this time was that although Tom had been good friends with Elvis he had never actually been to Graceland, and by special request the mansion-turned-memorial was opened for Tom to take a midnight tour, in the process becoming visitor number one million and one.

With the extreme decline in media interest it was not surprising that the news of Donna and Mark's imminent addition to the family, thus making Tom a granddad, was pounced upon as the next big story. The Woodward's child was due on June 14, but Tom told chat show hosts that he hoped they would be able to share the same birthday. The manner in which he spoke about his first grandchild was more like an expectant father: "You know I'm dashing home to California as fast as possible to be home for the big event. I've got to be with the family. I'm hoping for a boy, naturally, but we don't know which it will be."

Tom's career underwent yet another facelift as he prepared for his first tour of the UK in almost a decade since his enforced tax exile. He told the press: "I'm especially happy because I'm going to the people. Sure, we're sold out in London but we're also going to places where most performers don't go – Birmingham, Manchester, Glasgow, Liverpool, Brighton, Newcastle and South Cornwall. You know most people can't come to London so we're going to them. That's why I like this trip back home." When asked whether he was excited about the Queen or Prince Phillip attending his concerts Tom brushed it off, saying: "Listen, *I* am about to become a *grandfather*! I feel like a *king* now!"

Five days after Tom's 43rd birthday, Donna gave birth to a baby boy at 4.00 p.m. on June 12, 1983, calling him Alexander John. Tom was overjoyed, crowing to the press: "My grandson is the apple of my eye. He's like a second son to me. He makes me feel younger – he's fantastic. I feel more like a second-time father than a first-time grandfather." Tom pointed out that now he had money and security he was going to make sure that baby Alexander wanted for nothing – which was a far cry from both Tom and Mark's childhood in Pontypridd. "I'm so proud of my grandson that I want to show him off to my relatives back home. I'm looking forward to buying him expensive toys and taking him on trips that I couldn't afford for my son."

True to his word Tom overhauled his Bel Air home, turning it into a regular playground for his grandson, by installing a tree-house, playhouse, a slide and swings. As he grew, Alexander was given the very best tricycles, bikes and toys, even graduating to an extravagant electric jeep when he reached his fourth birthday. Tom was addressed as 'Grandsha' by Alexander, so that even in glossy Bel Air a little bit of Welsh could be instilled into his upbringing. As a relatively young grandfather, Tom indulged himself in endless games with the toddler, building a strong rapport between the generations. "It's a new experience and still being a young man, it's even better. I can enjoy my grandson and still think about when he's old enough to come out with me on the road and see what I do. You know, you can almost recapture when your own child was a baby."

With this new lease of life, Tom embarked on his first British tour since 1974. More than 400 eager fans queued at Heathrow airport for hours to welcome home their hero. Linda was travelling with him, but slipped away just after the plane landed so as to avoid the excitable crowd and prying press.

And what better way could there be to celebrate his long-awaited homecoming than with a family party? On September 10, Tom took over the Celtic Manor Hotel near Newport, Gwent, inviting nearly 100 relatives. He had been filming promotional TV in London during the day and was flown to Wales immediately afterwards for the evening event. Generously he had arranged for coaches to pick up his various aunts, uncles and cousins, some of whom had never even met him, from the surrounding areas in Wales. Cousin Kath Woodward describes Tom's typical patience as his entire extended family queued up to speak to their famous relative, "He never missed anyone out, you could sit there all night and he'd still come and see you."

Three sold-out concerts then followed at the new venue of St. David's Hall in Cardiff on September 11 and 12. All the tickets, priced at £30 each, were snapped up in just 48 hours and the proceeds were donated to a charity for miners suffering from 'Black Dust' in memory of Tom's beloved father. The singer was honoured with a civic reception headed by Lord Tonypandy in the grand surroundings of Cardiff Castle and footage from the critically acclaimed concerts was broadcast as a Christmas special for ITV.

Tom and his band then launched into a triumphant 15-day UK tour incorporating 20 performances, all to full houses. During this time Gordon Mills arranged for Tom to appear at a photo call on October 9 with the London Welsh Rugby Football Club. The club had approached MAM for some form of involvement and although Tom was unable to attend an actual match, he provided financial backing for the London Welsh Mini Rugby Tournament for players under the age of 16.

Tom's return visit was recorded for a Welsh programme for the HTV channel titled *Welcome Home Tom* and narrated by Arfon Haines-Davies. Tom was filmed giving a guided helicopter tour over Treforest and its surrounds, where he pointed out places where he once worked and commented on the new one-way system and overpasses. After landing he revisited the site of his first concert, the Wood Road Social Club, followed by a stroll across the road to his old school where he was allowed to ring the bell, then on to his birthplace, 57 Kingsland Terrace, before finally returning to 44 Laura Street. Jack Housler, the present owner of the house in which Tom grew up, currently rents it out to five students from the nearby university. He is well used to all the attention, as Tomologists (their preferred title) often make a pilgrimage from as far away as New Zealand and China.

While Tom was over in the UK Linda realised the extent of her homesickness, and they decided to purchase a house just a short drive from Pontypridd. Linda had previously been staying with her sister and brother-in-law, looking after her ailing mother while Tom was on tour. She now felt that it would be more suitable to have a permanent base of her own in Wales. The couple now planned for Linda to travel back to Los Angeles to visit her husband and conversely Tom would use their new property as a base for future UK tours. "Our house is near Cowbridge," he said in an interview with *Australian Woman's Weekly*, "which is just up the road from where we both come from. I love it there. It's an old market town set in beautiful countryside, within 20 minutes drive from Cardiff, the capital of Wales. And it's got some great pubs."

Bidding a reluctant farewell to Britain Tom returned to the US where he played to a packed concert hall, Resorts in Atlantic City, over the Thanksgiving weekend. As was the case worldwide, the tickets sold out quickly and no less than 5,000 people were turned away disappointed.

The immense difficulty of obtaining a ticket was alleviated if you were a member of a fan club, or better still a president. The various interlinking organisations at one stage proved to be so efficient that members could join a 'travel club' which would help arrange accommodation and restaurants for foreign visitors at each stage of the tour. The last night of a run of concerts in any one town was famous for being 'club night', which would be supervised by Lloyd Greenfield. On these special occasions the fan clubs were allowed privileges such as backstage visits for the club presidents and superior seating for the members. Those in the know were aware that the fan club presidents would receive specific T-shirts to identify them at concerts. It was mainly due to these 'gifts' that Tom would be able to recognise the presidents who worked hard to promote his image, and greet them by their first names. There were rumours that Gordon would sign up to each new fan club chapter as an anonymous member, in order to ensure that they were operating in an appropriate fashion.

One activity that was certainly not considered appropriate behaviour for a fan club was communicating with the press. When the president of the Tiger Tom Club was featured in a newspaper article, the club was officially disbanded shortly afterwards, even though their bank balance apparently showed a healthy profit of $2,000.

Overall the clubs were very generous to their hero, displaying their undying love for him by decorating his dressing room and leaving all manner of presents for his delectation. The different clubs began competing to outdo each other in extravagance and daring – some would even stretch to providing a lavish buffet for Tom and the musicians when they came off the stage.

★   ★   ★

Tom was agreeing to ever more interviews, either on television or for newspapers, but without a strong-willed PR man like Chris Hutchins guiding him he started to roam back to taboo subjects, expounding on his notorious sexism and sexuality. Tom has never denied his male chauvinism, but short of promoting his latest country album or single, if the journalists are to be believed he did not have much else to talk about. "I wouldn't cook to save my life," he boasted in an interview with *Woman's Own*. "That's my upbringing; my father kept out of the kitchen – no place for a man. I don't like being in a kitchen . . . It's nice to sit at the table and have the meal brought there. I'm sure women don't like being in the kitchen, either . . . it's just part of their life. Somebody's got to do it." Whether these remarks endeared him to their female readership or alienated them completely is impossible to say, but either way, with such expressions of his archaic value systems, he had pretty much dispelled the last fragments of dignity he had clung to in the eyes of the music press.

Linda had become conspicuous by her absence at almost every public occasion, with Tom instead being joined by Freda, Sheila or Mark. Interviewers could not fail to notice this, and encouraged by the fact that Tom was often rumoured to be having an affair, were always curious as to the truth behind Tom and Linda's marriage. In the past Tom had tried to keep his private life relatively quiet, gently implying that he and his wife had a special bond because they had met so young. In the early Eighties however he became far more willing to detail the exact nature of their time together. "Our relationship is still fresh, because I am away touring so much," he told journalist Trudi Pacter. "If I had a nine-to-five job and I was home every evening, then I think sex could get a little ordinary for us. But being continually on the road builds my hunger for Linda. And hers for me. When I get home things are very hot and sensuous. And they stay that way the whole time I'm here. For the sexual act is a kind of reassurance for us both. And Linda is very comforted by the fact that I still dig her."

Having declared that he and his wife were still actively in love, Tom then found it acceptable to admit his true urges. "For me, sex is the most important thing in the world," he continued in the same interview. "Every time a pretty woman walks into the room I look at her and I react to her. Any man who denies he functions the same way is either a liar, or there's something wrong with him." In another interview he blamed his dalliances on high testosterone levels: "I'm no angel, I admit that – but I'm no better or worse than any other man." When he was then put on the spot in a chat show Tom abruptly became very defensive, citing his exceptional circumstances as an excuse. "Ask any man in the audience, 'Are you faithful?' And they would say they are faithful, it's the first thing you say. But not every man is on the road nine months of the year."

"I am a *man*. I am a *married* man, so I have to be discreet," Tom told magazine journalist Donald McLachlan in a particularly candid interview.

"Men aren't the most angelic creatures on the face of the earth, now are they? . . . Most men can, and do, get away with a great deal more than me because of the publicity. If I do anything, if I take anybody out, there are pictures and there are always people talking to the gossips. *Everybody* knows about it. That's why I always have to be very, very careful."

With regard to how it affects Linda he had already formulated a stock answer. "Fortunately for me, my wife is a very clever woman, and she knows me very well. So she did a deal with me. She simply said this: 'As long as you keep coming home, as long as things are good between us when you *are* home, then what you do when you are away is up to you. What I don't know, I don't think about. But if anything ever comes back to me – then you're in trouble . . .' "

Marion Spence-Fox confirms that this was the attitude of her close friend and indeed one shared by all the wives left at home while the band was touring. "You just turned a blind eye to it. You don't listen to it, you don't believe it; you can't believe what you read in the papers. Most of it's rubbish anyway – it's all made up. Linda would just ignore it." Vi Trenchard, Linda's mother, did her best to dissipate the flames fanned by the press about her daughter's reclusiveness. "It's not a question of Tom banning all photographs. It's Linda's decision. She is basically very shy and hates the limelight. I know over the years there have been stories about Tom and other women, but the proof of their love is that they are still together after all these years."

"I just don't see what it has got to do with me," said Linda in one of her rare interviews. "Why should I be bothered with it? Tom's the star, not me." It seemed that Linda was content to be by herself while her husband toured, providing he was attentive on his return. "If she comes to the show, she'll sit in the back," said Tom. "She used to come to see me much more than she does now . . . Linda certainly doesn't like to be reminded all the time of what happens when I perform. She likes to be with me when I'm not working. And she doesn't ask questions."

That Linda did not like to join Tom on his tours appeared to be a source of relief to him. "Linda's shyness works for me because I have such a hectic time when I'm on the road. If I had a wife who wanted to go out all the time, being at home would be no different from the rest of my working life. And that wouldn't do at all."

Indeed Linda was wise to avoid the tabloid papers who frequently ran articles on Tom's latest conquest, be it genuine or a hoax. In November 1990, the *News Of The World* ran a feature on a Australian girl called Sallyanne Williams who claimed that she had been seduced by Tom in 1983. Her story described how the superstar had approached her parents to gain permission to take Sallyanne, then just 17 years old, on holiday, promising faithfully that he would look after her properly. She was allowed to go on the trip and for just over a week was taken shopping and watched movies during the day, then entertained Tom during the night. Sallyanne remembers that Tom made it clear to her that he would not leave his wife because of the financial ramifications and then abandoned her after their time together.

Sallyanne suffered a miscarriage shortly after her alleged affair with Tom and believes that the baby would have been his as she was a virgin when they met. Nearly two years after their 'holiday' she saw an Australian newspaper article which said that Tom was trying to reach her, and so she contacted his offices. After falsely accusing her of confirming their affair to the press, Tom gave Sallyanne 500 US dollars. Her family were furious about Tom's actions, with her father threatening, "If I'd got hold of him I'd have wrung his neck."

As 43-year-old Tom was still purporting to be a ladies' man, and all too happy to host the Miss Universe contest that year, he felt it necessary to take care of his natural ageing process. There is a small 'z' shaped scar underneath his chin which is supposed to have originated from 1983. One explanation for this scar is that it is the result of minor surgery to remove excess fatty tissue which was giving Tom a double chin. This is certainly feasible, especially considering that the singer's vanity would not allow cameramen to film him from underneath for *This Is Tom Jones*. However Sue Abbot, another fan who claims to have been intimate with Tom, has another rationale for this 'z' shaped mark. She alleges that a man approached Tom while he was drinking quietly in a bar and accused him of having an affair with his wife. Before Tom could do anything the jealous husband broke a bottle on the counter and stabbed it into Tom's throat, narrowly missing a vital artery, but scarring him for life.

Other than straightening his crooked nose and capping his rotten, yellow teeth, the only surgical enhancements Tom will admit to are a "few nips and tucks to get rid of the creases". He went to great lengths to explain why he hadn't had more done in the Birmingham *Evening Mail*: "[This surgeon] was a good bloke – told me the truth and lost himself a couple of thousand. 'Tom,' he said, 'you can't defy gravity. If I lift your eye bags up, the rest of your face will fall, and they'll all see the whites of your eyes.' I could imagine it – standing on stage like a blinkin' ghost all starin' like. I left it." Tom often maintains this self-mockery by pointing to his 'lived-in' face and joking that, if his appearance is the result of an expensive facelift, then the surgeon should be struck off the list.

Perhaps in an attempt to sweeten his public persona, Tom spent a great deal of time in 1984 on charitable projects. On February 2 he appeared in a benefit concert at the Luther Burbank Center For The Performing Arts, to help raise enough money to pay for the mortgage of the struggling facility. Although he charged a small fee for the event, his two shows raised some $90,000, kick-starting the targeted $3.5 million venture.

On March 19 Tom was then presented with the Humanitarian Award of the Boys Brotherhood Republic in New York for his services helping underprivileged children – he had donated a pair of skin-tight, sweat-drenched stage trousers to one of his fan clubs for raffling. Crossing the pond Tom generously gave the UK equivalent of $60,000 from his Atlantic City concerts the previous November to less fortunate children in his native Wales.

Sporting events were also to benefit from Tom's goodwill. It was noted that the singer had donated more than any other celebrity in supporting the British Olympic team in the Los Angeles summer games. Also, Tom posed for some publicity shots sparring with light heavyweight Ricky Womack while the American Olympic boxing team held their trials in Las Vegas. "I leapt at the chance," he commented. "I always wanted to be a boxer. I could never take it up because of the fear of injuries. You can't turn up on stage with two black eyes."

The heavy promotion achieved its goals and Tom acquired a couple of moderate hit singles in America's country chart in 1984, the plaintive 'I've Been Rained On Too' reaching number 13 and 'This Time' attaining number 30, while his album *Love Is On The Radio* came in at number 40 on the US mainstream chart. Tom's fan clubs seemed unconcerned by the shift of his music base and were actively encouraging their members to phone in to local 'oldie and country' radio stations and request Tom's records, which might have helped with his success.

Perhaps the highlight of Tom's year was finally fulfilling a childhood dream by starring as Dick Turpin in an episode of *Fantasy Island*. Producer Aaron Spelling gave Tom this sought-after opportunity after hearing Tom singing to raise money for one of Spelling's favourite charities. "Time was when Dick Turpin was England's most wanted man and I have always had a yearning to play him," Tom told the press. "It didn't seem like work. Holding up all those beautiful ladies in coaches seemed to come easy to me."

The episode about the highwayman was called *Lost and Found – Dick Turpin's Last Ride*, and starred the regular *Fantasy Island* stalwarts Ricardo Montalbán and Christopher Hewett. This time Tom's Welsh accent is acceptable as he plays Jack Palmer, a certified public accountant from Cardiff, whose fantasy is to be the notorious rogue Dick Turpin. Each week the half-hour show saw its guest star's wish granted, and so Tom was magically transformed and sent out into the woods on his trusty steed, Black Bess, to act out his role. After holding up a stage coach he sets off in

"Think I'd Better Dance Now!" *(Rex Features)*

Tom escorts Lorna Mills at her son Gordon's funeral at St Peter's Church in Hersham, near Weybridge on August 5, 1986. *(Rex Features)*

Katherine and Jonathan Berkery. *(Rex Features)*

Jimmy Tarbuck: "It's an enduring friendship, it's a friendship I treasure." *(David Redfern)*

Tom and The Treorchy Male Choir raise a glass. *(Mirror Syndication Int.)*

Freda drinks to her son's success. *(Rex Features)*

Chris Hutchins: "I think the whole bit with the cigars was his way of asserting himself. That's when he felt important, when he had a big cigar in his hand and a big ring on his finger." *(Neal Preston/Corbis)*

Tom and Linda in the Nineties. *(Rex Features)*

More like brothers than father and son. *(Rex Features)*

Tom collects his OBE with Mark, Emma and Alexander in March 1999. *(Rex Features)*

The two Tommy Scotts. "I was singing with someone who'd sung with Elvis and half-way through I just starte to go out of tune. I said to Tom, 'I can't believe I'm actually doing this, I've just realised who I'm standing here with!'" says the Space frontman. *(Ken McKay/Rex Features)*

The undeniable chemistry of Tom Jones and Cerys Matthews of Catatonia.
(Richard Stonehouse/Camera Press)

Robbie Williams: "It was quite a magical evening. It was absolutely amazing. People say that even heroes can let you down, but he didn't, it was just like, 'Wow! You're Tom Jones and you're amazing!' He was just outrageous brilliant." Brit Awards 1998. *(Richard Young/Rex Feature*

pursuit of saving his kidnapped wife Roxanne, yet even disguised as Dick Turpin, Tom still manages to sing a song to the delight of all the women in an 18th century village pub. Faced with pacifying his wife, who is frustrated by his roving tendencies, Tom barges into her bedroom to steal a passionate embrace. But they are stopped short because Turpin's name has been plastered on the 'Wanted' posters around the village and he has been tracked down by redcoats. After managing to lose them in a chase scene, Tom returns to rescue his sweetheart and jumps to the safety of reality, concluding that he prefers the quiet life after all.

The programme was aired on ABC on April 7, 1984 and although it did little to prove Tom's acting abilities, negotiations were reportedly soon underway for him to appear in the popular Eighties glitzy soap opera, *Dynasty*. "We're keen to extend his acting career and *Dynasty* is his favourite show," Gordon said. "The producers have made a series of approaches. Right now, we have an open invitation from the producers. We hope some agreement can be reached."

The idea was for Tom to start off in a cameo role which had the option of being extended if he increased the ratings. Nancy Reagan was also supposedly being courted by the producers, who hoped to combine the sex appeal of Tom with the regal qualities and acting experience of America's first lady. It would have also entailed the eventual screen pairing of Tom and the show's star Joan Collins, after Tom refused the role in *The Stud*. "I've always wanted to be in the movies, but until now I've lacked the confidence," Tom was quoted as saying in the papers. "But now, I feel the time is right and it would be great to start with a guest spot on *Dynasty* opposite Joanie . . ."

Despite his good-natured but largely superficial TV acting work, even Tom realised that he was still a long way off his ultimate dream of becoming a serious actor. "I've done a few light-hearted television movies, but I'd like to do a serious role. Directors don't look at singers as actors, though, and it's a matter of persuading the powers that be." And so for the time being he settled back once more into his touring routine.

Life was not going to resume quite as normal though, as Caesar's Palace had been hit badly by the recession and was unable to renew Tom's annual contract. This meant that he would have to relinquish the hotel's luxury two-tiered suite which featured a king-sized bed, a long conical chandelier above the circular dining table, mock roman plaster pillars and porcelain statues. Instead Tom moved to the rival MGM Grand in 1985 where he was fortunate to maintain his phenomenal fees, variously estimated at $200,000 per week.

In keeping with his on-off country image Tom was often to be found playing at venues such as the Allen County Fair in Ohio, but the regular fairgoers were unsure what to make of the replacement for their usual country bill and just over half the usual numbers turned up. The fair's organiser, Don Klingler had taken a gamble when he booked Tom for $50,000 and later told the local paper, "I had been confident it would be a sell-out. I guess we didn't draw from a cross section of the 10 county area like we have with some of the other talent. Jones was superb, but brought in a generally older crowd . . . we hope to break even."

Part of the problem the Allen County Fair experienced was that although Tom was recording exclusively country material, he persisted with the standard rock'n'roll numbers in his live act. He opened his shows with contemporary covers like 'I'm So Excited' before launching into Prince's 'Purple Rain', which was hardly the type of music that was likely to appeal to country fans. Tom had tried to keep up with the times by making a promotional video for 'It'll Be Me', but explained that he had encountered further difficulties in marrying the two genres: "It was too country for MTV. If I get one hot single going that's more rock, I'll make another one." As Tom's career dragged on into 1985 he seemed desperate to change the channel he was stuck on.

Meanwhile, Tom was concerned with protecting the assets acquired with his hefty income. He had spent £140,000 safeguarding his Bel Air mansion. "The house in Los Angeles that I bought from Dean Martin used to have live-in security guards when Dean was there," he said to *People* magazine. "I couldn't live like that. But I was forced to build a wall around the place because I got a bit fed up with people just turning up and having picnics on my front lawn. I also installed panic buttons that link directly to the police. I put those in every room. But you still get odd things going on."

On one rather embarrassing occasion the high-tech electronic gates leading into the estate jammed open, just as two tour buses pulled up in front of the house for a photo opportunity. As Tom does not employ a guard, the gawping tourists were able to stroll right into the property grounds. Linda immediately called the neighbourhood security patrol, who swiftly removed the unwanted guests.

However, Linda's smart thinking was unfortunately not mirrored by her mother, who was less used to such invasions of privacy. Over on a visit from Pontypridd, Vi Trenchard set off one of the numerous panic alarms by mistake in the early hours of the morning, instantly summoning an armoured squad car to the star's residence. When the agitated Vi leaned out of an upstairs window and called out, "What do you want?" she heard the threatening command: "*Freeze!*" Vi was so scared that she dressed hurriedly, putting her trousers on back to front, and went to find Linda, while the security force searched the house for the non-existent burglars.

Tom had kept a gun since his friendship with the late Elvis Presley. He admitted to chat show host Michael Parkinson that he would sometimes keep it on his person, especially if he was "out in the sticks where there are a lot of hillbillies about and a lot of guns around." When John Lennon was murdered by psychotic Beatles fan Mark Chapman in December 1980, Tom was deeply affected and became even more conscious of the vulnerability his public position invites. To this day he will carry a gun if he feels uneasy for any reason, but would only use it in self-defence.

This heightened sense of security did not necessarily mean that Tom wouldn't grant the odd special request from an unknown source to meet him backstage. A particularly endearing example of this was Karrie Harmer's encounter with her hero in 1985. Karrie was a mentally handicapped woman living in St. Catherine's Nursing Home, Ontario, who had totally ceased to speak as a teenager. She had been watching Tom on television one afternoon when one of the other residents changed the channel. To everyone's amazement Karrie suddenly shouted: "That is Tom Jones, and he is my favourite! You turn it back or I am going to get mad!" After this incident Karrie's sister Eva Longhurst felt she must contact the famous singer to let him know the extraordinary effect his appearance had on this fan. A once in a lifetime meeting was arranged between Tom and Karrie after a concert in Kitchener.

Tom's 20th anniversary in show business occurred on March 1, two decades after 'It's Not Unusual' hit the top spot. His fan clubs across America celebrated the monumental achievement by pooling their money to purchase a full-page advertisement in *Variety* magazine, congratulating Tom. In return, members of the Florida, Los Angeles and Atlantic City fan clubs were invited to attend a celebrity party at the Catskills' Concord hotel.

This period commemorating the longevity of Tom's career also saw the final farewell of previous MAM stablemate, Gilbert O'Sullivan. Gordon's appeal against the 1983 judgement in favour of Gilbert was initially heard in December of the same year, but not concluded until November 1984. Gilbert and MAM finally settled out of court in March 1985, agreeing to streamline the payout of £1,983,520. This was in addition to the six-figure remuneration for which Gilbert had previously fought and won. Just a few weeks later, MAM tellingly merged with Chris Wright's globally successful Chrysalis Group. It was the end of an era.

16

PUPPET MAN

IN THE EARLY EIGHTIES Tom had resoundingly upheld the merits of country music. Although this had been rewarded with the occasional appearance on the specialised country and western charts, it also meant that many of Tom's country records were never even released overseas. It was a situation that he came to regret but his hands were tied, as he explained to the *Sun*: "I was signed to Polygram in America and they put me in the country music division. I'd signed for five albums over five years back in 1981 and they were releasing country things in the States. But I couldn't get a record out in Europe." To the *News Of The World* magazine Tom described how, by doing the first album, *Darlin'*, in a country vein, he had been "digging my own grave. I wanted to sing contemporary songs, but publishers weren't sending me any. My image hurt me again."

When Gordon approached Tom to see if he would like to take up the option to record a sixth country album for Polygram after 1985's *Tender Loving Care*, the singer wisely refused. It would have been the easiest route for the 45-year-old to take, guaranteeing him a healthy income from the label and country sales. Balanced with the ongoing live performances in Las Vegas, this would have been at least a *comfortable* way for Tom to continue working. But Tom had an inkling that enough was enough, and if he wanted to rejuvenate his fading career, something needed to be done.

With the luxury of hindsight – not to mention Tom's comeback over the next few years – it was no surprise that Tom would disparage his early Eighties career move to country in those later interviews with the *Sun* and the *News Of The World*. Tom's public condemnation of his former record company was only made possible by one fortuitous turn of fate.

In the spring of 1986, Tom received a demo from the London office of the American record label, CBS. The tape contained songs intended for a musical which had been written by acclaimed producer Mike Leander, with words by his long-standing writing partner Edward Seago. The title of the upcoming musical was *Matador*.

Matador was highly intriguing to Tom. The drama, set in the Spanish Civil War of 1936, tells the story of the pauper Manolo Benitez, who against all odds rose to fame as El Cordobés, the greatest bullfighter Spain had ever seen. Based on the book *Or I'll Dress You In Mourning* by Larry Collins and Dominque Lapierre, the spirited subject material was perfect for a lavish stage production or film treatment. *Matador* was initially presented in the form of a soundtrack album, and it was by far the most interesting proposal Tom Jones had received in a long, long time.

This was not the first occasion that Mike Leander had made his material available to the MAM camp. As well as being responsible for discovering the now disgraced rocker Gary Glitter, with whom he co-wrote 11 Top 10 singles during the years 1972 to 1975, Mike had also been extremely successful as a songwriter in other genres, including 'Lady Godiva' for Peter and Gordon and 'Another Time, Another Place' for none other than Engelbert Humperdinck.★

"Mike and I were pop songwriters and we had an ambition to write a show," says Eddie Seago today. "We started talking about it seriously in 1984. We were originally going to write about the life story of El Cordobés, the legendary bullfighter. He was the guy who did it differently; he had an attractive story. He was called the rock'n'roll bullfighter, and his story was very appealing. Mike and I both had houses in Majorca, which was also why we leaned towards the Spanish theme."

"It was something that they [Mike and Eddie] needed to do," remembers John Springate, a former bass player and vocalist with The Glitter Band, who later played the part of the bar owner on the *Matador* album before becoming a renowned songwriter and producer in his own right. "They'd gone through writing three-minute pop songs . . . I think really it was more of a challenge to do something totally different."

Mike and Eddie were admittedly new to the world of theatre, and made a few errors along the way as they began to compose tracks based on the structure of El Cordobés' life story. "We made the classic mistake of writing the songs before we wrote the script for the show," Eddie recalls. "We reached a point where we'd written maybe 10 or 12 songs and we had contacts at CBS Records (as it was then), and we initially started by looking for a record deal. CBS liked the idea and we struck up a deal with them and went to record these songs with all unknown theatrical people. It was an album concept at that time."

Muff Winwood, the head of A&R at CBS' London office, suggested that the two writers needed a big-name celebrity to help publicise *Matador* once recording was complete. "Having got the record deal and having

★ Sadly Mike Leander died of cancer on April 18, 1996.

made the album, we reached the point where there was no promotional angle for the album. Nobody knew anything about the show, there was no selling point and what we needed to do was get a name involved to promote it." Eddie remembers sitting round a breakfast table with Mike and Muff, running through a list of potential candidates to flourish the matador's muleta. The part necessitated a mature male singer with a vast and expressive range, who would look good in traditional Spanish dress; Queen frontman Freddie Mercury was at one stage the favourite for the role.

"Eventually I remember saying, 'Well, what about Tom Jones?'" says Eddie. When Eddie and Mike had started writing songs together back in the Seventies, Tom Jones and Engelbert Humperdinck had been two of their greatest heroes. Both writers loved to compose for big, dynamic voices, and although their joint ambition of composing for Engel had been accomplished in 1974, they had never been able to work with Tom Jones. Although there was no question that Tom had both the right voice and look for the part, he was a bit of a gamble for the writers of *Matador*. After all, he hadn't had a sizeable hit in the UK for over a decade.

Mike and Eddie were convinced that Tom was the man for the job, and were more nervous that the star would turn down the role than whether or not he was out of vogue. "What happened was we sent the actual songs for the lead character, El Cordobés, to Tom's manager Gordon Mills, and we got a very favourable reaction," says Eddie. "I got a letter saying, 'This is some of the best material we've heard in 12 years.' So Tom agreed to do it and play the lead part on the record."

Leaving aside those sections of the album in which Tom's character is not singing, Mike and Eddie travelled to Britannia Sound Studios in Los Angeles, where Tom recorded the vocals for 'I Was Born To Be Me', 'A Boy From Nowhere', 'I'll Dress You In Mourning', and segments of 'This Incredible Journey' and 'Dance With Death'. In agreement with CBS, it was decided that the dramatic 'A Boy From Nowhere' would be released by Tom as the first single from the album.

As Tom awaited the single's release, he addressed new issues with the press. "People like to think of an entertainer as being human," Tom had said in May to the *Tampa Tribune*. "And the more they know about you, that you are a normal human being, it's better all round. I'd rather people would see and know me as I am rather than thinking, 'I wonder if he's gay; I wonder if he's this; I wonder if he's that.' My life is very much open."

In fact, with the promise of a career turnaround with *Matador*, life was looking very bright all of a sudden. Tom enjoyed having his family with him whenever possible. Mark had been promoted to production manager, and Tom's mother and sister were frequently present in the audience at his

Las Vegas shows. Young Alexander also made an appearance from time to time, waiting in the wings with a glass of water for his grandfather. On one endearing occasion in Lake Tahoe, no-one was able to prevent the little boy from toddling towards Tom onto the stage where all could see. Tom laughed and requested that the spotlight was turned onto his cheeky grandson, who jigged along to Tom's signature tune 'It's Not Unusual'.

On June 1, 1986, Tom was one of many distinguished guests including Ursula Andress, Sammy Davis Jnr. and B.B. King in a special tribute documentary entitled *Elvis: The Echo Will Never Die*. Gordon and Tom also discussed plans to film his own TV special on July 18 at the Marbella Club in Spain. However, for reasons beyond their control, this pro-gramme was to be postponed indefinitely. Similarly, fate would take a hand in ensuring that Gordon would never see the culmination of the *Matador* project.

★ ★ ★

Gordon's stomach ulcer had been troubling him on and off for as long as he could remember, certainly ever since he had first known Tom. In 1984 he had experienced a few harmless twinges and considered having an operation to remove the ulcer, but eventually decided against it as he was too busy to take time off. So when the twinges returned during one of Tom's recording sessions in early July 1986, Gordon thought little of it but decided to have a medical check-up just in case.

On July 11, Gordon's doctor confirmed that, aside from the ongoing stomach ulcer, there was nothing to worry about, and he was declared fit and healthy and allowed to go home. But the pains did not subside, and Gordon returned to the doctor the following week. This time the diag-nosis was far more serious. Gordon had incurable stomach cancer. Just three weeks after complaining of his recent discomfort, Gordon Mills was dead.

The suddenness of the prognosis and hopelessness of the situation brought an almost surreal atmosphere to Gordon's final days. An unsuc-cessful operation was performed in the hope that he might live a little longer. Ensconced in Cedars-Sinai Medical Center in West Hollywood, a hospital much patronised by the show business elite, Gordon was attended by his entire family and many members of his staff who had served him over the years. Setting aside the unhappiness that had characterised much of their life together Jo Mills, currently in the throes of their divorce, flew to Los Angeles to see Gordon for one last time. Annie Toomaru, his new partner, slept in his hospital room for the duration.

Tom was devastated and at a loss to know how to handle the situation. "He was no longer there," he recalls of his personal bedside vigil. "There was no hope; he was dying in front of me." Drifting in and out of consciousness, Gordon could at least recognise his best friend, and when he was able, the eternal gambler joked weakly on his odds of recovery. Ever concerned for his friend, Gordon's last words to Tom were: " 'If you ever get a pain in your stomach go and get it checked out.' He was thinking about me even then, as if I should learn by his mistakes."

Gordon finally passed away on July 29, 1986. His body was flown back to England for the funeral at St Peter's Church in Hersham, near Weybridge. Tom cancelled his imminent shows to be present, returning to the area his fellow Welshmen had once called home from home. Although he arrived wearing dark glasses, his distress was visible to all and he was unable to hide his tears. All of Gordon's five children attended. Jo Mills and Annie Toomaru were momentarily united in their grief. Neither Engelbert Humperdinck nor Gilbert O'Sullivan were present to pay their last respects, the former having flown out from London's Heathrow Airport to Los Angeles that very morning. Gilbert at least sent a wreath in memory of his one-time mentor, with just the two words: "Deepest Sympathy".

Tom was a pall bearer and he delivered an emotional eulogy. His valediction to his greatest friend betrayed his distraught state of mind as he struggled to express his feelings to the congregation. His moving speech was reported in the press the next day.

"I don't know where to start, oh God, oh God, Gordon changed my life – he was my manager and my closest friend. Oh God, oh God. He was the finest man I ever met . . . Gordon had simply said to me, 'You do the singing, I will do the rest.' He shaped me, he moulded me – I owe him everything."

"He was just a part of my life," Tom added later. "He taught me just about everything. He groomed me . . . he said he would guide me to become larger than life. There are parts of me which he totally created. We became much more than brothers . . . he took care of my life and now I will have to learn to deal with it."

On August 5, Gordon was buried next to his father in nearby Burvale Cemetery, Hersham.

Later Tom reflected on his two most devastating losses to the *Daily Star*: "When my father was alive, I always thought that I was alright, you just always expect your parents to be there. Then, when he went, I started believing that I would be next. Losing Gordon was a great shock too. He died within three weeks of knowing he had cancer and no one had time to prepare. I found it very hard to deal with. I'd lost such a great friend and manager – someone I had become totally dependant on since the Sixties."

Publicist John Moran echoed the disbelief of everyone involved in

Gordon's business endeavours, when he was quoted in the *Pontypridd Observer* the following month: "Gordon was supposed to go out in a car crash at 200 mph, not this way."

"I don't like showing my feelings," Tom admitted to the *TV Times* three years later. "I cried when my manager died. I couldn't control myself and I don't like getting out of control."

Perhaps this loss of control could go some way to explaining the unforeseen bitterness that was to follow over the next year. At the funeral Tom had made his honourable intentions towards Gordon's grieving relatives quite clear with the promise: "I would just like his family to know that if they ever need me, to call me and I'll be there." But, in May 1987, Gordon's mother Lorna Mills was interviewed by the *Sun*, and revealed the stark truth about Tom Jones. "My son made him what he is – but he has never once had the courtesy to see how I or Gordon's family are doing. There has never been a phone call or a visit. It seems as though he doesn't want to know the Mills family now Gordon has gone. He has cut us out of his life completely. I hope that when he reads this he will realise how hurtful his actions have been."

Tom has never commented on his treatment of the Mills family and, in addition to Lorna, both Jo and her daughter Beverley have made their wounded feelings blatantly clear in a previous biography. Jo had been pending divorce but was now unexpectedly left a widow, and the one reminder of the good times shared with Gordon was their beloved house in Weybridge. Ironically Gordon and Annie Toomaru had been planning a trip to England to reclaim Little Rhondda when the fatal illness struck, but now the house was put on the market by the Mills family. Barry Briggs, a potential buyer remarked to the authors of this book that his visit to the property in 1986 was akin to walking back in time. As he was shown round the empty shell of a house by one of Gordon's daughters, it seemed like nothing had been changed since its fevered occupation in the early Seventies. The purple paint was peeling from the walls and the incongruous recording studio extension harked back to a long outdated era when such ugly architecture was tolerated. It was clear even to an outsider that a vast, irreparable chasm had been left in Gordon Mills' wake.

Cynthia Woodard of The Blossoms summed up Tom's situation as well as anyone: "Johnnie, Tom and Gordon came over [to Los Angeles] together in one package. They were all one body and so when Johnnie and then Gordon died, it was like losing an arm and a leg."

Cynthia had pinpointed the crucial question of how Tom was going to cope without his best friend and mentor? Many career-minded individuals would throw themselves wholeheartedly into their profession in order to overcome their grief, but this was virtually out of the question for Tom since the one person he relied on for career guidance had gone.

The answer to the problem lay with his own flesh and blood. "Mark, my son, was with me and he was doing my lighting for me so he was travelling with me," Tom said many years later to Radio Two. "He was always throwing his two penneth in about why don't you do this song, or have you heard that?" It seemed only logical for Mark to look after his father's business interests, at least as a temporary solution. "I didn't know whether it was going to be a permanent thing. I was glad that he wanted to take it on, I mean, I could trust him for start. But I mean could I put my trust in him as far as where we were going to go?"

Most of those who knew Mark Woodward, however intimately, were surprised that he was prepared to take on Gordon's role, as although he had always been present throughout the latter part of his father's career, Mark had never shown much business-driven ambition. Big Jim Sullivan bluntly voices the general opinion of all concerned: "Mark was the most unlikely managerial type you could ever imagine in your life!"

But spectacularly rise to the challenge Mark did. "He's my boss and I care for him more than you can believe," the dutiful son explained the following year to a TV interviewer. "It's up to me to make decisions for him, with respect . . . it's a difficult situation." Mark went on to say that it was an honour for him to represent his father's interests as well as they had been in the past, and that he hoped to improve on them in the future.

Mark had been well trained for the job. He had felt privileged to be what he described as his father's general 'Mr Fix-It', with duties ranging from chauffeur, valet, lighting director and personal confidant. "I can't complain," he'd said three years earlier to Teresa Skelly. "Life has been very good to me, I haven't had to struggle for anything. It annoys me to hear the way some people talk – you'd think I'd never done a day's work in my life. I've done what many sons of working-class close-knit Welsh families do; go into the family business. I never really thought of doing anything else. Show business has been my life, ever since I can remember Dad has been a celebrity."

Reports surfaced soon after that Mark's takeover was almost brutal in its efficiency. According to certain sources, the telephonist was answering the phone "Tom Jones Enterprises" in the Santa Monica based office just one day after the funeral. Not everyone saw the abrupt change as a bad thing though, as Cynthia Woodard recalls, "Like his father he was a good person to work for. He was someone you could talk to if you had a personal problem."

Typically of any management shake-up, Mark felt it was necessary to dismiss many of those closest to Gordon and replace them with some new, fresh faces. He wanted a clean slate, which was completely understandable, but this obviously ruffled a few feathers along the way. In order to clear a path for Mark's wife Donna to join the fold in the role of publicist, two major sackings occurred within a strikingly short space of time.

Both Annie Toomaru and John Moran had been personally devoted to Gordon and it was evident that their allegiance lay solely with the late manager. When Gordon died, Annie had been his mistress for the best part of five years, but was also a much-loved and appreciated member of MAM's staff, fulfilling a specific role for Tom as his personal assistant. She was present at Gordon's funeral and comforted Tom in his grief, but was astounded when just two days later she was asked to leave her position by the company's accountant without a proper explanation.

Annie did not mince her words when interviewed a few months later by the *Sun*. "Tom Jones is a ruthless, self-centred creep. I am stunned at the way he has treated me, and everyone connected with Gordon. Gordon built him from nothing, made him what he is, and yet Tom has treated his friends and his family like dirt . . . The funeral was a great strain, and all I wanted to do when I returned home was immerse myself in work to get over it. But when I got back to my office there was a strange atmosphere. There were rumours of a witch hunt against Gordon's people, but I didn't believe them. We had all worked hard for Tom – why should he ditch us now?"

In fairness to Tom, he was probably too distraught to think about such employment details and the unpleasant business was tactfully taken out of his hands by his son. However, in Annie's eyes this did not excuse the fact that not only did neither Tom nor Mark have the courtesy to provide a reason for her sudden dismissal, but incredibly, her wages were also stopped. "They stopped my salary from the day Gordon died, which was a desperately callous way to treat Gordon's memory. I actually had to take this multi-millionaire singer to court to get the measly three weeks money they owed me for working after his death." The period of notice requisite to most honourable working contracts wasn't even discussed.

Annie wasn't alone in this perceived purge of Gordon's people. Publicist John Moran was the next to be sacked one month later. With Annie and John out of the picture, Mark and Donna Woodward were free to handle business as they saw fit, without interference. Before the year was out, three long-serving musicians were also let go, similarly without an explanation.

★   ★   ★

In much the same way he had allowed Gordon to organise everything some 20 years earlier, Tom chose to sit back and let his son take control of his career. "It's great having him there," Tom has since said about his son. "A lot of kids don't want to do what their fathers do, or be involved in the family business. It's a nice feeling, because it reassures you they like what you do." As much respect as Mark had for his father's status in the music world, he was able to stand back and look at the Tom Jones image objectively. "He's made me aware of things I didn't even think of, like my middle-of-the-road image. I just got on with the job, and you don't see yourself as others do."

Mark recognised that Tom was incorporating modern music in his live shows and suggested that perhaps he should record a song from a fresh genre, and leave the country stuff fully behind. The problem was not convincing Tom, but simply finding something suitable. "I sometimes record a song people wouldn't ordinarily associate with me," Tom said to journalist Pete Mikla. "Because if I decide I like a song, I will do it no matter what type of song it is. I never specifically decide that I'll get more heavily into rock or ballads, I just do what all artists do and look for challenges and new ways to express myself."

In 1987 life began to look up for Tom. He featured in an edition of *Star Portraits* which profiled his extensive career, including video footage of his live performances and an in-depth interview. Following endless years of bitterness he even managed to patch up his rocky relationship with Engelbert. After Gordon's death there seemed no point in continuing the feud.

Engel contacted Tom and suggested that they should meet after one of Tom's shows in Vegas. Tom categorically told Engel: "You were the one who split from Gordon. Whatever your idea was about Gordon it was your own. It was nothing to do with me. Let's leave Gordon at rest and leave it at that." Together they managed to spend some $3,000 on champagne and laughed at old times. Tom then visited Engel one night after his show, and although they did not pursue the rekindled friendship, at least they were no longer at loggerheads.

Professionally Tom was being slowly suffocated by the two equally damning perceptions people had of him: he was either a Las Vegas cabaret act attracting hundreds of pairs of flying knickers, or a country crooner wallowing in self-pitying ballads. It was a similar problem to that faced by many successful bands from the Sixties and Seventies, whose current records were not up to their earlier work and whose live concerts relied almost entirely on songs that were now described as 'golden oldies'. The annual tour brochures painstakingly produced by MAM, and now Tom Jones Enterprises, had carefully documented Tom's career until the late Seventies, but handily omitted much of the current decade. Tom said hopefully in an interview once, "If you've been around a long time, you get rediscovered."

In the aftermath of Gordon's death, the last thing on anyone's mind was Tom's next single release. Maybe the most important role that Mark could fulfil was to guide his father gently back into action in an attempt to resume business as usual. While Tom had taken a necessary breather from the public eye, the *Matador* project with Mike Leander and Eddie Seago had been satisfactorily completed. It was time for its launch, and based on the deal the composers had struck with the singer, some hefty publicity was now required.

"'A Boy From Nowhere' was chosen to be the first single and to Tom's credit he came over and promoted it," says Eddie Seago today. "He was a real trouper, he did whatever he was asked to do. Of course he got every TV show in the book." This was almost an understatement, for during April and May 1987, it was virtually impossible to turn on the television in the UK without seeing Tom plugging 'A Boy From Nowhere', and by default, *Matador*, on every chat show under the sun.

The new single was performed for the first time on British TV for Des O'Connor's primetime slot shortly after Tom's recovery from a bout of bronchitis. Appearances followed on the UK's foremost chat shows, including Michael Parkinson's *One To One*, *Daytime Live* with Alan Titchmarsh, *Wogan* with Terry Wogan and *Good Morning*. Children's television was also targeted, possibly in an attempt to catch the attention of the mothers or grandmothers who might also be watching, and Tom was seen with Matthew Corbett and his puppet Sooty, and a young Phillip Schofield on children's Saturday morning TV. Tom did not seem to appreciate that he was appearing before a much younger audience than usual, and was filmed talking about drinking, smoking and sex.

Tom tirelessly performed his new song to audience after audience, who gave the Spanish-tinged, blistering but sedate ballad of tribulation a glowing reception. The engaging subject matter was so perfectly suited to Tom's voice and image that all those fans who feared they had lost their hero long ago to Nashville rushed to buy the single, and propelled it straight to number two in the charts. It was held off the top position in the UK by another notably mature act, Starship with 'Nothing's Gonna Stop Us Now'. Amazingly the single was not even released in America. But that hardly marred Tom's hearty British comeback, nor did the song's unusual theme or the *Matador* story, which in some ways seemed to mirror Tom's own ascent to fame and fortune.

"I feel very close to his character," Tom explained. "There's not much call for bullfighting in Wales, but in a way El Cordobés and I come from similar backgrounds. We both had great dreams and ambitions. I think you get starstruck at an early age and you want to escape from routine." Headlines were splashed about Pontypridd's very own 'Boy

From Nowhere'. Landing with a bang straight back into the limelight can only have helped Tom sweep away some of his sadness at losing his manager.

Perhaps the most telling part of Tom's storming re-entry into the pop charts in the UK was his first appearance on *Top Of The Pops* for 15 years since he had promoted 'The Young New Mexican Puppeteer' in 1972. Tom was as thrilled as he had been the first time around. "It's the thought of being on *Top Of The Pops* after all these years that amazes me. I thought that they only had bands in weird clothes playing synthesisers on the show these days!" Unusually for the Eighties the BBC asked Tom to perform live, but unfortunately the filming date clashed with his return to Los Angeles, and he had to make a quick lip-synched performance after all. "I can't wait to see how it turns out. The really fantastic thing is that the last time I was on *Top Of The Pops* everyone thought I was the outrageous one, in tight trousers, with my shirt unbuttoned. No one could believe that anyone could go on the TV and be so suggestive. Now I'm the traditional one and everyone else is causing a stir," he said to Fiona Webster.

However, all was not strictly as it seemed on the *Matador* front. During Tom's exhaustive promotion of the single and its parent album he spoke to each and every interviewer at great length about the possibility of his taking on the lead role as El Cordobés in the forthcoming stage production. This was not something he had ever discussed with Eddie Seago and Mike Leander.

"It's a big decision, a bit of a gamble, I'd have to shut up shop here if the show was a success," he said gamely to the *Radio Times*. "I'd be taking a loss financially. But it's a brand new thing for me and I'd like to try it." He also spoke at length to Mavis Nicholson, the feisty host of *Mavis On 4* who veritably laid into Tom for his womanising and neglect of his native country. On the subject of his potential theatrical departure he explained to her that if he decided to go ahead and sign up for it, it would entail six months to a year of solid work in the UK, and for that long a stretch of time he would have to bring his family back to the country. He described it as a big decision which he was not looking forward to making, but in tandem he was still enthusiastic.

"I'm very excited about the whole project – the material is the best that's been given to me since I don't know when," he said to the Birmingham *Evening Mail*. "I've always liked big, gutsy ballads but good ones are often hard to find these days. That's the problem for someone like me who doesn't write his own songs. As soon as I heard this stuff I knew I wanted to do it." In the same interview he added a slight note of caution: "If this were a film I would definitely do it – but I'm unsure about committing myself to a long run in the theatre."

Any serious possibility of Tom taking on the lead was news to Eddie Seago, who recounts his version of events thus: "The promotional angle was that Tom would go on a chat show, sing the song, and in the chat the host would obviously ask him how it came about, talking about the musical, the forthcoming show etc. It became, 'Oh, you'll be playing the matador . . .' It was kind of assumed. I always thought that it was PR when he said it. But there was never any real discussion with Tom about the show. It was a vague thing and it was kind of left. I don't think that Mike and I felt that he would want to be in the show, because you don't earn much money from being in shows and the guy was earning a fortune in Las Vegas and other places."

As time went by and it became embarrassingly apparent that Tom would not be performing on stage as El Cordobés, he began to invent excuses, among them the likelihood that the musical directors of *Matador* might get in trouble with the "animal rights people" if they put it on stage. Two years later his story had changed somewhat, and on Danish TV Tom launched into a long explanation of how El Cordobés himself was not aware of the musical and had threatened the producers with legal action. In reality, the real-life matador wanted to correct the story to accurately reflect his character as a man anxious to prove himself to his supportive sister, rather than the love interest Mike and Eddie had written into the plot. Above all, Tom felt that the script was not commercial enough and its necessary re-write about a fictitious matador would lose the original essence that had so attracted him in the first place.★

Despite the growing difficulties on Tom's side, the original studio cast recording of *Matador* fared well and reached number 26 in the UK charts, no doubt helped by the phenomenal success of 'A Boy From Nowhere'. Tom's performance on the album was praised by magazines like Q, but Eddie Seago and Mike Leander were somewhat unfairly accused of being "kitsch" and "unintentionally comic" with their plot-line of "breathtaking banality".

Matador in its revised version finally hit the stage for a 10-week period in a theatre in Lincolnshire, Illinois, followed by a run at the Coconut Grove Playhouse Theater in Miami. *Matador* then moved to London's West End to open at the Queen's Theatre on Shaftesbury Avenue, where John Barrow was cast in the lead role that Tom had so recently boasted about playing.

Eddie remembers that Tom was upset when he wasn't invited to the opening night party of the show's American début. "I got feedback and

---

★ According to Eddie Seago, the truth behind El Cordobés' discrepancies with the stage script was that he was an elusive character who never turned up to meetings and never finalised the contract because he didn't like or understand his percentage deal.

suddenly it occurred to me that of course we should have [invited Tom], but there were other people involved at the time with whom the responsibility lay to ask people to the function." Instead Tom attended the charity preview in London, helping to raise £10,000 for the Motor Neurone Disease Association, but no more was said about his potential involvement. *Matador's* success was limited, partly because of the massive expenses it incurred, but also because of poor timing. It coincided with the Gulf War.

On a brighter note, *Matador* won the Laurence Olivier Award for Best Choreography in 1991. Tom also benefited from a second, smaller slice of the pie, when the follow-up single from the soundtrack album, 'I Was Born To Be Me' managed to reach UK chart number 61 in January 1988. The single was accompanied by Tom's next attempt at a promotional video which was visually reminiscent of the dramatic set for *Dracula*, but was a little uninspiring and slow-paced.

Making the most of his recent success Tom appeared at the Albert Hall in May 1987 where, dressed in black matador-style trousers, he was described by journalist Nancy Culp as being, "Camp in a peculiarly macho way." 'It's Not Unusual' was re-issued at the end of May on the strength of Tom's apparent comeback and became an eccentric club anthem during the summer. Tom marvelled at the irony of the situation. "I did *Top Of The Pops* in 1987 when they re-released 'It's Not Unusual'. It was the same studio as when it first came out in 1965 and I'm there miming to the same record and looking down at the kids on the dance floor and they look like the same people who were there in 1965."

On May 15, the Variety Club laid on a celebratory lunch for Tom to present him with an award for his longevity in show business. Ronnie Cass, the scriptwriter who had frequently worked with Tom made a touching speech highlighting his fellow Welshman's career. Tom was visibly moved, especially when talk shifted to the late Gordon Mills. Tom apologised to the audience, "You will have to excuse me – I feel very, very emotional. It's very difficult to accept the things people say. They say such lovely things."

The Woodward family who endured enough personal tragedy during the Eighties, were to suffer another blow. Linda's mother, Vi Trenchard, whose health had been deteriorating since the late Seventies, passed away on June 5, 1987. She had always stood up for her daughter and son-in-law, often telling the press and anyone who cared to listen, "I honestly knew he would become famous eventually. His voice was too good for him to get nowhere." Her death was another traumatic experience for the family, but their spirits were lifted not long after when Donna gave birth to her second child, Emma Violet, on September 15 at 8.35 p.m. Tom shared his personal joy with the papers, explaining that it helped to ease the pain of Linda's miscarriage many years before: "She wanted a daughter, but now we have a granddaughter and that has filled the void."

Continuing with the constant media promotion, Tom agreed to participate in *It's A Royal Knockout: The Grand Knockout Tournament* – a charity fundraising, royally led version of the madcap British TV game show, *It's A Knockout*. Presented by Rowan Atkinson, Barbara Windsor, Sue Pollard and Les Dawson, the four teams were captained by Prince Andrew for the World Wildlife Fund, his then wife the Duchess of York, Sarah Ferguson for the Homeless, Prince Edward for the Duke of Edinburgh's Award Scheme, and Princess Anne for Save The Children. Tom was accompanied by Chris De Burgh and Cliff Richard in Princess Anne's winning team, which she had dubbed "the strong silent type".

Tom had to dress as 'Romeo' and shimmy up a rope to save his 'Juliet' for one of the farcical games, but the singer lost his grip and fell back into the icy water below. "It's for charities that need to be supported, so I thought I'd help out," he said, but he later admitted to his son that he found it more nerve-racking than performing in front of thousands of fans at Wembley. In the event, *It's A Royal Knockout* was something of a disaster for the Royal Family, coming under fire from all manner of critics, royalists and republicans alike, for ridiculing the already troubled House of Windsor.

In 1987 Tom was once again reunited with his old friend Jimmy Tarbuck on stage at the London Palladium. Jimmy had compèred at the establishment since 1965 and when ITV started a new series of *Live From The Palladium*, they could not think of a better opening act than Jimmy Tarbuck introducing Tom Jones, followed by a duet from the pair on 'Johnny B Goode'. "It's an enduring friendship, it's a friendship I treasure," says Jimmy today. "He's very, very loyal, very generous and absolutely besotted with his grandchildren."

The one thing Tom would never do was forget his roots, and on December 2 he returned to Pontypridd to ceremoniously turn on the Christmas lights. It was the first time that he had been to his hometown in four years and the queue of fans stopped the traffic dead. Tom visited the Historical & Cultural Centre by the twin bridges where he presented the town mayor Glyn Gold with a signed photograph, to hang amongst the collection of the other famous children of Pontypridd. Tom quipped in the *Pontypridd Observer*, "It's great to be home again. I didn't expect such a large turnout – are they keeping the pubs open or something?" He was also presented with a symbolic key to the town welcoming him home whenever he wished, but rumour has it that when Tom charged a hefty £3,000 fee for the fleeting visit, the mayor requested the key back like a spurned parent.

Tom was able to attend these pre-Christmas festivities in Pontypridd as he was currently filming an hour long special at both the HTV studios in Cardiff and on location in nearby Castel Coch. The programme was called *Born To Be Me*, and scriptwriter Ronnie Cass enabled Tom to document his own career from his humble beginnings as a coal miner's son, through 'It's Not Unusual', and up to his recent comeback with 'A Boy From Nowhere'. The special was shot during November and December, just in time for a Christmas airing. It reportedly earned Tom a cool £1 million.

Born To Be Me comprised clips of Tom walking the streets of Pontypridd interspersed with sketches of him singing his own hits and other covers spanning the ages. He takes us first to the grocery shop where almost 45 years ago he had stood on the orange box as a toddler to perform, and explains how Mr Hughes the grocer would encourage the folk standing listening to pay little Tom for his efforts. The camera then follows him on a stroll down Laura Street with Mark, Donna and Alexander; baby Emma is wrapped up warm out of sight.

Within the show, Tom managed to fulfil a childhood fantasy, singing 'Thunderball' in a James Bond-style sketch. But perhaps one of the most enjoyable sections for him to record was the lively reunion between Tom and The Treorchy Male Choir, where they are filmed harmonising in a bar with pints of beer in their hands. "It wasn't easy," said Tom, "but then it isn't easy to sing with a tear in your eye and a lump in your throat." Bob Griffiths also recalls the time fondly, "We had a great time − it was marvellous."

17

THINK I'D BETTER DANCE NOW

H AVING SATURATED the market with personal appearances and guest
spots in order to revive his career, Tom could now afford to be a little
bit choosy with the offers that flooded in. In February 1988 he refused to
pose nude for *Cosmopolitan*'s centrefold, excusing himself on the grounds
that he was too shy. At the end of May, he did agree to appear in two
charity events; a concert in Santa Monica raising money for 'Share' and an
ITV telethon appeal to help deaf children.

While Tom returned to his usual stints in America, Mark took stock of
his father's career and sensed that a drastic change of image was needed to
truly kick-start his future. John Hudson, a respected producer who had
worked on the *Matador* recordings, succinctly sums up Mark's perceptive-
ness: "Mark is not musical – manager's aren't musical. But the thing is,
they've got a feel for things."

Mark now watched his father from off stage with a critical eye, pinpoint-
ing the changes that were required to help Tom re-establish himself further.
The first thing he wanted to do was to kill the overtly sexual image. Time
after time he repeated his frank statement to the press: "I want to redress the
balance, the way in which people see my father. I want the public gaze to
move about three feet upwards and remain always with his voice," hoping
that it would eventually have some effect. Mark was sometimes invited onto
chat shows with Tom and used the opportunity to explain, "There's more to
it than that, you know, he's not a Chippendale dancer – they come and go.
There's got to be more substance to have a long career." And on that note,
he warned his father not to encourage the knicker throwing, by simply not
picking up the lingerie and playing with it.

Mark advised his father on his physical appearance too. Tom cut his
thick curly hair slightly closer to his head and lengthened his sideburns
a little. The desperately tight, unfashionable trousers were replaced by
looser but more garish outfits. For television he now wore dark, comfortably tailored trousers and large, brightly coloured double-breasted jackets,
on stage he dressed in the same outfit, but all in black. Finally Tom began

to reappear in style magazines in a positive light once again.

But preparations for a new, improved Tom paled into insignificance when he continued to be plagued by unpleasant throat pains. Initially he had thought that it was just a bad bout of laryngitis, but after soldiering on for a while, worrying nodules were discovered and he had to cancel a large portion of his current tour to check into Cedars-Sinai Medical Center in West Hollywood, just as Gordon had done two years earlier. Under the utmost secrecy Tom was booked in for an operation to scrape his right vocal cord to identify the nature of the problematic nodules. He later described the frightening investigative surgery as, "Gruesome . . . Not only was there a chance of not singing again, there was a real possibility the nodes were cancerous."

After the operation the tissue removed was analysed, and Tom was ordered not to utter a single sound for a fortnight. Fortunately the growth proved to be benign, but Tom was not yet out of danger. "I was scared because when they operate there's no guarantee your voice will return to the way it was," he confided in the *News Of The World* magazine. "For the next two weeks I lived a nightmare, I was weak and powerless. It was terrifying to realise that I wouldn't know what else to do if I couldn't sing. Singing is so much a part of my life. When the doctor finally gave me the OK for me to try my voice I was petrified. I will never forget the immense wave of relief when it sounded the same."

While Tom recuperated from his throat operation, the wheels of his next assault on the pop charts were already in motion. Earlier that year on one of his promotional appearances for 'I Was Born To Be Me', Tom had featured on a new show that was rapidly on its way to cult status. *The Last Resort*, headed by trendy presenter Jonathan Ross signed up many mind-blowing acts over the years, but Tom was one of the very first celebrities approached to headline the first series. Graham K Smith, the show's producer, tells of their enthusiasm: "There were two people we always wanted to get on *The Last Resort*; Michael Caine and Tom Jones. Jonathan Ross and I went down to the London Palladium to see Tom Jones and we met him."

It was a gamble for Tom to go on such an unestablished show, but he and Mark felt the exposure to a young audience could only be benefi-cial. The result was, in Graham's own words, "one of those rare TV moments". Later explaining his choice of material for the show to jour-nalist Johnny Dee, Tom said, "It was *The Last Resort*'s policy not to plug your latest single. So Jonathan Ross asked me to do something up-tempo. I told him that I did 'Kiss' in my show. It wasn't unusual for me – every year I put new songs in my show to keep things up to date, the year before I did 'Purple Rain'." Both songs were written by and had previously been hits for the artist known at the time as Prince. Tom settled on 'Kiss', which had been a number one for its composer back in 1986.

The image of him decked out in a tight black leather ensemble and performing such a raunchy song certainly harked back to the explosive days of Tommy Scott & The Senators, but Tom was not mocking himself or revisiting an era. He was simply doing what came naturally. The singer finished the show by duetting with the audibly tone-deaf Jonathan Ross on 'It's Not Unusual'. The host's hero appeared on the show a couple more times over the following year and the two struck up a good relationship, but it was that first broadcast of Tom singing 'Kiss' live on television that was to have far-reaching consequences.

Watching the show on television that night was Anne Dudley, a talented composer, arranger and producer, based in Hertfordshire, England, who was then part of an acclaimed experimental pop band called The Art Of Noise. "I was watching *The Last Resort* one particular Friday evening and Tom Jones was on," she recalls today. "I hadn't really thought about Tom Jones as a serious pop star for ages until that moment. He'd done a lot of cabaret and I thought he was lost to Las Vegas, but he came on and he did this storming version of 'Kiss'.

"It was a revelation really because he looked wonderful, dressed in black leather looking about 15 years younger than he is. He sounded terrific and I thought maybe I'd underestimated Tom, because he must be very much 'up' with what's going on in pop music to have found this song in the first place, *and* he'd done a version of it which made it sound like the song suited him. So from that moment I changed my mind about Tom Jones and thought what a great voice, what a shame that he's not doing anything."

By pure coincidence Derek Green, the A&R man from Anne's label China Records, had also seen *The Last Resort* that night. He telephoned her with the suggestion: "Why don't you do a cover of 'Kiss' with The Art Of Noise featuring Tom Jones?" The Art Of Noise had previously revived 'Peter Gunn' with its original 'twangy' guitarist Duane Eddy and 'Paranoimia' with the computerised TV character Max Headroom, so Anne was intrigued and to her amazement Tom was open to the idea too, despite his current contract with Polygram.

Rather than meeting up in a studio, the singer requested a backing track which Anne set about recording with J.J. Jeczalik, the other half of The Art Of Noise. The tape was sent over to Los Angeles where Tom lay recovering from his recent operation but he was unable to work on it until his voice had fully returned. At this stage Anne felt that the complications of time and distance might interfere with the future of the project. "I didn't think it was going to be very satisfactory really," she admits.

"Usually when you let things go, things happen that you don't really want to happen. I think I probably underestimated Tom's experience and professionalism and he recorded a very good vocal without any particular direction from us." Some time had passed before Anne received the tape back complete with Tom's vocal, noting how he made much of the phrasing his own, emphasising lines like, 'Think I'd better dance now'. Pleased with the result she then decided on a musical change which became intrinsic to the finished track. "I did a brass arrangement for it, because I always thought Tom's voice seemed to go fantastically well with brass," says Anne.

With some trepidation the tape was returned once more to Tom Jones Enterprises and Anne awaited the final judgement from Tom. The feedback was excellent and the track was released, without the two parties having had any face-to-face contact. "So I had the great pleasure of actually meeting Tom when we were planning to do *Top Of The Pops*. That was the first time I'd met him."

Although he had enjoyed recording the vocals, Tom had probably been too preoccupied with his voice and health scare to realise the full potential of the funky new pop track. "I was doing 'Kiss' in my live show, not really thinking about recording it, because Prince had already had a big hit with it," Tom said in 1996. "The Art Of Noise saw me do it, approached me and asked if I'd record it with them. I said fine, but not really thinking that that would be the one that I'd been looking for. I just thought it would be good for their album, and it would be good to work with them.

"Then, when it was finished, everybody agreed that it sounded like a single and we put it out. All along, there was this song, and I wasn't really thinking it was the one I was looking for. I thought, if this doesn't do it, then I'd better get back to the drawing board again."

"They thought it was going to be a novelty, but it wasn't," Tom said to Mike Ross. "Once it came out, then the realisation hit people that we were serious about it. It wasn't just techno pop meets Vegas." He needn't have worried as 'Kiss' turned out to be a huge success. Reaching number five in the UK charts in November 1988, the following January the up-tempo track narrowly failed to hit the US Top 30. Tom gladly did the usual rounds of promotion, often with Anne in tow, including a memorable *Top Of The Pops* appearance with The Art Of Noise when the 48-year-old grandfather amazed the audience by climbing on top of Anne's grand piano and on the cue of 'Think I'd better dance now' performing a hip-swivelling dance.

Not only did Tom appear on almost every chat show to advertise his latest single, but he made a third attempt at filming an accompanying video. The snappy cut-out shots of Tom dancing in shades and a cool hat not only improved sales but also won him the Breakthrough Video Award from MTV that year.

So what did the song's composer think of Tom and Anne's interpretation? Tom later met the diminutive genius in a nightclub, and was taken aback when Prince actually thanked him for covering the track. Never one to miss an opportunity, Tom pursued the conversation. "So I said to Prince, 'If you ever had something you feel I can do, let me have it.' He said, 'Yeah, of course.' They were hoping to have had something ready for [my next] album but Prince said that there was nothing new that was suitable."

After the immense impact made by 'Kiss' Tom launched himself straight into his next project – an all-Welsh musical production of Dylan Thomas' *Under Milk Wood* – in November 1998. Directed by Sir Anthony Hopkins, the cast performed live on stage in aid of The Prince's Trust in the presence of His Royal Highness. Tom played the rather fitting role of Mr Waldo, a jack-the-lad drinker and womaniser, singing one song, 'Come And Sweep My Chimbley'. He also appeared on the double-CD soundtrack which was recorded in George Martin's studio and released by EMI.

Tom was ecstatic about his sudden resurgence in the world of pop music, and admitted that he shuddered when he watched video footage of his old concerts, "I looked like a bloody banshee out there," he laughed. Having successfully broken away from the lean country period, Tom was keen to continue in this new-found niche, telling the papers that he wanted to record "anything that has fire in it", rather than background muzak. Cynthia Woodard recalls the impact 'Kiss' had on the concerts: "In the audience newer faces were coming in, a different generation, but they still screamed and hollered! It didn't change drastically – they enhanced it by bringing in a new age group."

Tom Jones was not only attracting younger fans, he was now beginning to appeal to other famous pop stars as well, just as he had recently captivated Anne Dudley. Michael Jackson was the next celebrity convert. The self-styled King of Pop was a regular visitor to Quincy Jones' house which was just down the road from Tom's, and he had always promised himself that one day he would pluck up the courage to pay a surprise visit. "That's just the way he is," Tom clarified to journalist Johnny Dee. "He came round to my house one night totally out of the blue. He was driving the car, it was him and his sister La Toya. He just buzzed the gate and I looked at the monitor and there he was."

Tom had met Michael years ago when he was the child singing sensation of The Jackson 5. Now he was entertaining him in his house. "If I'd known he was coming I'd have baked a cake," Tom laughed, taking a light-hearted view on the bizarre scenario. "MTV was on and he was analysing all the videos. Whether he was being naïve or he just didn't know, but Mick Jagger was on and he said, 'That guy can't move very well can he?' I think he was pulling my leg. He's a wind-up merchant, he's winding us all up, he's having fun." Michael admired Tom's extended display of gold records and pictures he had taken with other famous friends. Then he left as abruptly as he arrived.

In 1989, Tom appeared in another documentary about one of his friends. This time he featured alongside Paul Anka, Johnny Cash and Roy Orbison in the tribute: *Jerry Lee Lewis – I Am What I Am*. After experiencing further pain in his throat that April Tom did not take any chances and cancelled a show on the 19th, but on the 21st was given the all clear to continue with his regular touring.

Hot on the heels of 'Kiss' Tom had switched record labels and signed up with Jive Records, a London based subsidiary of Zomba Records which specialised in soul and rap artists such as DJ Jazzy Jeff and the Fresh Prince. "So I signed with Jive Records in England, told them I wanted to do a contemporary album, and they said fine," said Tom.

For the ensuing album Tom worked with vibrant young producers including Barry J. Eastmond (previous credits including Chaka Khan and Anita Baker) and Timmy Allen (Hi-Five) in a bid to maintain the young audience he had attracted with The Art Of Noise collaboration. Tom was keen to take advantage of new developments in recording pop songs and was fascinated by the complex layering of synthesised sounds.

The album as a whole went to UK number 34 early in May 1989. It was released under three different guises, known alternatively as *Kiss*, *At This Moment* and *Move Closer*. The last title was from the 1985 Phyllis Nelson hit, and although Tom's management felt that he could produce a sufficiently different sound to attract sales, his smoochy version only managed to hit number 49 in the UK charts. The promotional video did little to aid its cause as it was very slow and uneventful, simply featuring Tom with intermittent flashes of couples romancing each other and women dancing.

A more successful video released this year was of concert footage filmed at Hammersmith Odeon entitled *Tom Jones Live At This Moment*, directed by Declan Lowney and produced by Zomba in association with Jive Records. Tom wore his ubiquitous black trousers, but dazzled the audience with a sparkling red jacket. After the show, he was filmed coming off stage drenched in sweat, bundled into a waiting car and whisked away while he tellingly sought reassurance from Mark about his performance.

In June 1989 Tom also took part in an event called 'Our Common

Future' which was broadcast to over 100 countries by satellite. Tom's contribution was filmed in the Norwegian capital of Oslo, and he was joined by artists performing from different corners of the world including Sting in Rio de Janeiro, Brazil and Stevie Wonder in Warsaw, Poland.

★ ★ ★

Tom's undying fans had for years campaigned to award him with a star on the Hollywood Walk Of Fame. This long celebrated stretch running down Hollywood Boulevard, Los Angeles is inlaid with pink marble stars embossed with bronze inscriptions bearing the names of celebrities from stage and screen and an icon symbolising their respective profession. Nominations, which are usually made by a celebrity's record company or film studio, must be approved by the Walk Of Fame Committee. Each year the 10 to 15 most qualified artists of those put forward become eligible to receive a star. The criteria is based upon professional achievement, career longevity of five years or more and contributions to the community, but there must also be a guarantee that if selected the celebrity will attend the ceremony. An additional proviso is that the submission must be accompanied by a $3,500 fee as a contribution to the cost of the event, hardly a condition to add credibility to the accolade.

The American fan clubs had been trying to persuade MAM that Tom deserved the honour back in the early 1980s, but Gordon, well aware that Tom's image was at an all time low, and an award of this nature could only highlight this, had always put them off. The resilient fans adopted a new tactic – instead of trying to persuade Tom's management to foot the bill, they decided that they would raise the money themselves, then proudly present their favourite star with his very own star. Fan club president Florence Coleman devised a plan whereby each club only needed to raise a minimum of $65, but sadly just 48 of the 75 clubs participated and they were unable to raise the full amount required. It seemed Gordon had anticipated the outcome correctly after all.

With the revival in Tom's popularity after the success of 'Kiss' the project was resurrected. When the fee was finally raised by the fans the ceremony was organised for June 29, 1989. Tom's star, number 1883, was to be situated outside Frederick's of Hollywood, apparently at the owner's request, so that the well-known but decidedly downmarket lingerie shop was able to capitalise fully on Tom's knicker-throwing reputation. The frontage of Frederick's is bedecked with lurid pink canopies and inside the shop there is a museum of famous lingerie. The surrounding area, once the centre of glittering Hollywood, the movie capital of the world, had by 1989 lost any sheen it might once have had.

The neighbourhood is in parts little more than a building site prowled by tramps and prostitutes.

It was not surprising therefore that fans later claimed Tom Jones Enterprises had tried to discourage them from attending the ceremony, even though they were responsible for realising the event in the first place. Nevertheless, a small crowd, undeterred by either the surroundings or Tom's management, arrived outside Frederick's to cheer on their hero, only to find that Fleetwood Mac's star had already claimed the prime location outside the front door. To add to the indignity of the occasion, Tom's star was relegated to the last space on the far left of the shop front.

Tom duly turned up at 12.30 p.m. on the day, accompanied by Mark and Donna, Freda and Sheila. Johnny Grant, the self-appointed Mayor of Hollywood, emceed the half-hour ceremony, opening with a brief speech designed to impress upon everyone the importance of the award. "Once the star's in the pavement, it's there forever," he pointed out, to no-one's great surprise. Carmen Goglia from Gift Of Fame Enterprises presented Tom with a monogrammed blue robe and a replica of the star. A double-decker tour bus decorated with balloons and a banner declaring 'We Love Tom Jones' drove past, while overhead a plane spelled out 'Tom Jones Day' with its jet stream. Tom himself then said a few words before throwing handfuls of navy blue garters, provided by Frederick's and trimmed with black lace, a gold star and Tom's name, out into the crowd.

Frederick's, decorated for the occasion with mauve flags, had a field day, but Tom and his crew let slip signs of embarrassment and did not stay for long. Donna released a press statement shortly after, belatedly acknowledging the hard work involved: "It is important to note that Tom is one of the very few celebrities to be nominated and supported solely by his fans. The applications and necessary fees were handled and raised by the members of the many Tom Jones Fan Clubs throughout the United States." Although Tom Jones Enterprises may have appeared somewhat ashamed that they had not initiated and financed the award, and also of its tacky setting outside a lingerie shop, the star at least stands as a testimony to the devotion of Tom's following. Another test of loyalty – in the form of another major scandal – was about to come.

For the first time in his 25-year career, one of Tom's adulterous lovers was not going to stand for being loved then discarded. Tom had first met Katherine Berkery, a 24-year-old shipping clerk, in Regines nightclub-cum-restaurant, New York, back in October 1987. Two years later she brought a paternity suit against Tom, alleging that he was the father of her young son Jonathan.

Katherine truly believed she had been treated harshly by the ageing pop star, with whom she had spent four nights after their first encounter. Determined to make Tom publicly admit he had fathered her child she sold her story to a number of papers and magazines. For her the truth about Tom's apparently callous behaviour was just as important as any financial settlement.

Journalists Graham Dudman and Paul McMullan secured a lengthy interview with the incensed mother, in which she described her time with Tom as follows: "At a party after a concert he invited me over to his table for champagne . . . Next night I was ushered backstage at his show. After an hour or so of drinks in his dressing room I went back to his hotel in a limo with him and we had sex . . . There was nothing kinky or unusual about our lovemaking but it was also nothing special.

"He would set the mood by playing a selection of his own songs on a reel-to-reel tape recorder he kept in a silver briefcase. I found that very funny and rather conceited. I hardly left his side for the next two days and nights . . . He never once mentioned his wife and I had no idea he was married." Katherine went on to say that the sex had been unprotected as neither party had been concerned about catching AIDS, and Tom had never asked if she was on the contraceptive pill.

Six weeks later, Katherine discovered she was pregnant and immediately tried to contact Tom. After numerous frustratingly unreturned messages, she was finally given an abrupt brush-off by a member of Tom's staff. Realising that she was not getting anywhere, Katherine was resolute that she wouldn't let Tom get away without taking any responsibility for his role in her pregnancy. When Jonathan was born in autumn 1988, she registered the baby's father as Tom Jones and approached celebrity divorce lawyer Raoul Felder, who had made quite a name for himself for his aggressive hounding of errant celebrities. The word on the street was that the lawyer kept piranhas in a fish tank in his New York office. He was just the man for the job.

Tom failed to appear for the initial hearing of the case at the Manhattan Family Court and was ordered by Judge Judith Scheindlin (who herself later found fame with real life cases in the American TV programme *Judge Judy*) to appear on July 21 for the next stage of the hearing. Tom faced arrest if he remained absent from the proceedings.

He denounced the claims in the press, issuing the following statement: "I'm disgusted and depressed by these lies and I flatly deny that the child is mine. I am the victim of an irresponsible and scurrilous allegation." Some papers also featured a brief quote from the mortified Linda, bravely insisting, "My husband has completely denied any involvement with this girl. I love him just as much as I ever did and he loves me."

The acrimonious suit stretched from July to September, and at one stage

Tom was ordered to take a blood test to biologically prove or disprove his paternity. When the result came back from the laboratory, the papers took great delight in reporting that it was 99.9% conclusive that he was the baby's father. It was all Judge Scheindlin needed to rule that Tom had lost the fight, and she initially decided that he should pay Katherine a fairly nominal amount in child support.

But Raoul Felder did not house pet piranhas in his office for nothing and immediately announced plans to appeal for an increase in the monthly payment to the region of $2,000. His case was helped by Katherine's further revelation to the press that after the first ruling in her favour, she had been offered £50,000 by Tom's people to drop the suit. As a result, in the early part of September 1989 Katherine was given a massive undisclosed settlement in addition to a monthly maintenance pay-out of $2,791 until Jonathan reached the age of 21. Katherine was delighted with the outcome of her case, but if she had thought that Tom would now admit to his indiscretion in the media, she had a big disappointment in store.

As late as 1998 Tom was still adamantly denying his clinically proven fatherhood of Jonathan Berkery. "Well, you have to understand that we get letters and calls from women claiming all sorts of things," he told the *Daily Telegraph*. "There is one woman in Belgium who thinks I should own up to having her child, and she writes to me all the time and sends tapes and things telling me about her life. But I never even met the woman." So how could he then explain his DNA test? "We settled that case with a lump sum payment." Yes, but were the results correct? "Well we couldn't disprove them . . . At least, it's natural. I mean, the sex. At least these things are all about natural stuff. You know, nobody's suggesting that I had sex with kids. Or sheep." While Tom seemed inclined to circumvent the issue with flippancy, Katherine herself was far more succinct. "I now realise I was nothing to Tom," she was quoted in the *TV Times*, "just another chick."

So what of Linda, who faced the terrible knowledge that it had been legally proven that her husband had fathered a child out of wedlock, decades after her tragic miscarriage had prevented her from ever bringing a brother or sister to Mark into the world? For a while according to many media reports, divorce seemed imminent. Pictures of Tom looking old and haggard appeared in the papers and on TV, and speculation flew about how a potential marriage annulment settlement would compare to the recent paternity figures.

After much presumed heartache, nothing concrete appeared, and the matter, like so many others before, seemed to have been quietly swept under the Woodward family carpet. Incredibly, Tom's indiscretion and the delicate balance of a marriage which must surely have been stretched beyond breaking point, did not prevent him from speaking without any visible tact at all to the *TV Times* barely three months after the Berkery hearing.

"[Linda] accepts that I will have affairs, although she doesn't go along with it. She doesn't say, 'Oh, it's all right.' She just tells me, 'Be careful.' I've never wanted to have affairs, they've just happened. It's better if they don't. But I'm always honest about the fact that I'm married and that it's never going to change. It's putting your cards on the table before you play the game . . .

"My wife really wants me there with her, but I'm away touring a lot. When I'm home, I reassure her by doing all the right things, I talk to her. I listen. I think she's as happy as she can be. I've never asked her. She knows her limitations. She's not a very confident person." Such a plain-spoken admission of guilt, not to mention his condescending attitude, would surely have been the final straw for any modern day marriage. But it was obvious to all concerned that this wasn't a normal marriage by any stretch of the imagination, and Linda wasn't just an ordinary wife.

Three years later, Tom brushed off this difficult period with Linda in a throw-away comment to the Birmingham *Evening Mail* that showed slightly more humility. "You should have heard her at the time! It came down to the fact that I was a careless, stupid old beggar who should have known better. Now the episode's never mentioned." One might ask why Tom would speak so openly to a journalist who would print his words nationwide when the subject was 'never mentioned' at home.

Why Linda chose to stay with her roaming husband remains her own private business, but it is interesting to note that Tom's own opinions on the subject of divorce are pretty austere. "I like stability and organisation," he said to Janie Lawrence in 1999. "I can't see that when people get divorced and they're still friends and play cards together that they could have ever been in love to start with. If we ever fell out I would never want to see her again. That's because love and hate are very close."

"Linda is a Welsh wife, they don't run screaming for their lawyers when their husband plays around. They grin and bear it," Vernon Hopkins once said. Wendy Watkins, however, has a different, less downtrodden memory of this enigmatic lady. "She's not the cowering, simpering, whimpering wife hiding underneath the table or anything. She's got a personality of her own."

It was shortly after the culmination of the Katherine Berkery paternity suit that Tom invested in a seven-bedroom Welsh farmhouse, by the name of Llwynddu House, near Ystradowen, Cowbridge. This was to be Linda's new home.

The property cost £575,000 and included a separate games wing, conservatory and tennis court. High-tech security equipment was installed to protect Linda in her luxurious hideaway at the end of the quarter-mile long driveway. Ystradowen itself is a very quiet, isolated scenic village surrounded by acres of farmland. In stark contrast to Treforest, the village has developed relatively recently and does not share the cramped rows of houses, one on top of another, spreading up the hillsides.

Tom spoke at the time about how Linda had never truly felt 'at home' in the States. "We had a pool and lots of servants but Linda would rather do her own housework and look out of the window at the British countryside even if it is raining." Despite strong statements to the contrary from Tom Jones Enterprises, there was much speculation that this move signified the end of Tom and Linda's marriage. No one was in any doubt, however, that they were now living apart on a more permanent basis.

High on the agenda at Tom Jones Enterprises at this time was a move to strengthen their hold over the numerous fan clubs that had diligently supported Tom for so many years. In the summer of 1989, during the thick of the Berkery suit, a letter was received by all of the clubs which caused immediate uproar. The letter★ berated the clubs for their insistence on meeting the star after his shows, and furthermore dictated precisely what presents they were allowed to bring for their idol. It went on to say that the fan club structure was being given a major overhaul so that only three would remain. The tone of the correspondence alone surprised the various presidents, who were understandably outraged.

"Contrary to what you may hear, very few artists ever visit with their fans, due to a tremendous demand on their personal schedules, of which you have no knowledge, nor should you speculate in this area," the fan clubs were strictly informed. "Your main function . . . is to support the artist in his endeavours, by word of mouth, by radio station call-ins, and record purchases . . . It is nobody's business who gets backstage for what reason . . .

"It is in your best interest to know that gifts more appreciated and used are fruit, home-made food items, towels and champagne." The general behaviour of the fan clubs was also reprimanded. "There are also criticisms that have come to us that reveal pettiness, selfishness, and a warped sense of 'understanding' of Mr Jones' business, and it is most annoying for the management staff to have to spend time with these 'issues'."

Initially it was the break-up of the clubs that caused the most concern. President of the American chapter, Bridge Across The Pond, Nancy Rosas, is still amazed at their gall over a decade later. "I had the club for 25 great years," she said in a recent online interview. "But a lot of the fans

★ Published in full in Stafford Hildred and David Gritten's 1990 biography of Tom.

were really upset. One went to a concert in Atlantic City and brought up the issue with Tom. He acted like he knew nothing about it. Of course, I'm not blaming this on Tom. He probably did know nothing." Another president felt so insulted, especially after the fan clubs had so recently solely financed Tom's Hollywood star, that she leaked the offending letter to the press, and American and British papers ran brief articles echoing the widespread disbelief. Sylvia Firth, president of the Tom Jones Appreciation Society, recalls that the more reserved British fans did not really feel that the letter applied to them, as it had only really been the American clubs that had gained access to Tom's dressing room and decorated it with goodies. "The clubs in America were whittled down not long after that, that's why there are only three of us now," she explains today.

Shortly after the scandal first broke Tom appeared on television and in an attempt to calm the situation insisted that the letter was intended only to discourage the fans from spending so much money on him. But the upset wasn't to end there. Tom's new management also decided that it was high time for the knicker-throwing tradition to cease once and for all. They made it clear that they felt it degraded the singer, especially as he was fast approaching his 50th birthday.

"He hates it. We all hate it," said publicist Donna Woodward to Patty LaNoue Stearns. "There's a handful of women who do this and it has become a ritual, and he, being the gentleman that he is, doesn't want to kick them back in their faces, so he tries to do it as gracefully as he can." But Tom had been slow to appreciate that the on-stage panty antics did nothing for his dignity, and an end to this ritual was unlikely to occur overnight.

"I used to encourage it," he admitted to journalist Neil Bonner. "I had fun and games with the ladies in the audience and, frankly, I couldn't see the wood for the trees. I didn't realise at the time that it was getting in the way of my music. Not only that, but it held up the show and must have been quite boring for all the men. Now I just want people to listen to me." Obviously there are always going to be the die-hard fans who cannot resist hurling a lacy offering, but Tom himself now tried to discourage such behaviour. "Mark brought to my attention that only a handful threw their underwear so I shouldn't pander to them. He said, 'You can't stop it, but don't pick the bloody things up and wipe your brow with them,' like I used to."

When the hoped-for change in his fans' attitude did not happen quickly enough for Tom's liking, he decided to target the press, blaming them for encouraging the panty throwing. "This stuff with the sex and the underwear has gone on for a ridiculously long time because the press always insists on it, reinforcing the expectations of a certain type of fan . . . It also has become a gauge of the musical success of each show, as in 'the audience was really hot because two dozen pairs of underwear were on the stage.' "

As well as discouraging the knickers, Tom was instructed to refrain from giving his fans his habitual deep French kisses. "I've been warned by doctors against all this kissing on stage, because you never know what you might catch."

18

FUNNY FAMILIAR FORGOTTEN FEELINGS

Tom's FIRST YEAR of the new decade was quiet, despite celebrations for his 50th birthday. When he wasn't touring as normal, much time was spent in his new house in Cowbridge. Meanwhile Mark and Donna searched for a new record label. As a direct result of Tom's dissatisfaction with former labels, notably Polygram, the contract with Jive Records had been a one-album deal and so had already expired. The press circulated rumours of a possible 'soul album', and after the success of 'Kiss' Tom received some well-meaning songwriting offers, including one from Michael Hutchence of INXS, but nothing transpired. Eventually Tom signed to Dover Records, a subsidiary of Chrysalis, harking somewhat back to the closing days of MAM.

Tom had pondered his half-century milestone back in 1981: "I think I can do what I'm doing, the way I'm doing it, until I'm 50 . . . After that I'll slow down, maybe change the act a bit, mellow it. Not because I think I'll feel different but, honestly, I'd feel a bit ridiculous leaping about up there at 50." This premonitory speech no longer rang true and Tom showed no signs of slowing down. Instead he rescheduled his prophetic retirement. "I'd rather be 50 than dead. I hope I reach 90," he said to Peter Robertson. "I don't mind getting older because there's nothing you can do about it, except keep as fit as possible. When you're 50 you can't be 20 so you can't try and compete. I intend to grow old gracefully. I don't want to look ridiculous. I hope that when it looks funny for a man of my age to be leaping about, I hope I don't feel like leaping about the place – that my performance will suit my age."

Pictured exclusively for *Hello!* magazine six months previously, Tom had betrayed his age with an unbecoming pair of large black rimmed specs and his greying hair closely cropped. He also began to speak publicly in a manner his former vanity would never have allowed. "I must confess, sometimes I walk past a mirror and think, 'Who's that? It can't be me!' I don't feel as old as I look."

While Tom seemed happy to make fun of himself in the public eye, for some reason he now felt he was in a position to criticise other mature pop stars of his era. Mick Jagger, Cliff Richard and Phil Collins were his immediate targets. His remarks were printed in *Options* magazine, one of many papers that eagerly jumped on the bandwagon in 1990. "They have watery voices with no weight. I don't understand how they do well or what people think they're listening to – especially the females. If they'd been born in Wales they wouldn't dare get on stage."

Tom first dismissed The Rolling Stones frontman. "He knows he doesn't have a good voice so he does the best with the tools he has." He was less aggressive about Cliff Richard, "He's a mild person and that's the way he sings." But Phil Collins suffered the full wrath of The Voice: "A monotonous, piercing sound with no sex or warmth."

Changes within the band set-up were not yet complete, and The Blossoms, who had been with Tom for 21 years, were the next on the list to be let go. Fanita James remembers that she received a telephone call out of the blue from Mark, saying, "This is one of the hardest things I've ever had to do . . ." Mark went on to explain that however sad he was to lose his former surrogate mothers, Tom Jones Enterprises had decided to downsize Tom's band in order to project a modern, younger look. Cynthia Woodard confirmed that four other musicians were also politely asked to leave at around the same time. It was truly the end of an era.

Tom also bade a sad public farewell to another old friend this year, joining in *Liza's Tribute To Sammy*, a concert dedicated to the memory of Sammy Davis Jnr. who had lost his battle against cancer on May 16, 1990. The tribute was held at the Royal Albert Hall and sponsored by American Express, who produced a lavish limited edition programme. On the inside cover was the immortal line from the song that Sammy had first made his own on *This Is Tom Jones*: "I know a man Bojangles, and he danced for you . . ."

Just one year after the Katherine Berkery scandal had died down, in December 1990 the *News Of The World* published reports of yet another affair. This time Tom was linked to Californian journalism student Cindy Montgomery, who at 21 years old was less than half his age. According to the paper, Cindy's mother Gladys (cousin of Angela Lewis of The Blossoms) had introduced the couple at a Las Vegas concert earlier that year. Supposedly Tom's current bodyguard, Chris Montgomery (no relation) was said to be dating Cindy's fellow student Karen. The Sunday tabloid speculated on the expensive gifts that Tom had bought for his latest lover and romantic holidays they had enjoyed together, but the main focus of the damning report was that Linda had apparently caught her husband canoodling with Cindy in their Los Angeles home. That Tom was reputedly being so blatant with this affair spurred on fresh allegations of a marital split, but Linda's sister Rosalyn Thorne spoke out: "They're not getting divorced. My sister is with her husband in Las Vegas. It's not true."

Rosalyn went so far as to claim that 'Cindy' didn't even exist and was just a jokey nickname for the butch blond minder, Chris Montgomery. But one of the claims from the *News Of The World* cut a little close to the mark. Tom was supposed to have arranged for him and Cindy to spend some time together at London's Inn On The Park hotel during the week while he recorded his new album.

One aspect of the story was undeniably true; Tom was indeed in the throes of working on his next musical project. The role of producer for the proposed follow-up to the *Kiss* album was initially offered to songwriter and arranger Terry Britten. As he was unavailable the project was passed on to John Hudson, the owner of Mayfair Studios, who had briefly worked as a mixer on *Matador*. The record company's brief to John was to recreate the electronic feel of *Kiss*.

John found this suggestion rather inconsistent with Tom's previous vinyl style, and so suggested to Dover that he should bring in musicians and record the songs given to him live. Dover balked at this, saying it would prove to be too expensive. This policy of cutting the costs also extended to the location of the sessions. "The record company didn't want me to go to America to record the album, because of cost, we could get a better deal here and also the musicians that I said I'd use were based in London," John recalls. So instead of flying out immediately to meet Tom in Los Angeles he was forced to work along the same lines as with Anne Dudley, laying down a backing track and then taking the tape to America for Tom to overdub the vocals at his leisure. Unlike Anne, who was fortunate enough to have heard Tom perform a version of 'Kiss', John had no idea how the singer was going to interpret the songs or even which key he would sing them in.

John's undoubted talents were stretched to the limit. "Before I met Tom I'd more or less planned the whole thing. When I met Tom it was a bit difficult for me because I had started a plot and I had to carry on." When John had laid down the backing tracks and was eventually ready to record in Los Angeles, he first met Tom in his Bel Air home. "The funniest thing about going to his house was when we got back to his place after a long brunch, the maid and the butler had gone home for the day and I said I could really do with some decent coffee. I said to Tom, 'I'll make some coffee if you point me in the right direction.' He said, 'I don't know where anything is!' They had two kitchens; a butler's pantry and a big kitchen with a stove in the middle, and nobody knew where the coffee machine was!"

The recording sessions, booked in Los Angeles' Larrabee Studios, were riddled with problems. On John's arrival he found the building locked and unmanned, the crew were late and the pianist couldn't sight read. The only saving grace to emerge from the first day's work was the technically dazzling replacement keyboard player, whose day job was working with Michael Jackson. Finally, with this last minute addition, the pieces began to fall into place.

"At that moment, even before Tom had arrived, I realised that this was how we should have planned it. The guy was so brilliant and when Tom arrived and started singing it was just so amazing." John returned to London with Tom's vocals and built up the songs around them. After a return visit to Los Angeles, and a reciprocal visit from Tom to London, the project was finished after four and a half months, or so he thought.

John felt that he had learnt much in the way of studio etiquette by the time he had finished with Tom. "Tom hadn't been in the studio for quite some time. He's a great showman, that's what he's best at. But when you're recording a song and it's a new song you've got to not cabaret it up, because you've got to sing the melody. We'd already discussed this the day before. Tom had said, 'I'll probably be over singing and losing the tune – you must stop me and tell me, because I'll get carried away.' So on one of the tracks I stopped him; he was really getting into it. I said, 'You started cabareting it up a bit there, you should really just stick to the tune. Do you want to do that again?' He said, 'But that was how I sang it, see!'" John felt it would be best not to argue the point with the superstar and so let it go. He was a little more strict with the album's executive producer, Tom's son Mark. "I had to ask Mark to leave the control room because he was on the mobile phone all the time!"

Even after all John's hard work, it still seemed that the follow-up to *Kiss* needed a little something extra. "They had completely finished everything that I did and I think by then they had realised that the album needed a little bit more soul, it was a bit electronic," says John, bringing to mind the comments he had made to Dover right at the very beginning of the project.

Tom takes up the story in an informative interview with A.J. Barratt: "When I signed with Chrysalis last year, we started getting the material together for the album and finished recording in January. As we were finishing it off, Van Morrison shows up . . . I got a message through Chrysalis and a few other people saying, 'Van Morrison would like to speak with you,' so I said, 'What about?' and nobody seemed to know. So I gave him a buzz, and he said he had this one song, 'Carrying A Torch' that he had recorded, but when he played it back he thought 'Tom Jones'. He said, 'I'd like to play it and some other stuff I've got to you,' and I said, 'Well, come over tomorrow,' and he brought a cassette.

"The one he was interested in was 'Carrying A Torch' and I loved it, and there were four songs [on the tape] I felt I could do . . . Working with him was great. We did the songs live in the studio and I haven't worked like that since 1971." In addition to the synthetic songs already recorded with John Hudson, Tom went into London's Town House studios with Van in February 1991 and taped the four songs he liked at the very last moment.

"It was the most hectic session I've worked on in a long time," remembers studio chief engineer Alan Douglas, of the Van Morrison session. The collaborators had booked 12 hours studio time in total, but partly because they were working at a last-minute frantic pace, and partly because the instruments were recorded live and not overdubbed in sections, the songs took only six hours in total to complete. Van surveyed his compositions taking shape, acting both as producer and backing guitarist. The result of this session combined with John's labour of love was a proposed 12-track album, with one of John's songs omitted to make room for the four Van Morrison compositions.

Because of the immense difference in studio styles between John Hudson's 'modern electronic' brief and Van Morrison's traditional live approach, it was painfully obvious early on that there was going to be little continuity on the album. "They [Van's songs] were so uncomputerised they didn't match the rest of the album, so they got me to remix his tracks," John remembers. "I did make a few adjustments, because the tracks were a bit of a free-for-all . . ." The problems that had dogged John with the creation of the new album even stretched to this remixing, as all the computer discs that were sent to him from Van's studio for remixing had been re-formatted and all the editing Van had worked on thus far was mysteriously lost. When finally he had dealt with this latest calamity, John felt that Van would have been pleased with the result, not that the acclaimed singer/songwriter was ever informed of the studio mishap!

Tom Jones shared much in common with Van Morrison, and it was evident from the start that the pairing was going to produce very interesting listening. Both men were of Celtic descent and had broken into the music industry at around the same time. Van had travelled to London from Belfast in order to make his mark on the Sixties music scene, in a similar manner to Tom's pilgrimage from Pontypridd. When the two first met back in 1964, Van was in a group called Them, and like Tom, he was struggling to obtain a recording contract. Both men struck lucky with the same label, Decca, and from 1964 through to 1965 they appeared occasionally together on the same live bill.

"We toured together in the Sixties," Tom explained to *Sunday Life* magazine. "In those days a bunch of people played in the same show. My first show with Van was in the Birmingham Town Hall. It was just before I released 'It's Not Unusual'. I had seen him a bit around London but we hadn't really had any contact since then."

Once the album, now newly titled *Carrying A Torch* after one of Van's contributions, was ready for release, John Hudson, who received the credits as producer, engineer and mixer for his devoted diligence, was able to reflect on the question of whether or not he considered the finished project to be a success. In retrospect, and especially after the last-minute contribution from Van Morrison, he would have preferred that his initial requests had been taken into more consideration by the record company, so that he could have produced a more rootsy, acoustic album, in keeping with Van's songs, rather than revisiting *Kiss*'s past musical territory. "Some of the tracks sound a little bit contrived and now I think that the record company and management would agree with me," he admits today. But the greatest shock of all was still to come.

"It cost £280,000 to make and after we'd finished it, Chrysalis in America announced that they weren't going to release it! I couldn't believe it. I got loads of phone calls from the fan clubs in America; they tracked me down having heard about the album, and they wanted to hear the tracks and know when it would be released. It was just such a shame, there were some fantastic tracks on it." Chrysalis' reasons for not properly backing this very important album in Tom's career have still not been fully explained, but EMI's takeover of the company in 1991 may have been to blame, as might the fact that *Carrying A Torch* had already gone over budget and promotion costs overseas were likely to be high.

Still, Tom set about promoting his latest album in the UK with vigour. The first single, 'Couldn't Say Goodbye' was released at the end of January, scraping in at number 51. A video accompanied the rather middle-of-the-road offering, but despite the MTV award bestowed on his promo for the 'Kiss' single, it was only very basic, with Tom and an animated dancing girl superimposed on an artistic collage of autumn leaves.

Carrying A Torch did not make a huge impact on the UK charts, reaching number 44 in April 1991, while the title single stopped at number 57. Tom noticed a slight change in the critics' perception of his music, some concluding that he had finally decided to age gracefully, rather than compete with the youngsters in the current pop scene. The highest acclaim he received was for his collaboration with the respected Van Morrison, with one reviewer remarking, "The four tracks, recorded live over two days [sic], aren't the finest songs Morrison has ever written, but they do stand head and shoulders above anything else on this album." Van included his own versions of these somewhat lyrically repetitive compositions for Tom, ('Carrying A Torch', 'I'm Not Feeling It

Anymore', 'Peace Of Mind' and 'It Must Be You') on his album, *Hymns To The Silence*. Released later in September of that year it fared substantially better than Tom's CD, going straight into the UK charts at number five.

Among Tom's promotional appearances for *Carrying A Torch* was one of his most memorable TV performances ever. On March 15, 1991, Tom took part in the third annual charity fundraising telethon, *Comic Relief*, 'competing' against comedian Lenny Henry in his outrageous Theophilus P. Wildebeest guise in 'The Battle Of The Sex-Gods'. Producer Richard Curtis announced the event as, "A battle of the codpieces. We hope to set up phone lines so the public can ring in and tell us who they think is the sexiest. We hope Tom Jones won't be offended . . ." Roughly one third of the money raised would go to a British charity project, with the remaining two thirds donated to African Relief Aid.

Never before had such a golden opportunity to publicly laugh at himself been presented to Tom. Decked out in identical T-shaped medallions and *Comic Relief*'s trademark flashing red noses (worn hilariously as cod pieces), Theophilus P. Wildebeest and Tom Jones competitively duetted on an overly raucous version of 'Can't Get Enough Of Your Love'. Tom, who had squeezed himself into a skin-tight black leather ensemble, was visibly having the time of his life as he sparred musically with his very own spoof. As their duet came to a climactic ending, the two were showered with knickers, and the viewers were invited to phone in to vote for the hunkiest 'Sex-God'. Tom eventually won the competition, raising thousands of pounds for charity with by far his most entertaining contribution ever.

"With Lenny, I thought I'd just go right over the top," Tom later reminisced to Gill Pringle of the *Daily Express*. "I've always said over the years that I don't take it seriously. People say, 'Oh, Tom Jones, you know, Medallion Man, open-necked shirts, and all that.' *Comic Relief* gave me the perfect opportunity to show that I don't really believe it all."

Tom's next major TV appearance was in a BBC documentary called *Omnibus: Tom Jones – The Voice Made Flesh*. The programme, part of the on-going critically acclaimed Omnibus series, aired on Good Friday and was an intelligent précis of the singer's career. Tom was interviewed in some depth, including on the subject of his ever in-question marriage, to which he responded, "I've never had a serious affair. It's never been questioned that I would leave my wife for anybody else." It had never been more apparent than now, with this frank discussion and *Comic Relief*'s self parody that Tom was a man to be taken at face value. Now in his fifties, he was unlikely to change.

Soon after the documentary was broadcast, Tom revisited old ground once again, presenting the Wood Road Social Club with a commemorative Harp Lager Plaque, an award commonly given to sights in Britain that have a place in pop history. Although his latest musical offering had not fared well in the charts, the streets came to a standstill as the crowds gathered outside the antiquated club that had given Tom his first break. Tom presented the plaque to committee man Charlie Ashman, who had paid him just £1 for his début performance back in 1957.

Carrying on the good work Tom had started with *Comic Relief*, he now went on to perform at Amnesty International's 'The Big 30', celebrating the human rights organisation's 30th anniversary. The fundraising concert was shown on MTV in America and helped to boost popular opinion of Tom, but infuriatingly for the well-meaning singer, many reviews of this concert concentrated entirely on the on-stage knicker-count, just three years after his management had gone to great lengths to discourage such behaviour. On May 12, 1991 Tom then appeared at Wembley Arena for 'The Simple Truth' benefit concert, this time raising money for Kurdish refugees. This performance was also televised on MTV, and once again helped to raise the public's esteem of the millionaire superstar.

Unfortunately, as had proved to be the case so many times during Tom's lengthy career, no sooner had he risen in the public estimation than he was dragged straight back down again, as yet another former member of staff left his employment and decided to spill the beans. Bodyguard Chris Montgomery quit his job of four-and-a-half years following a row with Mark in April 1991. Chris' agent, Jackie Evans, secured him a two-article deal with the *News Of The World*, and the printed allegations soon became known as the 'Listerine Exposé'.

The best remembered of the many 'revelations' in this latest exposé centred around the brand name mouthwash, with which Chris claimed Tom soothed his sore masculinity the morning after a heavy night. Chris, 10 years Tom's junior, had taken on many roles including chauffeur, cleaner and cook, but predictably it was his tales of Tom's insatiable appetite for women that stole the headlines. Throughout the years, many fans have begrudgingly acknowledged that beautiful young girls are often planted in the front row seats of a concert to stir up enthusiasm and generally boost appearances. Chris fuelled this belief by adding that he would be sent as a 'booty scout' by Tom to select a couple of the women to join them backstage.

"Mr Jones especially enjoys the spectacle of two women performing with each other," revealed Chris in the first instalment of his story. "His biggest fantasy is girls together. He's obsessed with it and talks about it all the time. If a girl he's persuaded to go to bed with him agrees to bring along a chum, he's in seventh heaven. He reckons all women take to it like ducks to water." Chris also told the paper how he would provide Tom with his required sex aids and pornography.

Chris claimed that Cynthia Woodard was one of the many who had an affair with Tom. "They had a passionate affair on and off for three years. Cynthia was a lovely girl – huge. But then The Boss likes big girls. The problem was that she also snored like a train and could rattle the walls with the noise." Cynthia remembers today that when she first laid eyes on the article she couldn't help but burst out laughing. She thought the allegations were outrageous, but remarkably she doesn't bear a grudge against Chris Montgomery and describes him as a "very sweet man".

Another of the suggestions in the *News Of The World* exposé was that Tom used TV star Victoria Principal's husband, a famed plastic surgeon, to operate on him during the time of Chris' employment, and pointed out that Tom has two tell-tale facelift scars under his ears.

As he had grown older, Tom's thick curly, dark hair began to show signs of greying and almost immediately he started dyeing it. The result was quite unnatural and as Linda bluntly told her husband, he looked like he had just had a bucket of soot thrown over him. But Chris Montgomery claimed that Tom took more drastic steps to reverse the thinning of his hair, describing in graphic detail five painful scalp operations Tom underwent. "Eventually he decided to go the whole hog and have scalp reduction operations. A strip of skin was taken from the centre of his scalp and then the skin on each side, which is blessed with nice thick hair, was pulled over to cover the balding bit – and then stapled into place. It was all done under local anaesthetic – in fact usually Mr Jones fell asleep," explained Chris. He continued to horrify the readers by adding that, "He performed on stage several times with 50 or 60 of these metal staples still in his head." The operation supposedly cost Tom £750 each time, but it was so successful that Tom gave up dyeing his hair and allowed himself to go grey 'naturally'.

In the second day's instalment Chris attacked Tom's family, paying particular attention to his manager son. "Mark also weighs in after interviews if he thinks he's said something that doesn't go with the new image. And he'll always have an opinion on what Mr Jones should sing . . . Worst of all for a man who loves women, Mark's trying to stop his legendary girl chasing. He's known for years what his dad gets up to. He turned a blind eye to it then, but since a paternity suit when a girl successfully claimed Mr Jones is the father of her son, Mark has nagged and nagged him about girls. I've had to smuggle girls out of the back of the house so Mark wouldn't see them and give his dad a hard time." Tom's response to the *Daily Mirror's* question of why he didn't sue his ex-minder for provoking this latest scandal was simply, "Because he's got no money, that's why!" So much for the all-empowering loyalty clause.

Tom's final outing for the year was in an extraordinary TV musical adaptation of *The Ghosts of Oxford Street*. The story was the concept of punk Svengali and Sex Pistols manager Malcolm McLaren, whose only previous involvement in this genre was the 1979 feature film *The Great Rock'n'Roll Swindle* based around the exploits of the Pistols.

"[Oxford Street] has a fascinating history, dating back to when there were public executions at Tyburn Gallows where Marble Arch is now," Malcolm McLaren, also the narrator of the musical, explained to *Hello!* magazine. "One of my favourite characters is Gordon Selfridge who made a fortune and then blew it all on wine, women and gambling. I felt Tom Jones would be ideal for the part and fortunately he agreed."

Typecast again, Tom indeed plays the role of the unscrupulous founder of the *Selfridges* emporium, who eventually quit his life's work at the age of 84. Included in his part were the songs 'Money' which he performed in the Christian Dior perfume department of the store, and 'Nobody Knows When You're Down And Out'. An array of musical celebrities participated in the tribute to the 200th birthday of London's most renowned shopping street alongside Tom, including Sinéad O'Connor, The Happy Mondays, Kirsty MacColl and The Pogues. *The Ghosts Of Oxford Street* was screened on Christmas Day on Channel 4 in the UK.

1991 had been a year of diametric opposition within Tom's career. On one hand he had done a great deal of work for charity, yet on the other the unexpected failure of *Carrying A Torch* and Chris Montgomery's stinging accusations had almost certainly tarnished his carefully reconstructed image. Nevertheless, his status with his fans would never be diminished and this year they queued in the biting cold British weather to reserve tickets for a concert in Plymouth *a year in advance*.

A droll start to the new year came with tidings of an interesting 'development' in Tom's fan base: he had garnered himself a gay following. To Tom's chagrin, boxer shorts now joined the lacy offerings hurled on stage during his concerts. Jimmy Somerville, the singer from pop group The Communards, fully expected this new aspect. "I'm not surprised gays find Tom sexy," he said. "I'm just surprised it's taken so long for Americans to wake up to it. Tom Jones is sex on legs." During this time reports also surfaced that Tom was making friends with the albeit straight, affluent Hollywood youth, namely Luke Perry and Jason Priestly, teenage stars of *Beverly Hills 90210*, with whom Tom would be seen in trendy restaurants on more than one occasion.

On May 23, 1992 Tom participated in a mammoth Welsh celebration entitled the 'World Choir'. This was the first ever gathering of 160 male choirs from around the globe, comprising some 8,000-strong voices brought together in the Cardiff Arms Park, in aid of the Lords'

Taverners Campaign for handicapped children and the Welsh Rugby Union's project to develop youth rugby.

Other guest artists included tenor Dennis O'Neill and operatic soprano Dame Gwyneth Jones, with the 200-piece band from the Welsh, Irish and Scots Guards conducted by the renowned Owain Arwel Hughes. The televised event drew a magnificent crowd of around 30,000 people.

"As a Welshman, singing at the Arms Park is a thrill and it should be quite a night," Tom predicted prior to the event. "It will also be a challenge singing in front of thousands of other Welsh people, because as you know everyone in Wales thinks they're good singers." Tom's assigned minder for the day, Richard Adler, recalls that although Tom was polite to all around, "He was visibly petrified of the task ahead. He spent the day coughing and clearing his throat, preparing his voice in anticipation of singing what he considered to be slightly operatic material."

After what proved to be a nerve-racking but wholly successful occasion, Tom accepted an invitation to perform as the special guest at the 22nd Glastonbury Festival on June 28. The famous Glastonbury event is the largest of its kind in Europe with four different stages showcasing performers from all genres of music. Tom appeared at sunset on the final day of the Somerset revelry. Recent collaborator Van Morrison had just come off the stage, warning Tom that the 75,000 rock fans watching weren't terribly enthusiastic.

"I thought, 'Great, let's do this and throw caution to the wind and dive in at the deep end,' because I had heard about the Glastonbury Festival, but I had never actually been there," said Tom to Brendon Williams. "I did the 'Green Green Grass Of Home' and ended with 'It's Not Unusual', which was unbelievable . . . When we were into the second or third song kids were coming from all over the place. It was like they were coming from over these hills, like we were being invaded and it was a fantastic feeling."

But this was to be only an introduction to his musical affiliation with the youth of the time. Twenty-one years on from the culmination of *This Is Tom Jones*, and over a decade since *Coast To Coast*, Tom commenced filming for a new TV show exploring the multiple roots of contemporary music.

Graham K Smith, who had previously worked with Tom on *The Last Resort* and then again on 'The Big 30' Amnesty International concert, approached Mark with a vague outline of a possible TV programme which Tom could present. The two of them, along with Donna, worked closely on the show's format which would involve Tom interviewing fashionable and established pop personalities as well as performing classic standards of all musical genres. There was a broad theme to each instalment, depending on the style of music the featured guest specialised in.

Initial titles for the series banded around by the trio included *Influences*, *Keep Your Knickers On* and *Saturday Night*, to reflect the projected primetime viewing slot, but eventually everyone settled on the name which seemed to reflect Tom's own current standing in the music world: *The Right Time*, a fitting Ray Charles song. The series of six shows was shot at Central Television Studios in Nottingham that June with a new episode completed every five days. During the filming Tom stayed at the Stapleford Park Hotel in Leicestershire, but he also maintained a large luxury caravan on-site for entertaining purposes. However, unlike the notorious trailer used on *This Is Tom Jones* at least Linda was seen visiting this time.

Tom was delighted with the guests his management had chosen and secured, and the material he would be performing on-screen. "For the first time they've given me the chance to do the stuff I want to do – gospel, blues, soul and Celtic. I've been seen as a narrow balladeer, but what I like are performers who sing big strong songs, straightforward stuff, sometimes right over the top, just like me."

The first of the shows to be broadcast was devoted entirely to the history of the pop genre. The set was designed to be youthful and bright, but nothing could quite match the colours of Tom's loud suits, which he changed at least once every episode. As an opener, Tom sang with his resident featured vocalists, True Image, who had previously made their name with Mica Paris the year before and also guested on *The Cosby Show*. In this first instalment, as with the majority of the series, there was a happy balance between performance and interviews with Tom's guests for that week.

As an interviewer, Tom came across as rather wooden, although his skills improved as the series progressed. His first attempt was with Marcella Detroit and Siobhan Fahey of Shakespear's Sister, and without a studio audience this part seemed quite stilted. The duet that followed, a T. Rex cover, was more successful, although Tom hadn't really established enough of a rapport with the two ladies to fully pull it off.

This continued to be the case for the next two interviews, with Andy Bell of Erasure and then EMF. In the latter piece the members of the group are heard to snigger when Tom compliments them by saying he performs their hit 'Unbelievable' in Las Vegas, and comment that that is "the apex of our career!" But once Tom hits the stage to duet on the same song with EMF, the balance shifts entirely.

Dressed in a trendy sports top, Tom totally steals the show from the young lads, who don't really get much of a look in on their own song.

Towards the end of the performance the stage becomes crowded with dancers and Tom is physically mobbed by an enthusiastic participant, who jumps onto the ageing singer's back. Tom deals with this sudden turn of events extremely professionally, continuing to sing despite the unexpected bouncing extra weight. To all intents and purposes it looks like the audience have stormed the stage, and Tom's rather sedate TV showcase has been turned into an unruly youth concert.

"It was absolutely spontaneous, it was one of those great moments," enthuses the show's producer, Graham K Smith. "Obviously EMF were at the height of their popularity at the time and, encouraged by Mark, Tom had become quite adventurous with his modern covers in his live gigs, and he had started doing 'Unbelievable' in his sets. EMF were so chuffed and so delighted. We invited them to come on the series and they could not believe they were going to be on Tom Jones' show. When they came down for the recording we had a big crowd there, and at the end there was a stage invasion and the audience jumped on Tom! It was great. Tom was all smiles and really enjoyed it." Following this first episode, the TV critics were divided on whether such on-stage antics improved Tom's show or whether they perhaps just underlined his age, playing on the self-effacing image that had been introduced the year before with *Comic Relief*. Either way, Tom's return had certainly made an impact, and EMF were so pleased with the recording of their duet that they used it as a B-side for their next single release.

The second show was less climactic, basing itself on a spiritual theme and featuring Tom's now standard 'Purple Rain' with Pink Floyd's Dave Gilmour on guitar, an interview with Al Jarreau, and a performance by Mica Paris. An interesting close to the show was Tom performing U2's arrangement of Woody Guthrie's 'Jesus Christ'. Staying with the flavour introduced by Al Jarreau, the following show covered soul music, with a beautiful working of Otis Redding's '(Sittin' On) The Dock Of The Bay' by Tom and True Image. Tom was evidently more at home with this genre and was visibly more relaxed interviewing Sam Moore from Sam & Dave and duetting on their 1966 track 'Hold On I'm Coming'. Female vocalist Cyndi Lauper would not normally be linked with the soul style, but her collaboration with the show's host on Ike and Tina Turner's 'River Deep Mountain High' was, aside from the EMF spectacle, surely the most dynamic pairing Tom was to see in this series. An unusual and exceptional trio followed, with Tom joining Daryl Hall of Hall & Oates and Sam Moore once again for a rousing 'Soul Music'. The music making did not end there as all the performers involved took part in an after-show jam in the television studio bar.

Tom was unlikely to forget his foray into country music, and the fourth show in the series was allotted to Country & Western. The programme comprised interviews with Bob Geldof and Lyle Lovett, and country-tinged performances of U2's 'With Or Without You', 'Green Green Grass Of Home' with added fiddles and an unusual version of 'Danny Boy' accompanied by a harpist. Tom's presentation of 'Cotton Eye Joe' with legendary Irish folk band The Chieftains should go down in history as more than just a lively end to an oddball TV programme. The Chieftains actually taped four tracks with Tom that day, including accompanying him on 'Green Green Grass Of Home', but sadly their input was edited to fit into the half-hour slot with just one song remaining.

"We were on [*The Right Time*] as his guests and we struck up a great relationship," recalls The Chieftains founding member and spokesman, Paddy Maloney fondly. "We did a medley. We were out in his caravan on-site and we were having a great time. They edited this piece and decided to do it again, and in the meantime we'd had a few pints at the bar . . . Needless to say when we came out to do it the second time it was much better! Let's just say it had liquidly loosened up brilliantly . . . The fun we had afterwards, it just went on and on and on . . ."

For the penultimate programme Tom was able to revisit his rhythm'n'blues roots. After opening with the raucous 'Shake, Rattle And Roll', Tom introduced his first guest, Joe Cocker and their interview concentrated on the influence Ray Charles still had on contemporary music today. Tom's other featured artist was Curtis Stigers with whom Tom duetted on 'Take Me To The River'. After their brief chat Tom sang 'Shotgun', using the middle eight to introduce the instruments individually as if they were ingredients in a recipe.

As a special climax to the series Graham, Mark and Donna secured a coup, booking Stevie Wonder, a very special hero of theirs who had previously appeared on *This Is Tom Jones*. Feeling honoured to have Stevie on the show, Tom dedicated the entire half-hour slot to him and the majority of the show centred on them jamming at a piano, duetting on 'It's Not Unusual' and Stevie's 'Superstition' among other favourites, and amusingly forgetting the words. Tom comes across as wholly reverential, yet strangely subdued, almost as if his star status had been swept from under him. Regaining his balance somewhat Tom concluded the series singing an uplifting version of 'Heaven Help Us' with The London Community Gospel Choir.

No Tom Jones extravaganza would be complete without a bit of scandal. The producers were scathingly criticised in the press for not allowing Tom's older fans to be present in the audience. Some of the mature devotees were actually turned away at the gates. Series producer Richard Holloway was unmoved, stating: "We're looking for a younger audience and it is inevitable some people are going to be upset. They can't blame Tom. It was our decision." Graham backed up this policy by intimating that the audience was merely appropriate for the featured guests.

Despite media scepticism, *The Right Time* was generally well received. "Tom is not a presenter," concedes Graham, reflecting on the star's performance on *The Right Time*. "Let's make no bones about that – that's not what he does. But he's a fantastic singer with bags of charisma . . . I'm sure ITV would have been very, very happy with an old-fashioned Tom Jones in a tuxedo, belting out 'Delilah'. They would have been very happy with that, but that was not the show that Tom or Mark wanted to make."

Graham had found the easy-going Tom such a pleasure to work with that even he was caught off-guard the first time he realised just what a star the Welshman actually was. "When it came to the launch, we did it in The Groucho Club in London. It's a showbiz den and basically, the main bar area is one of those places where it's full of media types who are always fascinated by who's coming in, but feigning disinterest all the time. They have to be above it all. The only time I've ever been into The Groucho Club and a hush has descended was when Tom Jones came in."

The Right Time was initially broadcast on ITV in the UK and later found its way across the Atlantic, where it was shown on VH1. Even though the ratings weren't brilliant, and the series wasn't renewed, at least Tom had finally gone some way to dispelling his medallion man image of years gone by. "I have always loved many different sorts of music but a lot of my fans don't realise that," he said. "I jumped at the chance of making the show because I was given total freedom to do what I liked. It gives me a chance to win my credibility back. I am well aware that I was in danger of becoming a buffoon because of the knicker throwing antics of some fans. My message to them is: 'Listen to my music and keep your knickers on.'"

Although the series was discontinued, at least one major result came out of the musical pairings on set. Tom was later contacted by Paddy Maloney of The Chieftains. The Irish group, who had previously worked with artists such as James Galway, Elvis Costello and Van Morrison, had decided that they would like to record a cross-over collaboration album with numerous rockers including Sting, The Rolling Stones, Ry Cooder, Mark Knopfler, Roger Daltrey and Sinéad O'Connor. Paddy had remembered covering the traditional song, 'Tennessee Waltz' in the original medley with Tom on *The Right Time*, and thought it would be an ideal track for the album, which was to be called *The Long Black Veil*.

The unforgettable recording session took place one afternoon at Frank Zappa's studio, imaginatively named the Utility Muffin Research Kitchen in Los Angeles. "Frank was a great friend and I loved his studio," Paddy

311

recalls. "I know Tom had a great admiration for Frank as well. When we went to do the recording, old Frank was quite ill, he died a year later, but he was there in the background, pretending not to be listening in. Almost without separation we recorded the song. We just sat in a circle and Tom just sang away and after two or three takes, there it was." Tom had been scheduled to leave the studio at 2.00 p.m. to get to the David Letterman show, on which he had been due to be a guest, but he had been enjoying himself so much with his fellow Celts that he stayed, drinking and chatting until quite late into the evening. Fortunately, he was able to catch the Redeye by the skin of his teeth and just about made the show in time, a little the worse for wear.★

Tom remained on television screens throughout 1992, presenting an episode of *Viva Cabaret* with American comedienne Sandra Bernhard, with whom he shared a flirtatious competitive duet. Unfortunately this further attempt to blend with a young audience went down very badly with certain critics who chastised Tom as being "rather sad" because of his advancing years. However, this did not deter the general public who continued to celebrate his comeback. A new hits compilation album sold well and Tom's worldwide concerts were impressively attended. Suddenly the 52-year-old was being hailed, at least in the UK, as a living legend.

What better way to immortalise such a star than to make a cartoon version of him? Tom was invited to do the voice-over for his own character in *The Simpsons* when the writers, who were all big fans, decided to incorporate him in a story-line. In the plot Marge Simpson, a closet Tom Jones fan, is romanced by her boss who kidnaps Tom Jones in an attempt to seduce her. In the end Marge's husband Homer wins the battle for her attentions and Tom's character, dubbed by the real singer, serenades the happy couple with 'It's Not Unusual'. This very different departure for Tom was aired on November 5, 1992, gaining him some much younger fans to add to his ever-expanding collection.

Tom was still relentlessly performing live and on December 1, 1992 at the New Empire Club on London's Tottenham Court Road, his audience was literally held captive as a bomb warning on the street outside forced them to stay in the club. There Tom calmed their nerves with an extra hour's performance. Five days later he was seeing in Christmas at the Town & Country Club, raising money for Capital Radio's nominated charity.

★ The long-term project of *The Long Black Veil* took a couple of years to complete, but was eventually so successful that it became The Chieftains' first ever album to chart in the UK when it was released in February 1995, débuting at its number 17 peak, and also attaining number 22 in the US. Tom also appeared in the accompanying film to the album, entitled *The Chieftains: The Making Of The Long Black Veil* that same year.

1993 was undoubtedly the year of charitable work for Tom Jones. Starting as he meant to go on, at 8.30 a.m. on Wednesday, January 6 he opened the annual Harrods sale in Knightsbridge, South West London, in aid of a newly formed cause, ChildLine. The Harrods press kit for the event ran as follows: "The singing star has responded to the invitation of Harrods Chairman Mr Mohammed Al Fayed to open the most famous sale in the world on behalf of ChildLine, the charity dedicated to eradicating child abuse. Mr Al Fayed, who has supported ChildLine since its foundation, is donating £50,000 or one per cent of the day's takings (whichever is the greater) to the charity.

"Mr Jones said, 'I have opened in Las Vegas more times than I can remember, but I have never opened the Harrods Sale. I am delighted to do so, not just because it is a great international event, but because it will give a tremendous boost to ChildLine. The charity is very special to me and it is having to fight for its financial survival.'"

Esther Rantzen, the charity's founder and chairman, arrived with Tom in some style, in an open landau carriage drawn by two black stallions. Nearly 1,000 hungry shoppers queued outside the department store doors prior to the event, and Tom took the opportunity to announce the release of his forthcoming single, the profits of which were to be donated to the same cause.

During the rest of the first week in January, Tom travelled from Los Angeles to London to spend time working on behalf of ChildLine, asking no fees for himself. "ChildLine is in bad financial shape at the moment, so a lot of people are trying to keep it afloat," he said. "I try to do as much as I can. I'm not attached to any particular charity, but when Esther Rantzen rang to ask me if I would make a record for ChildLine, I agreed immediately." One of the main features of the charity is a free telephone line dedicated to advising and supporting abused children who have nowhere else to turn. Their chief problem was that out of the thousands of daily phone calls made, only one third could be answered because there weren't enough funds to man the phones properly, a problem they still face today.

Producer Dave Stewart, best known as one-half of Eurythmics, was invited to transform the much-loved Beatles' track 'All You Need Is Love', the charity's anthem, into a vehicle specifically for Tom – some would say an impossible task. Dave took up the challenge enthusiastically, choosing to add his own signature electronic flourishes to translate it into something appropriate to the Nineties. The recording sessions were disjointed and took place in three venues around the world. The backing track was initially recorded in France, then Dave met up with Tom in Los Angeles to lay down the vocals. During this time British singer Kiki Dee happened to contact Dave out of the blue and so was roped into singing backing vocals for Tom. The final mix took place in London.

"When [Esther Rantzen] suggested the song I thought it was perfect; lyrically it's perfect," said Tom. "The only concern I had was to get it away from the way The Beatles did it . . . when The Beatles did the songs, they put their stamp on them so much, sometimes it's difficult to try to put it into another pocket, another beat. That's what Dave did. I just sang it."

The accompanying video was to prove equally important for the public image of ChildLine. Released exclusively in Woolworth's as a two-part film, the first section was simply the promotional video, while the latter half showed behind-the-scenes clips, titled *The Making Of All You Need Is Love*. On December 1 the previous year, Tom had been filmed playing the pied piper to a host of happy children, touching his toes and leading the conga as they merrily danced around him to the music. His scenes were interspersed with myriad British celebrities interacting with the kids including Jeff Banks, Michelle Collins, Darren Day, Ulrika Jonsson, Cleo Laine, Julia Sawalha, Alison Steadman, Bonnie Tyler and Desmond Wilcox.

"So many people have donated their time and talents to make this video," said Esther Rantzen. "All the artists' royalties and Woolworth's' profits will be donated to ChildLine, the free national helpline for children in trouble or danger. By buying the video you are helping us to comfort and protect these children – thank you, and thank you also to all the brilliant talented people who made this video possible." 'All You Need Is Love' débuted at number 19 in the UK charts in the first week of February 1993. The result of the single and its accompanying video was a £100,000 cash injection into the worthy charity.

Inspired by the current showing of *The Right Time* on VH1 in America, Tom then appeared as a guest star on *The Fresh Prince Of Bel Air*, which was first shown on February 8. He played a guardian angel who lifted one of the main characters, Carlton, out of his depression. "After 30 years in showbiz it's nice to do something different and fun," Tom remarked to the press. Another appearance around this time was on the notorious Howard Stern show. The programme's infamous presenter, never one to mince his words, went straight for the jugular, asking Tom if he felt guilty each time he cheated on Linda. For once Tom had the common sense and dignity to leave the room and cut the interview short. He returned shortly after-wards, telling Stern in no uncertain terms: "There's things you don't talk about. You do what you have to do."

Tom resumed work on his next good cause for 1993, accepting Sting's personal invitation to perform at the fourth Annual Rainforest Foundation Benefit concert on March 2. Joining a host of other pop stars including

George Michael, Tina Turner and Bryan Adams, Tom reportedly stole the show at New York's Carnegie Hall, blasting out an enthusiastic 'It's Not Unusual' accompanied by Sting on bass guitar. Sting admiringly described Tom's fantastic reception soon after in an interview: "I love playing the bass and not to have to sing at the same time is a fantastic holiday for me, but to back up Tom Jones – I could have joined the touring band I was so happy . . . He's a fantastic artist and people like that don't go away, they are just rediscovered."

Tom then swung straight from the Brazilian Rainforest to the Homeless, recording a cover version of The Rolling Stones' 'Gimme Shelter' for the Putting Our House In Order project. The brainchild of Food Records boss Andy Ross and gig promoter Jon Beast, this new campaign to raise funds for various homeless charities such as Shelter had already supported a number of one-off benefit concerts over the UK and an auction of pop memorabilia. The climax to the whole crusade was the release of not one but 12 different versions of 'Gimme Shelter', each as a B-side to a two-and-a-half minute spoken word interview on the merits of the project by the featured artists.

Andy Ross and Jon Beast were only able to engineer such an unusual feat by exploiting a loophole in the eligibility rules of the UK singles chart. This was to put the interview on each single's A-side and use the same catalogue number for all 12 releases, so that the sales of all the different formats would count as one chart entry, almost certainly guaranteeing a hit. "At one stage we had thought of putting out four or five singles and clogging up the charts with different versions of 'Gimme Shelter'," Andy Ross explained. "But the danger there was that a number of retailers might end up not stocking the lot. And it would also cut into the profit margin quite seriously . . . It's certainly something that's never been done before, but they [Gallup, compilers of the UK charts] couldn't see any reason why we couldn't get away with it."

Jon Beast continues: "The whole idea was originally to get all our mates in bands, like EMF, the Poppies [Pop Will Eat Itself], The Wonder Stuff and Carter [The Unstoppable Sex Machine] to record some sort of charity single and shove it into the indie charts, but it sort of spread out from there." After 10 months of kick-starting the concept, Andy and Jon secured the agreement of such diverse artists and bands as Jimmy Somerville, Voice Of The Beehive, Heaven 17, Samantha Fox and Sandie Shaw to all record their own version of the track. At the last minute, The Rolling Stones also donated a previously unreleased live version of 'Gimme Shelter' recorded on their European tour in 1990, and generously waived their publishing royalties, thus donating a sizeable amount more to charity.

The majority of the different versions of the song saw bizarre pairings of artists with bands from often opposing musical genres. Tom Jones was twinned with grungy rockers New Model Army, and the unusual blend saw a remarkably good match, that made excellent use of Tom's powerful vocals. As had become the norm for Tom these days, he did not meet up with the band in the studio and a tape was sent over to him in Los Angeles to add his part. Still, somehow a respectable musical rapport was established, resulting in what was certainly the most outstanding version of the Stones' classic, bar of course their own. Aside from Tom and the band's resolute input, the track also featured an authentic, bluesy harmonica introduction by Mark Feltham and was given the honour of being produced and mixed by Chris Kimsey, who had worked with The Rolling Stones for many years.

Possibly due to the gritty brilliance of this particular interpretation, Tom and New Model Army were invited to film a promotional video for their song one Saturday afternoon at Shepherds Bush Green, West London. The outcome of the filming was a very rough looking, grainy video showing Tom and the band performing determinedly against the chilly elements, which somehow only served to heighten the desperate effect of the music, and indeed the cause itself. Hard-hitting facts and figures relating to the plight of the homeless were superimposed at regular intervals over the footage, underlining the urgency to the charitable project.

'Gimme Shelter' was released in various formats by Food Records on April 13, 1993 and reached number 23 in the UK charts two weeks later, remaining in view for a further four weeks. Sadly the Putting Our House In Order registered charity folded in 1996, but at least it had done a good job of raising both money and awareness for homeless people with the record-buying public.

Although Tom's public image had been elevated to practically mythical status by his virtuous dedication to charitable causes over the past couple of years, his recording contracts with Jive and then Chrysalis had long since expired. Rumour has it that the very next day after the Rainforest benefit concert, Mark was contacted by nearly every major label, hoping to place Tom on their books and capitalise on his now established respectability. The phone call that Mark eventually chose to follow up was from the boss of Interscope Records, Jimmy Iovine, whose considerable credits included production work with Bruce Springsteen, John Lennon, Patti Smith and U2.

The Los Angeles based Interscope began life in the Eighties predominantly as a rap label, and rapidly gained the distinction of being the home of gangsta, featuring acts like the late Tupac Shakur, immortalised after his murder in a gang related drive-by shooting. Wisely diversifying as time went on, the label expanded to incorporate innovative bands and artists like No Doubt, Nine Inch Nails, The Wallflowers and Snoop Doggy Dog. Tom was understandably delighted when he signed with the eminent label, and proudly announced to his fan clubs that he was going to start work on a new album that very autumn, featuring songs written by the likes of Prince, Bruce Springsteen and Stevie Wonder, and aiming for a spring 1994 release.

While Tom was preparing to go into the studio, he was given the honour of being awarded a fellowship of the Welsh College of Music and Drama. Photographs appeared in the press soon after of Tom proudly wearing a graduate's robe and cap at the ceremony held in Cardiff. It did not go unnoticed by more uncharitable critics that Tom's fellowship had been granted despite the fact that he had left Treforest Secondary School without any qualifications, and was still unable to read music properly. But Tom was delighted nonetheless, proclaiming, "I often played truant then left at 15. This gives me as much satisfaction as any of my records."

Closing off the remarkable year, Tom recorded a sentimental, gospel-tinged version of the song 'Mary's Boy Child' for *David Foster's Christmas Album*. Although to this day one of the fans' biggest hopes is for Tom to record a Christmas album of his own, this contribution remains the closest he has come to fulfilling that request. In addition to the recording, Tom also appeared on the *David Foster Christmas Special*, aired on December 10 on NBC TV.

So as the latest chapter in Tom's life came to an end, it remained to be seen whether the 'charity year' of 1993 was simply a carefully orchestrated move on Mark's part, or in fact a genuine change in career direction to greater things. All too often pop stars are condemned for their large financial donations to charity, with the more cynical critics suggesting that it is merely an image-boosting method of tax evasion. But no-one could argue that Tom hadn't given freely of his time over the recent period, which for a star of his ilk could surely be seen as, at the very least, an equal-rating currency to hard cash. Either way, Tom's ongoing contributions to social causes were beginning to be noticed in all the right places, and the future was looking very bright.

19

THE LEAD AND HOW TO SWING IT

O N FEBRUARY 3, 1994 Tom opened for business as usual on stage at the newly relocated MGM Grand in Las Vegas. On the other side of the Atlantic, his recently recaptured UK fans were delighted to hear that he was planning a 26-date tour of the country, and for the first time ever, Tom was also going to perform in Russia. The Welshman even managed to amuse his home country with an advertisement depicting a photograph of his face superimposed on a beach and the equivocal quote: "Tax-exile Tom gets his head out of the sand for the homeland."

By far the most important item on Tom's agenda was the recording of his new album, which took place over the first half of the year and was then released in the autumn, slightly later than had been previously intimated to the fan clubs. Mark was well aware that promotion was all important to any of his father's contemporary musical endeavours, especially after his most recent album, *Carrying A Torch*, had fallen so flat in the few countries where it had been released. Quite rightly Mark decided to go for broke with the new project, and the publicity started months before recording was complete, with Tom and his son filmed routining the music in Larrabee Studios, Los Angeles; for better or for worse the very same site that had seen the making of *Carrying A Torch*. One thing was decided from the outset: whatever the musical outcome, the new album would be released in the US market – Tom's first new material there for an incredible six years.

Following on from Tom's on-going trend of collaborations with The Art Of Noise, Van Morrison and New Model Army, he and Mark decided to go the same route, but with a different twist for the new album. This time, Tom would 'collaborate' with a different producer on each track.

It was essentially up to Tom who he chose to work with and he made his selections purely on the basis of the bands he liked. Trevor Horn, renowned for his work with ABC, Frankie Goes To Hollywood, and more recently Seal, was the first producer requested by Tom, followed in swift succession by Flood (U2, Nine Inch Nails), Teddy Riley (Michael

Jackson, Bobby Brown) and a host of others.

"We went for these producers, the ones we knew were exceptional and making records today," said Tom, of the next stage of negotiations. "They in turn picked from the material we had, and some of the songs came from the producers themselves." In broad terms, the music agreed on (some covers, some originals) embrace three major marketing bases – contemporary dance, alternative rock and modern adult-orientated-rock.

Tom expressed his wishes on the cover versions he wanted to record, and ended up singing Yazoo's 'Situation' and 'A Girl Like You' by The Wolfgang Press, with whom Tom performed on a one-off gig later in October. Flood, also known as Mark Ellis, produced 'A Girl Like You'. "I was given a choice from 20 songs, and I picked the one that stuck out by a mile, the only one worthy of doing anything with," he recalls. "To me doing something like this is very much a challenge because you have someone who is almost stereotypical of a certain style . . . you had to make sure you could bring something new to it."

Once recording was under way, Tom's next task was to find a suitably snappy title for the project. *The Lead And How To Swing It* did not exactly roll off the tongue, and when Tom proudly settled on it as a definite he found he had to explain its meaning on every single occasion. It is based on an enigmatic saying often uttered by Tom's late father, and 'Lead' is lead as in metal, as opposed to say, the lead instrument of an orchestra, which was a common misconception. "It's a way of explaining something," Tom patiently reiterated, over and over again. "This is the lead and here is how to swing it. If you've got a problem, tackle it. Well, *I'm* saying – these are the songs and here's how I sing them."

Another unusual feature of the album was the cover, which memorably depicts Tom in a vibrant red plastic outfit on the reverse, but most outstandingly, standing screaming in a string vest and Sta-Prest trousers on the front. Apparently the photographer's concept was for Tom to wear clothes reminiscent of working on a building site, in order to tie in with both the title and his previous employment prior to megastardom. This did not really go very far to explaining just why a bikini-clad girl was present in the pictures alongside Tom . . .

Tom was delighted with the results of both the music and the design, not least because he had been so personally involved. "It's been a long time since I made a great album," he said to *Sunday Times Magazine* journalist Robin Eggar in 1994. "Not since the Sixties. I can sing anything but whatever I do, I inject soul into it, so it has to be hot." Although the album certainly had its moments, particularly with Trevor Horn's brilliant 'If I Only Knew', as a whole it must be said it suffers due to the lack of continuity brought about by using several different producers.

The Lead And How To Swing It was released on November 26, 1994, six weeks after the first single, 'If I Only Knew'. The album reached 55 in the UK but made no impact on the US market at all. Australian fans were rewarded for their long support of Tom with a second bonus CD featuring highlights of a live London concert, comprising 'Unbelievable', 'Take Me To The River', 'Walking In Memphis', 'Green Green Grass Of Home', 'It's Not Unusual' and 'Kiss'. Two singles were lifted in promotion for the regular album, the veritable opus of 'If I Only Knew' and 'I Want To Get Back With You', a duet with Tori Amos produced by Richard Perry and Thom Panunzio.

The story of 'If I Only Knew' as far as Trevor Horn is concerned began with a simple phone call. "Jimmy Iovine had just signed Tom to Interscope Records and they were looking for a single," Trevor remembers today. "Jimmy had this very obscure rap track and it had that hook, [sings] 'If I Only Knew'. Jimmy asked me if maybe I'd do something with it, because he said if I could make it into a single, I could have Tom on ZTT Records outside of America. It was an interesting proposition for me. I'd always been a bit of a fan of Tom."

The song had originally appeared on the eponymous 1992 début album by the American group Rise Robots Rise. Trevor's first job was to address the expletives within the song's original lyrics and make them suitable for a mainstream release by Tom Jones. "I took all that stuff out and re-wrote bits of the rap. I think the original thing wasn't even called 'If I Only Knew' – the hook only came up at one point in it and there were three or four rap verses, so instead we came up with the whole idea of Tom going up the Himalayan mountain."* Trevor's new chorus ran along the lines, 'Up north where the snow grows colder I travel onward 'cross the border/ Looked up a girl that I once knew frozen I found that I was chosen to be the follower of the deity.'

Having established the way in which he wanted to produce the song, Trevor invited Tom round to his Bel Air house and played him the basic rhythm track. The two wondered at that stage whether it would be feasible for the 54-year-old singer to include the rap in his version. Tom tried his best, but the results were initially unsatisfactory. "Although Tom had sung the chorus brilliantly, he hadn't quite got some of the phrasing in the rapping (as I wouldn't really expect him to), so I did something I'd never done before. I sort of re-shaped some of his vocals so that they sat more in time, so that they were more like a rap." After two months of hard work he met up again with Tom, this time at Trevor's Sarm West studios

---

* From its initial conception by Rise Robots Rise, the song had in fact been titled 'If I Only Knew'.

in London, England. Tentatively he played Tom the vocal changes, which greatly pleased the singer, and together they redid all the vocals with Tom eagerly learning from Trevor's demo.

"I must say I found Tom incredibly easy to work with," reflects Trevor about the actual recording. "He was a little bit edgy at first but then he just went for it. It was very impressive. He took to it like a duck to water. If he really wanted to rap it probably wouldn't take him long to learn how to do it."

One product of the very first meeting at Trevor's house was the extraordinary bloodcurdling scream that introduces the track. "It was a sort of ad-lib that Tom did, but I liked it so I joined about three of them together so it held an incredibly long note. I thought it was almost like a male animal making a sexual noise that it was ready to mate! The funny thing is when I saw Tom do the song in Vegas, he'd really worked on that because he said to me, 'I'm gonna be able to do that part when you see me do this live.' I said, 'I'll be very surprised if you can because it's actually three takes put together!' I did it so you can't hear the joins." Much to Trevor's surprise Tom has since trained himself to sustain the full-on howl for his live performances.

If there are two songs that symbolise why Tom is regarded as hip today, they are 'If I Only Knew', with its tighter than tight brass, relentless funky beat and almost irreconcilable rap, and the similarly super-cool 'Kiss'. It is interesting to note that Trevor Horn has been linked to Anne Dudley since their acclaimed production team took over the pop world of the early Eighties, leading to Trevor's label ZTT housing The Art Of Noise at the beginning of their career. 'If I Only Knew' narrowly missed the Top 10, charting at number 11 in the UK on November 12, 1994 – Tom's last hit of this stature had been 'Kiss' at number 5 in 1988.

Much to Trevor's disappointment (and to the potential detriment of Tom's career), Jimmy Iovine changed his mind about releasing Tom to ZTT for territories outside North America. "I had terrible fights with Interscope after that about really getting him onto ZTT," Trevor says ruefully. Further problems were to haunt the track as the song's composers, Joe Mendelson and Ben Nitze, were unhappy with their 70 per cent royalties and set about claiming sole authorship, stating: "Apart from six minor word changes, Tom Jones' version is substantially identical to the original. We were extremely pleased that he covered it so well, but the credits should be the same as in the US, where the writers get sole authorship." After threatened litigation the matter was resolved and the track was credited to Mendelson and Nitze's group, Rise Robots Rise.

Finally taking note of his previous success with 'Kiss', the single release for 'If I Only Knew' was accompanied by a trendy, amusing video showing clips of a youth watching Tom on television and operating the 'Lazee-Walker™'; an automatic dog-walking system whereby the dogs' leashes were attached to an inter-linking overhead track winding around the local neighbourhood.

The follow-up single to 'If I Only Knew' was 'I Wanna Get Back With You', a ballad which featured Tori Amos' vocals on the chorus, although it was generally described as a 'duet'. In the same month that *The Lead And How To Swing It* was released, Tori's current album, *Under The Pink*, was certified platinum, and a joint appearance of Tori and Tom could only have benefited him. However the pair were never seen together, either in Tom's promotional video for the duet, or performing live on stage. Without a visual union of this strength, the single completely failed to chart.

Although Tom missed out on capitalising on Tori's success and standing, he now became quite vocal about another female pop star with whom he would have liked to share a microphone. Apparently his admiration for Madonna was reciprocated. "We're signed to the same record label," he said to the Birmingham *Evening Mail* in November 1994. "When she heard that one of the ladies who works for the company was coming to see me Madonna said, 'You just gotta get me an autograph.' So I sent my picture to her – and in return, she sent a signed CD to me. I'd like to work with her because I think she's a very bright and ballsy lady . . . If fame happens, it happens. But with her it was calculated. She trained for stardom. She learned to sing, she learned to dance. I admire her for that." Given Tom's traditional views, it was highly unusual for him to be quite so praising of a female contemporary.

Tom toured England in November, performing at the Birmingham NEC on Saturday 14th to enthusiastic audiences. Earlier that day he had arrived at the Priory Square shopping centre in an open-topped bus and switched on the town's Christmas lights, raising money for the intensive care unit at the local children's hospital.

From Birmingham to Berlin Tom continued to enjoy his revived cult status and was invited to host the first MTV European Music Awards from Germany's capital on November 24. The event was staged at the Pariser Platz against the backdrop of the Brandenburg Gate. Tom particularly enjoyed starring in the TV advert for the award ceremony in which he let his sense of humour shine through, dressing up as Aerosmith star Steve Tyler, Icelandic singer Björk and Prince. "The stars themselves weren't available for the commercial so we thought it would be fun for me to do impressions of them," he joked to the press. "The Björk look – complete with hair buns and baggy jumper was my personal favourite. I'm even thinking of keeping the hairstyle on a permanent basis."

Among the stars that attended the event was the British boy band Take

That who collected the trophy for the best group. Robbie Williams, one of the band's young singers who was at that stage thinking of embarking on a solo career, was particularly impressed to be mingling with the likes of Tom Jones. "It was about that time that I decided that I could drink lots," laments Robbie today. "He had been drinking until about three or four o'clock in the morning and he looked like the front cover of *Health & Fitness* magazine and I looked like 'Garbage Bins Monthly'. That was the first time I really realised that he was a legend."

Although Tom's professional image had been sharply smartened up by Mark and Donna, deep down he had not changed his wicked ways, at least as far as the press were concerned. Reports had surfaced the previous year that Tom had broken off a sporadic two-year affair with blonde Texan Nicole Hall, who had been just 18 when they met. After the success of 'If I Only Knew', Tom was then linked to 23-year-old dancer, Lisa Edwards, who followed the well-trodden steps of many a spurned lover and enjoyed her 15 minutes of fame, boasting to the *News Of The World* about the 25 condoms Tom had ordered on room service at the Park Lane Hotel in Mayfair.

In 1995 Tom made a brief guest appearance in a James Melkonian directed film called *The Jerky Boys*, starring comedians Kamal Ahmed and Johnny Brennan. Tom's spot takes place in a nightclub with the two stars looking on as he sings 'Are You Gonna Go My Way', a massive UK hit for Lenny Kravitz in February 1993. Tom has since adopted this song as his own including it in most of his live performances.

Early in the year Tom duetted with Dwight Yoakam on 'The Last Time' at the House Of Blues on March 8, which was televised on American TV on March 31. He also performed at the opening night of the Coconut Grove supper club in San Francisco on March 27, the club charging diners $500 per head to raise money to fight leukaemia. Tom then appeared at concerts in Ostende fundraising for handicapped children on May 24 and 25.

But by far Tom's most celebrated one-off appearance this year was for veteran Hollywood performer Bruce Willis' surprise 40th birthday celebration weekend. On April 8 and 9, Bruce's wife, actress Demi Moore invited 140 relatives and celebrity friends including Arnold Schwarzenegger, Geena Davis, Mike Myers, Clint Eastwood and Woody Harrelson to a spectacular party. Previously, when Bruce had thrown a party for his wife, he had hired an entire amusement park for the occasion, so everyone involved wondered what on earth Demi would do to top it. Sparing no expense, Demi flew all her guests out to Dynomite Lounge in Ketchum Sun Valley, Idaho for a weekend of winter sports.

As Bruce's favourite performer is Tom, Demi chose 'What's New

Pussycat' as the theme for the whole affair, and everyone received a commemorative black baseball cap with the song's catchphrase title printed on it. Tom's appearance was kept secret prior to the occasion. He recalls: "[Bruce's] wife, Demi Moore called my office and asked if I would sing at the party. She put the whole thing together as a surprise. I did about an hour and 10 minute show and then Bruce came on stage and we sang 'Midnight Hour' and 'Great Balls Of Fire' together. Bruce also played harmonica. It was great fun."

Again mixing with other stars, Tom was next involved in a competition to help raise money for the National Trust's Centenary along with Phil Collins, Sting, Michael Caine, Sean Connery, Joanna Lumley and Elizabeth Taylor among others. Seventy celebrities in total were given a blank white T-shirt and invited to doodle on it in the style of their own choosing. The collection, which became known as 'Off Your Back', was then auctioned by Phillips at Dyrham Park near Bath on September 28. Tom's highly imaginative design of a Dalmatian drawn entirely from dots was held up as a shining example of creativity, unlike actor Hugh Grant who was criticised for simply scrawling 'lots of love from Hugh Grant'.

Pressing on with what he knew best, Tom embarked on a mammoth tour entitled 'Three Decades Of Cool' in the autumn of 1995. The trip encompassed the ubiquitous US domestic dates, Tom's first return to Japan in 21 years and a comprehensive tour of Australia.

Shortly after the tour yet another sex scandal broke worldwide in the tabloid press. This time he had supposedly been involved in a three-way orgy with actress Michelle Ferrara aged 27, and her 21-year-old model friend Linda Johnson, whom he had met at a nightclub and taken back to his suite at the Ritz Carlton Hotel in Sydney, Australia. Just months after their encounter Michelle Ferrara sold her sordid story to the press although this meant explaining that Tom had refused to actually have full penetrative sex as he was terrified of catching AIDS.

As part of his annual medical test every January for insurance purposes, Tom is reputedly required to take an AIDS test. He himself admits, "If someone's going to have sex, then it should be . . . safe. Not that the AIDS scare is going to stop me kissing. There's no evidence to show it can be passed on by kissing." When Tom appeared as a guest on Emma Freud's programme *Pillow Talk*, he spoke openly about how Linda used to give him free reign with other women as long as she never found out. But now, he continued, with reference to the AIDS crisis she says, "don't do it because you can kill yourself and me."

On *Ray Martin At Midday* during the same period, Tom revealed that, contrary to earlier statements, his voice is actually insured each year with Lloyds of London. He explained that if it was damaged temporarily then he would be paid for the missed work but if he lost his voice permanently, the compensation would run into millions.

Although by all accounts Tom was fighting fit, sadly by the end of 1995 his 82-year-old mother Freda had been taken ill with the onset of breast cancer and a series of strokes. Her dying wish was to return to Wales to spend her last days in familiar surroundings, so Tom set about looking for a suitable property in which to house his mother comfortably. Despite his efforts she had already deteriorated too much to make the tiring journey safely across the Atlantic and indeed was bed-ridden. Close cousin Kath Woodward reported on the traumatic turn of events. "Tom is shattered. He's making sure she is comfortable with the best care money can buy . . . he's always been so close to her and cries on the phone in calls back home. Freda's wish was to return home to live out her last days and Tom was negotiating to buy a bungalow. She is so ill that she cannot be moved and can barely recognise anyone."

Tom was distraught but still intended to fulfil her last request. "She is so proud of me still, and – though her mind wanders a bit – she still knows us all. She told us that she wants to be buried in Wales, and I shall get my father out of the ground in Los Angeles and take him back with her. That is what she wants, and that is what she will get."

As a reflection of the changing circumstances, Tom considered putting his Bel Air mansion on the market in December 1995. Mark and Donna were also planning to make the move back to England, where they would prefer their children to be educated. This was a sad end to the year and the Tom Terrific Fan Club, sensitive to Tom's personal situation, gave him a touching Christmas gift by naming a star after him.

Still, business had to plough on as usual and Tom's management arranged for him to join in the technical revolution and take part in an on-line interview broadcast over the internet. Late in December numerous websites began to emerge featuring Tom. They marked the first stirrings of a brand new fan base.

★   ★   ★

One former fan remained singularly unimpressed with Tom's career revival and was determined to let the world know. Katherine Berkery, who had successfully won her paternity suit against the singer in 1989, felt that their son Jonathan should also reap the benefits of Tom's recent change of fortunes.

Katherine, now the manager of a home furnishing business and living in Fort Lauderdale on Florida's east coast, had recommenced her media campaign back in 1994, re-selling her story of love and rejection to the tabloids. Although Tom's one-off settlement and subsequent monthly maintenance instalments had enabled Katherine to buy a house and send Jonathan to private school, part of her new argument was that her son needed to know who his father was, and he couldn't understand why Tom didn't visit or even call. The timing of her tabloid splash was cleverly based around Jonathan's sixth birthday and the papers pictured the singer's illegitimate child with a toy microphone.

Speaking out for the first time since the well-publicised legal proceedings, Katherine made her feelings clear. "Jonathan may well not exist as far as Tom is concerned," she told Caroline Graham. "It makes me mad when I read interviews with Tom about how important the family is to him. That's rubbish. *We* are his family, too, but he doesn't give a flying damn about us."

Katherine had spent time in deep discussion with her new lawyer, Howard Weiss, and together they stunned the Tom Jones camp with an appeal to increase his monthly payments. Soon enough, a Florida judge ruled that the original 1989 New York Agreement was in fact void in the sun-kissed state and could be retried. The case duly went to court on April 23, 1996 where Florida's Fourth District Court of Appeals sided with Tom in a bid to keep his financial records private, but approved Katherine's petition for increased financial help for her son.

Once again, although Tom was forced to accept the court's decision, he continued to deny the claim that he was the child's father. This further incensed Katherine, who continued to express her implausible demands to the press. "I don't want Tom to come into Jonathan's life as a part-time father. If he wants to see him now it has to be regular."

Tom had not been present at the hearing and during the spring period had been busy working on a new album for Interscope. In complete contrast to his last project which comprised slickly produced pop, Tom set about recording a set of authentic-sounding covers of classic soul and R&B songs. They included 'Can't Stand Up For Falling Down', 'Do Right By Me', 'Trick Or Treat', 'Down To The Nightclub' and 'Do You Get What You Deserve'. Particularly excited, as the project was his own idea, Tom boasted to the press that it would be: "More soulful, with lots of leakage and distortion. The big problem for me is always finding the right songs. My versatility sometimes goes against it. It's a handicap."

Overseen by producer Steve Jordan, Tom launched into the recording sessions with vigour, giving his chosen collection of material the full big band treatment with brass, strings, backing singers and an exciting rhythm section. The personnel included Waddy Wachtel and Cornell Dupree on guitar, Bernie Worrell on keyboards and bassist Pino Paladino. Producer Steve Jordan also played drums and The Memphis Horns were also lined up and arranged by Willie Witchell.

The album was recorded at New York's Hit Factory, with most of the musicians playing live to tape together. Despite Tom's enthusiasm for the music, to his disgust Interscope failed to see it as a commercially viable product and refused to release it. There then began an extended series of negotiations and the argument dragged on for quite some while.

Tom felt bitterly let down by his record company and complained vociferously in the press. "Well, it is disappointing when you do an album like this," he griped to the *Sun-Herald* in 1997. "We were in the studio having a great time, making a bunch of great music, and I'd get into the booth and listen back to what we were doing and it was like, 'Shit, yeah, this is happening, this is the real deal.' I was really excited about it, I thought it was going to be great." He continued the story in the *Ottawa Citizen*, explaining the record company's unexpected reaction. "Interscope was not thrilled. The thing is, because of my voice, we wanted songs that were powerful, with interesting lyrics. We got to the end of it and we had 26 songs on tape. It should have been, perhaps, 10 or 11 for a proper record, but Steve and I couldn't decide which ones to cut, so we sent them the whole thing."

Interscope, a label famous for its contemporary chart-hitting sounds, weren't prepared for an album of straight R&B standards. "They called it 'too authentic' which sounds strange but I can understand what they are getting at. I mean, these are the Nineties and, as much fun as the songs were to record, I can see that they may not be the sort of thing people want to listen to."

But Tom's main bone of contention was that Interscope had given him free rein to record his follow up to *The Lead And How To Swing It*, yet had not provided him with any guidelines as to what they might and might not release. "The disappointment is for the time spent on it, you can't help but think you've wasted your time. Also, Interscope told me to do whatever I wanted on this album. So where was someone during the recording saying, 'Well, we don't have a single here yet'? Why the hell wasn't someone there?"

As time progressed, it was apparent that the two parties had reached a stalemate. "They told me they'd put it out, but they weren't very enthusiastic about it. I thought that if they'd put it out they'd just throw it out there. We've asked to be released from our contract and they've agreed." This material has sadly remained unreleased to date, but more to the point, despite his hearty comeback with 'If I Only Knew', the dependably bankable Tom Jones was left high and dry without a record contract.

Fortunately another project was waiting in the wings to take his mind off his shelved album. Tim Burton, film director and producer of classics such as *Beetlejuice*, the first two *Batman* films and *Nightmare Before Christmas*, teamed up with scriptwriter Jonathan Gems to create the first movie to be inspired by a 1962 series of bubblegum cards, *Mars Attacks!* Tim was a well-known fan of Tom's, often using his songs in films (notably *Edward Scissorhands*, which features three of the Welshman's hits), and had always dreamt of casting Tom in one of his movies.

"Tim and Jonathan both really like Tom Jones. Tom epitomises performers in Las Vegas and was really cool at the time," says Jeanne McCarthy from the casting team, who all went to see Tom in concert at the Universal Amphitheater. Afterwards Tim went backstage to outline his proposal, which would essentially be Tom's big-screen début. Tom was beside himself with excitement and immensely flattered by the attention. "To have a director like Tim come to my show and then approach me about a script and ask if I'd like to do it was a bonus. It's gratifying to get the thumbs up from the young people. They tell me I'm awesome, and I'm the man and I'm telling you it's a great feeling after all these years."

Demands on Tom to 'act' in *Mars Attacks!* were limited however, as once again he was literally asked to play himself. But his importance within the film was vital. "I play a bit of a hero in it. The Martians come into the showroom where I am singing, and I lead people to safety," he explained. Here Tom sells himself short, for he also single-handedly flies a plane carrying the leading lady as the planet explodes around him. He remains the last man standing, rather dubiously, clutching an eagle and petting a baby deer, watching a new day dawn from a cliff top, before the familiar strains of 'It's Not Unusual' signify the close of the film.

The accompanying cast consisted of a tremendous list of Hollywood A-list members including Jack Nicholson, Glenn Close, Danny De Vito, Michael J. Fox and Pierce Brosnan. "It was a little risky to have 22 lead roles but . . . it looks stupid just to have a handful of people fighting a huge global invasion," said Jonathan Gems. Financing so many top drawer fees would have been virtually impossible and so each star agreed to receive a slice of the profits rather than a set fee for his or her appearances.

Tom again thoroughly enjoyed the film-making process, even though this time he was involved in an on-set mishap. "They used real explosives for filming. One bang was more powerful than expected – and it set my hair on fire," he revealed. "When I mentioned to the director what had happened, he said, 'Well, you'd better be even more on your guard tomorrow because we're using flame throwers.' I think that remark showed that there's not much sentiment in movie making. There is an awful lot of money involved and people are constantly concerned with the bottom line." Perhaps Tom's brush with Hollywood had finally quenched his thirst for acting, leaving a slightly bitter aftertaste.

Despite all the celebrity roles and extravagant special effects, *Mars*

Attacks! opened on December 13 in America and Boxing Day in the UK to mixed reviews. Some critics loved the cult vibe of the bizarre star-studded offering, but Stephen Dalton panned Tim Burton's latest offering: "It should have been a blazing satire on pre-millennial alien paranoia and sharp reinvention on Z-grade monster movie themes with Nicholson relishing his multiple comic roles, while raygun-toting Martians wipe out mankind . . . Hugely enjoyable though it may be in parts, *Mars Attacks!* is a messy, soulless, runaway, headless dinosaur of a movie."

After all the excitement had died down, Tom busied himself with an 'odd job' or two to tide him over while he was without a record label. He appeared in a high-profile British television advertisement for the sports clothing company, Reebok, which was estimated would net the children's charity Barnado's close to £1 million. More than a dozen famous names including Sting, Sir Richard Attenborough, Jarvis Cocker and Robbie Williams appeared together in the £4.5 million production, which features the football-crazed stars dreaming of being soccer personality Ryan Giggs for the day.

Tom returned to Australia during the month of April, and guested on numerous chat shows, also duetting with Australian singer John Farnham on 'A Long Way To The Top' at the 35th Annual Logies (a television award ceremony). The singers then presented the award for Australian Top TV Personality of the Year to Ray Martin. Over the summer months Tom then continued to tour extensively, including appearances in British venues.

Unsurprisingly, Tom was invited to perform at the 75th Royal Variety Performance which was filmed at London's Dominion Theatre and screened in the UK on November 10. Tom was the star guest of the event, performing a total of five numbers alongside Lionel Richie, Joan Rivers and Eternal in the presence of Prince Charles. The Prince had recently been hitting the headlines with the failure of his marriage to Princess Diana, and Tom was quite outspoken on this issue. "I still try to keep up appearances because I want to hold my marriage together," he said candidly to the *Radio Times*. "It's a shame what's happened to the Royal Family. It must be a big pressure to live a squeaky clean life, but if you're Royal that's the job and you have to do it. I think they've let themselves down. I didn't like that Princess Di interview on *Panorama*. When she started talking about those other guys I thought, 'My God, this is the Princess of Wales.' I would never go on television and spill my guts like that." Tom evidently failed to spot the double-standard; the constant stream of his quotations in the press, freely admitting his own affairs with Mary Wilson, Marjorie Wallace and others, and discussing his own lax marital 'arrangements'.

By the end of 1996, over 20 years after he had first arrived in California, Tom had finalised plans for putting his Bel Air home up for sale. The asking price on the property ranged in reports variously from £3 million to $7.9 million. Tom had undoubtedly experienced some good times playing Lord of the Manor at Dean Martin's old residence, but had somehow never seemed to fit in despite the numerous photo shoots posing in and around the building. "Last January at the American Music Awards I met the fella who lives next door – a show business lawyer – and he said we should definitely get together one night," said Tom in December 1996. "I haven't seen him since. I suppose I could make an effort, but I like to be with the family when I am in Los Angeles and don't need to search for anything else."

It was no great secret that Linda had been unhappy in Bel Air before she returned to Cowbridge for the majority of her time. Although the couple had previously seen each other only on a 'visiting' rather than a 'cohabiting' basis due to the tax bill Tom might face on re-entering the UK, now it didn't seem to be an issue. Rumours began to circulate at this point that Tom would be returning to his homeland and leaving sunny California behind once and for all.

There were other reasons prompting Tom's desire to uproot from his adopted US home. "The riots five years ago scared the hell out of me," he admitted. "Parts of the city are like the Third World. I've lived there for years, but I've never seen anything as bad. Mark doesn't want his children growing up in Los Angeles and I agree with that . . . Mark wants his children to go to schools in Britain so it means that I will have to come home if I want to be near my grandchildren."

To round off the year on a more pleasant note, Tom filmed a TV special entitled *One Night Only*; a live, studio-based concert with guest performances from Mark Knopfler, Bryn Terfel and Toni Braxton. Tom showcased three decades of hits from 'It's Not Unusual' through to 'If I Only Knew', and also sang some of the contemporary tracks he had by now incorporated into his current concerts; 'Are You Gonna Go My Way' and 'Take Me To The River'. The programme was directed by Declan Lowney, who had previously worked with Tom on *Live At This Moment*, and aired over Christmas in the UK, later released on home video for all to enjoy. The video includes three bonus tracks not featured on the television broadcast and stands as a fine example of a mature entertainer at his best and sparkling in concert.

Over the same Christmas period, the *Green Green Grass Of Home* documentary was also broadcast to celebrate the 30th anniversary of the release of the song. New interviews with Peter Sullivan, Vernon Hopkins and Tommy Pittman were interspersed with footage of Tom's neighbours, family and school friends, reminiscing about Tom's Welsh background and phenomenal rise to superstardom. The finer nuances of the title song were also analysed, with natives of Pontypridd going as far as to suggest that the 'Mary' of the lyrics may have been a member of a local family, when the song was in fact penned by Claude Curly Putnam Jr. many years before Tom's own cover version. If nothing else, this documentary certainly proved just how much the people of Wales had taken 'Green Green Grass Of Home' to their hearts.

Tom Jones Enterprises started off 1997 with a bang, formally announcing that only two of the fan clubs remaining in America after the 1989 culling were officially endorsed by Tom's management. They were named as Tom Boosters and the Tom Terrific Fan Club, while the Tom Jones Appreciation Society continued as the authoritative organisation in the UK. Yet approval did not mean that any of these clubs received regular advance notification of Tom's movements or indeed any other typical fan club privileges. The newsletters often rely on press cuttings and news sent in by fans around the world, and are then padded out with the usual competitions, pictures and titbits. They provide as good a service as they are able, but it is odd for a star's management not to promote their personality via fan club circulars.

Tom and Linda were busy celebrating their 40th wedding anniversary when reports wildly overestimated the couple's fortune to be somewhere between £100 million and $459 million, placing Tom as Britain's third wealthiest rock star after Paul McCartney and David Bowie. Ridiculous as it might seem considering this speculation, Tom was still without a record contract and continued to accept short term projects to maintain his cash flow.

The advert for the 'Angels' underwear range from the Victoria's Secret chain of lingerie shops was perhaps the most enjoyable odd job for Tom. His role was to play 'God', taking charge of half a dozen 'angels', all of them supermodels clad only in skimpy lingerie. Tom was only too pleased to relive the 'difficulties' they encountered during filming when he appeared on various chat shows. "Well these girls are six foot tall to start with and on the day wear big heels, you see. So, I'm standing there for photographs, you know, I'm five foot ten and a half inches and then you know, maybe six foot with shoes . . ." Daniella Pestova, Tyra Banks, Karen Mulder and Stephanie Seymour from the advert were hungrily photographed by the press when they accompanied a smug looking Tom to a New York show business party.

Tom was fortunate to be invited to work on a far-reaching musical project during this time as it was the only way he was able to appear on a record after the unsatisfactory split from Interscope. Anne Dudley was heavily involved in the British film *The Full Monty* as the musical producer, orchestrator and remixer. The low budget film was about a group of unemployed Sheffield steel workers who turn to stripping as a livelihood when the factory closes down. Originally the climax of the movie featured the Joe Cocker version of 'You Can Leave Your Hat On', but it came across as a little old-fashioned and Tom seemed an ideal candidate to add a bucketload of his distinctive masculinity to the soundtrack.

Having previously worked with Tom to immense success, Anne initially approached Mark Woodward to ask if his superstar father would like to update the song for the film. "Mark thought that we were definitely going down market," she reveals today, referring to the cheap and cheerful nature of the project. "He said to me afterwards, 'Had it not been you we wouldn't have entertained it at all!' " Despite his usual heavy touring schedule Tom managed to find a free day to attend the recording session in Newcastle and between them they produced an outstanding cover of the Randy Newman original.

Both the film and single were released at the end of the summer 1997 to unanimous acclaim from critics and public alike. The album's sales soon went gold in the UK, America, Italy and New Zealand, achieving platinum and multi-platinum awards for sales in Spain, Australia, Singapore and Canada, and ultimately winning an Oscar for Best Original Musical or Comedy Score.

In sharp contrast to this overwhelming success, Tom was dogged by throat troubles during August and September, forcing him to cancel two months of shows. Initially the singer was diagnosed as having a bad attack of laryngitis, but it soon emerged that he was suffering with a burned vocal chord from acid-reflux. Tom took the time to explain this affliction on chat shows towards the end of the year. "I had what's called reflux in the stomach. It's like a gas acid build-up and it came up in the middle of the night, and it got onto my vocal chord. So it actually burned my right vocal chord." The doctor advised Tom not to talk, drink or smoke for a while in order to recover properly.

By October Tom was fit enough to participate in a BBC single simultaneously intended to justify the expense of a TV licence and benefit their related charity Children In Need. Former Velvet Underground luminary turned New York low-life chronicler Lou Reed allowed the television channel to use his 25-year-old song 'Perfect Day' free of charge and all the musicians waived their royalties in favour of the needy charity.

The performance comprised 27 well-known singers including Reed himself, Bono, David Bowie, Susanne Vega, Elton John, Boyzone and Tom, whose one line is heard in the closing chorus. Tom flew to London in between dates on his current American tour to record and film his contribution for the accompanying video at the BBC TV Centre. The stylish film interspersed shots of the stars with clips from sunrise to sunset at the scenic Hampton Court Gardens, embodying a perfect day. The single raised £1 million within its first three weeks of sale, going straight to number one in the British charts.

While Tom's management reshuffled the concerts he'd missed due to the acid-reflux, the singer was asked to make a personal appearance in November at a private party akin to Bruce Willis' birthday. The celebrity was Mel Gibson, but this time the surprise was for the guests, not the host. "His wife threw a party for him and she asked if I would go along with my band and play," marvelled Tom. "I said, 'Is it his birthday?' And she said, 'No, just a party.' Mel came in to see me before I went on and told me the guests didn't know about the surprise."

In November Tom's friend Michael Hutchence, the extrovert frontman with INXS, died in ambiguous circumstances in an Australian hotel room. Eight days after his death, the funeral was held on November 27 at St Andrew's Cathedral in the heart of Sydney, with a PA system broadcasting the ceremony to the thousands of mourners in the adjoining square. The 2,000 strong congregation was littered with celebrities, including Kylie Minogue, Jason Donovan, Helena Christianson, Diana Ross and Tom, who had become firm friends with Michael a few years earlier.

Tom spent much of 1997, as ever, tirelessly touring. He performed 180 concert dates worldwide, commenting on the hectic schedule: "It's been a good year. It started off really well, I toured most of America. I went to Las Vegas five times. Two weeks at a time, as we spread the Vegas shows out these days." Along with the new songs Tom had embraced into his current set list, he had also over the last year or so taken on a fresh, new backing band to appeal to the younger generation. The tight knit group comprised Graham Ward on drums, Steve Spence on bass guitar, percussionist Sal Rodriguez, Wally Minko on keyboards and a brass section of Glen Berger, Matt Fronke and Fred Simmons. Three sassy new backing vocalists, Christi Black, Darelle Holden and Sharon Hendrix provided the flirtatious light entertainment in between tracks. It was far removed from the crew of the Seventies and the line-up was still prone to changes, somewhat lacking the former friendly continuity of days gone by.

20

RELOAD

NINETEEN NINETY-EIGHT proved to be to be the year when Tom truly received the recognition due a mature singer of his ilk who had so successfully reinvented himself. His public profile was boosted in an assortment of appearances early in the year. On January 11 he presented the People's Choice Award for Lifetime Achievement to Whoopi Goldberg. The televised ceremony touched the hearts of fans of both celebrities, as Tom took the popular actress/comedienne by the hand and led her to the stage, simultaneously serenading her with 'She's A Lady'. Tom then rekindled his friendship with Jonathan Ross, making a joint presentation at the Annual Comedy Awards Show. Tom also took the opportunity to remind the audience of his latest venture, 'You Can Leave Your Hat On'.

The same song was again plugged on January 17 when Tom co-hosted the British National Lottery with camp compère, Dale Winton. As Tom announced the rollover jackpot totalled £14.3 million, he joked, "How many pints could you buy with a million pounds?" He then narrated a filmed report on how South Wales had changed due to lottery fund donations from the Arts Council to the Welsh College of Music and Drama, where Tom had previously received his honorary fellowship. He also interviewed three athletes from Pontypridd whose ambitions had been furthered by individual lottery grants. Never one to miss a publicity opportunity, Tom closed the show by announcing a UK tour commencing later that year in November.

At the annual BRIT awards celebrating British pop music on April 12, Tom and Hugo Spears, who played the character of 'Lunchbox' in *The Full Monty*, together collected the award for Best Selling Soundtrack. "I'd like to thank Miss Anne Dudley for asking me to be part of *The Full Monty*, and getting me to record 'You Can Leave Your Hat On'," said Tom in his acceptance speech. "I would like to say that it is great to be a part of *The Full Monty* because not only is it the biggest British movie ever made — it's also the best," he concluded to the backdrop of flying knickers.

But the real highlight was when he duetted with Robbie Williams on 'You Can Leave Your Hat On', followed by 'Land Of 1000 Dances' and Steve Harley & Cockney Rebel's 'Make Me Smile'.

No-one who witnessed this incredible combination of masculine sexuality and adulation was likely to forget it. Robbie was clad provocatively all in black leather and high-heeled boots, an outfit reminiscent of Tom's own youth. "It was inspired by Tom, he did wear it once," Robbie laughs, "even down to the Cuban stacks!" Robbie's dancing was also very much part of the act, as his exaggerated pelvic thrusting both imitated and idolised his childhood inspiration. "He *was* a bit flirtatious," Tom later admitted. "I think Robbie Williams is great, and I get off on the respect of young performers." At the ceremony, comedian Ben Elton aptly rounded off the raucous performance by describing the pairing as, "Two of Britain's premier pop muscles in action."

"It was quite a magical evening," says Robbie. "It was absolutely amazing. People say that even heroes can let you down, but he didn't, it was just like, 'Wow! You're Tom Jones and you're amazing!' He was just outrageously brilliant." Robbie was so taken with what became known as *The Full Monty* medley that it was used as the B-side for his upcoming single, 'Let Me Entertain You'. Following the collaboration Robbie and Tom were to be seen together several times on television in hefty promotion of their respective careers. "We did loads of interviews with each other and we were like a double act, it was very funny," Robbie remembers.

The BRIT Awards had gained much media attention ever since the Jarvis Cocker incident in 1996, when the Pulp frontman attempted to upstage Michael Jackson in protest against his Christ-like posturing, dropping his trousers in the process. But this year the limelight had undoubtedly been stolen by Tom and Robbie and the ripples made by their impact continued to circulate for some time. "When Tom Jones and Robbie hit the stage, the ceremony came alive," wrote TV critic Caroline Garbett. "Their fabulous rendition of the hits from *The Full Monty* was a real treat, eclipsing even Fleetwood Mac's mini concert. If only we'd had two hours of Tom and Robbie – now that really would have hit the headlines."

There were suggestions that the partnership might reconvene in the months that followed. "If *The Tom Jones Story* is ever made," fantasised Tom to chat show host Des O'Connor, "I think Robbie Williams would be the best person to play me. He'd be great, he's definitely got the energy and enthusiasm and even has some of the moves." When the idea was put to Robbie, his response was typically reverent. "It is an absolutely amazing accolade. It's quite phenomenal that he should say that."

Another megastar to pay his respects to Tom this year was the Godfather of Funk, James Brown. On May 1, 1998 he attended Tom's show at the MGM Grand. Tom spotted James Brown among the sea of faces and greeted him from the stage, crying out, "I feel good!" When James egged him on with, "Do it, do it!" Tom obliged with a rousing rendition of 'I Got You (I Feel Good)'. Another musical celebrity, Neil Diamond, was also in the audience and similarly introduced, but this time without a song. Following the show the three stars met backstage in Tom's dressing room prompting a flurry of headlines. "You know," Neil Diamond quipped to *Rolling Stone*, "we're thinking of touring stadiums as the Three Baritones."

Two weeks later the music world was saddened by the loss of one of Tom's great mentors and friends, Frank Sinatra, who died of poor health on May 14. Tom was devastated. "We used to play Las Vegas together . . . He'd always been very polite and very nice to me. Very gracious." Frank Sinatra's reciprocal admiration was once demonstrated when he stopped his own concert, spotting Tom among the audience, fondly announcing, "He's number one in the world today, and I'm his number one fan."

At the end of May Tom performed at the Grand Casino's Mari Center in Marksville, Louisiana. Earlier in the day he had been presented with a tribal necklace by the chairman of the Tunica-Biloxi Tribal Council and was now showing it off. "I've got this wonderful neck thing I was given," he said during the concert. "I'm wearing it. It was a gift and I think you should always wear the gifts you are given." Tom received another gift just one week later when Planet Hollywood gave him a leather bomber jacket to celebrate his 58th birthday. He performed a relaxed concert at the restaurant in Tennessee, before donating a signed stage shirt and a pair of trousers to add to their display of memorabilia from shows and movies.

Eighteen months after first putting his Bel Air mansion up for sale, a buyer was finally found when actor Nicolas Cage and his wife Patricia Arquette fell in love with the house that had once belonged to Dean Martin. After finalising the multi-million dollar deal, Tom's primary concern was the destiny of his beloved red telephone box from Pontypridd. When questioned on its fate, he replied, "[Nicolas Cage] had the pool area altered, so he has lifted the telephone box out of the ground. He was going to move it to another one of his houses, but I told him that if he doesn't want it, then I'll take it off his hands!"

Recent reports had suggested that Tom's next move would see a return to English shores to be closer to his son and family, who were now quietly residing in Henley-on-Thames, Oxfordshire. In the summer months of 1998 Tom surprised fans by investing in a new home on Mulholland Drive, Beverly Hills. This notorious celebrity hideaway in the mountains offers affluent seclusion behind luscious foliage, with the occasional glimpse of luxury peeping through the trees. Tom's $2.7 million acquisition boasted five bedrooms, a family room, formal dining room, library, a pool and spectacular views across Los Angeles. Despite the prosperous fraternity of the neighbourhood, Tom did not anticipate getting to know his new neighbours. "Everyone thinks that here in LA all the stars hang out together," he said, "but people have become more and more closed in. I've yet to find a clique that I can settle in with like I did in London 20 years ago."

On Sunday July 5, 1998 Tom was once again the main attraction at an all-star concert in aid of The Prince's Trust, entitled 'Party In The Park' to reflect its location in London's beautiful Hyde Park. Appearing alongside energetic young acts like Boyzone, All Saints and Natalie Imbruglia, Tom's half-hour set included 'Vaults Of Heaven', 'Hard To Handle', 'It's Not Unusual', 'Delilah', 'You Can Leave Your Hat On' and a puissant rendition of 'Kiss' in front of the 110,000 strong crowd.

At the party backstage after the event Tom upheld his reputation as a party animal, drinking many of the younger stars under the table. "I was there till five in the morning as usual, could have been six," he tried to remember in a later interview. "Of the other performers, I think only Boyzone were still at it. They're good lads, they enjoy a drink." Faced with an enormous hangover the following day he hobnobbed with the Prince of Wales himself at a special charity preview of the musical *Dr Doolittle* at the Apollo Theatre in Hammersmith, London. The 'upmarket' socialising continued with a contribution to the latest Andrew Lloyd Webber project, *Whistle Down The Wind*, for which Tom recorded a gospel-flavoured version of 'Vaults Of Heaven' with The Sounds Of Blackness Choir. The ensuing album heralded the launch of a new musical production and marked Andrew Lloyd Webber's 50th birthday.

As the autumn approached Tom finalised lengthy negotiations with two separate record companies, and after several lost years signed up with both Virgin Music's V2 label and Gut Records. In preparation for recording sessions for a new album, some of Tom's September concerts were cancelled in advance, citing recurrent respiratory problems as well as schedule.

Gut Records was a relatively young venture headed by former radio and TV plugger Guy Holmes. After initial success with Right Said Fred's novelty hit 'I'm Too Sexy', Gut built up a respectable reputation, nurturing promising new acts like the Liverpudlian band Space. Gut had already been partially responsible for the rise in Tom's career with the release of a certain single.

In March 1998, Tom's legendary status had received a further boost when Space teamed up with the Welsh vocalist from Catatonia, Cerys

Matthews, for 'The Ballad Of Tom Jones'. The song was written by Space frontman Tommy Scott, whose very name ironically conjures up Tom Jones' own previous incarnation from the days of The Senators. "I used to have a song years ago called 'A Little Tom Jones', and because I didn't make it that song just got lost," Tommy recalls today. "I always wanted to do a song about Tom Jones because I think he's brilliant."

Tommy had never been one for shying away from song plotlines that ventured slightly left of centre. "We'll never write ordinary love songs. We're more likely to write, 'I met a girl and she's in love with me so she poisoned my entire family.'" Typically 'The Ballad Of Tom Jones' revolved around a pair of feuding lovers who resolve their murderous intentions after hearing Tom singing on the radio. Their tribute to The Voice runs as follows: "You stopped us from killing each other, Tom Jones, Tom Jones . . . I owe my life to 'What's New Pussycat'; 'Delilah' stopped me hating you and wishing you were dead."

Found on Space's second album, *Tin Planet*, 'The Ballad Of Tom Jones' reached number four in the UK charts, aided by an eye-catching cinematic video. Suddenly Tom's name was everywhere again, but this time it was not his doing. When word reached him in America, he was highly amused and also flattered. "You know you're doing something right when they start recording songs about you," he joked. Tommy Scott then got the shock of his life during one promotional appearance with Cerys. "We did one of those morning TV shows, and he [Tom Jones] phoned us from Las Vegas. At first I didn't believe it was him, I thought it was a setup, but he said he loved it! That's when he said we'll have to get together and do another song. I thought he was just being polite . . ."

There was another link at this stage between the two Toms as Tom Jones had lately taken to covering Space's 1996 hit 'Female Of The Species' in his live sets. The irony of this choice was that Space had actually written the track with Tom's vocal style in mind. Tommy Scott didn't find out that his hero was incorporating the song into his performances until he actually attended one of the concerts: "I just couldn't believe it. My wife had bought me tickets to go and see him for my birthday. I didn't have a clue he was going to do that song, I heard the first few notes and I didn't even recognise it! I went, 'My God, he's playing "Female"!' The housewives next to me were all singing the song but they didn't have a clue who I was. I just thought it was brilliant."

Unfortunately Tom wasn't always lucky or astute enough to recognise a good opportunity when it presented itself, and during the year had turned down the option of recording the lead vocals for the Beautiful South's next single. The song in question, 'Perfect 10', turned out to be a smash hit, reaching number two in October 1998 with the band's lead singer,

Paul Heaton, doing his very best Tom Jones impersonation.

As it happened, Tom had been far too busy with the sale of Llwynddu House in Cowbridge for around £700,000, almost £100,000 less than his original asking price. Local estate agents, Watts & Morgan, had been given strict instructions not to advertise it publicly, and a spokesman for the firm said, "We were told to be very discreet in selling the property. I don't think Tom wanted hoards of fans flocking to the place pretending to be would-be buyers just to get a look at where he lived. There was a lot of interest in it and the purchasers are delighted with it."

The plan was for Tom and Linda to maintain only one residence; the new property in Mulholland Drive. Having resigned herself to yet another move, Linda resettled back into the American way of life, adding her own personal touches to her new home. "She likes to do her own decorating," says Marion Crewe, "putting her own things away; she's very artistic." The couple remained reluctant to rule out the possibility of ever returning to Britain on a more permanent basis, especially as Mark, Donna, Alexander and Emma showed no signs of returning to Los Angeles. First cousin Idris Jones maintains to this day: "Linda is over in America right now but I think that she and Tom will eventually move to England to be near the grandchildren."

As was the case during the Seventies when Tom first uprooted and moved permanently to America, he was left wide open to attacks claiming that he had abandoned his Welsh homeland. But this time, having re-established himself as a major pop figure in Britain, there followed a public outcry which was exacerbated by wildly damning reports in the press.

The allegations of desertion necessitated some form of refutation from Tom, and he became fiercely vocal about his roots, using every possible opportunity to state his defence. At a concert in Wales during this period, after performing 'A Boy From Nowhere' Tom turned to the audience, holding up an offending article entitled 'Tom Quits Wales'. "Whoever wrote this article cannot be Welsh . . . No matter where I sing in this world, Wales is right here," said Tom, with his hand on his heart. He further detailed the logic behind his decision to sell his Welsh property to the papers. "When you are born in Wales then Wales is always inside you. It will always be there and you don't have to own a house for that. I tried. I bought the house and thought I would be able to use it, but it turned out that I was travelling too much. The reason that I sold the house in Cowbridge was that I was never there."

In Wales, and particularly Pontypridd, there are two schools of thought. The first, echoed by the national papers, was that Tom had pretty much left his roots behind. Even Tom's cousin Margaret Sugar admits, "We're all very proud of him y'know, but we don't see him very much anymore."

But in contrast, many others believe that Pontypridd's town council have not done enough to support their native hero.

Local Tomologist Mike Webb, who has made many attempts to give Tom his dues, presents a sturdy case: "I always felt strongly that Tom hasn't had recognition in his home town. He hasn't even got a plaque outside his own front door. I thought it would be nice to do an exhibition – the council don't *say* they're not supportive, just that it's got to be done their way. They don't approve of rock 'n' roll, so they pulled the plug on us."

The debate over Tom's debt to his hometown continues to this day. Councillor Brian John, current Mayor of Pontypridd, feels that it should be a two-way relationship. "He's never associated himself with Pontypridd, he doesn't live here, you see," he points out. "Tom never comes into the town and nobody sees him. I suppose he could give a donation, but the thing is you can't get hold of the guy, he lives in America and you never see him anyway."

Councillor Colin Gregory finds it a little irksome that the name of Pontypridd is constantly used by Tom in his personal promotion yet he has never given his townsfolk any financial help. Gregory has taken it upon himself to write to the superstar requesting a millennium gift of a £1 million. "I just think about the amount of money he has got and the great need in Pontypridd," he said in 1999. "I have just come back from a tour of the States with the town's male voice choir, and after seeing [the wealth of] Las Vegas – well, the two just don't compare."

To be fair, there is in fact an underpass on Mill Street in Pontypridd's town centre, on which the names of previous inhabitants who have achieved fame with their musical talents are engraved. The colourful, informative mural depicts baritone Sir Geraint Evans, The Pontypridd Male Choir and international soprano Gillian Humphreys among others. Tom Jones is a pop star, not a 'serious' musician, but he does at least warrant a mention. Unfortunately, as anybody who knows anything about him can see, Pontypridd's tribute to him is inaccurate: "Tom Jones from Treforest has become an international star since 'It's Not Unusual' reached number one in February 1965." That Tom's major breakthrough came on March 1, St. David's Day, appeared to have escaped them.

The Welsh tourist board have also become embroiled in the dilemma, having omitted any mention of Tom from their visitor's guide to the nation. Infuriated fans failed to realise that fellow countrywoman Shirley Bassey had also been ignored, indicating an oversight on pop stars rather than a dig at Tom personally.

While so much was being made of Tom's patriotism, few gave more than a second thought to his original Welsh backing band who, some 30 years after being collectively discharged, reformed in the summer of 1998.

Band leader and bassist Vernon Hopkins had briefly made contact with Tom after Gordon's death to offer him a new song he had written, but nothing materialised and any hope of rekindling the former friendship was lost. Vernon began working with keyboardist Vic Cooper again at the end of 1997, performing at various venues in Switzerland. After 10 months as a duo they persuaded drummer Chris Slade to rejoin them. This was some coup as after his time with Tom, he had gone on to work with such great acts as AC/DC, Pink Floyd and Led Zeppelin guitarist Jimmy Page among others. Calling themselves 'The Squires' once more, the old friends completed the line-up with Ricky Purcell, a vocalist who had previously been with a comedy band called The Fortunes.

As the reincarnation of Tom's former group rehearsed and started lining up regular concerts, the original singer himself was being criticised for having a 'faceless band' on stage with him. When asked, "Why don't you introduce the band any more?", Tom answered honestly before thinking of a witty reply: "Because I can't remember their names . . . They don't want anyone to know where they are, particularly their mothers and the FBI."

Tom's stage set was in a constant state of renewal, with the singer regularly introducing contemporary songs to his inevitable selection of past hits. "I want to please everyone," he told journalist Lisa Wilton. "I don't want one half of the audience going, 'There was too much rock'n'roll and too many kids there.' But then I don't want the kids saying there were too many old people there either. I try to do a good mix, and not let the kids come down to the front too soon and [anger] the older people sitting in the front, because the older people tend to get those bloody front tickets."

Tom was spotted wearing earpieces for the first time on his 1998 tours. He made a point of explaining to his audience that they were not hearing aids but were instead a feature of his new sound system, replacing the unsightly large black speakers on stage. Tom would round off this clarification with the reassuring quip, "I'm not going deaf – senile maybe!"

Eighteen months after the success of *Mars Attacks!* Tom was offered another exciting opportunity to feature in a movie. Acclaimed actress and director Anjelica Huston, most recently famous for her role playing Morticia Addams in the two big-screen versions of *The Addams Family*, envisaged a film based on the number one Irish book *The Mammy*, part of a semi-autobiographical trilogy by Brendan O'Carroll. The author teamed up with experienced scriptwriter John Goldsmith to produce the screenplay.

The story is set in the Irish capital of Dublin in 1967 and centres on a widow, Agnes Browne, struggling to cope with the burden of raising seven children. After reading and considering the plot, Anjelica Huston decided to make a vital change to the content. "In the original material, Agnes has a passion for Cliff Richard, but I thought Tom [Jones] was the perfect object of desire . . . He has raw, sexual power." Anjelica had first met Tom at a celebrity party in Los Angeles a decade earlier, and was delighted when he agreed to be involved in the project.

Initially Rosie O'Donnell was cast in the lead role of Agnes, but pulled out just a few weeks before filming commenced. Unable to find a suitable replacement at such late notice, Anjelica realised that the answer was for her to take on the part herself. The author also got his own character, playing a drunkard called Seamus, whom Brendan describes as a "silent, Charlie Chaplinesque narrator who pops up in nearly every scene".

Tom's scenes revolve around a concert in Dublin, attended after some complication by Agnes, and a brief trip to her home to return some lost property. His stage footage was filmed on August 6, 1998 at the Gaiety Theatre, and as an authentic touch, members of the British fan club, the Tom Jones Appreciation Society, were invited to attend as extras in the audience, on the proviso that they came dressed in the appropriate Sixties attire. More than 10,000 teenagers also applied for the part of 100 extras seated in the front row, watching Tom perform 'It's Not Unusual', 'Green Green Grass Of Home' and slightly incongruously for a film set in 1967, his 1971 hit, 'She's A Lady'.

Tom's other main task was to recite a small speech to Agnes, who is sitting in the audience. Brendan was greatly moved when he saw the culmination of his life's work spoken by such a major star. "I cried. I just cried," he choked to the press. "I was sitting in the front row of the Gaiety Theatre and I think a lot of the people cried as well, because the way he said it was just so moving." Conversely, an insider on the film-set does not recall Tom's speech through such rose-tinted glasses, as apparently the would-be actor kept getting his small amount of dialogue wrong. "Tom only has two lines, he has to deliver a brief dedication to Anjelica's character before launching into 'She's A Lady', but he just couldn't get them right." To cover up his excruciating embarrassment at these simple errors, Tom joked to the audience, "It's these teeth. They keep falling out."

After five hours filming Anjelica was satisfied with Tom's performance after which he treated the patient crowd to a mini concert in order to thank them for their hard work. "It wasn't a big stretch for me," he admitted afterwards. "Being a singer (and not an actor), I think it's easier to play yourself than somebody else. I've never got into a heavy role playing another character."

"It's a funny, beautiful film, and Tom was fantastic during filming,"

Brendan summarised to journalist, Jason Lamport. "He didn't stop the whole time he was here. We became great friends, he has a wicked sense of humour and we just cracked jokes whenever we had a spare minute. He gave everyone the time of day and wouldn't let me put my hand in my pocket to buy a beer – and even his fee didn't break the bank. He's a big man in every way. He's very generous, very patient and very talented. I'm sure he can only help make the film a hit."

Problems dogged the title of the film, which was changed to *Agnes Browne* before its projected release the following year. Anjelica realised that there were difficulties with the language barrier between traditional Irish dialect and American English. "It was unanimous that *The Mammy* was not going to go over as a title in America," she recalls. "People thought it was the new *Jolson Story* or something." There would have been further confusion as the summer of 1999 saw the release of an Egyptian horror movie called *The Mummy*. Tom attended the premier of the re-titled film, *Agnes Browne*, on May 21, 1999, the final night of the Cannes Festival directors' fortnight, after which he performed an impromptu concert on the beach. The general release date was set for December 3, 1999 in New York and Los Angeles.

★   ★   ★

To publicise his forthcoming UK tour in November and December 1998, Tom made a number of appearances on British TV including *TFI Friday* and another *Royal Variety Show*. He was also interviewed by Sir David Frost on behalf of British Airways, with the conversation broadcast in-flight to all those passengers who cared to tune in. As a result of such heavy promotion, the series of concert dates was sold out months in advance.

However, issues arose about the poor standard of the merchandise available at the tour. Unhappy fans complained bitterly to Tom Jones Enterprises that the overpriced tour programme they had purchased was exactly the same as the one just two years previously. Similarly official cassettes sold at the concert venues were also outdated and repetitious.

Situated in an imposing suite of corporate offices on Santa Monica Boulevard, Los Angeles, Tom Jones Enterprises should perhaps by rights be known as 'Tom Jones & Son'. Sadly, as seems to have become the norm with this particular organisation, the disgruntled fans received no response, let alone an explanation.★ To this day an official Tom Jones website has not been established on the internet, although there are an abundance

---

★ On one particular occasion when the authors requested some basic information in research for this book, the genuine response from the sole employee available that day was to utter the unforgettable line: "I don't know – I mean, I only work here!"

of fan homepages dedicated solely to The Voice. The only properly endorsed means of finding out Tom's latest news is via the V2 and Gut Records websites, which have only recently included Tom in their listed artists. K Space, who were responsible for advertising *The Lead And How To Swing It* in this medium, still print an 'official' e-mail address for the singer which expired long ago.

So the unfulfilled Tom fans took the matter into their own hands and created a series of electronic mailing lists in which they swap news and opinions, and chat about their favourite pop star. Although there is absolutely nothing they can do about it, Tom Jones Enterprises does not approve of these independent ventures, a feeling which was voiced by the president of one of the three 'authorised' fan clubs. In an attempt to disparage the validity of the mailing list in question, a flyer was distributed to members of the club, which in part read: "I know some of you have subscribed to this list on the Internet. As I mentioned in our March newsletter I don't support this list nor does Tom's management. Do not give out any information regarding Tom . . . to this list. I list on our website what I feel fans around the world need to know to promote Tom . . . Anything unofficial on the Internet is not worth belonging to." Its tone was highly reminiscent of the scandalous letter circulated to all fan clubs back in 1989, and surely did not encourage a harmonious atmosphere, let alone pave the way for an inspired move into the 21st century.

Two events made Tom's winter UK tour especially memorable. Before his greatly anticipated performance at the Cardiff International Arena, he attended a ceremony at the local Queen Street Station, unveiling a 100 tonne Valleys Line train that had been named in his honour. The other, more amusing occurrence happened on the second night in Belfast where Tom made a speech about *The Full Monty*, the film which had rapidly become synonymous with male strippers. As Tom turned to acknowledge his band members and introduce 'You Can Leave Your Hat On', the lights were raised to reveal eight of Tom's technicians posing, as per the climax of the movie, in their full naked glory, with only hats to preserve their modesty.

Just prior to Christmas, the 58-year-old singer of raunchy material was featured in yet another sex romp scandal. The latest candidate claiming to have succumbed to his manly charms was Christina James, and her explicit story which detailed the usual plethora of sexual antics gained extended publicity in the tabloids.

Christina was soon joined by TV actress Cassandra Peterson, who in 1981 had reinvented herself as Elvira, Mistress Of The Dark, and whose story was rudely exposed in America's tabloid *The Globe* shortly afterwards. Not only did the paper print claims that the former showgirl had lost her virginity to Tom in 1972 when she was just 19, but that the dastardly singer had left her writhing in agony, and she had attended the nearest hospital for stitches in her most intimate place. Cassandra's manager Mark Pierson explained for this book that, similar to Tom's recent treatment on 'shock jock' Howard Stern's notorious radio show, Elvira had been coerced into revealing this sorry saga on air in exchange for promotion of her latest movie. "On the show you are opening yourself up to whatever he wants to bring up," says Mark. "So he brought up the Tom Jones story to dig the dirt. It was picked up on by *The Globe*, who ran the story. The quotes were false but the story is true . . . It's not something she wants to expand upon."

This time around damage limitation for Tom took the form of celebrating the last new year of the century with two television performances and a live concert. He actually appeared at the famed House Of Blues in Los Angeles, but thanks to pre-recording was also able to ring in the new year on Jay Leno's *Tonight Show* in America, singing 'Midnight Hour' on the stroke of midnight, and duetting with Cerys Matthews from Catatonia on the *Jools Holland Show* in England. When asked if he minded working during the holiday period Tom responded, "Even if we were at our house, I'd be bloody singing anyway. We might as well make a party out of it, and the House Of Blues is a good place to do it. My whole family's coming."

"Old Tom's still got it. He's an amazing man with a brilliant voice," said a slightly bemused Cerys after the event. "He's a complete entertainer. He always gets the crowd going. You can't really fault a man who's willing to go on stage in a brightly coloured flamenco catsuit, can you?"

So what were Tom's hopes for the year ahead? "I want more of the same next year. I'd love to have a hit record. If bands say they don't want that, they're lying. You can't get paranoid about it, but you still have to strive for it . . . I want to keep moving, trying different things. That's what I want for 1999."

Early in the new year, Lloyd Greenfield, who had retired from his job as Tom's right-hand man in America just two years previously, became yet another of the singer's close associates to lose his fight against cancer. Tom was absolutely devastated as he had worked closely with the well-loved funny man for nearly 35 years. But his distress was not to end there.

Shortly after Lloyd's funeral in New York, Mark called his father to inform him that his oldest friend Dai Perry had also passed away, his death caused by a heart attack. For Tom, the horror of losing two close friends in such a short space of time must have mirrored the quick succession of Elvis Presley and Johnnie Spence's untimely deaths. Without hesitation he cancelled his upcoming concerts in New York and Connecticut to make the painful trip back to Pontypridd to pay his respects.

It was well known that Dai had suffered from ongoing heart trouble, and had in fact had a bypass operation several years earlier. Yet no one was prepared for the burly bodyguard's death while walking on Graig Mountain, an old childhood stamping ground of his and Tom's. Keith Williams, resident of Pontypridd and regular at the Wood Road Social Club, recalls: "Dai didn't have another job after being Tom's bodyguard because of his heart trouble, but he would keep fit by walking up and down the hills where he lived. This was his passion.

"The day before he died he went into the Wood Road Social Club and it was like he had a sixth sense, he put on his very best clothes and everyone commented how good he looked. He said that he'd never felt better. The next day he was found dead up a mountain."

Dai and his partner Glynis McKenna had last seen Tom in August 1998, when the star had arranged for the couple to fly out to Las Vegas for a holiday. Now Tom was in the unthinkable position of joining more than 200 mourners for his best friend's funeral.

Dai's sister Marion recalls the difficult return visit. "The night of the funeral, when Tom came here he just cracked up. He consoled us and went in the family car. He wasn't here for show. We were all crying." The loyal friendship had endured despite the professional split back in early 1975. "Dai wouldn't say anything detrimental [about Tom]; he put him on a pedestal. On the funeral wreath Tom put 'Friends Forever' and whatever David knew [of Tom's secrets], it went to his grave with him." Dai's mother Elsie Huish confirms this with absolute sincerity. "He'd never discuss anything with anybody, he was a true friend."

"It was a shock, a terrible shock," said Tom to *The Western Mail.* "I was talking with him two days before and he felt great. Because he'd had a triple heart bypass about five years ago I thought he'd be fine now, and it would give him a new lease of life . . . I had known Dave all my life. We were close as kids, we were close on the road. We went all over the world. We were like brothers. We got into trouble together and out of trouble together. It was a shock."

Coming to terms with the loss of his two great friends was helped a little by the public announcement in January of a prestigious award; an Officer of the Order of the British Empire medal (OBE). Other notable musicians on the British Honours List were David Essex and Dusty Springfield, who was tragically too ill with cancer to accept the invitation to attend the Queen's ceremony at Buckingham Palace in March.*

"Good records are great, hit television shows are great, but to get an

---

* Dusty sadly passed away on March 2, 1999, just one month short of her 60th birthday. Tom sent a wreath to her funeral in memory of all the work they had done together.

award from the Queen is a truly special honour," beamed Tom. "An OBE is something that you can keep and display, it's for services rendered over a lengthy period of time. It's not just awarded for one record or one appearance, like when you win a Grammy . . . This is for my contribution to music."

He was only too glad to pose in morning dress for photographs with Roger Moore, who received a Commander of the Order of the British Empire for his inexhaustible work with UNICEF. "I didn't bring a hat because I thought it might mess up my hair," laughed Tom. Although the OBE was a good step towards recognition for Tom's contribution to music, his fan clubs have for many years campaigned to see their hero receive a knighthood. Tom himself has never really seemed that concerned. "What do you have to do to become a Sir? Cliff is clean living to the nth degree. I couldn't become a knight if the qualification is to live like him."

While Tom himself had helped to raise thousands of pounds for charity over the years, his fan clubs had done as much as they could to match him in this respect. The three official clubs all hold regular raffles of stage shirts, trousers and jackets donated by Tom to raise money for the charities he supports. These include the Welsh Marie Curie Cancer charity and the American Cancer Society in memory of Gordon Mills, and the American Lung Association in memory of Tom's dad who died of respiratory diseases. Sylvia Firth, President of the authorised British club, chooses another obvious beneficiary. "All the money we've raised for the last three or four years has gone to ChildLine," she says.

In February, Tom himself helped to fundraise for cancer research in an unusual setting. *Men For Sale* was the first British TV programme featuring a host of male celebrities including Tom, Julio Iglesias and teenage pop band 911, being literally auctioned off to members of the studio audience, who paid hard cash to the charitable cause for the privilege of a night out with the star of their choice. Although Tom's name was used heavily in promotion for the show, unfortunately he did not actually appear in person, and the bidding which started at £300, took place over a premium rate phone number.

Professionally Tom had never seemed so much in demand. Although *Agnes Browne* was not due to go on general release until the end of the year, Tom's presence was felt on a seemingly infinite number of contemporary film tracks, including his take on 'Fly Me To The Moon' on *Deep Impact*, 'Green Green Grass Of Home' on *The Young Poisoner's Handbook*, 'It's Not Unusual' on both horror spoof, *Lake Placid*, and British comedy, *Little Voice*, and last but by no means least, a cover of the Seventies classic 'Kung Fu Fighting' recorded with techno band Ruby for the action movie

Super Cop. He was also heard on American adverts for Kraft Deluxe macaroni and cheese with 'What's New Pussycat', and Cornetto ice cream with a tempting 'Help Yourself'.

The charitable work continued, perhaps with renewed meaning after the passing of his friends. Tom donated another stage shirt to be raffled in aid of the Wired For Sound Group, which raises funds for deaf children who have had cochlea implants at the Princess of Wales Hospital in Bridgend, South Wales. Later in March, Tom also donated autographed lyric sheets for 'It's Not Unusual', 'Thunderball' and 'Delilah' to an auction called 'Hits Under The Hammer', raising money for two children's charities, Nordoff Robbins Music Therapy and Norwood Ravenswood. On March 28, Tom then began to rebuild his bridges with his home country, flying to the BBC studios in Wales to film his part for a new television advertisement, *BBC Wales And Proud Of It*. Tom spoke the potent line, previously coined by Catatonia, for the film: "Every day when I wake up I thank the Lord I am Welsh."

While Tom was assuring the world of his roots, in Las Vegas his image was being immortalised in wax for Madame Tussaud's new exhibition in the gambling city's Venetian hotel. The original waxwork in the London display had been removed from the gallery in the early Eighties during Tom's decline, but with his revival, his new model in Las Vegas proudly stands alongside other greats linked to the cabaret circuit, including Frank Sinatra and Elvis Presley.

Another sad death shook the music world when Linda McCartney succumbed to breast cancer on April 17, 1998. A tribute concert was organised by Chrissie Hynde of The Pretenders for April 10, 1999 in the Royal Albert Hall. The 4,000 tickets were almost immediately sold out, the proceeds going to Lady McCartney's favourite animal rights charities. Tom joined Paul, Chrissie, George Michael, Elvis Costello, Sinéad O'Connor, Neil Finn and M People's Heather Small for the emotional occasion.

"I have known Paul since the Sixties," Tom told the *Evening Standard*. "I only met Linda a couple of times and I did not know her really well but she was a great lady and Paul is a great guy." Tom performed 'She's A Lady' and 'When A Man Loves A Woman' in memory of the much loved vegetarian activist, and sang 'Green Green Grass Of Home', clutching a bunch of Welsh daffodils and backed by Sinéad O'Connor, Chrissie Hynde and Des'ree.

Tom pressed on with his Welsh drive, singing at the Wales vs. England final for the Rugby Five Nations on April 11 at Wembley, London. The crowd was delighted to sing along to Tom's rendition of 'Delilah', before he was joined by the Welsh Male Voice Choir in singing their national anthem. Fellow Welshmen, opera star Bryn Terfel and comedian Max Boyce were also present, supporting their team in front of the 79,000 rugby fans, the Queen, Duke of Edinburgh and Prince of Wales. "I'm just glad I can be at the match and singing," said Tom. "I'm normally out of the country performing, but this is a perfect opportunity to be at a Five Nations game – it's fantastic. This is the best team we have had for a long while and as I always say, I don't care who wins as long as it's Wales!" Spurred on by the excessive display of patriotism, Wales did indeed win the match.

To round off Tom's Welsh involvement for the meantime he headlined alongside Shirley Bassey at the Voices Of A Nation concert celebrating the new Welsh National Assembly. Other acts appearing on May 26 were Shakin' Stevens, Michael Ball, Charlotte Church and Bonnie Tyler. The government had initially envisaged a £2 million publicity drive using the names of Tom Jones, Sir Anthony Hopkins and actress Julie Christie among others to support the cause, but as Cardiff West MP Rhodri Morgan pointed out, "The problem is that – by and large – celebrities don't live in Wales. In 1979 there was a huge list of celebrities who supported devolution, but the 'No Campaign' turned it very effectively by asking how many of them lived here."

Tom's opinion of the Welsh situation is divided. "I don't like separatism completely," he said to the *Sun-Herald*. "I don't think Britain is big enough to split up into small countries. I think it would be nice for a region of a place to be able, as far as taxes are concerned, to do their own thing locally, like a council. It would be good for Wales if they could have certain things that they could deal with themselves, like Scotland has done."

Meanwhile, in America on April 28, Tom was featured on the prestigious *60 Minutes II* programme for which he was interviewed in depth by Vicki Mabrey. The film crew had followed him around the globe for several months and the programme received a generally good reception when it was aired on CBS in America.

Although the general opinion of Tom had been heightened by his OBE and work for good causes this year, it was difficult not to criticise the extortionate prices set for concert tickets in the Australian leg of his tour over the summer. For the privilege of one-and-a-half hours of pure Tom Jones at Melbourne's Crown Casino, fans were expected to pay between 179 and 295 Australian dollars. There was no feasible explanation for the tickets to be priced so high as the venue held some 2,000 people, which by default lost any valuable sense of intimacy for the spectators. Tom alienated some Australian fans as a result of the same apparent greed shown by Gordon Mills back in the Seventies on the Far Eastern and South African tours.

★ ★ ★

After many months of furtive negotiations, in mid-1998 Tom had finally agreed to a one-album deal with Gut Records, with an option to do more if the first proved to be successful. But this wasn't destined to be just any old album; there was a twist.

"My son said, 'What about doing an album of duets, because every time you sing with someone else it causes a bit of a stir.' I said, 'Yeah, great if we can get enough people to do it,'" Tom later told the *Metro*. Others have since claimed the rights to the concept, namely the record label itself. "The idea came about last year," says Rob Partridge, spokesman for Gut Records. "It was after Space and Cerys Matthews joined forces to sing 'The Ballad Of Tom Jones' that someone suggested an album of duets with the singer." Another reason cited for the new musical direction was the immense success of Tom's memorable duet with Robbie Williams at the previous year's BRIT awards. The idea itself was not a new one. In recent years many stars, including such diverse names as Frank Sinatra and Elton John, had released albums of duets, and in the early Eighties Tom had flooded the market with collections of songs with his guests from his *Coast To Coast* TV series.

Gut chairman Guy Holmes was so enthused by the project that he took on the role of executive producer together with Mark Woodward, and assumed a personal responsibility for spreading the word prior to the event. "Tom has a remarkable ability to reinvent himself for each succeeding generation," he said. "We know the esteem in which he is held by stars who weren't even born when Tom made his first records."

It was apparent from the outset that Tom was hardly going to have a problem securing enough acts to collaborate with, as his contribution to *The Full Monty* had by now become the stuff of which legends are made, and his public profile could not be higher. With people like Robbie Williams and Tommy Scott frequently declaring him as a musical divinity, Tom had never been in greater demand, or granted such respect in his own country. He had come a long way in the last 15 years.

An impressive selection of stars agreed to the project without hesitation. Tom was elated, and a huge sense of adventure encircled Gut Records' brightly decorated offices in West London. "I'm very pleased these artists have said 'yes' to the invitation," Tom enthused early on. "Every one of them is fresh and strong, no matter what kind of music they do, or how long they've been around. I'm absolutely thrilled to be having this experience."

Producer Stephen Hague, previously noted for his work back in the Eighties with mainstream pop acts The Pet Shop Boys and Erasure, was lined up for the recording sessions, most of which took place between March 20 and April 14, 1999 in RAK Studios. For acts like The

Cardigans, who are of Swedish origin, Tom travelled to Stockholm and recorded an entire song in the space of a single evening to fit in with their hectic schedules. Stephen Hague was generally in control of the sessions, but as with the studios, some artists insisted on working with their own producers. The majority of the songs planned for the project were to be cover versions of relatively contemporary tracks, with one or two especially written tracks thrown in.

To start the recording for the as yet untitled album Tom chose to cover the Talking Heads' Top 10 hit 'Burning Down The House', which had first been laid down on vinyl in 1983. Tom recorded this choice with The Cardigans. "The first track we cut was the single, 'Burning Down The House', which I sang once to get the balance right before Nina [Persson of The Cardigans] arrived at the studio," he told Phil Gould of the *Mercury*. "After one recording they said, 'That's it.' Nina came in and listened to the track and said, 'Oh my God, I'm going to sound like a little moth.' They told her not to worry but said my voice was actually ten times louder than hers."

Tom was to experience similar vocal imbalances with many of his chosen partners, but, once tweaked, this particular pairing is arguably the best of the entire collection, as Nina's beautifully cool, clipped phrasing contrasts spectacularly with Tom's rough-edged funk interpretation. Another song in which he found himself slightly mismatched in lung power was with INXS' 'Never Tear Us Apart'. This he chose to record with soft-voiced Australian singer, Natalie Imbruglia, who was still basking in the glory of her recent huge hit, 'Torn'. Tom described the recording of 'Never Tear Us Apart' to Q magazine: "Initially, I did attack that song with more vigour, but the producer told me to ease up because Natalie was so quiet. So I handled it a little more . . . sympathetically."

Although Tom was confident in his duets with most of the artists featured on the album, he was a little wary about James Dean Bradfield, the strident singer with the immensely popular Welsh band, Manic Street Preachers. Bradfield, blunt-spoken and a hero with the UK music press, was picked to join Tom on 'I'm Left, You're Right, She's Gone', a song Elvis Presley recorded during his early days on Sun Records. Tom later remarked on British television that he had been a little anxious prior to this particular session as Bradfield has a high vocal range. Aside from the rising climax at the end of 'Delilah', Tom has found that his voice has lowered with age, and tried to avoid specifically high songs. He was concerned as to the key that would be used for the song, yet he needn't have worried as the resulting track works well with a dash of compromise from two powerful singers.

The Welsh influence did not end there. Tom also recorded Three Dog

Night's 'Mama Told Me Not To Come' with another Welsh band, The Stereophonics, on whose behalf he collected a consolation trophy at the Mercury Music Awards later in the year. Cerys Matthews from Catatonia had previously sung the flirtatious 1961 Ray Charles and Betty Carter duet 'Baby It's Cold Outside' with Tom on the *Jools Holland Show* at the close of 1998. The track was reprised for the new album, and the obvious chemistry between Tom and Cerys positively drips out of the speakers in this beautifully orchestrated big band version of a classic track.

Still staying with the Celtic theme, Van Morrison provided a traditional feel with his own track, 'Sometimes We Cry', which he both contributed for the album and duetted on with Tom. This track is notable for the ease with which the two mature stars fall into musical pace with each other, almost as if the *Carrying A Torch* sessions had occurred only the previous month.

No duets project was going to be possible without another repeat pairing of macho strutting, and Robbie Williams was invited to sing once more with Tom on a fast and furious version of Lenny Kravitz's 'Are You Gonna Go My Way', which had long since become a staple of Tom's stage performances. Interviewed for this book just minutes before going into the studio with Tom, Robbie seemed bewildered that he had again been approached by Tom's management, and extremely flattered that his name was beginning to be linked with his childhood idol on a more permanent basis. "I just jumped at the chance to do it," he said, before launching into an enthusiastic impression of Tom's stage version of the song in question.

Tommy Scott from the band Space had also previously been linked to Tom, with his reverent duet with Cerys Matthews, 'A Ballad Of Tom Jones'. He became involved with Tom's new album right at the very beginning of negotiations for all the artists and set about writing two new original songs for the collection.

"I wrote this song called 'Little Did He Know' for Tom Jones and I had to go and sing it with him and it was terrifying," Tommy laughs today. "I was singing with someone who'd sung with Elvis and half-way through I just started to go out of tune. I said to Tom, 'I can't believe I'm actually doing this, I've just realised who I'm standing here with!' " 'Little Did He Know' was recorded at Abbey Road but sadly did not make it onto the finished product. The same fate befell the other song generously contributed by Tommy, but at least this one left a lasting impact, for it was called 'Reload', and soon became adopted as the title for the album itself. Tommy and his band eventually ended up on the album performing a bizarre, psychedelic take on The Kinks' 'Sunny Afternoon', which has since become a much performed version in Tom's public appearances.

Mick Hucknall of Simply Red also appeared on television with Tom to showcase his duet, Sam & Dave's 'Ain't That A Lot Of Love'. A slightly different ending occurred to this track, as shortly after the release of *Reload* Simply Red put out their own version of the same song. Mick was interviewed later on *Entertainment Weekly* for Sky News, explaining that he had hoped that his take with Tom would have been slated for a single release, but when Tom's management refused, Mick's own producers removed Tom's vocal from the track and remixed it to reflect a more garage-type feel.

Tom performs a heartfelt version of Portishead's 'All Mine' with the British band The Divine Comedy. "I didn't want to record this with Portishead because they've already done it, so there is no chance of taking it to the next level," he told *Select* magazine. "I knew Neil Hannon [The Divine Comedy's vocalist] would be great singing this song . . . In fact he helped me with this song. I kept going sharp, and he told me to, 'Think flat, sing it below where you think the tune is.' He helped me a lot."

The other tracks appearing on *Reload* are as numerous as they are impressive. Gladys Knight & The Pips' 'You Need Love Like I Do' with Heather Small from M People and a storming cover of Iggy Pop's 'Lust For Life' with The Pretenders. The George Baker Selection's 'Little Green Bag' is done moderate justice with The Barenaked Ladies and a cute cover of Fine Young Cannibals' 'She Drives Me Crazy' with Italian singer Zucchero comes across well enough. Portishead are connected once again to *Reload* with their take on the traditional song, 'Motherless Child' closing the album on a dark and contemplative note.

Tom chose to record his own song, 'Looking Out My Window' with the funk band, James Taylor Quartet. Co-written many years ago by Tom and Gordon Mills, this song appeared on the B-side of the 1968 single 'A Minute Of Your Time'. *Reload*'s re-take is a nice, if a little predictable, interpretation. Interestingly Gordon's credit as songwriter was dropped on the sleeve notes to the album.

But the track that has made by far the most impact since the release of this new material is 'Sexbomb', especially written for Tom by Mousse T. This proved to be the only track which, strictly speaking, was not a duet. Mousse, a German house producer, had just had a massive international hit with the track 'Horny' with Hot n' Juicy, which went to number two in the UK and number one in the US club charts. His work is known for its sexy lyrics, and although it has since been acknowledged that Tom was the 'Sexbomb' intended in this tremendously catchy track, he modestly insisted on changing the words slightly, in order to sing as if he were speaking to a woman. Tom Jones Enterprises foreboding knicker-throwing warnings were still visible on the horizon.

Although after the sessions there was a surplus of material to choose from for the album, not all the artists approached to work with Tom on *Reload* actually materialised. There had previously been much talk in the press of All Saints joining Tom for a duet, but their names were missing from the extensive cast list at the end of the sessions. Shirley Manson of Garbage had also been cited as a possible contributor, but something must have gone badly wrong, judging from her appearance on *Jo Whiley* on May 12, 1999. During a discussion on Tom's latest release she bitingly described how much she dislikes his 'tight trousers' image, summing up: "He makes my stomach churn."

Reload was released on September 27 by Gut Records in the UK, and V2 took over the distribution in Europe, Japan, and Southeast Asia. At this time no North American deal had yet been made, but at the time of going to press the news was *Reload* should be introduced into the US market early in the New Year. Gut swiftly realised that they could make a hefty profit from selling advance copies to Tom's American fans over the internet, so at least his work had been heard overseas by the turn of the century. Japanese fans received an unexpected bonus, with *Reload*'s début occurring there five days before the general UK and European release, and also boasting two bonus live tracks, 'Unbelievable' and 'Come Together'.

Although it seemed that Tom could not fail to strike a chord with an album so full of diversity that surely everyone must find one duet enjoyable, the reception for *Reload* ranged from the ecstatic to the dubious. Renowned rock journalist, Paul Du Noyer, pointed out in a review, "Lots of these younger artists cannot really compete with him in the vocal department. He is one of the most forceful singers and it takes someone of extreme power to balance that out." Many of Tom's fans stretching over the globe simply failed to recognise the majority of the stars featured on the album, and the more mature followers were uncertain how they should respond to a set so obviously aimed at the younger end of the market. Perhaps even more so than the production collaborations with *The Lead And How To Swing It*, this was an obvious exercise by Mark, Donna and Tom himself to bring Tom Jones, Las Vegas crooner, back into vogue with a certain fan base.

'Burning Down The House' was chosen as the first single from *Reload* and was released on September 13. It was given a superb launch with a live performance from Tom and The Cardigans on Zoë Ball's Radio One breakfast show the following morning. The single was accompanied by an artistic promotional video, directed by David Mouldy and featuring silver clad figures dancing to Tom and The Cardigans' performance set against a startling orange, black and white background. Although many remarked that 'Burning Down The House' was not the obvious first single, as opposed to the tongue-in-cheek autobiography of 'Sexbomb' or the guaranteed ratings of a duet with Robbie Williams, it proved to be an excellent choice for an introduction to the album, and rose rapidly to number six in the UK charts, his 16th Top 10 hit and his greatest success since 1988's 'Kiss'. Not surprisingly 'Burning Down The House' fared equally well in the Scandinavian countries in September 1999 and Tom made a promotional visit later in the month to pick up a gold record to commemorate the single's success.

Publicity for *Reload* started in earnest some weeks before its official release, and alongside the usual TV appearances came a new gimmick, which certainly attracted some attention across the internet. *Reload – The Game* was launched by Gut Records at the end of August and can be played simply through an internet browser. It was generally thought to be the first of its kind to link in with the launch of a pop music album. Running along the lines of a simplified arcade game, the brief is to race Tom's car along a winding road, collecting the collaborating artists along the way and transporting them to the studio within a set time limit. The player who scores the highest will win a signed silver disc of *Reload* and concert tickets.

A press release was duly issued by Tom Jones Enterprises to all fan clubs in the UK and Asia, praising the support of the fans and issuing a special request or two. "Tom's last release got tremendous response from his fans, and he very much appreciated all of their hard work in its promotion. Fans were so excited that they would call the radio stations demanding that they play Tom's music and even took the time to scout out local record stores to see where store management was placing his CD; making sure it had prominent positioning on store shelves, displays and in windows. All of the fans' efforts, no matter how small, by so many were very important and very powerful, and made the difference in making his new music a success."

While it seemed that his company was demanding quite a lot from the very people they had been known to dismiss in the past, Tom himself started an exhaustive stretch of TV appearances. Among others, he sang 'Sexbomb' on the UK version of *The Jerry Springer Show*, 'Sunny Afternoon' with Space on *TFI Friday**, 'Burning Down The House' with The Cardigans on *Top Of The Pops*, and 'Looking Out My Window' with the James Taylor Quartet on *The National Lottery*. Children's TV also got a look-in, with performances and interviews on *The Ozone* and *Live And Kicking*. Fans were given a rare opportunity to meet their hero as he was booked in to sign copies of *Reload* at the Virgin Megastore on London's

---

* This was a continuation of his relationship with *TFI* presenter Chris Evans, whose Ginger Productions company had filmed footage of Tom during *Reload*'s recording sessions.

Oxford Street at midnight on September 26. Tickets were available in advance on a first come first served basis, and 200 lucky fans met Tom, some travelling all the way from America in order to do so. Tom performed a short set of songs from the album and remained at the store signing CDs for the best part of two hours.

Further promotion for *Reload* continued when Graham K. Smith finally tied Tom down to a project he had first conceived shortly after *The Right Time. An Audience With Tom Jones* was filmed in front of celebrity spectators on September 19, 1999 and aired one week later on the 25th. Tom invited the mainly British TV soap stars to ask him preordained springboard questions, from which he would tell amusing tales from his life and career. With guest stars Tommy Scott, Mick Hucknall and Cerys Matthews, Tom was able to showcase several songs from *Reload* as well as the old favourites, which interestingly went down much better with the crowd. 'Sexbomb' was the obvious exception as everyone got up and danced in the aisles.

Tom's duet with the coquettish Cerys was one of the most remarked upon aspects of the show. The two shared a sensual connection as they duetted and cuddled on 'What's New Pussycat' and 'Baby It's Cold Outside'. The pair had recently been spotted sharing an intimate embrace at London's trendy Met Bar after the recording session for *Reload*. They also appeared together during London's Fashion Week held at the Roundhouse in Camden, North London. 'Baby It's Cold Outside' was released in time for Christmas in the UK and featured a rather remarkable promo video where Tom, a taloned Satanic figure, sets free a seemingly angelic, white-clad Cerys from a gilded cage atop a floating island somewhere in hell. Cerys then magically transforms into a black-clad vixen and cunningly manages to manipulate her captor back into the cage, where she leaves him trapped, commenting, "Bloody freezing, innit?"★

As *Reload* entered the UK charts at a dazzling number one, selling more than 80,000 copies in the first week and rapidly climbing to platinum status, Tom returned to the MGM Grand in Las Vegas for October and November stints. He was careful not to include any of his new material in his American act, well aware that fans were unhappy that his latest CD offering wouldn't be available in the US until several months after the rest of the world. Meanwhile London continued to celebrate his career with a one-off show, *Las Vegas In London*, starring Eurovision Song Contest star Andy Paul paying tribute to Tom Jones, Elvis Presley and Engelbert Humperdinck.

★ Instead of 'Baby It's Cold Outside', 'Sexbomb' became the second European release at the end of the year.

As Tom prepares for the millennium, two projects were launched to keep him at the forefront of the public eye. *Tom Jones 20th Century Masters: The Millennium Collection*, another greatest hits compilation was to be released in the near future. There was also talk of a future *Reload Part II* with an array of American artists and a rumoured session already booked with The Dixie Chicks.

It is only fitting that a star of Tom's calibre should bid farewell to the past century in high style, with hopes for his future burning bright. After rumours circulated that he would be singing for the Pope during the weekend before Christmas, sadly the pontiff did not attend the annual concert held at the Vatican, where Tom joined the Vatican's Swiss Guards choir for a chorus of 'Oh Happy Day' and 'Silent Night'. However, there was no question about audience attendance for his Millennium Eve concert held, no less, at the White House. President Bill Clinton was delighted to wield his saxophone alongside Tom, and his other star guests Will Smith and Quincy Jones. The tumultuous adventures of the last six decades truly climaxed on a zenith for the miner's son from Pontypridd.

Epilogue

WHAT'S NEW PUSSYCAT

"$\bigcirc$ N THE STREETS of Hollywood or Vegas, he looks like a thousand other mature gentlemen who suck in their guts, slip on some shades and play Mr Cool behind the wheel of an expensive convertible," Michael Sheldon aptly wrote in a recent article for the *Daily Telegraph*. So as Tom approaches his 60th birthday, what is it exactly that sets him apart from any other career-orientated man of his maturity?

For one thing, retirement seems to be the very last thing on his mind. Tom has many times admitted that he will never stop performing because he literally craves the 'pat on the back' guaranteed to him each and every time he steps on the stage. Still, the advancing years are a genuine concern.

"I'm not looking forward to old age because it will slow me down," he said to journalist Nick Krewen in 1998. "That's the only thing I don't like about it. Time is my enemy, because it's going to stop me from doing what I love to do. Thank God it hasn't affected me yet. So 60 doesn't bother me. Now, I don't know what I'm going to be like when I'm 70 . . ."

Tom will start his 61st year as he means to go on with a special birthday concert held at Cardiff's Millennium Stadium, hopefully featuring his new-found pop star friends Robbie Williams, Stereophonics, The Divine Comedy and Natalie Imbruglia. Welsh Labour Councillor Joyce Cass voices the opinion of many from his beloved homeland, wishing to see the opening of a special Tom Jones Museum or Memorial, appropriately situated to reflect his South Wales roots. "We must have a permanent tribute to Tom," she says, hoping for an all-star opening on June 7, 2000.

So how does the singer who has successfully crossed over more generations and musical genres than any other view himself? "I think I'm a cross between, or somewhere in the middle of Elvis Presley and Frank Sinatra. I'm not as rock'n'roll-ish as Elvis and I'm not as middle-of-the-road as Sinatra," he said, back in the days when both were still alive. Tom is plainly pleased with the way his life has turned out, and after everything that has happened to him, still appears relatively unaffected. "I'm a basic person," he reflects today. "I like what I do very much. And I've enjoyed it, I've learned things . . . I've gone to different countries. I've read a lot of history books. I've taken advantage of what success has given me . . ."

Tom refuses to see the onset of his sixties as middle age, let alone old age, and with a twinkle in his eye states that he doesn't see that his appeal should lessen at all. "You don't have to be 25 to have the X–factor," he justified to Cynthia Jardon. "In fact you can have more when you're older because you understand about life. If I do anything a little bit cheeky, it's tongue-in-cheek, but there has always been a sexual thing with me." Perchance this is not the kind of statement of which Tom Jones Enterprises would quite approve, but still there has always been, as there will pre-sumably always be, The Voice.

"For me, it's the easiest thing I can do. It's not like work to me. I love to sing," says Tom. "It's a very natural thing to me. The actual being on stage is fun, it's a charge, an 'up'." Although Tom has fully enjoyed the fruits of his success, he is the first to recognise that the gift of a good voice is not something to be abused. "You learn over the years things to do and not to do. You can't burn the candle at both ends all the time. You can do it once in a while . . . I think that's what happens with a lot of young bands when they start off. When you first start, you run a little too fast. You're so excited, you try to do too much. If you don't watch it, you can get burned out. If you get over those early years fairly unscathed, you can handle it," he says, clearly speaking from experience.

Tom prides himself that he can still sing with as much power as ever. Amusingly, he frequently describes the physical change in his vocal timbre as his voice 'getting fatter', reminding his fans that his sense of humour has developed almost as much as his singing technique. Having performed the same songs for over 35 years, it would be reasonable to suggest that the endless repetition might have brought about a lessening of motivation. However, Tom insists that this is not the case and that it is his fans and the audience who keep these old friends alive and well. "Each of the songs is so recognisable, I get instant applause when I start singing them," he explains. "When I see the audience, it lifts me up. It's like a test . . . I know that they are expecting certain things of me, so I know I had better deliver."

The bargain works both ways. Rising to the challenge of 'proving himself' night after night is the price Tom must pay for global recognition as a living legend. This kind of sycophantic compliment rarely affects the straightforward Welshman on a personal level, but he's eternally flattered by recognition on purely musical terms. "I can hear the influence of my voice on a lot of the material I hear today," he says. "I'm sure I've had an effect. When I started I was a bit of a misfit. There weren't many solo performers around, it was all groups. It's good to see these kids making it on their own terms, I admire what they do."

Such success has brought Tom wealth unimaginable to the son of a poor Welsh coal miner. Estimates of Tom's assets range dramatically, but a recent article in Q magazine drew attention to all the hard work that has gone into amassing this fortune, including an impressive concert tally of around 200 dates a year for 30 years or more. That often includes two performances a night. Taking into account all Tom's indefatigable work for children's charities over the last decade along with a multitude of television appearances and recording sessions – could he be the hardest-working man in pop?

Despite having seen so much, played so hard and scored so many hits, Tom still has a few regrets. "So many years have gone by with me doing the same thing," he confided to Lesley Salisbury in 1992. "I've done Vegas, I've done this, I've done that. I've been so busy I've lost track a bit. You get so involved in doing a show you sometimes lose the initial feeling you had. You always think there's plenty of time. But then, when you get older, you think, I could have done that, I should have done it when I had the chance!"

An interesting glimpse into Tom's psyche comes with two recurring dreams he has described in interviews over the years. One nightmare is fairly predictable, in that something happens which inadvertently stops him from ever singing again. He dreams that he has killed a person, hidden the body and is waiting for the police to discover his crime; a life sentence in jail would certainly put paid to any Las Vegas career. Perhaps more tellingly is the version where his accountant arranges a meeting with him to say that his finances have run out and he will have to get a 'proper' job and sing only as a hobby.

"I still have that dream," he says. "It bloody terrifies me. That's the thing that still sometimes plays on my mind. I'd hate to have to start all over again. I go back to the house where I was brought up – I take Alexander there – and it all floods back. Nothing's changed. And you're not always aware that you've moved on until you go back . . . I'm only too aware of what a lucky so-and-so I am."

Tom often relates how a memory of having to get up early to record a television breakfast show once put his good fortune sharply into perspective. Sleeping in the back of his Rolls Royce Phantom VI limousine, Tom was woken by his chauffeur. "I started moaning about the time and why the hell I had to be there at that time of the morning . . . and I saw this hod carrier, a young kid, working on the building." The shock of being so visibly confronted with his past as he reclined in his luxury car soon brought Tom to his senses. "I thought, 'Jesus Christ, you're in this big Rolls Royce, you've got a great number, what the ★★★★'s the matter with you? What's the big deal about going to work early once a week? You could still be up there on a ladder." It was quite a while before he took his life for granted again.

There can be no doubt that Tom has handled his immense fame in a manner of which his working-class parents would be proud. His patience with his fans borders on the legendary and rarely do any reports surface of aggressive behaviour brought on by pressure, arrogance or pomposity. "You can't be famous and expect to escape your fans. I like to sign autographs because I love what I do for a living. You can't just walk on stage, do your thing, walk off again and then expect it to be over," he says.

Chris Hutchins will never forget an incident where Tom was asleep in an hotel room and an imposing line of people formed outside his door, stretching all the way out of the building. "He was very good about it," marvels Chris. "He'd just stand there in his dressing gown and sign all these autographs." TV Producer Graham K Smith shares the same impression of the easy-going singer: "He's a pleasure to work with. In all the time I've known him, I've never ever seen him throw a wobbly."

Vernon Hopkins, former friend and leader of The Squires, sees things somewhat differently, giving voice to an aspect of Tom's make-up that many suspect but few will put into words. "He comes first with everything. It's a way of seeing life; totally and utterly selfish. There's no conscience."

Big Jim Sullivan speaks more on behalf of those who have known the man yet escaped his initially mercenary methods of climbing to the top. "One thing I've always liked about Tom is he knows where he's at," the guitarist says frankly. "He knows he's not an intellect, he knows he's not anything other than he is. Although you might not call it simple; he has got a simple way of life. That's the way he is."

It is also the way he is always likely to be, for Tom Jones is too set in his ways to change now and no doubt has a good deal of living left to do. He once described his definition of paradise to broadcaster Michael Parkinson as simply, "immortality". Mainly, though, after such unrivalled dedication, they can offer only pure, unadulterated admiration for the simple Welshman whose voice has made his dreams come true.

The final word must rest with The Voice himself:

> "I just hope I die with a bit of dignity, if at all possible.
> Thank you very much, that was *me*, and good night."

Bibliography

Books (on Tom Jones):
Hildred, S. & Gritten, D., *Tom Jones – The Biography* (Sidgwick & Jackson, 1990)
Jones, P., *Tom Jones – The Biography Of A Great Star* (Arthur Baker, 1970)
Macfarlane, C., *The Boy From Nowhere* (W H Allen, 1988)
Roberts, C., *Tom Jones* (Virgin, 1999)
St. Pierre, R., *Tom Jones: Quote Unquote* (Parragon, 1996)
Schwartz, B., *Tom Jones* (Grosset & Dunlap, 1969)

Books (General):
British Hit Singles (Guinness, 1999)
Clark, D., *Rock, Roll & Remember*
Concise Encyclopedia – A Quick Reference Guide (Grandreams, 1996)
Concise Encylopedia Of World History (Parragon, 1994)
Davis Jnr., S., Boyar, B., Boyar, J., *Why Me?* (Michael Joseph, 1989)
Encyclopedia Of Albums (Dempsey Parr, 1998)
Faber Companion To Twentieth Century Popular Music, The (Faber and Faber, 1990)
Garfield, S., *Expensive Habits, The Dark Side Of The Music Industry* (Faber, 1986)
Goldman, A., *Elvis* (Harmondsworth Penguin, 1981)
Grade, L., *Still Dancing – My Story* (Harper Collins, 1987)
Halliwells Film And Video Guide, 1999 Edition (Harper Collins, 1999)
Halliwells Who's Who In The Movies (Harper Collins, 1999)
Love, D., *My Name Is Love: The Darlene Love Story* (Morrow, 1998)
Q – Encyclopedia Of Rock Stars (Dorling Kindersley, 1996)
Repsch, J., *The Legendary Joe Meek: The Telstar Man* (Woodford House, 1989)
Rogan, J., *Starmakers And Svengalis: The History Of British Pop Management*
        (Macdonald Queen Anne Press, 1988)
Savile, J., *As It Happens* (Coronet/Barryes & Jenkins, 1974)
Short, D., *Engelbert Humperdinck – The Authorised Biography* (New English Library, 1972)
Talevski, N., *Encyclopedia Of Rock Obituaries, The* (Omnibus Press, 1999)
Time Out Guide To Las Vegas (Penguin, 1998)
Time Out Guide To Los Angeles (Penguin, 1999)
Warner Guide To UK And US Hit Singles, The (Carlton/Little, Brown, 1996)
Who's Who In The Twentieth Century (Oxford University Press, 1999)
Wilson, M., *Dreamgirl – My Life As A Supreme,* (Sidgwick & Jackson, 1987)
Worth, F., Tamerius, S. D., *Elvis: His Life From A-Z* (Corgi Books, 1989)

Fanzines:
Goldcoast Gals, Tom Jones Appreciation Society, Tom Boosters, Tom Terrific

Periodicals:
Annual Tour Brochures from 1969–1991

Newspapers & Magazines:
Daily Express, Daily Mirror, Daily Star, Disc, The Enquirer, Evening Standard, Financial Times, Globe, Hello!, Melody Maker, Metro, Mirror, Mojo, New Musical Express, News Of The World, Pontypridd Observer, Q, Radio Times, Record Mirror, Rolling Stone, Sun, Sunday Times, Telegraph, TV Times

TV & Film Appearances:
An Audience With Tom Jones, The Chieftains: The Making Of The Long Black Veil, Coast To Coast, Comic Relief, David Foster Christmas Special, Ed Sullivan Show, Fantasy Island (Lost and Found – Dick Turpin's Last Ride), The Fresh Prince Of Bel Air, The Full Monty, The Ghosts Of Oxford Street, Green Green Grass Of Home, It's A Royal Knockout: The Grand Knockout Tournament, The Jerry Springer Show, Jools Holland Show, Jo Whiley, The Last Resort, Live At This Moment, The Making Of All You Need Is Love, Mars Attacks!, The Merv Griffin Show, The Mike Douglas Show, Morecambe & Wise, Omnibus: Tom Jones – The Voice Made Flesh, One Night Only, Pillow Talk, Pleasure Cove, Ray Martin At Midday, Ready Steady Go!, The Right Time, Royal Variety Show, The Simpsons, 60 Minutes II (Tom Jones), *Sunday Night At The London Palladium, TFI Friday, This Is Tom Jones, Tom Jones Live At This Moment, Tom Jones Live In Las Vegas, The Tonight Show, Top Of The Pops, Viva Cabaret, Voices Of A Nation.*

Radio Appearances:
A Boy From Nowhere (Radio 2)

Places Of Research:
British Library, Colindale Newspaper Library, Flamingo Hilton Hotel, Institute Of Directors, MGM Grand, Office For National Statistics, Pontypridd Library, Pontypridd Historical & Cultural Centre, Pontypridd Registry Office

Discography

Due to the immense volume of Tom's musical output over the last four decades, it is an overwhelming task to list every product that has ever been available. The following is a comprehensive selection of his major releases, omitting only some superfluous re-releases and repetitive hits compilations.

Singles:
Chills And Fever / Breathless
Decca F 11966 August 64

It's Not Unusual / To Wait For Love
Decca F 126062 February 65

Once Upon A Time / I Tell The Sea
Decca F 12121 April 65

Little Lonely One / That's What We'll Do
Columbia DB 7566 May 65

With These Hands / Untrue
Decca F 12191 July 65

What's New Pussycat / The Rose
Decca F 12203 August 65

Lonely Joe / I Was A Fool
Columbia DB 7733 October 65

Thunderball / Key To My Heart
Decca F 12292 January 66

To Make A Big Man Cry / I'll Never Let You Go
Decca F 12315 February 66

Stop Breaking My Heart / Never Give Away Love
Decca F 12349 February 66

Once There Was A Time / Not Responsible
Decca F 12390 May 66

This And That / City Girl
Decca F 12461 August 66

Green Green Grass Of Home / Promise Her Anything
Decca F 22511 November 66

Green Green Grass Of Home / If I Had You
Decca F 12516 November 66

Detroit City / If I Had You
Decca F 22555 February 67

Detroit City / Ten Guitars
Decca F 22563 March 67

Funny Familiar Forgotten Feelings / I'll Never Let You Go
Decca F 12599 April 67

I'll Never Fall In Love Again / Things I Wanna Do
Decca F 12639 July 67

I'm Coming Home / The Lonely One
Decca F 12693 November 67

Delilah / Smile
Decca F 12747 February 68

Help Yourself / Day By Day
Decca F 12812 July 68

A Minute Of Your Time / Looking Out My Window
Decca F 12854 November 68

Love Me Tonight / Hide And Seek
Decca F 12924 May 69

Without Love / The Man Who Knows Too Much
Decca F 12990 December 69

Daughter Of Darkness / Tupelo Mississippi Flash
Decca F 13013 April 70

I (Who Have Nothing) / Stop Breaking My Heart
Decca F 13061 August 70

She's A Lady / My Way
Decca F 13113 January 71

Puppet Man / Every Mile
Decca F 13183 June 71

Till / The Sun Died
Decca FR 13236 October 71

Till / One Day Soon
Decca FR 13237 October 71

The Young New Mexican Puppeteer / All That I Need Is Some Time
Decca F 13298 April 72

Letter To Lucille / Thank The Lord
Decca F 13393 April 73

Today I Started Loving You Again / I Still Love You Enough
Decca F 13434 July 73

Golden Days / Goodbye, God Bless You Baby
Decca F 13471 November 73

La La La (Just Having You Here) / Love Love Love
Decca F 13490 January 74

Somethin' 'Bout You Baby I Like / Keep A-Talking 'Bout Love
Decca F 13550 September 74

Pledging My Love / I'm Too Far Gone (To Turn Away)
Decca F 13564 November 74

Ain't No Love / When The Band Comes Home
Decca F 13575 April 75

I Got Your Number / The Pain Of Love
Decca F 13590 July 75

Memories Don't Leave Like People Do / My Helping Hand
Decca F 13598 September 75

Say You'll Stay Until Tomorrow / Nothing Rhymed
EMI 2583 April 77

Have You Ever Been Lonely / One Man Woman, One Woman Man
EMI 2662 July 77

No-One Gave Me Love / That's Where I Belong
EMI 2756 February 78

Do You Take This Man / If I Sing You A Love Song
Columbia DB 9068 July 79

Come Home Rhondda Boy / What In The World's Come Over You?
Polydor POSP 371 November 81

But I Do / One Night With You
Polydor POSP 410 February 82

I'll Be Here Where The Heart Is / My Last Goodbye
Decca JONES 1 September 83

A Boy From Nowhere / I'll Dress You In Mourning / Dance With Death/
To Be A Matador
Epic OLE T1 April 87

It's Not Unusual / Delilah
London F 103 May 87

What's New Pussycat / Hard To Handle
London F 104 August 87

I Was Born To Be Me / A Panama Hat
Epic OLE 4 January 88
Kiss / EFL
China 11 October 88

Move Closer / 'Til The End Of Time
Jive 203 April 89

At This Moment / After The Tears
Jive 209 September 89

Can't Say Goodbye / Zip It Up
Dover ROJ 10 January 91

Carrying A Torch / Walk Tall
Dover ROJ 12 March 91

I'm Not Feeling It Any More / Something That You Said
Dover ROJ 14 May 91

All You Need Is Love / All You Need Is Love (Club Mix)
ChildLine CHILDCD 93 February 93

Gimme Shelter / Interview
Food CD ORDERA 1 April 93

If I Only Knew
ZTT ZANG 59CD November 94

A Girl Like You
Interscope 1994

I Want To Get Back With You / If I Only Knew
Interscope 981 98-7 February 95

You Can Leave Your Hat On
PID 421122 UK July 97

Perfect Day / Perfect Day
Chrysalis CDNEED 01 November 97

Burning Down The House / Unbelievable / Come Together
CXGUT 26 September 99

Baby It's Cold Outside / Remixes
CDGUT 29 December 99

Sexbomb / Remixes
VVR 5011173 December 99

EPs:
Tom Jones On Stage
Decca DFE 8617 March 65

Tom Jones
Columbia SEG 8464 December 65

What A Party
Decca DFE 8668 January 67

6 Track Hits
Scoop 33 7SR 5004 September 83

Albums:
Along Came Jones
Decca LK 4693 May 65

It's Not Unusual
Parrot PAS 71004 July 65

What's New Pussycat
Parrot PAS 71006 September 65

A-TOM-IC JONES
Decca LK / SKL 4743 January 66

From The Heart
Decca LK / SKL 4814 August 66

Green Green Grass Of Home
Decca LK / SKL 4855 March 67

Live At The Talk Of The Town
Decca LK / SKL 4874 June 67

13 Smash Hits
Decca LK / SKL 4909 December 67

The Tom Jones Fever Zone
Parrot PAS 71019 June 68

Delilah
Decca LK / SKL 4946 July 68

Help Yourself
Decca LK / SKL 4982 November 68

Tom Jones Live In Las Vegas
Decca LK / SKL 5032 April 69

This Is Tom Jones
Decca LK /SKL 5007 June 69

Tom
Decca LK / SKL 5005 April 70

I, Who Have Nothing
Decca LK / SKL 5072 October 70

She's A Lady
Decca SKL 5089 May 71

Tom Jones Live At Caesar's Palace
Decca DKL 1 1 / 2 November 71

Close Up
Decca SKL 5132 May 72

The Body And Soul Of Tom Jones
Decca SKL 5162 June 73

Somethin' 'Bout You Baby I Like
Decca SKL 5197 November 74

Tom Jones: 20 Greatest Hits
Decca TJD 1 11 / 2 March 75

Memories Don't Leave Like People Do
Decca SKL 5214 October 75

The World Of Tom Jones
Decca SPA 454 December 75

Tom Jones Sings 24 Great Standards
Decca DKL 7 1/2 December 76

Say You'll Stay Until Tomorrow
Epic PE 34468 April 77

What A Night
EMI EMC 3221 February 78

I'm Coming Home
Lotus WH 5001 September 78

Do You Take This Man
EMI SCX 6220 September 79

Rescue Me
Columbia SCX 6628 December 79

Darlin'
Polygram SRM1 4010 October 81

Tom Jones Country
Polygram SRM1 4062 1982

Discography

Don't Let Our Dreams Die Young
Polygram 814448 1983

Love Is On The Radio
Polygram 814701 1984

Tender Loving Care
Polygram 826140 1985

The Country Side Of Tom Jones
RCA Camden CN 2074 March 85

The Soul Of Tom Jones
Decca TAB 91 February 86

The Golden Hits: Tom Jones
London 810 192-2 March 87

Matador – The Musical Life Of El Cordobés
Epic VIVA 1 April 87

Tom Jones – The Greatest Hits
Telstar TCD 2296 May 87

It's Not Unusual – His Greatest Hits
Decca 820 544-2 July 87

At This Moment
Jive TOM CD 1 April 89

Move Closer
Jive 1214-1-J April 89

Kiss
Jive 301012 April 89

After Dark
Stylus SMR 978 June 89

Stop Breaking My Heart
Deram 820 773-2 August 89

Carrying A Torch
Chrysalis AAD 20 April 91

The Lead And How To Swing It
Interscope 92457-2 November 94

The Lead And How To Swing It / Three Decades Of Cool
Interscope 6544926492 November 94 (Australian release only)

From The Vaults
Mercury 314-558 186-2 1998

The Ultimate Tom Jones Collection
32 POPPVC 0412340172 1998

Reload
GUTCD009 September 99

Contributions:
Thunderball S/T
UA Records 4132 1965

What's New Pussycat S/T
UAL 4128 1965

Promise Her Anything S/T
1966

The Pink Panther Strikes Again S/T
UA-LA 694-G 1976

Matador – The Musical Life Of El Cordobés
Epic Viva 1 1987

Under Milk Wood S/T
EMI CD 791232 1988

The Ghosts Of Oxford Street S/T
BMG/RCA PD 57233 1991

David Foster The Christmas Album
Interscope 792 295-2 1993

The Chieftains: Long Black Veil
BMG/RCA09026-62702-2 1995

Super Cop S/T
Interscope INTD 90088 1996

Mars Attacks! S/T
WB/Atlantic 82992-2 1996

The Full Monty S/T
BMG 68904-2 1997

Whistle Down The Wind
Polygram 1998

Paul Anka – A Body Of Work
1998

Agnes Browne S/T
2000

Index

Roscommon County Library Service WITHDRAWN FROM STOCK